The
GERMAN
WORKER

6

The

GERMAN WORKER

*Working-Class Autobiographies
from the Age of
Industrialization*

Translated, edited,
and with an Introduction by

Alfred Kelly

University of California Press

Berkeley · Los Angeles · London

University of California Press
Berkeley and Los Angeles, California
University of California Press, Ltd.
London, England
© 1987 by
The Regents of the University of California

Library of Congress Cataloging-in-Publication Data
The German worker.
Includes index.
1. Labor and laboring classes—Germany—
Biography. 2. Labor and laboring classes—
Germany—History—19th century. 3. Proletariat—
History. 4. Germany—Economic conditions—
19th century. 5. Germany—Social conditions.
I. Kelly, Alfred, 1947–
HD8453.A1G47 1987   305.5′62′0922 [B]   87–5076
ISBN 0–520–05972–7 (alk. paper)
ISBN 0–520–06124–1 (pbk.: alk. paper)

Printed in the United States of America

1 2 3 4 5 6 7 8 9

To my mother
and the memory of my father

Contents

Illustrations

Acknowledgments

This book began several years ago as a whimsical idea while I was standing in line at the canteen of the Bayerische Staatsbibliothek in Munich. Books have a way of taking longer than we ever imagined, and this one might still be incomplete if it weren't for a good deal of help. My greatest debt is certainly to Suse Field and Otto Liedke. Each of them spent many hours with me, patiently answering hundreds of questions and advising me about sticky points in the translations. They have saved me from countless infelicities of phrasing and just plain blunders. Whatever deficiencies remain are a result of my not having had the wits to solicit their opinion, or stubbornly choosing not to follow their advice.

For helping me to locate the pictures, I am indebted to the staff of the Ullstein Bilderdienst in Berlin and to Herbert Kraft of the Archiv für Kunst und Geschichte in Berlin. John Fout of Bard College kindly supplied me with copies of some of the rarer women's autobiographies.

I would also like to thank the Translation Program of the National Endowment for the Humanities. The two-summer grant I received from them was of great assistance, as were the comments of their outside readers.

Laurie Moses and Theresa George accurately typed and retyped the manuscript—no small task with my terrible handwriting and propensity to mess up clean manuscript pages.

Finally, I would like to salute my friends and colleagues in the History Department of Hamilton College. They not only put up with me, but also make me believe that writing books is really worth all the trouble.

A Note about Currencies

Germany

1 mark (about $0.25)	100 pfennigs
1 groschen	10 pfennigs
1 taler	3 marks

Austrian Empire

1 guilder (about 2 marks or $0.50)	100 kreuzer

U.S. dollar equivalents refer to the pre–World War I exchange rates and should be considered only a rough guide. There is no meaningful way to measure any of these values against the buying power of today's dollar. The reader is referred to the discussion of wages and expenses in the Introduction, as well as to the context of each individual autobiographical selection.

Introduction

In the two generations before World War I, Germany emerged as Europe's foremost industrial power. The basic facts of increasing industrial output, lengthening railroad lines, urbanization, and rising exports are well known. Behind those facts, in the historical shadows, stand millions of anonymous men and women: the workers who actually put down the railroad ties, hacked out the coal, sewed the shirt collars, printed the books, or carried the bricks that made Germany a great nation. This book contains translated selections from the autobiographies of nineteen of those now-forgotten millions. The thirteen men and six women who speak from these pages afford an intimate firsthand look at how massive social and economic changes are reflected on a personal level in the everyday lives of workers. Although some of these autobiographies are familiar to specialists in German labor history, they are virtually unknown and inaccessible to the broader audience they deserve. My hope is that these translations will prove at once useful, interesting, and entertaining to a wide range of historians, students, and general readers. The purpose of this introduction, which is aimed primarily at those nonspecialists, is to enrich the reading of these autobiographies by placing them in their historical context and by sketching some of the major themes in the secondary literature.

The first question usually asked of workers' autobiographies is: Are they representative of the lives of the working class as a whole?[1] In the narrowest sense the answer to this question must

[1] On working-class autobiographies, see Georg Bollenbeck, *Zur Theorie und Geschichte der frühen Arbeiterlebenserinnerungen* (Kronberg, 1976); Ursula Münchow, *Frühe deutsche Arbeiterbiographie* (Berlin, 1973); and "Das Bild des Arbeiters in der proletarischen Selbstdarstellung. Zur Bedeutung der frühen Arbeiterbiographie," *Weimarer Beiträge* 19 (1973): 110–35; Adelbert Koch, "Arbeitermemoiren als sozialwissenschaftliche Erkenntnisquelle," *Archiv für Sozialwissenschaft und Sozialpolitik* 61 (1929): 128–67; Cecilia A. Trunz, *Die Autobiographien von deutschen Industriearbeitern* (diss., Freiburg, 1934); Bernd Witte, "Arbeiterautobiographien. Dokumente sozialen Kampfes oder Abenteuer der Seele," in *Arbeiterdichtung. Analysen-Bekenntnisse-Dokumentationen*, ed. Österreichische Gesellschaft für Kulturpolitik (Wuppertal, 1973), 37–46; Leo Uhen, *Gruppenbewusstsein und informelle Gruppenbildungen bei deutschen Arbeitern im Jahrhundert der Industrialisierung* (Berlin, 1964); Wolfram Fischer, *Wirtschaft und Gesellschaft im Zeitalter der Industrialisierung. Aufsätze-Studien-Vorträge* (Göttingen, 1972), esp. 214–23; Frank Trommler, *Sozialistische Literatur in Deutschland. Ein historischer Überblick* (Stuttgart, 1976), esp. 339–55; Mary Jo Maynes, "Gender and Class in Working-Class Women's Autobiographies," in *German Women in the Eighteenth and Nineteenth Centuries: A Social and Literary History*, ed. Ruth-Ellen B. Joeres and Mary Jo Maynes (Bloomington, Ind., 1986), 230–46; Juliane Jacobi-Dittrich, "The Struggle for an Identity: Working-Class Autobiographies by Women in Nineteenth Century Germany," in *German Women in the Eighteenth and Nineteenth Centuries*, ed. Joeres and Maynes, 321–45; Hermann Bertlein, *Jugendleben und soziales Bildungsschicksal* (Hannover, 1966) presents sixty autobiographical selections on youthful experiences and education; Wolfgang Emmerich provides a full bibliography of working-class autobiographies, useful biographical sketches of their authors, as well as short selections from the works themselves, in his *Anfänge bis 1914*, vol. 1 of *Proletarische Lebensläufe. Autobiographische Dokumente zur Entstehung der Zweiten Kultur in Deutschland* (Hamburg, 1974); Richard Klucsarits and Friedrich G. Kürbisch have collected short excerpts of working women's autobiographies in their *Arbeiterinnen kämpfen um ihr Recht. Autobiographische Texte zum Kampf rechtloser und entrechteter "Frauenspersonen" in*

be no. Anyone of any class—but particularly the working class—with the time, talent, and ambition to complete an autobiography is almost by definition exceptional. Out of millions of working-class lives we have only about a hundred autobiographies for this period, all but a handful of them by men. (Given the difficulties of defining who is, or still is, a worker, no precise count is possible.) Moreover, at the time that they wrote, some of these men and women had left behind the world of work—if not the working class—and become writers, trade union or party functionaries, or even state officials. There is, then, a gray area where the working-class autobiography meets the proud story of the self-made bourgeois. Only one of the authors (Otto Krille) in this book falls into the latter category. Four others (Franz Osterroth, Franz Rehbein, Ottilie Baader, and Adelheid Popp) had moved into the world of working-class politics and journalism when they wrote—though they still considered themselves part of the working class. As for the other fourteen, they were either still working, retired, or ill when they wrote.

But representativeness is not a single category of analysis. The appropriate questions are: Representative of what? Of a range of industries? Of working conditions? Of wages? Of living conditions? Of family situations? Of regions? To these more precise questions, we may fairly answer: yes, taken as a group, the selections in this book *are* representative of the wide range of experiences of the working class. We encounter traditional industries and modern industries; wretched working conditions and toler-

---

Deutschland, Österreich und der Schweiz des 19. und 20. Jahrhunderts (Wuppertal, 1975). By way of comparison, see John Burnett, ed., *Annals of Labour: Autobiographies of British Working Class People 1820–1920* (Bloomington, Ind. and London, 1974); Margaret Llewelyn Davies, ed., *Life As We Have Known It* (New York and London, 1975); David Vincent, *Bread, Knowledge and Freedom: A Study of Nineteenth Century Working Class Autobiography* (London and New York, 1981); on Russian workers, see Victoria E. Bonnell, ed., *The Russian Worker: Life and Labor under the Tsarist Regime* (Berkeley and Los Angeles, 1983). On the genre of autobiography, see Roy Pascal, *Design and Truth in Autobiography* (Cambridge, Mass., 1960).

able ones; and wages up and down the scale. There are people from all different parts of Germany (and Austria), living in all kinds of housing—both rural and urban—in a variety of family situations. All the "typical" working-class experiences are present in these selections: unemployment, high job turnover, long hours, low wages, grinding drudgery, child labor, crowded housing, alcoholism, sexual abuse, illegitimacy, home work for women, and so on. And in every case the autobiographies put a dramatic personal edge on the statistical reality.

Representative experiences are fairly easy to establish empirically. Determining representative attitudes is another matter. Our authors are acutely conscious of how typical their work and living conditions are, but they usually set themselves apart intellectually. Moritz Bromme, for example, talks about "we enlightened"—in contrast to the inert masses. There is an element of snobbery here, to be sure. Yet there can be no doubt that those who wrote autobiographies were more educated and informed than the vast majority of their fellow workers. The very fact that all but one of the men (Karl Fischer, the oldest) and three of six of the women were class-conscious Social Democrats suggests an unusual degree of awareness, as well as the ability to see beyond their immediate personal situations. Nonetheless, is there any reason to assume that those who are better able to articulate will therefore articulate idiosyncratic attitudes and emotions? Surely, the coal hewers next to Max Lotz, the women sewing collars next to Ottilie Baader, or the threshers choking in dust alongside Franz Rehbein would recognize their own distress in the descriptions of their more articulate neighbors. As individuals, those millions who had similar experiences to our authors are forever mute. If they are to be anything more than anonymous statistical objects, we must allow these few authors to speak for them. In short, there is no more reason to dismiss these autobiographies than there is to dismiss those of the upper classes. All autobiographies are the products of unusual individuals. Lower-class people certainly write less, but the greater uniformity of life imposed by poverty warrants wider generalization from each single work.

Although the genre of workers' autobiographies is rather small, the reader deserves a word of explanation about why these particular selections were chosen. Above all, I have been guided by the desire to provide the greatest possible diversity. Further, I have sought autobiographies that lend themselves to excerption—that is, books with chapters or long passages that can stand on their own. Some authors, who might otherwise merit inclusion, simply eliminate themselves because of the structure of their narratives: these may be either disorganized chronologically or topically, or else too heavily dependent on references to other parts of the text. Interest and liveliness have also been major considerations; given a choice, there is no point in including a dull selection when an exciting one on the same topic is available. When feasible, I have given preference to the more personal narratives and have avoided works whose real center is the party or union. These latter works are significant in their own right, but with their submergence of the individual into the workers' movement, they are only marginally autobiographical. The reasons why someone became politically involved are obviously of great interest; but I prefer to document the development of political consciousness in the more subjective context of individual experience and emotion. In such a context political consciousness reveals its problematic side and appears less an abstract given. Finally, in the case of works by women, there is simply less from which to choose. Were women represented in this book according to their numerical contribution to the genre, there would be only one or two women's selections. I have raised that number to six so that it is more in accord with the proportion of women to men in the work force at any given time. Personal preferences have certainly played their part in the final selections. Nonetheless, I believe that this book provides the reader a good feel for the whole genre of German workers' autobiographies.

I have arranged the translations in chronological order, based roughly on the dates of the central experiences each author is describing. This arrangement (like any other) is somewhat arbitrary, but it does have the advantage of giving the reader a sense of historical development, without obscuring the unevenness with which historical change is experienced by different individuals.

THE ORIGINS OF THE AUTOBIOGRAPHIES

Given the obstacles they faced, what prompted these workers to write autobiographies? It is not possible to say in every case, but where we do know something of the origin of these works, we usually detect the influence of either Social Democratic or bourgeois-reformist editors. At least initially, progressive members of the middle class were most instrumental in the development and popularization of the whole genre. Pastor Paul Göhre is the key figure here. As a young theological student in 1890, he had worked "under cover" as a common laborer in a Chemnitz machine factory. His widely acclaimed *Three Months in a Workshop* is one of the finest early descriptions of both factory work procedures and worker attitudes. In a country with little tradition of popular social novels, the book did much to alert the middle class to the psychological, as well as economic, dimensions of the "labor question." As one conservative reviewer remarked, "we were better acquainted with the condition of life of the half savage African tribes than with those of our own people."[2] (Only men worked in Göhre's factory; but his book stimulated Minna Wettstein-Adelt, a middle-class Berlin feminist, to describe her experiences among women workers in several Chemnitz factories.)[3] In 1891, Göhre was elected secretary of Friedrich Naumann's Evangelical-Social Congress (*Evangelisch-Sozialer Kongress*).[4] The congress counted among its members prominent cler-

[2] Anthony Oberschall, *Empirical Social Research in Germany 1848–1914* (New York, 1965), 81; see Paul Göhre, *Three Months in a Workshop: A Practical Study*, trans. A. B. Carr (London and New York, 1895).
[3] See Minna Wettstein-Adelt, *3½ Monate Fabrik-Arbeiterin. Eine practische Studie* (Berlin, 1893).
[4] On Göhre, see Oberschall, *Empirical Social Research in Germany 1848–1914*, 28–30, 80–82; and Horst Kern, *Empirische Sozialforschung. Ursprünge, Ansätze, Entwicklungslinien* (Munich, 1982), 102–4.

gymen and academics (including Max Weber) who were seeking an alternative to Social Democracy. These men believed that the working classes could be integrated into the modern industrial state by means of enlightened social legislation. One of their main concerns, therefore, was to arm themselves with empirical data about the status of the working class. (Naumann himself would later edit a worker's autobiography.) The congress's aims—and to some degree its membership—overlapped with those of the older Social Policy Association (*Verein für Sozialpolitik*), which sponsored pioneering sociological studies. Weber himself, in his massive study of the status of agricultural laborers in eastern Germany, relied heavily on the testimony of country pastors.[5] For a man like Göhre, who was sympathetic to Social Democracy and stood on the congress's left wing, interest in the lives of workers was a product of the interaction of Christian activism, progressive liberalism, and the newly emerging discipline of sociology.

The boundary between Social Democracy and the cluster of attitudes just described was fluid, and in 1900 Göhre joined the Social Democratic party (SPD). Three years later he was elected to the Reichstag, where his background aroused the suspicion and contempt of the Social Democratic leader, August Bebel. Intellectuals, Bebel warned, were "marauders who attack the party in the rear."[6] Surely Göhre did not mean to be a traitor to Social Democracy when, in 1903, he edited a sizable autobiography by Karl Fischer, a sixty-two-year-old unskilled laborer. Fischer had been moved by Göhre's book to record his own experiences in a variety of industries, including steel and railroads.[7] But Göhre's choice of publisher, the new Eugen Diederichs Verlag, was revealing. Diederichs was making a name for himself

[5] Weber's *Die Verhältnisse der Landarbeiter im ostelbischen Deutschland* (Leipzig, 1892) appeared as vol. 55 of the *Schriften des Vereins für Sozialpolitik;* see also Oberschall, *Empirical Social Research in Germany 1848–1914,* 31.
[6] Bollenbeck, *Zur Theorie und Geschichte der frühen Arbeiterlebenserinnerungen,* 245.
[7] Ibid., 108.

publishing conservative *völkisch* material, and in contracting
with Göhre he was certainly not intending to advance the cause
of Social Democracy. In fact, Diederichs instructed Göhre to de-
emphasize Social Democracy in the introduction, and to stress
instead "the need to fulfill our social duties."[8] The main purpose
of the book, in Diederichs's view, was to promote a true folk
community (*Volksgemeinschaft*) by introducing bourgeois readers
to an "unknown folk comrade."[9]

Diederichs need not have worried. Fischer was a man of patriarchal, preindustrial outlook. When he learned—to his dis-
may—that Göhre was a member of the SPD, he feared that his
book would be turned into a piece of Social Democratic propaganda.[10] Actually, the whole book was primitively written ("First
I did this, then I did that"), and gave the impression that Fischer
was simply a passive victim of his milieu. The reviewers liked
the book, seeing in it the genuine voice of a little man struggling
against adversity.[11] Göhre had clearly succeeded in his aim of
informing the bourgeoisie without alarming them with calls for
social revolution. He rummaged through Fischer's voluminous
manuscript and issued a sequel.[12]

Emboldened by the success of Fischer's book, Göhre was now
on the lookout for more manuscripts. In 1905 he edited the life
story of Moritz Bromme, a tubercular woodworker whose articles
for Social Democratic newspapers had caught the pastor's eye.
Bromme was an avid Social Democrat, but Göhre called the book
simply *The Autobiography of a Modern Factory Worker*. As he admitted frankly in the introduction, the words *Social Democrat* in

---

[8] Diederichs is quoted in Gary D. Stark, *Entrepreneurs of Ideology: Neoconserva-
tive Publishers in Germany, 1890–1933* (Chapel Hill, N.C., 1981), 100.

[9] Bollenbeck, *Zur Theorie und Geschichte der frühen Arbeiterlebenserinnerungen*,
112, 242–43.

[10] Ibid., 110; see also Trommler, *Sozialistische Literatur in Deutschland*, 342.

[11] Trommler, *Sozialistische Literatur in Deutschland*, 343–44.

[12] The sequel caused less of a stir. Many probably sympathized with Marie
Soslich, who reviewed Fischer's original volume for the *Preussische Jahrbücher*;
Fischer is interesting, she said, but enough is enough! See the review in the
Preussische Jahrbücher 114 (1903): 336–38.

the title might scare off bourgeois buyers! Similar concerns were on his (and probably Diederichs's) mind when he followed with two more autobiographies in 1909. Both authors—Franz Rehbein, a north German farm laborer, and Wenzel Holek, a Bohemian brickyard worker—were Social Democrats. But once again Göhre presented their stories as factual reports rather than propaganda. This pretense of objectivity, as well as the high price tags, angered Franz Mehring, the SPD's chief cultural critic. "A book for the bourgeoisie" was his contemptuous label for Holek's autobiography.[13] Mehring's judgment reflected a deep-rooted suspicion in Marxist circles that "bourgeois" publishers distorted the true voice of the proletariat by depicting workers as victims of their milieu. Victims of a bad environment (like the characters in naturalist literature, also a target of Mehring's wrath) could only wait passively for the liberating reforms of well-meaning liberals.[14] Whatever the merits of this argument, Mehring was at least right about the readership of the autobiographies edited by Göhre: it consisted largely of politicians, professors, students, and pastors.[15]

In the same spirit, *Die Neue Zeit,* the SPD's official theoretical organ, also attacked Adolf Levenstein, a factory foreman turned amateur sociologist. From 1907 to 1911, Levenstein conducted a huge opinion survey of workers in the textile, metal, and mining industries. In the eyes of the party, he was an outside meddler, exploiting his connections in the working class. *Die Neue Zeit* urged workers not to return Levenstein's extensive questionnaire.[16] Despite the opposition, Levenstein published the tabulated results of some 5,000 questionnaires, as well as some lengthy selections gleaned from his correspondence with the more articulate workers. Max Weber, who was perhaps slightly jealous, dismissed the ex-foreman as a rank amateur sociologist;

---

[13] Trommler, *Sozialistische Literatur in Deutschland,* 346.
[14] Bollenbeck, *Zur Theorie und Geschichte der frühen Arbeiterlebenserinnerungen,* 11.
[15] Ibid., 248.
[16] Kern, *Empirische Sozialforschung,* 107.

nonetheless, Levenstein's *The Labor Question* (1912) is a gold mine of information and is justly considered one of the pioneering works of modern sociological research.[17] It was, incidentally, Levenstein who discovered Max Lotz, the extraordinarily gifted coal miner whose story appears in this volume. The Eberhard Frowein Verlag, the publisher of Levenstein's correspondence with workers, saw as its task not the spread of Social Democracy but rather the discovery of hidden talent among the lower classes. By "finding the path into the human soul" on a "psychological basis," the press hoped to "contribute to the understanding of our social conditions."[18] Similar sentiments informed the work of other middle-class editors and publishers. In their eyes the autobiographies were "tales of woe" about "victims of the environment."[19]

As might be expected given their complaints about Göhre and Levenstein, Social Democrats viewed workers' autobiographies as part of the literature of agitation. It was not enough to use them as documentary evidence for socially committed scholarship, as did Göhre, Levenstein, and later Eugen Rosenstock, who published the autobiography of Eugen May, an itinerant turner. Rather, Social Democratic editors were frankly seeking educational and inspirational works by dedicated party people whose conversion to Social Democracy had been the central experience in their lives. Never were these workers presented to the reader as mere victims of the environment. One might call this the "If

[17] See Adolf Levenstein, *Die Arbeiterfrage. Mit besonderer Berücksichtigung der sozialpsychologischen Seite des modernen Grossbetriebes und der psychophysischen Einwirkungen auf die Arbeiter* (Munich, 1912); and his *Aus der Tiefe. Arbeiterbriefe. Beiträge zur Seelen-Analyse moderner Arbeiter* (Berlin, 1909). On Levenstein, see Kern, *Empirische Sozialforschung*, 106–11; and Oberschall, *Empirical Social Research in Germany 1848–1914*, 100–106, 131–32. On Weber's critique, see Max Weber, "Zur Methodik sozialpsychologischer Enqueten und ihrer Bearbeitung," *Archiv für Sozialwissenschaft und Sozialpolitik* 29 (1909): 949–58.

[18] Trommler, *Sozialistische Literatur in Deutschland*, 348.

[19] Franz Bergg, *Ein Proletarierleben*, ed. Nikolaus Welter (Frankfurt, 1913), 9. G. Braun, ed., *Im Kampf ums Dasein! Wahrheitsgetreue Lebenserinnerungen eines Mädchens aus dem Volke als Fabrikarbeiterin, Dienstmädchen und Kellnerin* (Stuttgart, 1908), 8.

only everyone were as aware as Comrade X!" literature. These works were published by either Dietz or Vorwärts (the two major Social Democratic publishing houses) and were aimed largely at proletarian, rather than bourgeois, readers. Short excerpts often appeared in Social Democratic newspapers. As books, however, they rarely reached their intended working-class audience, attracting at most a few middle-class readers. Among the works in this book, those by Ottilie Baader, Aurelia Roth, and Franz Osterroth are the most notable examples of such Social Democratic agitation. Overall it would be fair to say that the autobiographies had a modest influence on the progressive bourgeoisie but virtually no influence on the working class.

THE WORLD OF WORK

For the men and women who speak in these pages, work was the great, overwhelming reality of life. When we say that these people lived during the Industrial Revolution, we may be prone to conjure up images of homogeneous urban masses mindlessly tending machines in huge factories. While there is a tiny kernel of truth to these images, they are for the most part misleading. These autobiographies serve as a useful reminder of how complex and variegated the Industrial Revolution really was. In the lives of actual workers we repeatedly run across the older realities of work—the rural and small-town flavor, the small scale, the personal relations, and the mix of muscle power and craftsmanship. Even a self-styled "modern factory worker," like Moritz Bromme, had deep roots in the past, and the pattern of his life confounds any simple model of radical change during the Industrial Revolution.[20]

Occupational statistics confirm that the autobiographies do

[20] There is a huge literature on German industrialization. For a general overview, see W. O. Henderson, *The Rise of German Industrial Power, 1834–1914* (Berkeley and Los Angeles, 1975); Knut Borchardt, "The Industrial Revolution in Germany, 1700–1914," in *The Emergence of Industrial Societies,* pt. 1, ed. Carlo M. Cipolla, vol. 4 of *The Fontana Economic History of Europe* (London

give an accurate picture of the world of work. According to the census of 1907, some 72.5 percent (17,836,000) of all those employed in agriculture, industry, and commerce and transportation were classifed as workers (*Arbeiter*).[21] (The figure does not include the 1,736,000 servants.) Now this seems like a lot of workers in a total population of about 62 million in the Second Reich. But what is really being counted here are wage earners, over 40 percent of whom (7,283,000) were in agriculture. These *Landarbeiter* made up nearly three-quarters of those employed in the agricultural sector.[22] Given the immense regional diversity, generalizations about them are dangerous, but our two agricultural autobiographies (those by Franz Rehbein and Otto, the contract laborer) suggest two salient points. First, especially in the lands east of the Elbe River, landless workers lived in a distinctly premodern relationship with the landowners. Though nominally free, such workers were still subject to the old Servants Code (*Gesindeordnung*), which contained numerous feudal vestiges: payments in kind, service obligations, restrictions on mobility, informal employer police powers, and the like. Second, the impact of farm machinery was only just beginning to be felt at the turn of the century. The steam thresher had come to the countryside, but most farm labor was still the human (and animal) muscle work that was little different from previous centuries. Thus, in the daily life of the millions still working on the farm, the Industrial Revolution marked no radical departure from the past.[23]

Of the remaining 10,553,000 workers counted in the 1907

and Glasgow, 1973), 76–160; Friedrich-Wilhelm Henning, *Die Industriali-sierung in Deutschland 1800 bis 1914* (Paderborn, 1973). Of course, *German* workers were not the only workers in the Reich; see Richard Charles Murphy, *Guest Workers in the German Reich: A Polish Community in Wilhelmian Germany* (New York, 1984).

[21] Gerd Hohorst, Jürgen Kocka, and Gerhard A. Ritter, *Sozialgeschichtliches Arbeitsbuch. Materialien zur Statistik des Kaiserreichs 1870–1914* (Munich, 1975), 67, 69.

[22] Ibid., 67, 70.

[23] On agriculture, see Frieda Wunderlich, *Farm Labor in Germany 1810–1945: Its Historical Development within the Framework of Agricultural and Social*

census, 1,960,000 were in commerce and transportation and the other 8,593,000 in the industrial sector proper (which also included mining, construction, and handicrafts).[24] Although the number of industrial workers had more than doubled since the 1882 census (population had increased in the period by about one third), the impact of modern industry was uneven geographically. For the Reich as a whole in 1907, 42.8 percent of the population was supported by the industrial sector (up from 32.8 percent in 1882). In Saxony, the old industrial heartland, 59.3 percent depended on the industrial sector; whereas in rural East Prussia the figure was only 20.4 percent.[25] Moreover, industry should not automatically be equated with either large firms or large cities. Giant firms predominated only in the mining industry, where by 1907 the majority of miners worked for companies employing more than one thousand people. (It's no accident that the miner Max Lotz is one of the few workers to complain about being "just a number.") Elsewhere, the small and medium-sized firms held their own. In the 1907 census, firms with five or fewer employees still accounted for 31.2 percent of the industrial work force. A majority (57.6 percent) worked for firms with fewer than fifty employees, and a mere 4.9 percent for firms with more than one thousand employees.[26] City growth was far more spectacular than firm growth, but even as late as 1905 only 19 percent of all Germans (and even of those in the industrial sector, only about one-quarter) lived in cities of over 100,000 in population.[27] Industry remained predominantly a rural and small-city

Policy (Princeton, 1961), 8–27; Borchardt, "The Industrial Revolution in Germany, 1700–1914," 128–29; Richard J. Evans and W. R. Lee, eds., *The German Peasantry: Conflict and Community in Rural Society from the Eighteenth to the Twentieth Centuries* (London and Sydney, 1986), esp. chaps. 4–6; Robert G. Moeller, ed., *Peasants and Lords in Modern Germany: Recent Studies in Agricultural History* (Boston, 1986).

[24] Hohorst, Kocka, and Ritter, *Sozialgeschichtliches Arbeitsbuch,* 67.

[25] Ibid., 73.

[26] Ibid., 75.

[27] Ibid., 52; Barrington Moore, Jr., *Injustice: The Social Bases of Obedience and Revolt* (White Plains, N.Y., 1978), 180.

phenomenon. And, as the autobiographies reveal, many of those who worked in cities lived on, or maintained contact with, the surrounding countryside, sometimes working part of the year in agriculture.[28] To be sure, one was never far from a railroad line, but well into the twentieth century much of Germany looked, sounded, and smelled as it always had.

Nor should increasing mechanization obscure the continuing importance of brute strength. A great deal of traditional heavy labor was scarcely affected by the Industrial Revolution. As one historian has aptly remarked, "A vast amount of wheeling, dragging, hoisting, carrying, lifting, digging, tunneling, draining, trenching, hedging, embarking, blasting, breaking, scouring, sawing, felling, reaping, mowing, picking, sifting, and threshing was done by sheer muscular effort, day in, day out."[29] The truth of this observation is brought home to the reader repeatedly in this book. Think only of the rail lines, the symbol of the new age. They were laid out by labor gangs using picks, shovels, and wheelbarrows. And, as Max Lotz so poignantly depicts, coal, the fuel of the industrial age, was mined not by power machinery but by sweating hewers and haulers. To the unskilled in particular, work still meant what it always had—exhausting drudgery.

For skilled workers, the impact of industrialization was more complex and differentiated. Some crafts, like the making of wallpaper, hats, buttons, umbrellas, canes, soap, and light fixtures, were displaced by the new technologies and largely disappeared. Others, like the construction trades, were little affected by new machinery; while still others, like shoe making, shifted from production to repair.[30] Moreover, new, specialized skills, especially in the metal industry, emerged in response to the need to

[28] Peter N. Stearns, "Adaptation to Industrialization: German Workers as a Test Case," *Central European History* 3, no. 4 (December 1970): 303–31, esp. 306.
[29] Cited by Burnett, *Annals of Labour*, 25.
[30] Henning, *Die Industrialisierung in Deutschland 1800 bis 1914*, 126–32; Thomas Nipperdey, *Deutsche Geschichte 1800–1866. Bürgerwelt und starker Staat* (Munich, 1983), 214.

produce, maintain, and repair the vast array of industrial machines. Overall, the number of artisans (*Handwerker*) actually rose (both absolutely and relative to population) during the Industrial Revolution.[31] Of the 8,593,000 industrial workers in 1907, about 4,900,000 were classified as skilled.[32] Most of these workers had artisanal skills that had survived the Industrial Revolution either intact or as ancillary processes to machine work.

The survival of some artisanal skills, however, is not the same as the survival of artisanal status. By the end of the nineteenth century, the word *Arbeiter* was often applied casually to a *Handwerker*.[33] It had not always been so. Traditionally, the artisan was a proudly independent member of the petty bourgeoisie.[34] As a young apprentice he could look forward to becoming a journeyman at about age twenty. After two years of traveling around and seeing the world (*Wanderjahre*), he could settle down with a real chance of eventually becoming a master with his own shop. Snug within the legally protected monopoly of the guild, the artisan did more than work and run a business—he defended a way of life with all its cliquish traditions and provincial rectitude. The modern world, with its stress on innovation, acquisitiveness, and individuality, was a foreign intrusion. Beginning in the early nineteenth century, the craft guilds entered a long period of crisis and decline as they were sucked inexorably into the modern market economy. As fewer and fewer journeymen could realistically aspire to becoming independent masters, large segments of the artisan class slipped into wage dependency. Throughout the first half of the nineteenth century, the craft guilds fought a rearguard action against their perceived enemies—new machinery and industrial freedom (*Gewerbefreiheit*). But by about 1860, *Gewer-*

---

[31] Henning, *Die Industrialisierung in Deutschland 1800 bis 1914*, 131–32; Nipperdey, *Deutsche Geschichte 1800–1866*, 210–19.

[32] Lutz Niethammer, "Wie wohnten die Arbeiter im Kaiserreich?" *Archiv für Sozialgeschichte* 16 (1976): 61–134, esp. 112; Moore, *Injustice*, 180–81.

[33] Bollenbeck, *Zur Theorie und Geschichte der frühen Arbeiterlebenserinnerungen*, 31.

[34] Nipperdey, *Deutsche Geschichte 1800–1866*, 210–19.

befreiheit had triumphed in all the German states. Some informal vestiges of the old guild influence (the pride, the cliquishness, the *Wanderjahre*) persisted into the twentieth century.[35] Nonetheless, most artisans who came through the Industrial Revolution unscathed had been reduced to skilled workers competing in the free market.

Whatever the industry or skill level, hours were typically long, wages meager, and working conditions unpleasant or unhealthful. None of this was new, of course. In fact, all the evidence suggests that workers' lives were gradually improving during the Second Reich. Moritz Bromme is probably right that few workers of his generation (he was born in 1873) would have put up with the endless drudgery that had been routine for the older generation. In the 1870s, the typical workday outside of agriculture was about twelve hours. Although regulation of hours for adult men was excluded from the social legislation of the 1880s, the length of the workday drifted downward—to about 10½ hours in 1900 and to about 9½ hours in 1913. With a six-day workweek, this trend meant a reduction from a 72-hour week to a 57-hour week over a period of forty years.[36] Of course these are averages. Hours for those who worked irregularly or in particular industries (like coal mining) might be shorter; while hours for many workers (especially women—see below) could be much longer.

As the workweek shortened, average wages rose, going from roughly 500 marks yearly in 1871 to roughly 1,100 marks yearly in 1913.[37] What this meant in terms of real wages is a matter of dispute. The best recent estimate is that real wages rose by 79 percent in this period, although older studies peg the increase as

[35] Sixteen of the thirty male autobiographers examined in one study had gone on *Wanderungen;* see Jochen Loreck, *Wie man früher Sozialdemokrat wurde. Das Kommunikationsverhalten in der deutschen Arbeiterbewegung und die Konzeption der sozialistischen Parteipublizistik durch August Bebel* (Bonn-Bad Godesberg, 1977), 133.

[36] Gerhard Bry, *Wages in Germany, 1871–1945* (Princeton, 1960), 45.

[37] Hohorst, Kocka, and Ritter, *Sozialgeschichtliches Arbeitsbuch,* 107.

low as 35 percent. There is general agreement that most of the improvement occurred before 1900.[38] None of these statistics should be taken too seriously, but the general impression they give is confirmed by the anecdotal evidence of the autobiographies. A safe generalization would be that in the early part of this century a male worker making 12–15 marks per week was at the low end of the scale, one making 20 marks in the middle, and one making 25–35 marks at the high end. (See "A Note about Currencies" in the front of this book.) Skilled workers' wages averaged about one-third higher than those of the unskilled.[39] By way of comparison, a breadwinner's income of about 2,000 marks would mark the threshold of the middle class. But, as late as 1912 in Prussia, nearly 40 percent of the population earned (or was dependent on someone earning) fewer than 900 marks yearly, down from 67 percent in 1896.[40]

Of course, periods of unemployment might drastically reduce yearly wages. While official statistics show relatively low unemployment levels (averaging 2–3 percent) for the Reich, the impressionistic evidence of the autobiographies suggests that these average figures are deceptively low.[41] One historian quite sensibly recommends doubling the official rates to get a more reliable picture.[42] But the burden was not felt as an average. Some, especially the unskilled and those in construction, were disproportionately affected. Even in a good year, a third of the work force might face significant periods of unemployment.[43] With no state unemployment compensation available, it is no surprise that the

[38] Ibid., 107–8; see also the summaries in Dieter Groh, *Negative Integration und revolutionärer Attentismus. Die Sozialdemokratie am Vorabend des Ersten Weltkrieges* (Frankfurt, 1973), esp. 40, 85.

[39] Bry, *Wages in Germany, 1871–1945*, 363.

[40] Hohorst, Kocka, and Ritter, *Sozialgeschichtliches Arbeitsbuch*, 106.

[41] Jürgen Kuczynski, *Germany, 1800 to the Present Day*, vol. 3, pt. 1 of *A Short History of Labour Conditions under Industrial Capitalism* (London, 1945), 162–64.

[42] Peter N. Stearns, *Lives of Labor: Work in a Maturing Industrial Society* (New York, 1975), 111, n. 27.

[43] Ibid., 85–117 passim.

fear of losing a job and the depression of looking for work loom so large in many of these autobiographies. Judged by today's standards, the German working class was badly off indeed. But raw wage and unemployment data disguise a complex reality. Families of unskilled workingmen depended on the main breadwinner for only about 75 percent of their total income.[44] The rest of the money came in from the earnings of wives and children, the renting of beds to lodgers, and other miscellaneous sources—from the pilfering of coal piles to the sale of surplus garden vegetables. To all of this we must add the intricate informal exchange of goods and services that had always been an integral part of the culture of the poor.

Low wages and unemployment were not the only threats. Poor health often precluded the long, uninterrupted work life that was so essential to any measure of security. Two of our authors (Moritz Bromme and Franz Rehbein) were permanently disabled by their work; while one other (Fritz Pauk) was forced to take up a sedentary trade. Among the others, illness, injury, and fatigue appear as almost constant, unwelcome companions. These laments probably mirror the generally depressed state of health among the working class. Precise interclass comparisons are not easy to make, but the high infant mortality rates among the poorest families are surely indicative of overall health conditions. Of the 2,201 children born into the 268 Munich families studied by Rosa Kempf in 1911, 910 had died—a mortality rate of 41.4 percent. Working mothers had lost more of their children than their hausfrau counterparts (46.4 percent and 38.9 percent, respectively). These figures are probably fairly typical for the period.[45] By way of contrast, the mortality rate by age fifteen for

[44] Hohorst, Kocka, and Ritter, *Sozialgeschichtliches Arbeitsbuch,* 112. This figure is probably too high; see the discussion of women workers that follows.
[45] Rosa Kempf, *Das Leben der jungen Fabrikmädchen in München* (Leipzig, 1911), 218–20; Kempf's book was vol. 135, pt. 2 of the *Schriften des Vereins für Sozialpolitik.* See the discussions in Sabine Richebächer, *Uns fehlt nur eine Kleinigkeit. Deutsche proletarische Frauenbewegung 1890–1914* (Frankfurt, 1982), 72; and Ute Frevert, "The Civilizing Tendency of Hygiene: Working-

the population as a whole during the first decade of the century was about 26.5 percent.[46]

Poor housing, inadequate diet, and inferior medical care no doubt played their parts here. Yet workers believed that their working conditions were responsible for many of their health problems. Despite the introduction of factory inspection in all of the Reich in 1878, a good deal of work was simply dangerous. Machine accidents in factories and mines, or on farms, could maim or kill; while dust and toxic fumes led to general listlessness, prolonged disability, or early death. At the very least, the endless exhaustion of most work contributed to premature aging. Earning power for a man usually peaked in his thirties. From age forty on—just when a middle-class man would be entering his peak earning years—a workingman was struggling to keep pace, especially if he did piecework. A study of the metal industry, for example, found that in the early years of the century only 5–10 percent of the workers were over fifty.[47] Those forced out of work found themselves dependent on the Reich's health, accident, or old-age and disability insurance (enacted 1883, 1884, and 1889, respectively). To be sure, these laws were watersheds of social legislation and protected the individual against destitution in the short run. But long-term disability was another matter; one had to make do with a pension of perhaps one-sixth of average wages: "Too little to live on, too much to die on"—as the saying had it.[48] It is a telling fact that almost all workers went on disability

Class Women under Medical Control in Imperial Germany," in *German Women in the Nineteenth Century: A Social History,* ed. John C. Fout (New York and London, 1984), 332; see also Hartmut Kaelble, *Industrialisation and Social Inequality in 19th-Century Europe,* trans. Bruce Little (New York, 1986), 142–44.

[46] Hohorst, Kocka, and Ritter, *Sozialgeschichtliches Arbeitsbuch,* 33.

[47] Marie Bernays, "Berufswahl und Berufsschicksal des modernen Industriearbeiters," *Archiv für Sozialwissenschaft und Sozialpolitik* 35 (1912): 123–76, and 36 (1913): 884–915, esp. 35, 127–33.

[48] Ibid., 36, 914; see also Gerhard A. Ritter, *Staat, Arbeiterschaft und Arbeiterbewegung in Deutschland. Vom Vormärz bis zum Ende der Weimaren Republik*

pension, rather than old-age pension, for which one was not eligible until age seventy.[49]

It is no wonder that working-class families got their children into the work force as soon as possible. Child labor had been an integral part of agricultural society and was also one of the most publicized evils of the early industrial period. The law of 1878 did away with some of the worst abuses: those under twelve (under thirteen after 1891) were banned from mines and factories; juveniles could enter the work force only upon completing their schooling; and their hours were limited. Further restrictions followed in the next generation.[50] As the autobiographies clearly reveal, much of this legislation meant little in practice. Parents were desperate for the extra money that children would bring into the household; and children could always earn a few paltry pfennigs in unregulated home-industry jobs or in factories that hid children when the inspectors came. As late as 1903 there were still about 2 million school-age children working.[51] By the time they got regular, legal jobs, adolescents were already used to hard work and harbored no illusions about continuing their education. While the children still lived at home, the family assumed that they (especially the daughters) would turn over much of their earnings to the household.[52] In the families studied by Rosa Kempf, daughters brought in 30 percent and sons 13 percent of the total household wages.[53] Although the figure for

(Berlin and Bonn, 1980), 52; and Hohorst, Kocka, and Ritter, *Sozialgeschichtliches Arbeitsbuch*, 156.

[49] Henning, *Die Industrialisierung in Deutschland 1800 bis 1914*, 270; Henderson, *The Rise of German Industrial Power*, 233. Workers in the Austrian Empire had no state old-age pensions.

[50] Kuczynski, *A Short History of Labour Conditions under Industrial Capitalism*, vol. 3, pt. 1, 170.

[51] Richebächer, *Uns fehlt nur eine Kleinigkeit*, 49.

[52] Robyn Dasey, "Women's Work and the Family: Women Garment Workers in Berlin and Hamburg before the First World War," in *The German Family: Essays on the Social History of the Family in Nineteenth- and Twentieth-Century Germany*, ed. Richard J. Evans and W. R. Lee (London, 1981), 228.

[53] Kempf, *Das Leben der jungen Fabrikmädchen in München*, 124.

daughters is inflated by the nature of the study (Kempf was studying only families with daughters working in factories), the figures do indicate the economic importance of getting adolescents into the work force.

Like child labor, women's labor tends to slip between the neat statistical categories designed for an adult male work world. Despite middle-class (and often working-class) beliefs that women belonged in the home, millions of women were in the labor force. Of the 17,836,000 people classified as "workers" in the 1907 census, 6,422,000 (36.0 percent) were female. The majority (4,254,000) of these were in agriculture. Of the remainder, 605,000 were in commerce and transportation and 1,563,000 in industry. Women represented 18.2 percent of all industrial workers, up from 13.3 percent in 1882. (The change probably reflects an increase in domestic industry, not a massive movement of women into factories.)[54] To these numbers we must add 1,265,000 domestic servants and an unknown number of prostitutes (perhaps more than 300,000).[55] Still, the picture is incomplete. The census routinely missed countless women who were occupied full-time or part-time at home doing piecework, some of which might have been taken home from a factory (a practice prohibited in 1908). This world of home work is a statistical quagmire. Not only was it seasonal and irregular, but also, both employer and employee had an interest in concealment—the former to save on insurance contributions, the latter to save on taxes.[56] And then, there were any number of miscellaneous odd jobs for women: taking beer to a factory at lunch hour, washing dishes, cleaning apartment house corridors, tak-

[54] Hohorst, Kocka, and Ritter, *Sozialgeschichtliches Arbeitsbuch,* 67. On this issue, see Barbara Franzoi, *At the Very Least She Pays the Rent: Women and German Industrialization, 1871–1914* (Westport, Conn. and London, 1985), 17–39.

[55] In 1907, 98.78 percent of domestic servants were females; see Rolf Engelsing, *Zur Sozialgeschichte deutscher Mittel- und Unterschichten* (Göttingen, 1973), 232, 235–36. On the number of prostitutes, see Richard J. Evans, "Prostitution, State and Society in Imperial Germany," *Past and Present,* no. 70 (February 1976): 106–29, esp. 108.

[56] Franzoi, *At the Very Least She Pays the Rent,* 124–42, esp. 127.

ing care of boarders, or tending a neighbor's children. Moreover, some 70 percent of working women also did all of their own housework—no small task in the absence of modern conveniences![57] Unlike men, women had virtually no free time.

Sex segregation of work tasks—so much a part of agricultural society—carried over in new forms into industrial society. The majority of women worked, as they always had, with cloth, food and drink, and dirt. They made, cleaned, repaired, and ironed clothes; they cooked and served meals; and they cleaned up the messes other people made. In the other great branches of the economy—construction, metals, wood and paper, and mining—males predominated. When women did work alongside men, it was usually as unskilled helpers—packing boxes, stirring vats, filling bottles, fetching and sorting materials, folding papers, and the like.[58] Very few women had learned a skilled trade. What little money a family might have saved for an apprenticeship almost always went to the sons. In Rosa Kempf's study, 97 percent of working mothers were unskilled, and only 13 of the 125 children in skilled trades were girls.[59] Clearly, these parents did not want to "waste" money and time training a daughter who

[57] Jean H. Quataert, *Reluctant Feminists in German Social Democracy, 1885–1917* (Princeton, 1979), 39; Richebächer, *Uns fehlt nur eine Kleinigkeit,* 297, n. 4.

[58] Quataert, *Reluctant Feminists in German Social Democracy, 1885–1917,* 27–45; Franzoi, *At the Very Least She Pays the Rent,* esp. 17–39; Rosemary Orthmann, "Labor Force Participation, Life Cycle, and Expenditure Patterns: The Case of Unmarried Female Factory Workers in Berlin (1902)," in *German Women in the Eighteenth and Nineteenth Centuries,* eds. Joeres and Maynes, esp. 26–29; John C. Fout, "The Viennese Enquête of 1896 on Working Women," in *German Women in the Eighteenth and Nineteenth Centuries,* eds. Joeres and Maynes, 42–60; on the impact of the sewing machine on women's work, see Karin Hausen, "Technical Progress and Women's Labour in the Nineteenth Century: The Social History of the Sewing Machine," in *The Social History of Politics: Critical Perspectives in West German Historical Writing Since 1945,* ed. Georg Iggers (New York, 1985), 259–81.

[59] Kempf, *Das Leben der jungen Fabrikmädchen in München,* 13, 221. Even this small proportion is probably too high—inflated by the selectivity of the survey.

they hoped would make a good marriage and soon be out of the work force.

Many families considered domestic service the best preparation for marriage.[60] A good housekeeper might well make the difference between modest dignity and impoverished squalor in the working-class household. However, domestic service was shunned by experienced city women who preferred the higher pay and greater freedom of the factory.[61] Well-to-do households usually relied on unmarried girls from the provinces, who quit after a few years to get married. In the meantime these girls were at the complete mercy of their employers. Driven by the whims of an all-too-often tyrannical hausfrau, servants were on the jump fifteen, even eighteen, hours a day for wages that amounted to no more than three to four pfennigs per hour.[62] If, in addition, they were fending off unwanted sexual advances from the men of the house, their lives could become a nightmare. There was no easy escape, since servants were not even free laborers in the modern sense. The old Servants Code put almost total power in the hands of the employer. As Doris Viersbeck's autobiography shows, a girl who fell out with her mistress could forfeit wages and be ruined by a bad reference in her workbook. Desperate servant girls were the most likely group to fall into prostitution.[63] Yet despite its drawbacks, more women were employed in domestic service than in any other job outside of agriculture;

[60] On domestic service, see Oscar Stillich, *Die Frage der weiblichen Dienstboten in Berlin* (Berlin and Bern, 1902); Regina Schulte, "Dienstmädchen in herrschaftlichen Haushalt. Zur Genese ihrer Sozialpsychologie," *Zeitschrift für Bayerische Landesgeschichte* 41 (1978): 879–920; Engelsing, *Zur Sozialgeschichte deutscher Mittel- und Unterschichten,* 225–61.

[61] Wettstein-Adelt describes women who would rather starve than submit to the tyranny of domestic service; see Wettstein-Adelt, *3½ Monate Fabrik-Arbeiterin,* 95.

[62] See the tables in Stillich, *Die Frage der weiblichen Dienstboten in Berlin,* esp. 423–33; servants consistently reported that they worked more hours than their employers said they did.

[63] Richard J. Evans, "Prostitution, State and Society in Imperial Germany," 107–8; former barmaids were also numerous among the ranks of prostitutes.

and domestic service remained the typical transition from rural to urban life for women. In Hamburg, for example, about one-third of all employed women were live-in domestics in the generation before World War I.[64] Perhaps as many as one-half of all urban working-class men married women who had at one time been in domestic service.[65]

Women's wages reflected their subordinate position in the labor market. On average, they earned one-third to one-half less than men. In some trades, like printing, the difference was even greater.[66] Skill differentials are only a part of the explanation, for women typically received less even when they did basically the same work as men. The prevailing assumption was that women did not "need" as high a wage: their work was supposed to be supplementary or temporary—to help their family or to tide them over until marriage; and they had fewer expenses, being able to cook, sew, and clean on their own. Since these arguments expressed not only deeply held traditional beliefs, but also the employers' self-interest, they were impervious to empirical evidence. The millions of women supporting themselves or their families could consider themselves lucky if they made ten or twelve marks a week in the early part of this century.[67] Those swarms of prostitutes were a grim confirmation of the widespread belief that "a woman can always get by."

Sex distinctions were sharpened by regulation. Middle-class

[64] Dasey, "Women's Work and the Family," 229. In 1900, 12.4 percent of Hamburg households had servants, down from 17.3 percent in 1871; see Engelsing, *Zur Sozialgeschichte deutscher Mittel- und Unterschichten,* 240.

[65] Peter Stearns estimates (probably conservatively) that at least one-third of urban working-class females had been domestic servants at one time or another; see Stearns, "The Unskilled and Industrialization: A Transformation of Consciousness," *Archiv für Sozialgeschichte* 16 (1976): 248–82, esp. 260–61.

[66] Bry, *Wages in Germany, 1871–1945,* 368–69; see also Franzoi, *At the Very Least She Pays the Rent,* esp. 41–49.

[67] More than half of working women may actually have been making less than a subsistence wage of nine to ten marks per week; see Richebächer, *Uns fehlt nur eine Kleinigkeit,* 28.

factory inspectors, striving to protect women and "save" the working-class family, fought to keep unrelated men and women apart on the job. (However, no one said anything about the widespread sexual harassment of women by male superiors at work.) Beginning in 1891, the Industrial Code limited women's workdays to eleven hours in industry, assured their lunch breaks (so that they could run home to tend the family), and compelled a four-week leave after births. And the years before World War I witnessed an expansion of restrictions—keeping women out of certain jobs (like underground mining), prohibiting night work, and cutting the workday to ten hours. Care must be taken not to exaggerate the effects of this legislation. As stressed earlier, most women workers were employed in agriculture, home industry, or domestic service—all beyond the reach of factory regulation. Nonetheless, the cumulative effect of industrial legislation (as well as the attitudes that informed it) was probably to reinforce traditional sex roles. To reformers, successful regulation got women out of "men's jobs" and returned them to the home.[68]

Such attitudes toward women in the work force should not be dismissed as simply reactionary. For the working class, work was rarely the path to the independence and personal fulfillment characteristic of the middle-class professions. On the contrary, work usually equalled body- and soul-destroying drudgery; it was something to be avoided. Most working-class men (and probably women too) felt that it was the height of good sense and decency to subject as few family members as possible to the hardships of work. Accordingly, most women withdrew from full-time work when they married, staying in or returning to the labor force only if absolutely necessary. The better-paid skilled workers were generally able to keep their wives at home and

[68] On protective legislation, see Jean H. Quataert, "A Source Analysis in German Women's History: Factory Inspectors' Reports and the Shaping of Working-Class Lives, 1878–1914," *Central European History* 16, no. 2 (June 1984): 99–121; also Quataert, *Reluctant Feminists in German Social Democracy, 1885–1917*, 39–45; and Franzoi, *At the Very Least She Pays the Rent*, 60–81.

preferred to do so as a matter of pride. As Göhre observed, "If a man earns enough, he doesn't let his wife and children go into the works of his own accord."[69]

However, full-time homemaking was not a realistic choice for many married working-class women. Given the nature of women's work, precise statistics are impossible to come by, but clearly, a majority of wives were in the work force at least some of the time. Rosa Kempf found in Munich that in households where both husband and wife were present, 42.4 percent of the wives were exclusively hausfraus, 16.5 percent worked part-time, and 41.1 percent worked full-time.[70] (Of course, some of this work would have been domestic work.) Those who worked part-time contributed 10.3 percent to the total family wages; those who worked full-time, 28.3 percent.[71] Families with many children were in a special bind: they needed more money, but it was all the harder for the mother to find extra time. Of course, married women whose husbands were "work-shy," incapacitated, or dead (over one-quarter of the women in Kempf's study) were driven, along with their children, into the work force.[72] To judge by the autobiographies, the ideal of working people was a small family with the husband in a steady, skilled job and the wife a homemaker. Any deviation from this ideal (and how few families could measure up!) spelled hardship. But hardship was the reality.[73]

---

[69] Göhre, *Three Months in a Workshop,* 116. A survey of married women in the textile industry revealed that only 10 percent of the women worked because they didn't like housework (which is not to say that they liked the textile work!); see Stearns, "The Unskilled and Industrialization," 254.

[70] Kempf, *Das Leben der jungen Fabrikmädchen in München,* 13.

[71] Ibid., 124. In contrast, a 1909 survey by the Imperial Statistical Office reported the wife's contribution as 7.7 percent if the husband was unskilled, 3.5 percent if he was skilled; see Hohorst, Kocka, and Ritter, *Sozialgeschichtliches Arbeitsbuch,* 112; Kempf's figures are probably more realistic.

[72] In Kempf's study, wives who worked full-time had an average of 3.9 children, those who worked part-time 5.0, and those who were exclusively hausfraus 6.1; Kempf, *Das Leben der jungen Fabrikmädchen in München,* 218–20.

[73] On working wives, see Quataert, *Reluctant Feminists in German Social Democracy, 1885–1917,* 37–39; Stearns, "Adaptation to Industrialization," 326–27;

LIFE OUTSIDE OF WORK

Any discussion of life outside of work must begin with one overriding reality: after a worker had housed and fed his or her family, there was little money left for anything else. Food alone, at the turn of the century, represented at least one-half of the typical household budget.[74] By today's standards, that money did not buy a very interesting diet. If, in Ludwig Feuerbach's famous equation, "You are what you eat," then German workers had traditionally been composed largely of potatoes, dark bread, and beer. Scholars generally agree that diet improved dramatically—in both quantity and variety—during the course of the nineteenth century. Workers were eating increasing amounts of meat (especially pork), white bread, sugar, fruit, fresh vegetables, and milk.[75] But even as late as 1910, a male worker might consume several pounds of potatoes and bread daily, washed down by prodigious quantities of beer. Although beer is not the most efficient source of body energy, it does provide a significant number of calories, and it makes a plain, dry diet more palatable. (To subsume beer drinking under the rubric "The Alcohol Problem" would, then, be misleading. It was no accident that working-class drinking, of both beer and spirits, declined as diet improved.)[76] On the whole, workers were getting as much nourish-

Dasey, "Women's Work and the Family," 223–24, 243–44; Frevert, "The Civilizing Tendency of Hygiene," 326–27; Bernays, "Berufswahl und Berufsschicksal des modernen Industriearbeiters," *Archiv für Sozialwissenschaft und Sozialpolitik* 36 (1913): 906–9; Franzoi, *At the Very Least She Pays the Rent*, 103–23.

[74] Hohorst, Kocka, and Ritter, *Sozialgeschichtliches Arbeitsbuch*, 113, 118.

[75] Ibid., 120–21; see also Hans-Jürgen Teuteberg, "Wie ernährten sich die Arbeiter im Kaiserreich?" in *Arbeiterexistenz im 19. Jahrhundert. Lebensstandard und Lebensgestaltung deutscher Arbeiter und Handwerker,* ed. Werner Conze and Ulrich Engelhardt (Stuttgart, 1981), 57–73.

[76] On beer as a food, see James S. Roberts, "Drink and Working-Class Living Standards in Late 19th Century Germany," in *Arbeiterexistenz im 19. Jahrhundert,* ed. Conze and Engelhardt, 74–91, esp. 83–89; and Hans J. Teuteberg and Günter Wiegelmann, *Der Wandel der Nahrungsgewohnheiten unter dem Einfluss der Industrialisierung* (Göttingen, 1972), 143.

ment for their money as was reasonably possible. Actual famine was a thing of the past, though undernourishment—especially for those doing heavy labor—was still a fact of working-class life.[77]

The period from 1850 to 1900 may have been an "epoch of nourishment revolution,"[78] but there was no equivalent revolution in housing conditions. Housing for the rural poor had always been wretched. Urbanization usually got the animals out of the house, but in other respects marked little improvement. Urban dwellings were both crowded and expensive. Between a fifth and a third of the wages of big-city workers might go for rent. (Only a tiny minority of workers were home owners.)[79] For their money, workers were forced to squeeze their families into tiny, usually dismal, apartments. In 1910, 70.5 percent of all apartments in towns of more than 5,000 population had three rooms or fewer.[80] With the middle class taking the "big" apartments, most working-class families were getting by with one or two rooms. Crowding was at its worst in Berlin, where in 1905, 74.7 percent of the population lived in one- or two-room apartments. In 1912, 600,000 people (about 30 percent of the population) in the capital city were living five or more to a room.[81] This was

[77] Teuteberg and Wiegelmann, *Der Wandel der Nahrungsgewohnheiten unter dem Einfluss der Industrialisierung,* 141–47. Wettstein-Adelt claimed that the factory women she observed could have eaten much better had they not spent so much money on personal adornment; see Wettstein-Adelt, *3½ Monate Fabrik-Arbeiterin,* 15.

[78] Teuteberg, "Wie ernährten sich die Arbeiter im Kaiserreich?" 60.

[79] Niethammer, "Wie wohnten die Arbeiter im Kaiserreich?" 80. Lower figures, reflecting the percentage of rent in the total household budget, are found in Hohorst, Kocka, and Ritter, *Sozialgeschichtliches Arbeitsbuch,* 112. In the industrial city of Bochum, for example, only 5.2 percent of the skilled metalworkers were home owners in 1880; see David F. Crew, *Town in the Ruhr: A Social History of Bochum, 1860–1914* (New York, 1979), 173. On housing in the Ruhr, see S. H. F. Hickey, *Workers in Imperial Germany: The Miners of the Ruhr* (Oxford, 1985), 36–69; for a European-wide perspective, see Kaelble, *Industrialisation and Social Inequality in 19th-Century Europe,* 105–27.

[80] Niethammer, "Wie wohnten die Arbeiter im Kaiserreich?" 96.

[81] Ibid., 87, 90.

cramped enough under the best of circumstances. When "home" doubled as a workplace—as it often did for women—beds, chairs, and stoves competed for space with worktables and sewing machines. Dora Landé, who investigated the living conditions of Berlin machine workers for the Social Policy Association, described the proletarian apartment at its worst:

A living room and tiny kitchen: with two adults and three children, that means that everyone sleeps in the same room, all three children in one bed. This is very much the norm in proletarian circles, for the single room of such an apartment has space for, at most, three beds, one sofa, one table, and one wardrobe.[82]

Nor did such apartments have the amenities that were increasingly common for the middle class. Even as late as 1910, flush toilets were a luxury, the shared outhouse being the rule.[83] Electricity too was a rarity; and only about 15 percent of workers had gas for cooking, lighting, or heating.[84] Most got by with petroleum and wood. Even the better apartments were likely to be dark, damp, smoky, and either too hot or too cold. As Wettstein-Adelt remarked, if one accepts the premise, "Tell me where you live and I'll tell you who you are," then most of the workers could not even be called human.[85] It is no wonder that workers wanted to escape—to the tavern, to a suburban garden plot, or for a walk in the country. One of Levenstein's most consistent findings was that workers dreamed of owning a little house in the country.[86] In small industrial towns some workers were in fact able to live in outlying villages, where they could maintain settled, semi-rural habits.[87] But, especially in big cities, the usual pattern was

[82] Bernays, "Berufswahl und Berufsschicksal des modernen Industriearbeiters," *Archiv für Sozialwissenschaft und Sozialpolitik* 36 (1913): 901.

[83] Kuczynski, *A Short History of Labour Conditions under Industrial Capitalism*, vol. 3, pt. 1, 169.

[84] Ashok V. Desai, *Real Wages in Germany, 1871–1913* (Oxford, 1968), 27. Heating and lighting accounted for 4–5 percent of the total household budget; see Hohorst, Kocka, and Ritter, *Sozialgeschichtliches Arbeitsbuch*, 113.

[85] Wettstein-Adelt, *3½ Monate Fabrik-Arbeiterin*, 56.

[86] Levenstein, *Die Arbeiterfrage*, esp. 115, 123, 130, 187, 198, 212–13.

[87] Bernays, "Berufswahl und Berufsschicksal des modernen Industriearbeiters," *Archiv für Sozialwissenschaft und Sozialpolitik* 36 (1913): 900–901.

a restless, almost frenetic, housing turnover, as workers moved into, out of, and around town—responding to job changes, family additions, or some deep inner need for variety. In some German cities the majority of apartments turned over every year.[88]

Middle-class social reformers, like Paul Göhre, were alarmed by proletarian housing conditions. They feared that crowding, excessive mobility, and particularly, the frequent presence of lodgers would lead to the breakdown of the family.[89] At any given time, 10–20 percent of all households in the Reich had lodgers. The proportion was higher in the working class, particularly among hard-pressed families with children. In these families, lodgers were a significant source of extra income.[90] Most lodgers were single men, who rented just a bed, sometimes sharing it with a family member.[91] Under the best of circumstances they were taken into the bosom of the family and developed an avuncular relationship with the children. More often, they were a disruptive element, impinging on privacy and even molesting female family members. However undesirable such a family situation might have been, the fears of reformers were probably misdirected. There never was a golden age of the family, such as they envisioned. And even well-intentioned outside observers

[88] Niethammer estimates that some families spent 10–15 percent of their rent budget on moving expenses alone; see his "Wie wohnten die Arbeiter im Kaiserreich?" 114, and, for a table of apartment turnover in selected cities, 83.

[89] Göhre, *Three Months in a Workshop,* 37–38; Hickey, *Workers in Imperial Germany,* 48–51.

[90] Niethammer, "Wie wohnten die Arbeiter im Kaiserreich?", esp. 116, 118; see also Franz J. Brüggemeier and Lutz Niethammer, "Schlafgänger, Schnapskasinos und schwerindustrielle Kolonie. Aspekte der Arbeiterwohnungsfrage im Ruhrgebiet vor dem Ersten Weltkrieg," in *Fabrik. Familie. Feierabend. Beiträge zur Sozialgeschichte des Alltags im Industriezeitalter,* ed. Jürgen Reulecke and Wolfhard Weber (Wuppertal, 1978), 152–53; on income from lodgers, see Hohorst, Kocka, and Ritter, *Sozialgeschichtliches Arbeitsbuch,* 112.

[91] Female lodgers were not unheard-of. Wettstein-Adelt describes the wretched accommodations offered to her in response to a newspaper ad seeking a place to sleep in Chemnitz; see her *3½ Monate Fabrik-Arbeiterin,* 61–65.

were prone to misinterpret proletarian habits by applying idealized middle-class values.[92]

Viewed in historical context, the proletarian family was remarkably resilient. In fact, what the middle class viewed as family breakdown and rampant immorality are probably better understood as signs of continuity. Göhre complained that no worker over seventeen in Chemnitz was chaste. He pointed a finger at the dance halls.[93] What he may not have known was that chastity in the countryside had been just as rare. *Ländlich, Schändlich* (rural and shameful) was the old saying in the country, where sexual relations among the young had always been casual, especially at festival times. Peasant couples frequently did not marry until the young woman was pregnant or had already given birth. As the autobiographies suggest, the same pattern carried over into the industrial age. Almost every physically presentable girl had her *Schatz* (sweetheart), who gave her presents, accompanied her on walks and to dance halls, and not infrequently got her pregnant. Marriage usually followed, but not always quickly or even to the baby's father. Among factory workers there was no stigma attached to illegitimacy, but there is no clear evidence that illegitimacy was on the increase. For most workers, marriage and children remained the norm.[94]

The quality of those marriages is, of course, hard to judge. By

---

[92] Niethammer, "Wie wohnten die Arbeiter im Kaiserreich?", esp. 122–28; see also James H. Jackson, "Overcrowding and Family Life: Working-Class Families and the Housing Crisis in Late Nineteenth-Century Duisburg," in *The German Family,* ed. Evans and Lee, 194–200.

[93] Göhre, *Three Months in a Workshop,* 202–3.

[94] See the fundamental article by R. P. Neuman, "Industrialization and Sexual Behavior: Some Aspects of Working-Class Life in Imperial Germany," in *Modern European Social History,* ed. Robert J. Bezucha (Lexington, Mass., Toronto, London, 1972), 270–98, esp. 281–85; also Bernays, "Berufswahl und Berufsschicksal des modernen Industriearbeiters," *Archiv für Sozialwissenschaft und Sozialpolitik* 36 (1913): 902–6. The illegitimacy rate (for live births) in the Reich was 8.5 percent in 1901, 8.4 percent in 1906, and 9.1 percent in 1912; see Hohorst, Kocka, and Ritter, *Sozialgeschichtliches Arbeitsbuch,* 36; for an early discussion of working-class illegitimacy, see Othmar Spann, "Die

middle-class standards, the expectations were minimal. From the matter-of-fact descriptions in the autobiographies, one gets little sense that workers married in quest of romantic love or personal fulfillment.[95] Given the pressures of poverty, those goals would have been virtually unrealizable. Wettstein-Adelt was probably right when she observed: "In families that are either childless or blessed with one or two children, conditions are usually simple, but orderly, and marital harmony prevails. Where there are a lot of children, there is usually strife, distress, filth, and misery; and unfaithfulness on the husband's part is much more common."[96] A large family, Wettstein-Adelt lamented, forced the wife to neglect the family and enter the work force full-time.[97] The autobiographies provide a wealth of testimony about childhood hardship. But as they look back, most authors pay tribute to the struggling proletarian mother, who held the family together on a few marks a week and by sheer force of will.[98]

How successful a wife was at keeping the family together often depended on how much time and money her husband spent at the tavern. There appear to be no drunkards among our authors (writing an autobiography almost assumes sobriety), but stories of the horrors of alcohol fill these pages. Leaving aside barmaids (who were "professional drinkers"), alcohol abuse seems to have been largely a male problem. Like Frau Hoffmann, many a wife met her husband at work on payday in order to get her hands on the week's wages before he squandered them in the tavern. Just how many men drank up their wages is hard to say. Certainly, the potential for alcohol abuse was interwoven with the whole

---

geschlechtlich-sittlichen Verhältnisse im Dienstboten- und Arbeiterinnenstande, gemessen an der Erscheinung der unehelichen Geburten," *Zeitschrift für Socialwissenschaft* 7 (1904): 287–303.

[95] Koch, "Arbeitermemoiren als sozialwissenschaftliches Erkenntnisquelle," 151.

[96] Wettstein-Adelt, *3½ Monate Fabrik-Arbeiterin,* 42.

[97] Ibid., 43–44.

[98] Münchow, *Frühe deutsche Arbeiterbiographie,* 117.

fabric of working-class leisure. Taverns were refuges from home and work, social centers for card playing and gossip, resting places on Sunday walks, as well as the sites of club meetings and political rallies. Studies of workers' budgets at the turn of the century suggest that, on average, at least 5 percent of expenditures went for alcohol.[99] Göhre, who was something of a moralist, observed that being drunk now and then was not held against a man.[100] Yet Levenstein found only a small minority of workers who admitted that alcohol use was "indispensable" to them (5.6 percent of metalworkers, 5.9 percent of textile workers, but 19.7 percent of miners). Most workers claimed to prefer the pleasures of the family to those of the tavern.[101] A good deal of drinking is probably being covered up in these answers, but it is important to keep the whole alcohol problem in perspective. Beer and schnapps were a part of the diet, and they were often consumed out of desperation as stimulants (or rather, covers for exhaustion) on the job. With the improvements in diet in mature industrial society, alcohol consumption (especially of schnapps) was actually falling.[102]

Clearly, the overwhelming majority of workers looked forward to Sunday, not as a day of drunken excess, but as a relief from the tyranny of work. For someone deprived of open spaces, sunlight, and good air, a country *Spaziergang* (walk) was the most tempting Sunday recreation. A Berlin mechanic spoke for many when he said, "I'd like to go walking all day the way the rich people do."[103] Fortunately, woods and fields were only a streetcar's ride away for most city workers. A garden plot on the edge of town

[99] James S. Roberts, "Drink and Working-Class Living Standards in Late 19th Century Germany," 77; Hohorst, Kocka, and Ritter, *Sozialgeschichtliches Arbeitsbuch,* 118; on drinking in general, see James S. Roberts, *Drink, Temperance, and the Working Class in Nineteenth-Century Germany* (Boston, 1984).

[100] Göhre, *Three Months in a Workshop,* 199.

[101] Levenstein, *Die Arbeiterfrage,* 257, 269, 281, and 247–82 passim.

[102] Hohorst, Kocka, and Ritter, *Sozialgeschichtliches Arbeitsbuch,* 121.

[103] Bernays, "Berufswahl und Berufsschicksal des modernen Industriearbeiters," *Archiv für Sozialwissenschaft und Sozialpolitik* 36 (1913): 911; see also Levenstein, *Die Arbeiterfrage,* 354–81.

might also provide a little contact with nature, as well as a few welcome fresh vegetables. Young single workers were more likely to seek simple merrymaking, frequenting dance joints or cheap concert halls (*Tingeltangel* in the inimitable original) with their sweethearts.[104] Of course, at its worst, Sunday entertainment could degenerate into a tour of all the local taverns. But the German penchant for organizing clubs and associations ensured an abundance of wholesome entertainments—at least for men; women had little time to join in the fun. For the athletic, every town had its soccer, bowling, gymnastics, and (from the 1890s) bicycling clubs. There were choirs and bands for every taste and talent. And the intellectually inclined could choose (at least in the big cities) from an array of lecture series, extension courses, theater societies, and libraries.

Most of the autobiographers put particular stress on the pleasures of reading. To be sure, we are dealing with the more intellectual strata here (only 5.9 percent of the total males in Levenstein's overly precise but suggestive calculation). This elite was overwhelmingly skilled, urban, and male.[105] Still, there is good evidence that reading was an important element of many workers' lives. By the late nineteenth century, illiteracy had virtually disappeared in Germany;[106] and relatively cheap books and newspapers were plentiful. As the autobiographies suggest, there were still many poor readers, but even they might plow through trashy novels, popular calendars, or Sunday supplements. All the workers in the Chemnitz factory where Göhre worked read the

---

[104] For a description of a variety of such places, see Wettstein-Adelt, *3½ Monate Fabrik-Arbeiterin*, 80–87.

[105] Levenstein, *Die Arbeiterfrage*, 113. On working-class reading, see Dieter Langewiesche and Klaus Schönhoven, "Arbeiterbibliotheken und Arbeiterlektüre im Wilhelminischen Deutschland," *Archiv für Sozialgeschichte* 16 (1976): 134–204; see also Alfred Kelly, *The Descent of Darwin: The Popularization of Darwinism in Germany, 1860–1914* (Chapel Hill, N.C., 1981), 127–30.

[106] Of Prussian newlyweds in 1897, only 0.75 percent of the men and 1.25 percent of the women were classified as illiterates; see Hohorst, Kocka, and Ritter, *Sozialgeschichtliches Arbeitsbuch*, 166.

newspaper, even though only 3–4 percent of them were, in Göhre's judgment, intellectually aware.[107] The great majority of Levenstein's respondents claimed to be book readers. Their reading lists (even allowing for some bragging) are impressive tributes to self-education. Authors like Shakespeare, Schiller, Goethe, Maupassant, Zola, Bellamy, Tolstoy, Gorki, and Hauptmann turn up repeatedly on the fiction side.[108] August Bebel's *Woman and Socialism* (1879) was by far the most popular nonfiction book. There was also considerable interest in science (especially evolutionary theory), popular history, and anticlerical works. But party and union librarians routinely complained that workers showed little interest in serious political and economic works. Lassalle's speeches and Engels's *Origin of the Family* (1884) were reasonably popular, but even serious readers shied away from Marx. Clearly, the majority of reading was light reading of a kind hardly distinguishable from middle-class light reading. Most workers used their precious spare time to relax; a minority to better themselves; and only a tiny elite to increase their political awareness.[109]

CLASS CONSCIOUSNESS

The majority of authors in this book were class-conscious Social Democrats. For some of them the very writing of an autobiography was a political act, and their conversion to Social Democracy forms the intellectual and spiritual center of their story. Like the authors of religious autobiographies, they see their life teleologically, and they judge their preconversion years solely in relation to their present consciousness.[110] Of course, these men and

---

[107] Göhre, *Three Months in a Workshop*, 113.
[108] Levenstein, *Die Arbeiterfrage*, 382–403.
[109] See Kelly, *The Descent of Darwin*, 127–30.
[110] Pascal, *Design and Truth in Autobiography*, 95–98.

women were far more politically aware than their fellow workers. But to judge by election returns, there were millions who shared their convictions. From a tiny base of 3.2 percent of the electorate (males over 25) in the first Reichstag election of 1871, the Social Democratic party proved itself an increasingly successful vote-getter. In 1890, the SPD emerged from the twilight of illegality as the largest single party in the Reich. And in the election of 1912, the last before World War I, the party garnered some 4,250,000 votes, 34.5 percent of the total (more than double that of its nearest competitor, the Catholic Center party).[111] Some of these votes surely came from middle-class sympathizers, but there can be no doubt that the vast majority of male industrial workers considered themselves Social Democrats—at least on election day. For most workers, the development of political consciousness was tantamount to a conversion to Social Democracy.

Impressive as these election statistics are, they should not be taken as signs of a widespread, deep, or sophisticated commitment to Social Democracy. Actual party membership (a rough indicator of strength of commitment)—though growing—was only a fraction of vote totals, and overwhelmingly male.[112] Even among those 970,112 party members (in 1912), the rough-and-ready intellectual awareness characteristic of the autobiographers was confined to a minority. (Recall Göhre's and Levenstein's sobering assessments of intellectual awareness.) Those frequent complaints in the autobiographies about the ignorance and lethargy of the masses are probably well-founded.

None of this should be surprising. As is abundantly clear in the autobiographies, the obstacles on the road to class consciousness were formidable, even for the intelligent and ambitious. Those in power in Imperial Germany tried every means at their disposal—from outright suppression to the subtle lure of social

---

[111] Hohorst, Kocka, and Ritter, *Sozialgeschichtliches Arbeitsbuch*, 173–75, 179.
[112] Werner Thönnessen, *The Emancipation of Women: The Rise and Decline of the Women's Movement in German Social Democracy 1863–1933*, trans. Joris de Bres (Glasgow, 1973), 116.

welfare—to contain the growth of Social Democracy. From an early age, children learned in school that Social Democrats sought to deprive honest people of the fruits of their labor, while rewarding the lazy and shiftless. Like school, the military (to which all young men were subject) also provided the state an opportunity to inoculate its citizens against the "inner enemy." Kaiser Wilhelm told a group of recruits in 1891 that they might have to "shoot down [their] own relatives, brothers, even parents," should Social Democracy threaten public order. No Social Democratic literature was permitted in the barracks; soldiers were barred from taverns frequented by Social Democrats; and vocal Social Democrats were isolated from their peers and tormented into submission.[113] (With pardonable exaggeration, one might characterize the workhouse described by Ernst Schuchardt as the ideal of upper-class domination. There the worker is ruled by military discipline suffused with religious piety.) Despite its rigors, army service was for many men a welcome interruption in a dull life. Their selectively retained fond memories were psychological anchors in the existing order. But even when "free" and in the world of work, Social Democrats were still subject to harassment by employers, who were likely to regard Social Democracy as an economic pipe dream, contrary to human nature. Zealous agitators at the workplace could easily find themselves demoted, fired, and even blacklisted.

Hatred of Social Democracy ran deepest in rural areas, where millions still worked, lived, or at least had family connections or childhood memories. Peasants were generally suspicious of outsiders—especially, well-read and critically minded ones. As Fritz Pauk recalls of his rural childhood, the call "The Social Democrats are coming!" was enough to send him scurrying under the bed to hide. Moreover, the enduring powers of traditional institutions greatly inhibited Social Democratic organizational efforts in rural areas.[114] Few urban workers attended church, but in the

[113] Ritter, *Staat, Arbeiterschaft und Arbeiterbewegung in Deutschland*, 30, 31–33.
[114] On this issue, see Jens Flemming, "Landarbeiter zwischen Gewerkschaften und 'Werksgemeinschaft.' Zum Verhältnis von Agrarunternehmern und

country, where the clergy was still influential, village pastors and priests condemned Social Democrats as godless outside agitators. In town the worker was at least unconstrained at the ballot box; whereas those in the semibondage of estate labor voted under the overseer's watchful eyes (as Otto, the contract laborer, describes). Many workers with rural backgrounds internalized these negative images and were often astonished by their first contact with committed Social Democrats. Instead of the raving lunatics of their childhood fantasies, they encountered reasonable and decorous people who actually embodied many of the best "bourgeois" virtues.

Institutions were not the only forces constraining Social Democracy. Politically inclined men often faced vehement opposition from the women in their lives. A study of thirty-three Social Democratic autobiographers has revealed that not a single author was supported by his (or in three cases, her) mother in the decision to join the party. Wives usually reacted just as negatively.[115] There were, of course, Social Democratic women, and their numbers were increasing in the last years before World War I. (Until 1908 women were legally barred from full membership in any party, and even the most progressive men were still ambivalent about yielding any real power to women.) By 1914 there were almost 175,000 female party members, about 16 percent of the total.[116] But, as the party leadership realized, most of these women were the nonworking wives of highly committed male comrades. An independent decision by a woman to join the party was rare.[117] Indeed, as Wettstein-Adelt pointed out, it was even

---

Landarbeiterbewegung im Übergang vom Kaiserreich zur Weimarer Republik," *Archiv für Sozialgeschichte* 14 (1974): 351–418, esp. 351–56.

[115] Loreck, *Wie man früher Sozialdemokrat wurde*, 238–39.

[116] Thönnessen, *Emancipation of Women*, 116.

[117] See Richard J. Evans, "Politics and the Family: Social Democracy and the Working-Class Family in Theory and Practice Before 1914," in *The German Family*, ed. Evans and Lee, 258–88.

rare for a woman to call herself a Social Democrat out of real personal conviction.[118] Social Democratic women like Ottilie Baader and Adelheid Popp, both of whom achieved modest distinction, were unusual exceptions.

There were some immediate and practical reasons for women's greater conservatism and caution. Women were responsible for the tight family budget, and in a larger sense saw themselves as protectors of the family. They viewed party activity as a costly and risky threat. Why spend money on books, newspapers, or membership dues when the children need new shoes? And why risk being fired and impoverishing the family for a distant and perhaps unattainable goal? These are certainly fair questions, but the attitudes revealed in them run deeper than everyday pragmatism. The very structure of women's work tended to ingrain political passivity by narrowing and personalizing their views of economic relationships. If they did piecework at home, as was so often the case, they were isolated within a system that engendered self-competition and self-reproach: the harder I work, the more I make—it's all up to me! Unlike men, women had few opportunities at work or off work to exchange critical views, meet well-traveled outsiders, organize to define and defend their interests, or envision long-range alternatives to the present. Even in factories, where solidarity was physically easier, their greater vulnerability to sexual exploitation and personal favoritism bred docility. And after work, when the men might go to the tavern to talk politics, or just to grumble, women had to rush home.[119]

Women in domestic service were not only isolated, they were also likely to absorb a heavy dose of bourgeois values. Far from home and torn from their own families, servants sought acceptance into the bosom of their employer's household. Though usually rebuffed, they could at least pride themselves on their in-

[118] Wettstein-Adelt, *3 ½ Monate Fabrik-Arbeiterin,* 71.
[119] Christian labor organizations, with their more traditional appeals, had more success organizing women; see Franzoi, *At the Very Least She Pays the Rent,* 161–77.

timate knowledge of, and ability to imitate, the habits and prejudices of their social betters. By all accounts, there was widespread misery and dissatisfaction among servant girls. However, the patriarchal system in which they lived and worked deflected their criticism onto the personal shortcomings of the individual employer, while obscuring the systemic causes of their plight. Rich and poor appeared to them as fixed categories; one could only hope to work for a decent rich person. Servants defused their anger in lonely crying fits, gossip, and frequent job changes. Their only alternative reality was an escape into the fantasy world of dime novels. In a typical such novel—aimed expressly at servant girls—the master of the house would expel his evil wife and throw himself into the arms of the pure-hearted servant girl.[120] *Equality (Die Gleichheit)*, the Social Democratic women's magazine, routinely condemned these enormously popular books as reactionary fairy tales.[121] But it was a losing battle. Servants were hard to reach and virtually impossible to organize politically. When they left service to marry, as most of them did, these young women carried their primitive political understanding into millions of working-class households. There can be little doubt that they acted as a brake on the development of Social Democracy.

Limited political awareness or even passivity (of either sex) should not be equated with contentment or total identification with the upper classes. Official statistics indicate that labor unrest was growing after 1900. By 1913, the major trade unions counted about 3 million members, 85 percent of them in the Social Democratically oriented Free Trade Unions.[122] Work stoppage peaked in 1905 with the involvement of over half a million workers and the loss of over 7 million man-days of work. Thereafter, union leaders were more cautious with their treasuries in the face of well-organized employers; but the rising number of

[120] Schulte, "Dienstmädchen im herrschaftlichen Haushalt," 908–9.
[121] Richebächer, *Uns fehlt nur eine Kleinigkeit,* 115–18.
[122] Hohorst, Kocka, and Ritter, *Sozialgeschichtliches Arbeitsbuch,* 136.

peaceful actions (short of work stoppages) continued to reflect discontent.[123]

And these statistics are far from the whole story. Discontent and protest are more likely to show up in disguised form. They may be expressed pathologically in, say, drunkenness, depression, wife beating, or crime.[124] Or, more commonly, they may appear as attempts to control one's fate at the workplace. The majority of workers, quite understandably, disliked their work.[125] It was tiring, often monotonous, and in larger firms workers were subjected to degrading control numbers and fines, and encumbered by a host of petty regulations. High absenteeism (especially "blue Mondays"), a typically slower work pace at the beginning and end of the week, and the casual waste of company materials may reasonably be interpreted as expressions of protest.[126]

More dramatic was the high job-turnover rate—a fact of working-class life that leaps from the pages of virtually all the autobiographies. There is more here than just the vestigial wanderlust of the skilled artisan. The unskilled moved too, not just from shop to shop (like the skilled), but from one industry to another. Some workers moved around in search of better pay and conditions or a more congenial foreman; some were responding

---

[123] Ibid., 132–33; see also Carl E. Schorske, *German Social Democracy 1905–1917: The Development of the Great Schism* (Cambridge, Mass., 1955), 29–32.

[124] On the question of disguised militancy, see Dick Geary, "Identifying Militancy: The Assessment of Working-Class Attitudes Towards State and Society," in *The German Working Class 1888–1933: The Politics of Everyday Life*, ed. Richard J. Evans (London, 1982), 220–46; also Klaus Tenfelde, "The Herne Riots of 1899," in *The Social History of Politics*, ed. Iggers, 282–312.

[125] Levenstein found that only 15.2 percent of miners, 7.1 percent of textile workers, and 17 percent of metalworkers liked their work; see his *Die Arbeiterfrage*, 61, 68, 75.

[126] Bernays, "Berufswahl und Berufsschicksal des modernen Industriearbeiters," *Archiv für Sozialwissenschaft und Sozialpolitik* 35 (1912): 172–76; Wettstein-Adelt, *3½ Monate Fabrik-Arbeiterin*, 22–23; Hickey, *Workers in Imperial Germany*, 137–38.

to boredom or changing family needs. But reading between the lines of the autobiographies, one senses that these were often superficial reasons. Job switches often go unexplained, as though mobility is just taken for granted. Workers, even the more ignorant ones, seemed to sense that the only real freedom they could exercise in the free market system was the freedom to move around. Overall, the extreme mobility probably slowed the growth of Social Democracy by defusing individual anger and hampering organizational efforts.[127]

On the other hand, there were obviously powerful economic and social forces promoting the development of class consciousness. One of the great advantages of the autobiographies is that they provide a useful corrective to the widespread tendency to slide into abstractions in discussing the origins of class consciousness. When we listen to real workers—as distinct from middle-class theoreticians—talk about the origins of their class consciousness, what strikes us is the role they assign to the power of the spoken and written word. Revelations about the roots of exploitation and the liberating possibilities of Social Democracy are usually the immediate results of personal contact and pamphlet reading. To be sure, structural determinants are what make an individual receptive; no amount of persuasion could have converted a sixteenth-century peasant to Social Democracy. But the autobiographies do expose the problematic nature of structural determinants. Important concepts like mechanization and the division of labor—both central to the discussion of class consciousness since Marx—just don't come to life in the autobiographies.[128] As stressed earlier, only a minority of workers actually did stereotypical factory work; and by no means all of them found it alienating. Some people preferred the anonymity of large

---

[127] Stearns, "Adaptation to Industrialization," 327–29; Bernays, "Berufswahl und Berufsschicksal des modernen Industriearbeiters," *Archiv für Sozialwissenschaft und Sozialpolitik* 36 (1913): 884–900. It is possible that the autobiographies give a somewhat exaggerated impression of mobility; people who have done and seen more are probably more likely to write an autobiography.
[128] Uhen, *Gruppenbewusstsein,* 52–53.

firms and liked the hum of machinery.[129] As Göhre showed, there were dozens of informal ways of preserving individuality, team-work, and personal relationships within the modern plant. Print-ers and cigar makers, probably the most class-conscious of all workers, were by no means the most modern of workers. What they had in common was a subculture centered on the word. Printers spent their day making and reading words. Cigar mak-ers, whose work could be done quietly, entertained themselves by talking or having someone read aloud to them as they worked. General correlations (e.g., that the strength of Social Democracy varied with the size of the industrial sector) obscure the meaning of Social Democracy to the individual worker. In his (or more rarely, her) eyes, he was responding to persuasion, not reacting mechanically to his place in the economy. And in his eyes, Social Democracy was not just another party, not just a program appro-priate to his class position; it was an emotional revelation.

Several of the workers in this book (notably Max Lotz, Wenzel Holek, Franz Osterroth, and Otto Krille) write at length on the context and personal meaning of that revelation. There is no point in repeating their views here, but a few critical generaliza-tions may illuminate the context. The reader will be struck by the obvious religious undercurrents running through discussions of Social Democracy. For many workers, the conversion to Social Democracy had been preceded by the destruction of their tradi-tional religious beliefs. As one worker told Göhre, "Religion—there is no more of that among working men."[130] Levenstein did find a minority who believed in God, although it was usually not the Christian God, but rather a God identified with the natural order of the universe.[131] The rejection of Christianity usually marked the final emotional break with the dominant values of

[129] Bernays, "Berufswahl und Berufsschicksal des modernen Industriearbei-ters," *Archiv für Sozialwissenschaft und Sozialpolitik* 35 (1912): 159–71.

[130] Göhre, *Three Months in a Workshop*, 166. The statement is surely an exag-geration; on the continuing importance of religion in the lives of some work-ers, see Hickey, *Workers in Imperial Germany*, 70–108.

[131] Levenstein, *Die Arbeiterfrage*, 336–53 passim.

society. Social Democracy (the "new gospel," as Krille calls it) rushed into the emotional void left by the rejection of Christianity. In Göhre's apt words, Social Democracy was "a new conception of the world and of life; . . . the logical outcome of materialism and the practical application of the doctrine of a natural order of the universe substituted for that of a moral and divine order." [132] To the committed Social Democrat, the party was more than a political organization; it was a spiritual home, promising an entirely new world. A man like Moritz Bromme could live his whole life within the "alternative culture" of Social Democratic organizations. [133]

The reader may also be struck by the moderation of these men and women. Writing in 1899, Eduard Bernstein, the leader of the revisionist wing of the SPD, remarked that, "the desire of the industrial working classes for socialistic production is for the most part more a matter of assumption than of certainty." [134] Likewise, Max Weber saw in the workers' resentments and hopes little to distinguish them from those of the petty bourgeoisie. A peculiarly proletarian consciousness, he argued, was largely the imposition of middle-class theoreticians. [135] The autobiographies do offer some support for these views. Like parvenus, the workers parade their knowledge of the best of bourgeois culture from Schiller, to Darwin, to Tolstoy. None seems really familiar with Marx. Their socialism is a grab bag of half-understood propositions from Lassalle's speeches, Engels's *Origin of the Family,* Bebel's *Woman and Socialism,* newspaper articles, and popular books

[132] Göhre, *Three Months in a Workshop,* 108–9.

[133] The phrase "alternative culture" comes from Vernon L. Lidtke, *The Alternative Culture: Socialist Labor in Imperial Germany* (Oxford and New York, 1985). For a survey of the literature on workers' culture, see Gerhard A. Ritter, "Workers' Culture in Imperial Germany: Problems and Points of Departure for Research," *Journal of Contemporary History* 13 (1978): 165–89.

[134] Eduard Bernstein, *Evolutionary Socialism: A Criticism and Affirmation,* trans. Edith C. Harvey (New York, 1961), 107.

[135] Weber, "Zur Methodik sozialpsychologischer Enqueten und ihrer Bearbeitung," esp. 956–57.

on evolution. There is no coherent economic analysis, little talk of revolution, and only the faintest hint of international solidarity. Most often their main interests are short-term gains and personal improvement; while their calls for future justice and equality seem little more than echoes of radical democracy.[136]

But it would be a mistake to end on that note. These men and women did have a keen sense that they were being exploited, and they regarded the upper classes with a cold, objective contempt. For reasons good or bad, their rejection of capitalism and the prevailing class system was sincere. The dignity they sought for their children transcended a mere amelioration of present conditions. However vaguely, they envisioned a future where exploitation, selfishness, and cruelty had disappeared. If, in the meantime, they took advantage of the best of the present—whether its literature or its nobler political sentiments—if they fought for a higher wage and a secure old age, then they simply revealed their humanity.

A WORD ABOUT THE TRANSLATIONS

Translation is always a problematic craft, but the documents in this book confront the translator with unusual challenges. Few of these men and women are good writers by the standards of the educated classes. Lacking formal education, even the autodidacts among them write a prose that bears some of the marks of the *halbgebildeter Mensch* (half-cultured person). Their organization is often puzzling, their choice of words odd, their sentences and paragraphs either confusingly long or abruptly short. Most confounding to the translator is an intangible quality of awkward-

[136] On these issues, see also Guenther Roth, *The Social Democrats in Imperial Germany: A Study in Working-Class Isolation and National Integration* (Totowa, N.J., 1963), esp. 193–211; Moore, *Injustice*, esp. 208–26; Kelly, *The Descent of Darwin*, esp. 137–41.

ness, which seems to derive from an unevenness of style and tone. Within a few lines there are disorienting shifts from the colloquial to the overly formal and from High German into regional dialect. Yet there are a fair number of movingly eloquent passages scattered throughout these texts. It is an eloquence that does not just survive awkwardness; it seems, paradoxically, to thrive on awkwardness. In the most arresting passages of these autobiographies there is a directness and richness, born of passion and years of drudgery. Polished prose, written in a mood of reflective detachment, would eviscerate those memorable scenes that so command our attention: Karl Fischer's excavation site, Moritz Bromme's courtroom, and Max Lotz's pit baths, to name but three.

Lamentably, the translation is likely to be least successful where the original is most successful. What is uniquely valuable in these pages is rooted deeply, not only in language, but also in the intangibles of nationality (indeed regionality), historical era, and social class. Of course, awkwardness and eloquence (or even the marriage of the two) may be found in contemporary American English, as well as in the German of eighty years ago. But these qualities occur in different dimensions in the two languages. The search for a truly parallel awkward eloquence is fruitless and quickly degenerates into a parody of the original. Instead I have tried to translate as "innocently" as possible, trusting my first impression—pretending, as it were, that I was listening to the individual speak and had not yet heard everything. The accumulated effect, I would hope, is that the entire selection breathes the spirit of the original, keeping pace with the original, stumbling where it stumbles. To be sure, there is a tendency (I fear inevitably) to flatten the original. For the sake of clarity, I have broken up some overly long paragraphs; and thousands of tiny decisions about wording have, overall, scarred the eloquence and smoothed over the awkwardness. But, with any luck, most of those matchless passages have survived to haunt the reader in English.

I'm afraid that passages of regional dialect (that mine field for the translator) have simply disappeared into the colloquial. To seek equivalents in English dialects would be sheer affectation. What could they possibly be? Cockney for the Berliner? Appalachian for the Swabian? Down East for the Mecklenburger? The translator might flag the dialect with an asterisk, but with no enlargement of meaning to justify defacing the text. Then, too, obscure parts of obsolete tools and machines have a way of metamorphosing into generic blades, levers, or pedals. And regional soups, no doubt as foul-tasting as they are colorfully named, always seem to masquerade in English as "gruel." My hope is that these men and women have not come to sound suspiciously like a contemporary American academic. If nineteen individuals have found distinct voices in these pages, then despite the defects, I may claim some small measure of success.

The
GERMAN
WORKER

Karl Fischer,
Railroad Excavator

Karl Fischer (1841–1906), the son of an impoverished baker, was also trained as a baker, though he was never able to establish himself in his trade. Instead he drifted from one unskilled job to another, beginning as a farm laborer and ending up as a cleaner of locomotive parts in the state railroad shed in Osnabrück. This selection covers his early years in the 1860s, when he worked on a labor gang constructing the Halle-Kassel railroad line. For many years Fischer had been in the habit of keeping a journal. He was apparently moved to assemble his writings into a book by his reading of Paul Göhre's *Three Months in a Workshop,* and somehow the manuscript came into Göhre's possession (see Introduction). As Göhre had hoped, Fischer's autobiography attracted a fair amount of public attention. Some reviewers found his style tedious, others biblical; but all agreed that, despite his apparent total lack of culture, he had a keen eye for details. When Fischer reminisces, it is almost as though the earth itself were speaking—telling the epic tale of the industrial age. In the last scene it is dramatically clear that the railroads were the lifeline of the emerging Reich.

WITH THE EARTHWORKERS, HÜNEBURG

Then came the year when I had to report to the military for the last time. The army doctor had determined that I should be in the artillery, but I didn't pass the final physical examination and was rejected. I felt as though I'd been subjected to the worst possible disgrace. All my uncles had been soldiers; one had served with the rifle guards, two with the sappers, and one with the black hussars, but he had later gone into the navy. And now I was excluded. I was overcome by misery and didn't want any lunch. Instead I took my walking stick and went out into the Bischofröder Woods, and finally lay down in an ash pit and cried until sunset. So I had to continue taking jobs as a worker's helper. But then came the years when the Halle-Kassel railroad was being built; so I went to the railroad and did heavy excavation work.

Very soon a lot of outsiders showed up: East and West Prussians, Poles and Silesians, Pomeranians and Mecklenburgers, Brandenburgers and Saxons, Hessians and Hanoverians, and a few from Austria, South Germany, and the Eifel. All of them got work where I was working, and eventually I got to know them all by name. The people interested me as much as the work, and when I had the time and opportunity I liked to talk to and even more to listen to them. There were also a lot of local people there.

I was there for only a short time, and then I stopped and went one excavation site further toward Hüneburg, where I started work again. This was a high hill, probably almost one hundred feet high at the top. It was carted away from above in stages with two-wheeled carts, each pulled by two men. I began with this kind of work. I'd brought my own shovel and "shuffle." That's what they called the harness that you put over your shoulder with a strap attached to the cart. Instead of saying pull, they said

Translated from Karl Fischer, *Denkwürdigkeiten eines Arbeiters*, ed. Paul Göhre (Jena: Eugen Diederichs Verlag, 1903), 123–36.

shuffle, and the pair who pulled the cart were called shuffle people, and you called your partner your shuffleman. The shuffle- men were as different as the shuffles; many were excellent and some were better than the shuffles they had. A good shuffle was an important thing, and before you harnessed up with a partner, you first suspiciously checked out his equipment. Often you heard someone say scornfully, "What kind of shuffle is that sup- posed to be!" The shuffle was the best thing about some people, and it wasn't long before everyone knew who these people were. They wanted to do piecework with the carts so they could earn more, but they could no longer get a good shuffleman.

If two such people were harnessed together and shuffled all day, they barely earned what they would have at the daily wage rate. Then they usually fought with each other, and the next morning they watched to see whether anyone was missing. If someone was, they offered themselves, but were usually scorn- fully turned down. One man would excuse himself by saying, "I'm waiting for my partner; if he doesn't come I'll work at the hourly rate today." Someone else said to another: "I should shuffle with you? What will you give me if I do?"

"Well, what do you want?" the other man said.

And the first man replied, "Give me your daughter."

"Which one?" asked the old man.

Then the young one said, "The one who always brings you your meals."

The old man said, "Yes, yes, that's fine, you shall have her."

While the others were laughing, the old man had already hitched up his shuffle to the cart. But the young man said: "For- get it, hurry up and report to do wage work. I do want your daughter, but I don't want to strain my father-in-law so much today; I won't have that."

Someone else would refuse by saying, "No, I don't have any money with me, and if I shuffle all day with you I'll have even less this evening." And still another said to a man who showed off his fine new shuffle, "Your shuffle is good, but you're a do- nothing." Of course people like this were the least capable or the least skilled. Even if nothing else worked out, there were some that you really didn't want to harness up with. No one was forced, but if you didn't have a partner you had to work for hourly wages. If you wanted to earn anything it was very important to have a suitable and compatible partner; for this was piecework and was paid by the cartload. If you didn't want to miss any cartloads, you had to keep up a good pace all day. In two years there I changed partners only four or five times. I got along with all of them but one; and he was actually the one I shuffled with the longest. Sometimes he tried to make me believe and acted as though he was doing more than I was. But I knew better; he was actually the least skilled of all the partners I had, and finally when he angered me too much, I dropped him.

Many of those who started hauling soon quit and preferred to do other work that wasn't as difficult and that they could stand. The ground that we were excavating was composed of clay and stones, and it all had to be broken loose with pickaxes. In the first two weeks I must have had a half dozen shufflemen because I didn't know the ropes, and I had to make do with the very worst people; sometimes I even sought them out. After this I was harnessed up with a discharged hussar sergeant from Posen. I thought I really had someone good, but we didn't earn any more than we would have made on daily wages. The reason was that the man wasn't at all used to such work. It certainly was no fun when the loaded cart went rushing down the hill; you had to stay with it, and learn to be "all legs" when you went down with a full load. Alongside the path going down there was an up path for the empty carts being pulled up the hill; it had planks laid on it. For every cartload you got a token from the token dispenser; and in the evening you got credit for as many cartloads as you had tokens. The token dispenser watched closely, and if your cart wasn't properly loaded you didn't get a token. The whole time I was there he stopped and warned me twice, but he always gave me the token. He often snapped furiously at others, and some frequently didn't get a token. When we got back up to the loading place with our empty cart, the sergeant, like a lot of others, wanted to rest before getting back to work. But I noticed how some of the others did things: They quickly turned the cart around, positioned it, threw the harness off their shoulders with one hand and reached for their shovel with the other; and then they started throwing dirt for all they were worth until the cart was full again. It wasn't long before the last shovelful was in and one of them said "OK." They just dropped their shovels, and in no time they were both in their harnesses and shuffling away.

One evening after we'd been working together at least a week, I got very annoyed that we had so few tokens; and I told the sergeant firmly that we couldn't go on like this, and that we had to do better tomorrow. He agreed. The next morning he pulled himself together and at noon we had five more tokens than we had had at noon the day before. But just before the afternoon break when we got up to the top with an empty cart, he let go of the shaft and tipped the cart over the way you do at quitting time. I looked at him questioningly and he said, "That's enough for today, I can't do any more, my feet have given out." I could believe that because my own hurt too, but once again we'd earned nothing. I suggested that after the afternoon break we report to do wage work for the last quarter of the day, but he refused and said I should go home with him. I didn't want to, so he went alone. I went and turned in our tokens so that they could be recorded, and at the break I went to see the foreman. He was standing there leaning on a cart and looking at the embankment. Some of the foremen say *Du* to everyone; and some say *Du* to some and *Sie* to others. Others say *Sie* to everyone, and still others say *Ihr** to everyone; each has his own way. This one said *Sie* to everyone, and when I told him what I wanted, he said in a friendly voice, "Yes, hourly wage, hourly wage, where's the other fellow?" I said he'd gone home. Then he said: "Oh, I thought he wanted to do wage work too. I can't help it, I've got enough

**Du, Sie,* and *Ihr* are, respectively, the familiar singular, the formal, and the familiar plural forms of address. Among themselves, workers commonly used the familiar.

wage workers. The important thing now is to keep all the carts moving. Why did you ever team up with him? He's no man for you, don't team up with him again. If it's OK with you, go back to your place and dig up the ground and within an hour I'll send someone to help you. You can harness up with him tomorrow." So I didn't go to wage work, but I agreed to go back to my place and dig up ground. Later my new partner came, and he really knew how to use the pick better than the sergeant. The sergeant didn't come back until noon the next day, and he stood around all afternoon, then I didn't see him again. I was sorry for him, but I couldn't help him.

After the afternoon break we usually took only a few cartloads down the hill. Instead, one after another of us began to dig up the ground for the next day. Every section was about ten feet wide, and it was important to have honest neighbors on both sides who were content with the dirt they'd dug up themselves. But some were greedy, and when they loaded their carts they reached over too far with their shovels and pilfered from their neighbors on both sides. This often caused bitter arguments and sometimes brawls because these were impudent rascals. Usually a few strong words were enough; and everyone had his special way of repelling these encroachments. One would say, "Get back, you're coming over my border." Another said, "You're about to get it in the smacker with my shovel." Another, "Stay away from what I'm entitled to." Another, "Keep your long fingers out of here." Another, "Mind your own business and leave our ground alone, that's for us to carry away." Another, "You're coming too far over, you need to be a little more Christian." And while loading up, another would say to his partner, "Watch out on your side, he's coming over too far and loading some of our dirt, give him a whack on the head with the shovel." Another would say, "That's our dirt, we dug it up, you're regular thieves." Those who didn't want to or couldn't protest loudly enough were in a bad way if they had bad neighbors.

The hardness of the ground varied from place to place; in some spots it was easier to work loose than in others, and a lot of people complained that they had a bad place. But you got two pfennigs more per cartload for places where it was exceptionally hard to dig the ground up. Depending on how far away the place was, you got seventeen to twenty-three pfennigs per cartload. New cuts were always being made in order to go a stage deeper and then we only manned the carts. You didn't have to dig yourself; that was done by the day laborers who dug the whole day so that you could cart continuously throughout the day. Then you got only fourteen to sixteen pfennigs a cartload. If you wanted to earn one taler, both of you had to carry fifty cartloads when the rate was fourteen pfennigs a load; but when the rate was nineteen pfennigs a load, you only had to carry forty loads.* For every taler you earned, you had to pay six pfennigs for the health plan. Every two weeks there was a payday, and if there had been dry weather for the whole pay period and you could haul regularly, then you really earned something. But when the rainy days came, then you couldn't haul for three or four days; even a light shower made hauling immediately impossible. You could get the load down the hill, but you couldn't get the empty cart back up, because the wheels began to slip on the wet planks and slide right off. When this kind of weather was frequent, you had to go home, and some paydays you earned no more than your food costs. So there were good paydays and bad, although you weren't to blame for the bad ones. The boss was just as irritated by the bad ones as the workers were because the work wasn't proceeding.

On rainy days many of the workers went happily to the tavern; some of them went just because they couldn't spend the whole day in their rooms. No lodgings were provided, so everyone had to find a place for himself in town or in the neighborhood. Some spoke highly of their quarters, but others said they didn't even have enough room to sit down. And some slept on straw in barns or stables and got their own food as best they could. Then there

---

*If the taler is valued at three marks, the calculations are a bit off.

were some who were always bragging and carrying on, and talking and behaving as if they knew everything and could do anything. In the beginning I respected them and considered them the finest workers. But as soon as I got a really good partner whom I could work with properly, I realized what sort of characters these were. The very ones I'd judged to be most able from their talk couldn't keep pace, and in the evening they had fewer tokens than we did. There were always too few rainy days for them. When the weather was good and they'd shuffled for three or four days in a row, it was too much for them and they took off, three, four, five, and sometimes even more of them at a time. They'd get a keg of beer and lie down in the bushes and have a good time and sing songs. In the evening they came back to their lodgings at the usual time and acted as if they'd worked the whole day. Since many of them got a lot less money at payday than I did, I wondered how they could drink so much. But it was all very simple; they ran up debts until things got uncomfortable. Then they disappeared, cheating many poor landlords out of the board money. Moreover, some of these people had a wife and children at home, but they didn't care at all about them. Many poor landladies would come crying to the boss, and many of the grocers were left holding the bag. So after a while I saw what sort of workers these people actually were, what they could do, and what was wrong with them. They never finished a railroad but always left that to the other people.

They were usually short of people when they began to build a new stretch, and so everyone who came along was taken on as long as he had two arms and two legs. Later, when things slowed down a bit, the foremen took on some, but not just anyone. When I came to Hüneburg and asked the foreman whether I could start work, he looked at my shuffle and said, "Sure you can start, but you'll have to find a man to team up with."

One time a frail young fellow who looked very irresponsible and down-and-out came along and asked for work. The foreman asked him, "What are you?"

And the stranger said, "Sculptor."

The foreman misunderstood and said, "I don't want any brewers."*

"I'm a sculptor," the stranger said.

And the foreman said, "I don't want any sculptors either." The stranger said nothing and went away.

One time the two of us had to haul carts within the excavation. The ground was being broken up by the day laborers, and six to eight of them were standing there in a row. The wall wasn't very high and the foreman (it was a different one) stood up above. Along came a man from one of the nearby villages; it was obvious that he was a small farmer. He went up to the foreman and asked if he could get work. The foreman said, "Don't you have any work?" And the man said, "No, I do have something to do at home, but it's not enough; I can't support my family on it." Then in a loud, ringing voice the foreman said, "I believe it, and I'm very glad if I can put somebody to work." As he said this he turned to the side and looked up to the high embankment where a few men were standing. They were levelling a high spot and talking at the same time. Then the foreman continued, roaring like a lion: "But look over there. I have some people who aren't worth five groschen a day to me. I have to stand right over every one of them. That makes you lose all your desire to take on people you don't know." While he was cursing like this, one of the pickers below him whispered to his neighbor, "Theodore, blow!" I heard it and before I knew what he meant, Theodore made a little bugle call sound while he continued to dig and said quietly, "Trarara, Trara, Trara." But the foreman had heard it; he broke off, jumped around like lightning and bent down to Theodore. He held up three fingers as in a curse, gesticulated right under Theodore's nose, and shouted heatedly: "Yeah, I have your number, you don't deserve five groschen a day either. You just got here by mistake, and if you don't start digging better today,

---

* In German, brewer (*Bierbrauer*) and sculptor (*Bildhauer*) sound similar.

you're through." It looked dangerous. Anyone else might easily
have hit the foreman on the head or the hand with his pick. But
that was out of the question for Theodore. That wasn't his style,
for he never lifted the pick higher than a foot at the most.

This foreman got drunk frequently; the boss was very angry
about it and complained to the landlord at the foreman's lodgings. But the landlord said firmly that the foreman didn't take
any schnapps with him to work and that he couldn't get drunk
on the schnapps he did buy. The boss let it be known on the
whole excavation site that whoever gave the foreman schnapps
would be fired, no matter who it was. But they didn't catch
anybody. And one afternoon the foreman was drunk again. He
propped himself up against the embankment, and soon his back
and head bent over backwards so that he was lying half upright.
But he wasn't unconscious; he kept rolling his red head to the
right and then to the left. The boss came by and walked back
and forth in front of him a few times. Then he picked up a shovel
himself and cleaned off the empty cart track. When this didn't
rouse the foreman, he threw the shovel away and called his name
angrily: "Müller!" Müller winced a little, because he knew the
voice well, but he couldn't stand up. The boss called over a few
people and had him carried into the shed. He was still sitting in
there at quitting time, and the next morning he didn't come
back, having already been discharged. Soon another foreman
came; and soon after this the boss was walking through the cutting with another gentleman. They stopped right by our cart; we
heard the other man ask the boss, "You have another foreman;
the old one was just a peasant, wasn't he?" The boss nodded sadly
several times and then said in a haughty tone: "It wasn't so bad
that he was a peasant. I wouldn't have fired the peasant if he
hadn't liked to drink schnapps so much; a lot of foremen drink
too much!"

As they did later at the other sites, people would come to the
foreman asking for work, and when they were accepted, they
would immediately ask, "What will I earn?" These were always

people from the local villages who'd never seen a railroad in their lives. They wanted to make a quick estimate of how much they would make in a week, a month, or a year, and they didn't think of all the many factors. The answers they got were all the same and soon you got to know them in advance. Once when somebody asked about it, someone nearby called out, "You get two talers a day!" And the foreman added: "That's right, plus twenty-five groschen. You work first and then we'll see what you'll earn." Another foreman answered the question by saying, "I don't know; first I'll have to see how you work; and only then will I know what you'll earn." Another said, "What you earn depends completely on your work. If you work well then you'll earn money." Another said, "Work first, always work first, I don't promise people anything in advance." And foreman Hartung from Artern, who said *Du* to everyone, said, "You're asking too much for me to tell you that; I don't know you. I always say, the pay fits the man. If working is important to you, then start in working hard and don't think."

O Hüneburg, O Hüneburg, how my bones did ache! That was really hard work, I can assure you. If you didn't work there, you just don't know how it was. But money was the whole thing. You have to have it; that was the only compulsion, nothing else. The best payday that I had there, my partner and I each earned sixteen and a half talers less a few pfennigs; as usual the boss had deducted the health insurance. A merchant from town who was owed money by some of the men was sitting next to the boss, hoping to catch some of his debtors as they were being paid. As the boss counted out my sixteen talers, six groschen, and six pfennigs on the table, he turned to the merchant and said loudly and proudly, "That's really getting into the talers!" But the merchant just nodded sadly. He had other problems. It had been good weather during the whole pay period; and the Eisleben fair was the next week; you had to have money for that. Everyone went to the fair together, even the foreman and the boss; and for two days no one did any work but celebrated at the fair instead.

They all yelled out, "Time for the fun!" And the foreman Kunze said, "Man and beast have fun here." In spite of good weather each of us had earned only eleven talers in this pay period. But that wasn't the worst by a long ways.

On Sundays nobody touched a cart. But some of the day laborers had to work on Sunday, there was no way around it. Putting planks on the paths, or building and planking bridges over new cuttings—that could only be done when there was no cart traffic. After years of hard work we'd gotten down to the base and before us was the last wall of the last cutting. It wasn't much longer before the whole formation level was done; and before we'd carried the last cart of earth out of the hill, the track was already laid up to that point and then the roadbed continued on a level surface. Finally only a few carts were called for, and one after another the workers went away. Many of the outsiders stayed in the area and went to the mines. Since that time many of the comrades have probably worked their last shift in this world, including some of those I shuffled with. But Moritz Henschel, who'd just been discharged from the Twenty-seventh,* might well still be alive. And Wilhelm Kreidemeier, who'd served in the artillery, might still be too.

When the roadbed was completely done, a group of us were still busy on the hill cleaning up. One day just before noon three gentlemen came running fast down the track from the direction of town. One of them we knew well—he was the construction supervisor of our stretch of track—but nobody knew the other two. Each was trying to outrun the other two, and when they had just passed us, one of the workers said: "What can they want? Something must have happened." The three were already out of the hill, and when they had the open stretch before them, one of them pointed with his walking stick and shouted fervently: "It's passable! It's all done! My God, it doesn't have to be any more than passable!" Then the construction supervisor stopped, gestured wildly, and said with equal fervor, "It is pass-

---

*Presumably a regiment number.

able, that's not the question, but we still don't have any tele-graph line!" Then they ran further and you couldn't hear what they were saying. We didn't see them again either. But within a very few days there was already talk about the Battle of Langen-salza,* and then we knew what they had wanted. After this I had to worry about getting other work.

* One of the opening battles of the Austro-Prussian War (27 June 1866). The use of railroads to move men and materiel contributed significantly to Prussia's quick victory.

Ottilie Baader,
Seamstress

Ottilie Baader (1847–1925), the daughter of sugar refinery workers, was a Berlin seamstress who later became prominent in the Social Democratic women's movement. Her autobiography, published by the socialist Dietz Verlag in 1921, was written to inspire other struggling working women. The majority of her book deals with the women's movement, rather than her personal life. But in the first two chapters, which appear here, she tells of her early years in the 1860s and 1870s before she had discovered Social Democracy. Baader's account is very revealing of the ways in which sweatshop owners manipulated female employees. Organizing the working women of Baader's generation was an almost impossible task.

CHILDHOOD AND FIRST WORK YEARS

I hadn't intended in this memoir to speak of myself or of my own life. But from childhood on my life has been all work, and every-

Translated from Ottilie Baader, *Ein steiniger Weg: Lebenserinnerungen* (Stuttgart/Berlin: J. H. W. Dietz Verlag, 1921), 7–17.

thing that I'm going to relate here is based on this life of work and can only be properly understood on this basis. There is nothing unusual about my life. Thousands of working girls of my time lived and worked just as I did.

My parents lived in Frankfurt on the Oder where my father worked as a refiner in a sugar factory. The job required a knowledge of chemistry, which my father had been able to acquire thanks to his good schooling. His good education proved beneficial to me not only in my childhood but even more in later years. He himself never got much use out of it, and he never really got to show what he could do. I was born in 1847 as my parents' second child. There were two more children after me. I had only a few carefree childhood years, and the images that flash before me of those first seven years are loving and friendly. My mother was a hard-working woman with a gentle face, and we children never heard a sharp word from her. But she said many things that the long years of my life have not been able to erase from my memory, and I've often thought that the best things I have I learned from her. I can still see her sitting in the window of our room and sewing. She helped my father as much as she could, and then she would make filter cloths for the sugar factory. Sometimes we'd come running to her and show her little crimson spiders (we called them "love God cows") in our hands. She was delighted, but then she said, "Take the little animal right back where you found it, otherwise it will die." We never caught beetles and put them in boxes, and my older brother never tortured an animal either. I know that one time I caught a butterfly, a simple cabbage butterfly, and I enjoyed rubbing its wings between my fingers. Suddenly I noticed that the delicate shimmer was gone from the wings, and in astonishment I went to my mother and showed her. "Yes," she said, "do you know what you've done now? You've hurt it and it will probably die early. It's as though someone took your clothes and you had to run around naked. You could put on other clothes, but a poor little butterfly can't grow new clothes." One thing is sure—I never again rubbed the dust off the wings of a butterfly.

When I was a bit older, she and my father gave my brother

and me our first school lessons. We lived about a mile out of the city and didn't go to school regularly. But if we wanted to, we could go with the other children to the village school.

My mother put great store in imbuing her children with a sense of order. Every evening when we got undressed we had to check our things, and if there was anything wrong with our socks or our clothes, we had to bring them to her so she could mend them while we were in bed. One evening, being either tired or careless, I didn't bring her my sock, even though I knew very well that it had a hole in it. She probably checked for herself after I was asleep. The next morning I put the sock with the hole back on and ran off happily to school with the other children. But when I came home from school, my mother said, "You've got a hole in your sock!"

For a moment I looked at her without saying a word, and then I said quickly, "But nobody can see it!"

"Oh yes they can," she said. "You can easily see when someone has a hole in his sock!" She meant that you could see from a person whether he was careless about himself or his clothing.

My father had given up his position in the sugar factory and gone off to Berlin. He worked there at Borsig.* He'd intended to have us follow him when he'd gotten settled and found an apartment. He earned three talers a week, of which he regularly sent two talers to my mother; and there was always a groschen enclosed for us children. Nowadays fathers who work elsewhere go home every Saturday. That wasn't possible then. The post coach was expensive or you had to wait for a particular occasion. And so it happened that my father was gone for a long time. When he finally came home he was shocked by my mother's appearance, and he sent for the doctor. After the examination the doctor went outside with my father and told him that he would prescribe something for her and come back in two days to see if anything else could be done. But it was too late and very soon she died of galloping consumption. The oldest of us children was

* Borsig was a great locomotive works.

eight and the youngest three. But even misfortune like this needed company! It was bad winter weather and my father fell on the ice and sprained his right hand. And so all the work fell to me—a seven-year-old girl. The first thing I had to do was wash my dead mother and put her bonnet on her head. Then the people came and praised me and called me a "good child," and no one knew the horror I felt at the incomprehensibility of death. My father's wages were scarcely enough for the poorest life, so we didn't know where the money for my mother's funeral would come from. But in our hour of need the Borsig workers came to our rescue and brought us some money that they had collected among themselves.

My father never remarried. During my childhood and into my later years, the question was always asked, what would my mother say about something, what would she do? It grew to be a kind of obsession that certainly restricted our own development.

The circumstances now forced my father to work in Frankfurt again. But he never made enough to get a regular housekeeper for us. So we children were usually left to our own devices and grew up without any motherly or even feminine care. But we did get to know work and cares from an early age.

Only in my tenth year did I go to school. I'd learned reading, writing, and arithmetic from my father. According to the test, I was ready to go into the third class. It was a middle school housed in an old cloister, and at that time it was considered a good school. It was said that the girls there were educated above all to have "good manners." The ideal woman of the time was gentle, tender, and sweet; my father had particularly admired my mother for her sweetness and wanted his daughters to be like that.

I didn't go to school for long. When I was thirteen years old, our father moved with us to Berlin, and that was the end of my school days. I had to work and help support the family. There was no need for any big family council to choose the right trade for me, because there wasn't much choice for girls in those days. In school I'd always been praised because I could sew well, and most of all because I could make good buttonholes. So I was to be a seamstress. The wife of a journeyman saddler had a little shop on Neanderstrasse where dress shirts were made. All the sewing was done by hand, there being very few sewing machines in use. For a month I trained without any pay; after that I got three talers a month. Two years later I was already getting five talers a month, but then I remained at that level for several years. To make some extra money I took home cuffs to double stitch. Double stitching meant tiny, even, hand stitching. You got one groschen for each pair of cuffs. How often my young eyes must have closed, and how my back ached! I already had a twelve-hour workday behind me—from eight in the morning to eight in the evening with a short lunch break.

My memories of my first mistress are not too pleasant. I've never heard such shameless talk of the most intimate things as I heard from this woman. There was another seamstress there, a girl of the same stripe as this woman, and the two of them showed no restraint before me. My eyes probably popped many times when I heard all sorts of strange things, and then they would say, "OK, little one, you don't have to be listening to everything!" But these crudities went in one ear and out the other. I remembered only one thing that I didn't understand, and, in later years, after I'd learned many things in life, I would now and then suddenly understand a word that had stuck unconsciously in my memory. I had no idea what it meant when they said, "All the seamstresses are walking the streets!" Since I was a seamstress myself this seemed to have something to do with me. But I was too shy to ask about it, and so it was years before I understood the harsh truth. I've often thought how easy it would have been for an impressionable young thing like me to have been thoroughly corrupted by the thoughtlessness of this woman.

I stayed for several years in this place and worked along with my sister when she was old enough. She was bolder than I, and she made sure that we looked for other work. We found it at the Schwendy Wool Factory on the Gitschinerstrasse, but we were placed in different workrooms.

We did earn somewhat more here—two talers a week—but the conditions in this factory were horrible; and it was said that anyone who worked there for a few years had consumption. Our foreman was good, but he didn't have any power. There were no organizations representing our interests, nor were there any inspections. So we just had to accept the conditions.

We had to spin thick clumps of wool into thinner skeins. When the wool tangled and had to be straightened out, we weren't allowed to turn the machine off first. Instead we had to reach into the running machine and quickly take out the thick spots and then twist and knot the threads together so they would go through the eyes. This produced a lot of skinned hands and knees. There were many bad things there. The toilets were right next to the workroom. Since there were no sewers, the toilets often ran over and filled the workroom with an almost unbearable air. Young people had to work day after day in this air. Frequently we had to work at night too. That usually happened by inserting a shift in the night between Friday and Saturday. But then we didn't get Saturday off; we had to work through it like any other day. That meant in effect three day-shifts one after the other without any breaks to speak of between them. At night they gave us a cup of coffee—that is, a thick chicory broth that I couldn't keep down. I was so miserable that I stood at the machine half like a corpse. Even the boss noticed it. I can still hear him saying to the foreman, "How she looks. She's probably sick, isn't she?"

"Yes," the foreman said, "she just can't take the night work. It's too much for a decent girl." Later they didn't work us nights anymore.

This boss then introduced a new pay scale that was supposedly to our advantage. We were supposed to weigh the fully spun rolls, and we would get paid extra for everything over a certain amount.

Of course we were tempted by the prospect of making more money, and each of us tried to outdo the others in working. But then one of the working girls had an insight that was, for the time, quite remarkable. I can still see her, a pretty girl with reddish blond hair from Rixdorf, as she stood among us one day and said: "Kids, don't be so dumb! He just wants to see how much work we can do. If we really do make a few groschen more for a few weeks, then they will just take it away from us."

I was in this factory for two years. Then I did different kinds of work, including making coats. You've got to try all sorts of things if you haven't done a regular apprenticeship.

It was only later that I got any actual training, and even then it didn't last long.

THE SEWING MACHINE AND
WORKING AT HOME

It wasn't until the 1860s that the sewing machine industry in Germany was far enough advanced for machines to be in general use. This produced a great revolution in the work that women did, especially the manufacturing of white goods and shirts. The making of collars and cuffs (heretofore they had been a fixed part of men's shirts) now developed into a separate industry. At this time there were four or five companies in Berlin that produced large quantities of these articles.

As I said, I had tried all kinds of work. But now I learned to sew on a machine and worked in one of these factories on Spandauerstrasse. There were about fifty women working at sewing machines and about an equal number engaged in preparing the pieces for the sewers. Every sewer was teamed with a preparer and the pay was split between them.

The workday lasted from eight in the morning until seven at night without any significant breaks. At noon you ate the bread you'd brought with you, or else you ran to the canteen next door to get something hot for a few groschen. Together, the preparers and the sewers got seven, at most ten, talers a week. Since the machine sewing was more strenuous than the preparing, it was customary for the sewer to get 17½ and the preparer 12½ groschen of every taler. But before the division was made, they deducted the cost of the wasted thread and broken needles, which usually came to about 2½ groschen per taler.

The first stimulus for us to change these conditions came with the Franco-Prussian War. Immediately after its outbreak, business in the clothing industry came to a standstill. Women were let go and stood around penniless because they hadn't been able to save anything on their low wages. Our company wanted to take the "risk" of keeping up full employment during the slack time if we wanted to work for half pay. We had no conception of any organization and were in a crisis situation since most of the women depended on themselves for support; they lived, so to speak, from hand to mouth. So we agreed to try it for a week.

So we started the drudgery. But the result was pitiful. The full cost of thread and needles was still deducted from our half wages. The owner's brutal actions made us start thinking. We decided unanimously that it was better to quit than to work for such wretched pay, which you couldn't even exist on. We selected three women, among them me, to tell this to the boss. When our delegation announced our common decision, he tried to calm us by telling us that as soon as there was news of victory in the war, business would go back up and wages would climb. He carefully avoided saying that they would "reach their former levels." Luckily we had the presence of mind to say that the wages would never rise as fast as they had been cut and, moreover, that there was a full warehouse of articles produced at the lower wages. When the boss realized that he couldn't fool us so easily, he got so angry his face turned red and he screamed at us, "OK, then I'll pay you the full wages again! Are you going to work now?" We told him curtly, "Yes, we'll work again."

We ourselves were surprised by our success. And it was just as much a novelty to the owner that working women would get together and make common demands. He had been taken by surprise, but it was also true that collar makers were very much in demand at that time. Shortly thereafter the boss called me into his office and told me that I didn't have to fear that my participation in this matter would hurt me at work. As long as he had work, there would be a place for me. That sounded very good, but it really wasn't true. He began to find fault with my work, and it wasn't long before I got tired of this and left voluntarily. The unity of the women, which had brought us the success, did not last long. Business did not pick up very quickly after the news of the victory. But the owners had learned. They didn't act as brutally as before but rather proceeded more carefully. They negotiated individual wage cuts with women who were in particularly dire straits. Of course this generated mistrust instead of unity among the women, and it took many years before they understood what was happening and confronted management with closed ranks. For many women it was a long and hard path.

I now bought my own machine and worked at home. I got to know all too well the fate of women working at home. I pedaled at a stretch from six o'clock in the morning until midnight, with a one-hour lunch break. At four o'clock I got up and did the housework and prepared meals. There was a little clock in front of me as I worked, and I watched carefully that each dozen collars took no longer than the previous dozen. Nothing made me happier than being able to save a few minutes.

This went on for five years, years that went by without my noticing that I was young, years in which life gave me nothing. Many things had changed around me. My sister and then my brother had gotten married, and my youngest sister had drowned during a boating party. My father had not been able to work for a long time, and so my fate was the same as many single daughters who don't make their own happy life at the right time: they have to hold everything together, to be both mother and father at the same time, and support those family members who can't support themselves. I supported my father for over twenty years, and I was always able to work hard enough to have an apartment with a living room and a kitchen.

My brother's wife died when their first child, a girl, was still very small. I took the child in, and during the year I had her, she brought me much joy. She learned to walk with me. When my brother remarried, I had to give her back. My brother himself died a few years later, and I often had the two boys from his second marriage with me because their mother had to work.

I can't say that I was always very happy. I'd hoped for something else out of life. Sometimes I was just sick of life: Sitting year after year at the sewing machine, always the collars and cuffs before me, one dozen after another; there was no value to life, I was just a work machine with no hope for the future. I saw and heard nothing of all the beautiful things in the world; I was simply excluded from all that.

For a while things were even worse. The endless work made me ill and the doctor said I'd have to give up the continuous sewing-machine work. I started to work on aprons which also took some handwork. I also got a half-day position doing alterations on finished goods. That was some variety, but basically work went on as before.

As a young girl I belonged for a time to the Working Women's Society that Lina Morgenstern had founded.* They gave instruction in arithmetic, writing, and German, and it was completely free. But not all the teachers got there on time, and so we often had to waste our precious Sunday morning hours waiting. We told Frau Morgenstern that we'd rather pay for our instruction than waste time waiting.

At that time there was a lot of misery; unemployment was high and the cost of living was very high. At the tilting yard the bourgeois clubs set up stalls to sell hand wares, and in one of the working women's meetings we were told that we could bring our work there too. One of the women asked what you could earn there. The amount mentioned was so small that she said, "Then I'd rather remain a printer's helper in my print shop; at least I know for certain what I have there."

One time the members of Morgenstern's Working Women's Society said, "These women, these Social Democrats—Frau Stae-

*Lina Morgenstern (1830–1909) was a prominent social reformer and the editor of a magazine for housewives.

gemann, Frau Cantius, and all the others—they're supposed to be real hyenas." But a few others had the reasonable thought, "We can at least first hear what they have to say."

And there soon was an opportunity to attend a meeting where Social Democratic women spoke; I didn't hear them, but the impression they made prompted the women to say, "That's right, that's something you can stand up for."

Then when I first went to a Social Democratic meeting, I just listened. The people there spoke so plainly, so calmly, so matter-of-factly, that it was like a deliverance for me. But it was still a long time before I became a Social Democrat.

Franz Bergg,
Apprentice Waiter

Franz Bergg (1866–1913), the son of a coachman and a farm laborer, grew up in Königsberg and later lived in many parts of Germany. A cigar maker by trade, he had originally planned to be a waiter. The first part of this selection describes his short-lived waiter's apprenticeship at a fancy restaurant and casino in Elbing (near Danzig), about 1881. In the second part, Bergg takes the reader through a typical day of a Prussian army recruit in the late 1880s. An ambitious and obviously gifted man, Bergg was frustrated in his attempts to establish himself as a free-lance writer and lecturer. He also had a way of getting himself into trouble: he served a short prison term for embezzling Social Democratic funds; he was in detention in the army; and near the end of his life he served six months in a Luxembourg prison for causing a disturbance in the gallery of the Luxembourg parliament. His autobiography was written, at the suggestion of the prison director, as a way of passing the time in prison. The irony in these passages is heavy-handed, but still, as a stylist Bergg is among the most successful of our authors. He has, moreover, a fine sense for the subtleties of human power relationships.

75

APPRENTICE YEARS

I was now forced to choose a trade. I had no particular preference; our financial situation demanded quick earnings. In Königsberg there wasn't anything that suited me in the long run. Finally I applied through an ad in the newspaper for a waiter's apprenticeship in E[lbing]. I was accepted, and, with the barest necessities, I journeyed toward my destiny.

Saying good-bye to my brothers and sisters and my father didn't take long; I was never to see my father again. My mother went with me to the train. The train was just about to leave, and I had to run so fast to my compartment that I hardly had time to embrace my mother. The good woman cried and waved her handkerchief at me for a long time, until our view of each other was cut off by a curve.

Without any real pain, I set off into the unknown. I was just short of fifteen years old.

In comparison to Königsberg, E[lbing] seemed very small to me. My destination was the casino. There I presented myself to the headwaiter. As soon as I entered I felt intimidated by the view of the large luxurious rooms. A new world opened up to me. The casino was the meeting place of so-called fashionable society, the nobility of the town and surrounding area. There were landowners, officers, judges, lawyers, and high administrative officials. Outsiders required a special introduction.

The building's furnishings reflected its function—huge mirrors, marble columns, carved wooden balconies with golden bronze railings, and ornate stuccowork on the walls and ceilings. In my eyes they had a fairyland splendor. Each room—for billiards, smoking, cards, or reading—had its own color scheme. Huge chandeliers and charming wall lamps poured out a magical glow. Adjoining the inner side of the building was a large garden with terraces, verandas, arbors, fountains, and grottoes.

Translated from Franz Bergg, *Ein Proletarierleben,* ed. Nikolaus Welter (Frankfurt: Neuer Frankfurter Verlag, 1913), 38–54, 112–19.

There were Sunday morning concerts during the nice weather. Families came to enjoy an after-church drink and music. We had our hands full. Now and then there was an importunate "Is it coming soon? Hey, Hey, Damn it all, waiter," etc. That was *our* music. But I didn't have the slightest desire to listen to any other. I didn't envy the fortunate people who could luxuriate in the abundance of melodies. No, I admired our Viennese waiter who could thread his way between the tables and chairs with thirty glasses of beer on a tray, sometimes in a gallop, sometimes with the patter of a delicate little girl—as if in time to the music.

The garden emptied out after the concert. But usually a few families and even whole parties stayed for lunch. There was enough work. Rarely were there any new faces. Almost all the guests were members of the casino society and made themselves at home. The younger gentlemen, especially the lieutenants, thought that their annual dues entitled them to lord it over the servant staff. We often had to suffer for their thoughtlessness. The administration of the business was in the hands of a manager. But the headwaiter was the soul of the whole place. His wages rose and fell with the consumption of beer and schnapps. The waiters got six marks a month for their laundry money; for the rest they had to depend on tips. My wages were exclusively tips.

For the knowledgeable, who are not deceived by the dazzling, spotless uniform, the waiter is a lamentable creature. In the waiter you can see clearly what human society—with its institutions, its customs and traditions, its caste spirit and class prejudices, and especially its proudly stupid narrow-mindedness— can do to some of its members. The prostitute is by nature less of a slave than the waiter. She sacrifices only her body; the waiter is demeaned to a moral eunuch who lives under special social laws.

Our actual fate as waiters was embodied in the figure of the headwaiter. The absolute power of his appearance spread fear and trembling. His anger ruled us with a whip made of ox leather, the stinging greeting of which I first felt on the third of May, the eve of my birthday. What business had I hiding in the arbor, treating my friends to a glass of beer and drinking to my health as a birthday boy?! The beating I suffered reminded me that the world cared no more about me than to know that I had been born. The where, how, and when didn't matter in the slightest.

Our highest duty was to be in constant motion. So the rules demanded. It makes a bad impression and damages the house's reputation if the waiters sit down or even pick up a newspaper. Wouldn't it be frightful if the count and countess along with their most gracious daughter had to sit down on such shockingly desecrated chairs! The very thought that only a moment before those chairs had served as a resting place for a common plebian was enough to have a heartrending effect. Hadn't countesses and their daughters been known to faint when they saw masons up on scaffolds on the new wings of their mansions blow their noses and then touch the stones with unwashed hands? And these were the stones that had the honor to be part of His Grace the Count's residence.

In the beginning I was not called upon for any of the grand services. I served the guests who ordered from the menu. I was satisfied with the tips, and was soon able to send home fifteen marks. In return my mother sent my laundry and darned socks. On the advice of my fellow workers I quickly had a new waiter's uniform made. There was a special tailor who worked for the whole service staff of the casino. I paid for the uniform in a month. Obviously I saved my money. My brisk cheery manner soon ingratiated me with the guests. They called me by my waiter's name "Schorsch"—a eunuch has no right to his real name.*
The clientele that had been entrusted to me was composed of some older gentlemen from the court of justice and a number of younger officers and junior barristers. They liked billiards most of all. I had to stand by the whole time and see to the drinks. Often they played well into the night. Sometimes I fell asleep on

---

*Schorsch is the German pronunciation of the French name Georges; the intention is to give Bergg a "fancier" name.

a chair in the corner next to the billiard table. Then the boorish lieutenants would wake me up with a billiard cue. On nights like this when I didn't get to bed until four o'clock, I got hardly any sleep because we had to be up at seven.

Our beds were no good; the bedrooms were up under the roof and were in very bad shape. The place was a mess; it was barely swept out once a week. In the morning the beds were left unmade, and in the evening we just used them as they were. For the morning work we put on our worst clothes. I brushed the billiard tables, dusted, raked the sand on the garden paths, swept off the garden tables and chairs, helped clean the knives and forks, and practiced folding napkins and setting tables, etc.

Despite our strenuous work, we weren't given at all enough to eat. With our own money we often bought bread and fresh country butter at the local market and devoured them greedily. The notorious "waiter's hunger" took root only too naturally in us.

The waiters' conversations among themselves revolved almost exclusively around the most base sensuality. They indulged in all sorts of crude advances toward the maid; and the apathetic woman did nothing to stop them. One day in the cellar I surprised the headwaiter in an obviously compromising position with our kitchen supervisor. In his surprise, he would have gladly given me a thrashing, but she restrained him. After that he had a grudge against me.

Some of the waiters never tired of making fun of certain gentlemen with whom they had "interesting love adventures." These instances of unnatural sensuality were not infrequent, even among men who in their public life held important offices and were considered pillars of religion and morality.

When setting the tables, you had to pay attention to every detail: how the plate was placed on the table, and which plate came first; whether the fork was on the left and the knife on the right, and where the spoon was supposed to go; making sure the plate, the fork, or the knife didn't stick over the edge of the table. All these were matters of great importance with which I had to familiarize myself.

I still had no idea of "how one was supposed to eat." Whether one chews with the cheeks full or with the lips compressed; how and in which hand the knife and fork are held; whether a spoonful of soup should be touched to the edge of the bowl or the drops of soup allowed to fall back in, or in order to avoid both, whether it's allowed to hold your chin right over the soup. I was initiated into all these particulars.

The waiters put great stress on the strict observance of these rules—by other people. They kept a sharp eye on the fashionable people as they ate, followed all of their movements, and found fault with everything. Our Viennese waiter remarked, his eyebrows raised with significance, that no human being was capable of observing all the fine points of table manners. The whole business left me completely cold.

The holiday evenings held a special charm for me. A large Hungarian band—its members in national dress—arranged itself on the balcony of the great dining hall and played their wild, fiery, and yet so melting melodies.

At such times the very look of the dining tables was a pleasure. There were the blinding white tablecloths; the tasteful, multiply folded napkins; the big silver bowls and shimmering metal platters; the artistic, richly segmented centerpieces; the finely polished, nobly formed drinking glasses; the pleasingly arranged bouquets. In all its richness it offered a constantly shifting feast for the eyes. There were the ladies in the splendor of rustling silk; there was the sparkle of jewels, and the soft shimmer of fresh arms, necks, and shoulders, so charming as they moved. There was the wine playing in the crystal; the tinkle and ring of glasses and goblets; the constantly rising good cheer; the music; the festive speeches; the burst of jubilation. Yes, to me all this was the apex of worldly refinement and culture. Amidst all the glitter and beauty you didn't notice the actual ugliness of eating—the animalistic chewing, the grinding jaws, and the smacking lips. These were just a necessary part in this blissful affirmation of the life force.

The waiter too can really lose himself in the magic of these hours, because serving a preplanned dinner is much less demanding than taking orders from the menu. Everything goes smoothly. The waiter can stay calm; he doesn't need to keep in mind the prices of the individual dishes or the order of courses for each guest; serving at the so-called table d'hôte he really feels relaxed.

When he's clearing away the food, the waiter is sharply watched to see that on the way to the kitchen he doesn't stuff something into his always hungry mouth. However, every waiter has a special pocket that is always soaked with fat; he calls it his storeroom. While he's on the run, he quickly sneaks in a piece of chop or chicken. He can eat his treasure only after the coffee has been served. And where does he eat it? . . . Well, you can guess.

This self-degradation was part of the nature of the situation. They fed us short and bad rations, like hunting dogs. If you're degraded to the level of a beast, you act like a beast.

After the evening meal the mild spring and summer evenings lured the somewhat overworked guests out into the park to relax. The ladies in their rustling, shimmering skirts sauntered in the lamplight of the garden, like fairy-tale flowers of the night. Beside them and behind them were their eager admirers in black coats or colorful uniforms.

As a child I imagined that Prussian officers, in full consciousness of their lofty position, would talk only of extraordinary things. In this childish belief, as in so many others, I was to be disillusioned. I couldn't hear anything from these men but sarcastic remarks or stories about dogs, horses, women, and drinking bouts. At that time I didn't understand much about horses and women.

Among the ladies the art of conversing was a bit more developed. At the dinner table you could see that swallowing the tasty morsels eventually got to be a torture for the beautiful young women with the flushed and sweating cheeks. That was to the credit of the delicate creatures. Outside in the garden, free from the inhibitions of the salon, they could act more naturally. They enjoyed this freedom with a carefree ease; sometimes it went as far as a laughing looseness or even wantonness, which was very entertaining for the hidden observer. It goes without saying that the god "Amour" played his eternal role here too. Now and then in their conversations you heard a word or two about art or literature; at least the ladies showed that they—unlike the officers—knew about more than just dogs and horses.

When the ladies and gentlemen feast from the menu, the staff has all the more to do. The kitchen slaves are especially pitiable. For the guests, the great burden is choosing from the endlessly long menu; there were dozens of kinds of soups, roasts, fish, and fowl, as well as vegetables, fruits, and cheeses. Everyone is guided by his own taste and demands satisfaction. Thus, for example, one doesn't simply order an egg. No, one calls for scrambled eggs, fried eggs, or pickled eggs, in all stages of tenderness and doneness: almost hard, hard, very hard, soft, very soft, soft as a plum, with a runny white part but a soft yolk, with an almost half-soft yolk, with a yolk somewhat hardened at the edge, and every conceivable combination, calculated to drive the cook to despair. Each of these specially prepared eggs must suit, not only the taste of its gourmand, but also his mood of the moment. Otherwise there is an outburst that races like lightning through a lightning rod, from the headwaiter through the waiter, exploding on the heads of the kitchen slaves in the depths of the kitchen. Slaving away in foul air and almost intolerable heat, they are set upon, as if by a pack of hounds.

O you dear men and women who cook, you washers, cleaners of kettles, knives, and forks—those lucky people out there have no idea of the unreasonable demands placed on you! Of the orders that hail down on you, blow by blow, in a crisp commanding voice, hard and loud! Even a lamb would go raving mad; the so-called kitchen madness is unfortunately a very understandable fact, even if its cause cannot be discovered by the learned doctors.

The kitchen turns into a true hell if the queen of this stifling realm, the head cook, does not have the necessary peace of mind and soul. Hers is no bed of roses. It's as if she forms the central exchange of a telephone network that has connections in every direction and is being rung up every second. There's no way to avoid mistakes in the rush and chaos. What do these poor people know of the upper world, of the sunniest sunshine on the sunniest Sunday? Like the stokers and shovelers by the boilers and coals in the belly of a ship, they are tied to the stoves and pots in the steam and heat, at the mercy of the changing moods of the guests who don't think about them, of the waiters who scream at them, and of the fellow workers who get in each other's way and irritate each other. It's no wonder that quarrels, curses, and real fights are not infrequent.

Of course the waiters are hardly better off. They have to suffer the guests firsthand. Someone's egg is too hard; another wants his beefsteak broiled, not fried in butter in a pan. A third wants his chops garnished with greens. This person's schnitzel has been left on the fire too long, that person likes his with an egg and a slice of lemon. At the same table the very same soup will be praised as good by one and sent back as inedible by another. The ham is too smoked, the fat too fatty, the salt too salty, the pepper too peppery.

There are guests and families who are surrounded by circles of waiters because they keep sending back what they've ordered, either because they've misunderstood or are simply mean. If the kitchen refuses to take it back, as may well happen, the waiter is caught in the cross fire and becomes the scapegoat. He has no rights anywhere. Every guest is the boss. The real boss, whose interests are not always the same as the guest's, turns against the waiter, not the guest. If, as was the case with our manager, the real boss puts the power into the hands of the headwaiter, then he's allowed to play the role of tyrant.

It should be said to his credit that our manager was basically a peaceful man filled with dignified reserve. Only once did I see him strike an apprentice and that was in error.

As usual the manager's breakfast had been set before him at nine o'clock; before he'd finished he was called away. A waiter who was passing through the room saw the rest of the bread, butter, and ham on the table. He thought that the manager was finished and ate what remained on the plate. A few minutes later the manager returned and found his plate empty. Understandably, he got very angry and sent for the waiter who'd served him the breakfast. Thinking that no one else could be the guilty one, he said not a word, but grabbing the unfortunate and astonished fellow by the ear, he dragged him over to the empty plate and boxed his ears. The poor devil defended himself to no avail. The real guilty one, who had been seen chewing with his cheeks full, was able to keep the anger from being directed his way. And so the matter remained.

When we waiters were by ourselves and looked at each other, our whole lamentable condition became all too obvious to us. We'd actually sold ourselves, sold ourselves for tips! Oh, this custom! This jingling invitation to humiliation and subjection that suppresses a free humanity! It seduces the giver into arrogance and misanthropy; and it robs the receiver of the last vestiges of human dignity.

Tips are not really wages for work performed; they are compensations for special services. First you have to show yourself worthy of this dog's pay. We tried to do so by running, bowing, and fawning, and with a thousand little attentions of look, manner, and gesture. Like a little girl cleaning the head of her dolly, we rubbed nonexistent dust off every chair before allowing the ladies and gentlemen to sit down. We pitter-pattered and danced and turned in every direction. If Her "Grace" or His "Severity" dropped something, we plunged to their feet like shooting stars, frequently tipping over full glasses in our excessive zeal.

However, tips really have to be earned; and that is expected of the waiter; he gets them by cunning, wrangling, cheating, and extorting. Actions that were illegal were considered permissible, even necessary, by the waiters I knew. Just as the proprietors of such institutions—from the finest restaurant to the lowest tavern—have their own rules, so too do their employees have their own codes of ethics. From tips alone, none of these waiters could save up enough to buy the grand restaurant or fancy inn whose proud owners they hope to be after ten to twenty years of drudgery. They have to use special tricks to help out. Here's an example of one of them: a guest orders a bottle of five- or nine-mark wine from the wine list, and he's served a bottle that costs three or six marks. How is that possible? Well, all that's required is some dexterity and a lot of cheek. The waiter peels the labels off all the empty bottles of the better wines and saves them along with the marked corks. When a guest asks for a six-mark wine, the waiter takes a three-mark bottle, puts the right label on it, opens it "with tender loving care" on the bar, and serves it to the guest with the appropriate cork, which he also has handy. It's possible to do this for all wines with the exception of champagne, which is always served corked so you can't switch the corks beforehand.

Indeed, even if the guest asks for the bottle with the cork still in it, he can still be tricked. Metal foil around the cork makes the trick easier. Sealing wax around the cork makes it harder but not impossible. Although the color of the wax varies with the price, you don't exactly have to be a magician to have the right color on hand.

At the brewery where I washed bottles during my last year of school, beer that had come in kegs was put into bottles, marked with counterfeit labels of brands like Pilsener and Grätzer, and sold as genuine bottles of these beers.

I could give examples of dozens of such tricks and prove by them how even poor people are cheated.

I held out in my position for over four months. Then the slavery became too much for me and I thought about running away. There was no way that I could return home; I would have been ashamed to show myself before my parents and relatives without having completed my apprenticeship. Caught in this dilemma, I thought of my oldest brother who'd been working as a cigar maker in Hamburg for several years.

I wrote to the Hamburg city government and asked for my brother's address. A month later the postman brought a large letter with the stamp of the Hamburg police on it. I wasn't present when it came, and the letter aroused curiosity and suspicion. The manager sent for me, showed me the letter, and asked whether I was thinking of running away to America. I answered that the letter gave me the Hamburg address of my brother who hadn't written to me yet. That took care of the matter. I was happy as a lark. From then on I could think only of Hamburg; before me lay a road that would forever deliver me from the hands of the brutal headwaiter.

From my tips—that degrading payment—I'd saved almost eighty marks. My clothes were good enough. Even my confirmation outfit still looked respectable. I waited for a favorable opportunity to flee. Toward the middle of August it came. Under some pretext—I don't know which—the headwaiter had struck me again. I waited for the quiet midafternoon hours, went up to my room, and asked a friend to help me get my trunk down. He was willing to risk it only to the final staircase. From there I loaded the trunk onto my back, went softly down the last steps, opened the main door (which was right there), and staggered outside. I would have almost collapsed from nervousness; fortunately there was a worker coming down the street, and I asked him to carry my trunk. We crossed the square in front of the casino and went toward the cemetery. Where the street turned, I glanced back. I saw our cook in the window watching my departure with helpless astonishment.

The wife of the cemetery caretaker was our laundress and liked me. I was allowed to spend the night in their house, and I slept and dreamed pleasantly without being scared of the dead.

That same evening I had notified the police of my departure and also asked for my leaving certificate. They tried to talk and threaten me into staying. But I was firm. Then they flatly refused to hand over my papers. I went anyway. The next day a taxi took me to the railway station. I had a satisfied expression on my face when the coachman left me. I planned to arrive unannounced in Hamburg and surprise my brother. My first step was to buy a fourth-class ticket to Berlin.

The car was filled to the point of suffocation. Emigrants with children and infants, peasants, peddlers, and Polish Jews were sitting and standing all over the place. Mothers were squatting on the floor, offering their breasts to hungry little mouths. All the windows were closed in consideration of the babies, many of whom looked sick. My trunk tempted a young girl to sit down on it. She sat on half of it, leaned against the wall, and went right to sleep. I stood at the window and watched the unfamiliar changing landscape rushing past me. But my eyes got tired and my legs craved a rest. I sat down on the other half of my trunk, but so softly that the pretty girl wasn't disturbed; and I tried to go to sleep too. With the monotonous rattle of the train and the rhythmic shaking of the car it was not too hard. Soon I was asleep.

As I'd fallen asleep I'd put my arms around the neck and bosom of the sleeping girl. On awaking, or rather in that condition of inner wakefulness before your eyes really open, I felt the young full body of my neighbor under my hands; and I decided to extend this pleasant half-sleep as long as possible. The girl must have already been awake for some time, but she didn't stir, fearing that she would disturb me. I'd given her a welcome place to sleep, and with a tender and charming sense of consideration she now tolerated my hand on her breast.

My hands probably could have stayed there for a long time. But I had to decide to wake up. I opened my eyes, acted as though I were very sleepy, and while keeping the delightful feeling in my fingers, I looked around at my neighbor. I looked into two big blue eyes that looked down, filled with inexpressible tenderness and girlish embarrassment. I quickly withdrew my hands, sat up, acted confused, and excused myself. She thanked me with a moving innocence. We got to talking and had a nice conversation. The beautiful child had to get out at Bromberg. I watched her go with regret.

The next morning at about six o'clock my train got to Berlin.

I asked a policeman about the schedule to Hamburg. The huge man looked me over from head to toe and said that the first train was an express that left at nine o'clock and cost 23 marks; the second, a local with a fourth class, left at two-thirty in the afternoon and cost only 6.20 marks. "Thank you," I said, "I'll take the express."

I went up to the counter and asked for a ticket to ————. I didn't get any further. There was a heavy grip on my shoulder that forced me to turn around. It was the hand of the policeman I had just asked for information. Despite all my reassurances, he was suspicious and led me to the guard room. Here I told them everything they wanted to know and did not conceal the circumstances under which I had left E[lbing]. A check by telegraph substantiated my story. But it still seemed suspicious to the police that a very young person who didn't look like a man of private means wanted to take the express to Hamburg. I explained that with the local train I wouldn't get to Hamburg until nighttime; since I didn't want to notify my brother, I had to get there during the day, which would have been possible with the express. Then my trunk was searched thoroughly, and I was allowed to go. In the meantime, however, the express had left. One of the higher police officials consoled me and said that I shouldn't spend my hard-earned money so carelessly. I'd get to Hamburg with the local train too.

I went to a restaurant. Afterward I wanted to have a look around Berlin. In the restaurant a finely dressed gentleman approached me: Where was I going and when? He was going on the same train. As he spoke he handed me his card. "Hermann de l'Or," it said on it.

The distinguished man made a tremendous impression on me. Such a gentleman and yet so friendly, a true friend of humanity! He assured me that he knew Berlin and placed himself at my disposal for three hours. I was enthralled. We had a beer and set off on our way.

We went through the Brandenburg Gate and onto Unter den Linden. I liked the great bustle and admired the splendid buildings; I was especially taken by the waxworks. Suddenly my companion became thirsty. He knew a tavern where the beer was good. We went in.

There were quite a few customers there. Some were playing cards. My guide took a fancy to the game; he bet and won, in fact he won quite a lot in a short time. The one-, five-, and ten-mark pieces were flowing freely. I had an urge to try my own luck. I bet and in a few moments I was eight marks poorer. I began to get uneasy. My change was all gone. In order to get more money out I would have to get into my back pocket, the so-called rogue's pocket. I didn't dare do that in front of all these strangers. Suddenly I got suspicious. It was a very odd-looking crowd. There was a secret greed and expectation in the eyes of many of them. I had to get out of there. My companion sat there like a stump. I was dizzy. I struggled for air, jumped for the door, tore it open, and stumbled out. And to the station, to the station!

No one followed me. Monsieur Hermann de l'Or was a swindler. As I later discovered, his name means in plain German "Hand over the gold!" The game that was supposed to relieve me of my savings was notorious among card sharpers.

This was an enlightening experience for me. From Wittenberg I telegraphed my brother that I'd be arriving in Hamburg at 11:10 P.M. I told him he'd recognize me by my white trunk and umbrella. We wouldn't have recognized each other otherwise, because I was only nine years old when my brother left home.

The railroad station was brilliantly lit. I followed the crowd of people and stood at the exit, trembling with anticipation. Then a well-dressed young man stepped up to me and asked, "Pardon me, how do I get to St. Pauli?"

I told him that that was where I wanted to go too, and I didn't know where that part of the city was either.

He looked at me sharply and continued, "I'm looking for Kampstrasse."

"So am I."

"Number 24?"

"Exactly the number I want."

"The third floor, at Herwart the shoemaker's?"

There could be no more doubt.

"Yes," I cried happily, "Rudolf Bergg's—and that's you."

We fell into each other's arms and kissed. In this kiss I felt the complete bliss of brotherly love.[. . .]

IN THE MILITARY

In its main outlines the recruit's day goes as follows:

Early in the morning the noncommissioned officer on duty storms like a savage up and down the hall, ripping open the doors and roaring a hideous "Get up!" into the barracks rooms, for the soldier has to be terrified, even out of his sleep.

You jump into your clothes and in a few minutes they order, "Step out! Out!"

Some of the slow ones still haven't made it.

"Out! Out! Out!"

Curses, cussing, shoves, and kicks drive the slow ones into the hall. The corporals have enough time to throw some quick punches. "I'll make the beds for you all right!"

"Get out, you swine!"

Then they order, "Squads report!"

"Stand at attention!"

The corporals go to the sergeant for the morning report.

"Squads step forward!"

The sergeant also inspects the barracks rooms. Two or three straw mattresses are lying on the floor. The names on the bed lockers are noted down. Some of the beds are badly made: they're ripped open and it's noted down. Two or three lockers are not closed: all the things are dumped out onto the floor in a mess and it's noted down.

Now the sergeant goes into the yard where things are teeming as in an anthill. The drilling of recruits is in full swing. The lieutenant in charge of recruits also appears.

The command shouts resound like crazy and clash in shrill confusion. Every corporal has a lance corporal and some of the old hands to help him. These "staghounds" run behind the closed ranks and "correct" the recruits with their fists and their feet, without saying a word.

The companies vie with one another. The lieutenants and sergeants throw many a searching look toward the other recruit units to check their progress. Within the same company the corporals watch each other with jealous nervousness. In a few weeks the recruits will demonstrate before the colonel. At that time none of the companies, and neither the lieutenant nor the corporal, want to lag behind their colleagues.

These morning exercises last for two hours. A ten-minute break gives the recruits time to collect themselves for the following trials.

The sergeant has the miscreants he has noted down step forward. But how odd! He is more merciful toward them than toward the corporal. Of course the recruit laughs thankfully in his heart and thinks, "Say, you've got yourself a good sergeant." In reality a trick has been played on him, which is the custom in the army from the highest general to the lance corporal. Every superior sharply reprimands his immediate subordinate. Like an avalanche, a word of reprimand spoken at the top swells in its precipitous fall until, passing over the lance corporals, it smashes with raging power onto the recruits. The squad leader is rudely taken to task for every obligation both inside and outside. Every shortcoming in the company's conduct is put at his door.

The corporal would have to be a god in order to resist the brunt of everything. Unfortunately, he is, or was in my time, all too often a rough person whose raging instincts were given full rein in the barracks yard. It's no wonder that his anger at the often unjust blows exploded in an uproar of cussing and slapping.

And this thunderous violence is not even the worst.

More dangerous is that icy malevolence that gives a subdued command in a peculiarly altered barracks voice, the facial muscles playing like a hardened smile around the eyes; and then, with a sharp change back to a natural facial expression, it deals

out some kicks and slaps, only to flee once again behind the mask
of a sinister sneer before which a horse would rear back trembling.

With the intonation of a buzz saw that cuts through the recruit's every bone, the corporal commands that the untidy beds,
lockers, or rooms be put in order or cleaned up. But the "guilty
one" is not allowed to do the work himself; others are ordered to
do it. All at once the staghounds and some of the other old hands
act as orderlies for the recruit; they turn the straw mattress, man
the broom, or straighten the locker. Limp with exhaustion, the
recruit watches them work, a bottomless abyss before his eyes.
He knows what awaits him.

At the given moment the corporal leaves the room. Scarcely
has the door closed behind him when, as if on signal, there is a
momentary silence. But then it's as if a pack of wild animals has
smashed into the poor boy. That damn fellow is going to make
amends for their having to work on his account! They fall upon
the poor fellow with fists and boots and with brooms and
brushes. He's delivered helpless into the hands of his tormentors.
But the corporal has gotten his satisfaction. The squad's disgrace
has been blotted out.

What a subject there is here for the dramatic writer, a writer
who would have the courage to build a real barracks on his stage!

Down with the miserable soldiers' farces and their singing!
Down with the hollow barracks anecdotes and the humorous
sketches of military life! Low-down mercenary writers, worthless
bunglers—with their filth they betray and prostitute a crushed
people for a second time. When will there be a writer of genius,
a noble friend of humanity who dares bring about justice to the
thousands and thousands of martyrs whose bodies are ravished,
whose souls are whipped with flaming rods, and who are damned
in the most horrible sense to suffer without complaining?

Many a crushed human worm would take comfort from the
noble wrath of that blessed spokesman. Many a suicide would
find atonement—albeit too late—through the poet's sword of

judgment. This literary savior of the barracks slaves may never come.

But after this short digression, I come back to the regular day's work of the damned as I saw it in my years.

The young "remount," as the recruit is called, has to get used to the idea as quickly as possible that for the time being the recruit is inferior human material that "has to be kneaded." Even the old troops, the second- and third-year soldiers, do their part to make his fate all the worse. They have a sort of traditional right to do this.

During his early days the recruit has to request permission before he enters the room of the old troops. The "bluesacks" and "reserves" often like to keep him standing in the doorway or even order him to do deep knee bends, holding out his rifle at arm's length for their amusement.*

But the real hell breaks loose only when, after the colonel's inspection of the recruits, the recruit is assigned to the old troops in their barracks rooms and is incorporated into the company drills.

The whole company has to pay with exhausting repetitions for the tiniest error of the individual. The recruit who is uncertain in his duties catches it from behind with shoves and kicks so that he doesn't even see his tormentors. He's not allowed to look around during full drill, so he staggers on through the mistreatment like a drunkard. The captain even has his own ways to "kick into line the ones who've gone astray." He gives the command: "The man in the middle (whom he calls by name) turn! Straighten out! March! March!" At this command, which is quickly repeated five to ten times without waiting for the wings to align themselves, the company revolves around its natural center, the always-turning middle soldier, like a top set loose in furious anger; the soldier in the middle is dealt countless blows, shoves, and kicks in the intended confusion. A hideous picture!

---

* The standard (M98) rifle weighed about nine pounds unloaded.

Worthy of accompanying this "devil's dance" are torments like: "On the double, march, march! Up! Down! Up! Down! Lie down! Up! Form up right and left, march, march! Form columns! Form up!" And so on. Who could even name all the torments imposed as "duty" on the soldier? For example, "Heels up, knees bent." And all the while you're holding your rifle out! So that the corporal doesn't get tired of commanding, "Rifle forward! Bend! Straighten up! Bend!" and so on, they've invented the command "Continue!" So all the commander has to bother to do is watch a kind of death agony of constantly weaker, twitching cramps.

"Aha," they say when strength fails, "that fellow doesn't want to do any more. Look at the faces that guy's making! Look at that beast pant for air!"

If the soldier is actually at the end of his strength, if his hands can't extend any longer, if his knees and legs tremble and his rifle hangs in numb paralyzed hands, then a bayonet can goad him on. "Hands extended! Hands extended!" they say. Finally they rasp, "The fellow is lazy!" and he's reported to the captain.

Then there are extra exercises, one to two hours longer than for the rest of the troops. The first time the unfortunate creature even drops his rifle during this extra drubbing, he gets three days detention. If he collapses, he has to carry sandbags and bricks in his knapsack.

The soldier's self-confident, manly dignity goes to pieces under all the mistreatment, at least for the duration of his military service. In those days, being slapped and kicked was part of the proper barracks style.

Someone who'd been slugged had no need to blush in front of the others. All he had to consider was the physical pain.

When military service is over, the usual plain self-respect comes back into its own, and the reservist is ashamed of the despicable treatment he received under the fists and feet of the corporal. Indeed patriotic duty even compels him to say nothing to society about this inhuman treatment.

After lunch, which is spiced up for him more than once with the order to hold out a footstool, the recruit falls in for inspection.

This inspection is more fearsome than the hardest exercises. It's not only that the articles ordered up for inspection must be in perfect condition, the man himself is most painstakingly inspected down to the nails of his shoes. The corporals take pleasure in cutting all the buttons off the coat, jacket, and trousers, if in their opinion, just one button is loose.

"Battalion turn around! Right foot up! Left foot up!" The soldiers' shoe soles are inspected like the hooves of horses and oxen.

In the afternoon there are gymnastic exercises, climbing, and bayonet drills for two hours or longer. Woe to him who is just now learning gymnastics and is clumsy and slow at climbing!

Squatting down with rifle outstretched (often two rifles at a time); or pressing your knees through the ladder, with old bayoneted rifles goading the clumsy ones over the wooden fences and other three- to four-meter-high obstacles—that's considered obligation and fun. The staghounds prove themselves here splendidly; their constant howling is the strongest spur for your waning strength; it reminds you of a madhouse or a pit of trapped wolves.

After supper a savage witches' Sabbath breaks loose in the guard rooms. The corporals don't have enough hands and feet to impress their orders on you violently enough. Sometimes coal shovels help out, especially on the skulls of the Poles, until they can acknowledge their orders in German.

Suddenly, amidst the wild chaos you'll hear, "Over the tables! To the lockers! To the beds! Under the beds! On top of the lockers!"—and so on.

The pitiable soldiers shake, steam, and foam like overwrought stallions. The corporals sweat too, but they're enjoying their pleasure to the full. Often one recruit is ordered to hit another. Then there's another command, "Do a rifle drill!" or "Hold out a stool!" In the winter they like all this to happen right near a glowing hot stove so that the pitiable scapegoats collapse from exhaustion.

Bedtime puts an end to the wild brawl. Sleep should bring a few hours of peace. But for some it doesn't. Many recruits are pursued into their dreams by the orders of that unleashed pack of corporal dogs; they start to exercise in their beds, trying to climb ladders while they roar like beasts, only to tumble head over heels onto the floor.

In the early morning the mad harassment begins anew. The noncommissioned officer on duty storms along the corridor like a wild beast, ripping open the doors and roaring his hideous "Get up!" into the rooms, for the soldier has to be terrified, even out of his sleep.

Wenzel Holek,
Brickyard Worker

Wenzel Holek (1864–1935), the son of a Czech-German migrant worker, spent his early life working in the brick, sugar, and glass industries of northern Bohemia and Saxony. After a period in the wood industry, he gradually rose to the fringes of the middle class as a librarian and educator of working-class youth, first in Leipzig, then in Berlin. He gradually distanced himself from the socialist zeal that plays such a prominent role in this selection. Holek was stimulated to write his autobiography by the reading of Karl Fischer's book, which he had acquired through a middle-class teacher who had befriended his son. After being rejected by one publisher, Holek was eventually referred to Paul Göhre and the Eugen Diederichs Verlag. In the following selection Holek describes his political awakening in the mid-1880s, when he was working in a brickyard in Aussig in northern Bohemia. As in Germany during the 1880s, socialist activity in the Austrian Empire was dangerous and could have severe consequences. The petty rivalries between socialists and Czech nationalists, as well as the small-time politicking among the socialists themselves, appear almost laughable in retrospect. But the reader should bear in mind that

97

the battle for the hearts and minds of the workers was decided, not on a grand theoretical level, but in the local clubs, taverns, and shops, as described by Holek.

LIBERATION

Two years had gone by since I'd come to Aussig, and I hadn't realized a single one of the plans I'd made. One after the other, my castles in the air had come crashing down. My budget that I'd planned so carefully didn't balance with the assets I'd taken in up until now. I was in the same position as most finance ministers: my accounts showed a deficit. But unlike a minister, I couldn't get anyone to approve a supplementary budget. And yet we were as thrifty as possible. From the twelve or thirteen guilders that Luis and I earned in a week, I bought food, paid the rent, got whatever else we needed, and paid off the furniture; but we were always short of money. We didn't get to save anything even though we didn't take part in any amusements.[. . .]

Meanwhile the creditors were putting more pressure on my mother-in-law to pay off her old debts. I now realized that it would never be possible for us to pay the debts and I advised selling the house in Charwatetz. My mother-in-law was convinced she had to and followed my advice. My brother-in-law Kane, who was married to Luis's older sister, took over both the house and the debts. This brought Luis an inheritance of 137 guilders.

When my mother-in-law got back to Aussig, she brought word that my father was building a house again and had said that I should come for a visit. That really disturbed me. I was ashamed for having neglected my own family. But even this pushed my gloomy thoughts into the background for only a short while.

Translated from Wenzel Holek, *Lebensgang eines deutsch-tschechischen Handarbeiters,* ed. Paul Göhre (Jena: Eugen Diederichs Verlag, 1909), 195–223.

I couldn't help but think again and again how all my beautiful hopes had faded away like clouds of fog into the evening. The only wish that had come true for me was that Luis was at my side. Oh, how many evenings I spent speculating and brooding over my failure. But all in vain!

Added to this was my growing dissatisfaction with my humiliating situation with Schindler.* When I thought the whole thing through from every angle and recalled the indifference of my surroundings, how patiently and submissively my fellow workers accepted the miserable wages and all the injustice, and how there was no prospect for improvement in the future—when I recalled all this I would often fall into a deep melancholy, despite my youth. Even the fretsaw work that I did for a time to divert my thoughts elsewhere began to irritate me.

I'd taken the *Prague Daily* [*Prager Tagblatt*], a government paper, for a year now and I was thinking less highly of it all the time. The subscription cost only twenty-six kreuzers a month—probably so it would be accessible to the poor people and give them a good opinion of high society. This never-ending praise of the rich! Gradually the reports of parties, hunts, and pleasure excursions among the high and highest levels of society awakened in me a vague hatred for them. But I got just furious when they took out after the workers. How often it was that I threw the rag into the coal box! Finally I'd had enough and instead subscribed to a liberal paper. At least that's what I thought the *Narodni Listy* (in German, something like *People's Paper*) was. It was the organ of the Young Czech party.† To be sure, each afternoon's edition cost three kreuzers, but even so I stopped the *Prague Daily* and bought the *Narodni Listy* instead because I liked its style much better. Before long I had a very high opinion of this paper, since it seemed to me to be the most radical and free-thinking newspaper I'd ever seen. Occasionally I also read the

---

*Holek's foreman; see p. 102.

†The "Young Czechs" were radical Czech nationalists fighting against German domination in Bohemia and Moravia; the "Old Czechs" (see p. 107) were the more moderate nationalists.

Vienna General News [*Wiener Allgemeine Zeitung*], a German paper that I also liked a lot. Because my German reading was still not very good, I preferred the former paper since it was written in my native language.

One day this newspaper told its readers, especially the workers among them, that it had started a column for them in which they could air their complaints about wage and working conditions in industry (assuming of course that the complaints were true). I was amazed and read over the lines repeatedly. It looked to me like a good opportunity to be able to pour my heart out. I had enough material. It was just a question of what part of it I should make public. There I was, quite alone and unable to confer with or confide my plans in any of the people with whom I worked. Finally I very laboriously put together an article. I chose something that pertained to more than just local conditions but still could be based on them—factory inspection. In the essay I criticized the bad conditions in the industries that I knew about, and told how the factory inspections were (and actually should be) conducted. I hoped to awaken a general interest in this serious matter and especially to direct the attention of the workers to it. Yes, my hope was even so great and naive that I assumed that the authorities would have to intervene immediately in order to abolish the abuses. It was not long before I saw how deceived I was. Aside from correcting a few spelling errors, the editors published my article just as it was when I had sent it to them— so of course in the short run my enthusiasm for the paper went way up, for it was now in my eyes the only paper that didn't fear to represent the workers' interests. Had it been in my power I would have made all the workers read it.

One morning shortly thereafter we were beginning work as usual, digging out a long stretch of mud wall above the brickyard and putting in an embankment, when along came Römmler, one of the workers. He had once been a forester's assistant but now was a down-and-out alcoholic. He pulled out a leaflet and read it aloud to us. The leaflets were said to have been distributed at night in Türmitz, a small city about a half hour away from Aussig.

Today, after so many years, it's no longer possible for me to reproduce the entire contents of the leaflet here. But I do remember that in it the author tried to clarify for the workers their entire social position in state and society. Then it discussed the miserable economic condition of the workers. How they had to slave and toil year in and year out their whole life long and still had to suffer from want. How they were robbed of the greatest part of the fruits of their labor by the capitalist exploiters. How the rich, who did nothing useful in their life, led a comfortable and luxurious life at the expense of the workers. Then it touched on the workers' lack of any rights. How the freedoms of press and assembly were withheld from the workers so that they counted for nothing, even though they were the major factor in society. How those who had the courage to represent openly and fight for the rights and freedom of working people were chained and dragged off to prison, where they languished innocently for months, even years, while their families had to go hungry. And finally, the workers were called upon to unite, to rise up in order to be able to throw off the yoke of capitalist exploitation, to do battle against their oppressors, to destroy them! Down with the exploiters! Down with the oppressors, the tyrants of the working class! So far as I recall, that was the closing call!

We listened to the reader almost breathlessly. When he was finished reading, we stood there for a long while, speechless, looking dumbly at each other. Most of us had probably never heard such things and in such a tone. We couldn't even think, let alone speak.

Römmler put the leaflet back into his pocket. No one wanted to come out with an opinion on what it said. Probably because no one trusted anyone else. Finally Römmler himself spoke up; he didn't think much of anyone anyway, and he had a way with words; he was even a smart aleck with the bosses. "Yeah," he yelled in his bombastic voice, "it's high time things got moving. That's exactly right what it says there. If nothing gets started, it's not going to get better; mark my words!" Some said he was right, but others objected that we workers were poor and without any means, and so were powerless to carry anything through.

There was also mention of the army, the police, and the gendarmerie, which were always ready to suppress anything that got started. In short, the discussion moved within very unimaginative limits. Most considered themselves powerless as workers. The greatest pessimism came from the mouth of Heinrich, a former policeman and brush maker. He philosophized, "We were born for the wheelbarrow and we have to remain with it!"

Before long the foreman Schindler came running up. Römmler quickly told him the latest news and spiced it up with a few select lies: that the socialists wanted to divide up everything into equal portions for people, etc. Schindler asked to see the leaflet and showed great curiosity. But Römmler, who was just about to get it out, didn't give it up, and apologized for getting fresh once again. A short time later the factory police sergeant appeared. He also asked Römmler for the leaflet. Once again Römmler made his jokes, but he did hand over the leaflet. The sergeant reached for it eagerly and at once began to read it for himself; when he was done, he put it into his pocket and hurried away.

The message of the leaflet swirled around in my head. Although I hadn't the foggiest notion of press freedom and other rights, I deemed the rest of what it said—the part about the distress and misery of the workers—the absolute truth.

"So this is what the socialists think and what they want?" I asked myself again and again every time I thought about what I'd heard. The tone of it, being unfamiliar, did strike me as too harsh. But when I compared what was said here about the workers with what was written about their demands and character in the *Prague Daily,* I realized that most of the latter had to be a malicious lie, a falsification of the truth. I didn't trust that paper anymore anyway after I'd seen that its opinions were always on the side of the rich. The expressions that they used against the workers—"oily fellows," "traitors to the fatherland," "agitators," "subversives"—these just didn't agree at all with what I'd heard in the leaflet. But how was I to be certain who was actually right? Where was someone who really professed socialism and could explain to me its principles and its views of the workers' situation? There I was—at a loss. And for a long time I groped in the dark when it came to this matter.

In the meantime a weavers' strike broke out in Brünn. Although I was far removed from it, I still followed all the details through the newspapers, just as I then liked to do in other similar situations. The great miners' strike that had broken out earlier in the Durer mining district of northern Bohemia had already awakened in me the greatest sympathy for the strikers. From my own experience I knew the working and living conditions of the people there. I'd helped out in the pits there as a twelve-year-old boy, and not only had to observe the terrible misery, but also had to endure it myself. In my mind the workers were completely right when they stopped work and demanded better living conditions. From the bottom of my heart I desired the victory of the poor people.

And now the weavers' strike! The *Narodni Listy,* of which I was still an enthusiastic and diligent reader, dedicated a long article to the conditions of the weavers. It described the low wages, the long working hours, the poor housing, and the generally inhuman life of the weavers; and it represented these abuses as justifiable causes of the strike. According to a telegraph report, thousands of strikers had gathered in the marketplace, and with their hats off, had sworn not to go back to work until the demands had been met.

This description moved me a great deal. My sympathy for the poor people rose, and the anger within me against the rich stirred even more in my breast. In my opinion they alone were responsible for the misery of the workers.

Every day I waited impatiently for the moment when I could get the new edition of the newspaper. To me its contents seemed completely true! Above all, what would the outcome of the strike be? I completely devoured every line.

One evening I went to see my neighbor, the shoemaker Honsa. I'd recently gotten to know him through his brother, a carpenter; and I now had all my shoe work done by him. We got to talking about the strike and the newspapers. Of course at this opportunity I couldn't suppress my enthusiasm for the *Narodni Listy*, and I praised it as the best paper of all. Honsa smiled and squinted at me searchingly, and then he said quietly:

"There are papers that write even better."

"Really! And which ones?" I quickly burst out. I waited tensely for the shoemaker's answer.

But he just kept on nailing his boot and didn't answer me. I continued to press him, and he finally said that he didn't have any such paper now, and he also didn't know where it was actually published. But that still didn't satisfy me; and I pressed him further, asking where and from whom I could definitely get such a paper. For now I was on the trail of what I'd long been searching for. At last he promised to get a copy for me. "But I'm telling you, you must not talk about it with anyone!"

"Well, is it perhaps forbidden?" I asked, astonished.

"Not really. But not everyone needs to know." Honsa kept his word. That same evening he sent me the promised paper via his journeyman Zaruba, with still another warning not to tell anyone that he'd gotten it for me. I shook my head. Why were people so nervous when it wasn't anything forbidden?

It was a four-page paper of large format and carried the title *Duch Casu*—that is *Spirit of the Time*—an organ for the interests of the fourth estate; it appeared fortnightly and cost forty kreuzers for three months. Franz Hlawacek was the managing editor. Its place of publication was Prossnitz in Moravia. The paper was well edited; I, at least, was so taken by this first copy that I resolved that from then on, I would fear nothing and count myself among the "oily fellows."

At that time there was no parliamentary politicking of the sort that the working class does today, because the parliament was composed exclusively of members of the propertied classes; and since the workers still didn't have the right to vote and there was almost no political or union organization, parliament basically ignored the socialists.* So this newspaper contained mostly ar-

*Universal manhood suffrage was not introduced in the Austrian Empire until 1907.

ticles that dealt with workers' questions from the perspective of the economic theory of Karl Marx. This was the only Czech-language socialist paper that appeared in Austria in those days. Right there in that first issue that I'd just happened to come upon, there was, for example, an article explaining capitalism and its system of exploitation. It described how capitalism had to exploit the workers' labor power and expand rapidly. Then the conclusion was very encouraging; it said that this could not happen in the state of the future because then everyone would have an equal obligation to work, and equal rights to life.

I was dumbfounded, my mouth almost hung open. I sat there in amazement and kept looking at what was written there as if I couldn't quite trust my eyes. This was really another style, a totally different opinion and perspective than in the *Narodni Listy!* Of course I didn't understand what I read, for how was something like this possible? But still, wasn't it something completely just—this demand: equal duties, equal rights? Yes, so it should be, so it shall be! These and similar thoughts intersected in my brain and heightened my sense of justice more and more.

Then I devoured the survey of politics and the reports from the various regions and provinces, calling attention to bad wage and working conditions and other grievances. Every line that I read seemed true to me. For I myself had a large store of such grievances and was the daily witness of how other workers also experienced injustice.

I'd finally achieved what I'd striven for for so long! At once the dark scales fell from my eyes. In one leap my enthusiasm went from the Young Czech paper over to the *Duch Casu* and the idea that it taught and advocated: socialism!

When I brought the paper back to Honsa, I couldn't suppress the joy that filled my heart, and I had to praise openly the paper's courageous and truthful style. He looked at me carefully and then turned his gaze back to his work; he nodded and a soft smile crept over his lips. Then he said, "Yes, yes, that's something quite different from the *Narodni Listy,* isn't it?" After I'd pointed out and discussed a few of the places that especially interested me, I put down in front of him forty kreuzers and a filled-in postal money order form. I asked him to take it with him to the post office when he had a chance, because I'd decided to subscribe to the paper.*

Only now did he stop his work; he rested his elbows on his knees and looked at me with amazement and embarrassment; then he averted his gaze inward, thoughtfully, like one who wanted to search his conscience. After a short silence he turned back to me and said quietly, "And you have no second thoughts about the troubles that this could cause for you?"

But I'd already expected something like that from him, because I'd noticed even during our first conversation that he was afraid, though groundlessly I thought. Exasperated, I replied: "Why are you always talking about troubles!? The paper is censored and approved by the state authorities. So it's legal. Why should it be dangerous if you subscribe to it and read it? I just don't see the point!"

"That's true," Honsa replied. It seemed to me now that he found the whole subject unpleasant and regretted having let me in on the secret. "But," he continued, "I've often heard that after getting the third or fourth issue of this paper, people have their houses searched, and then . . . ?"

"And what if that *is* true?" I interrupted quickly. "That wouldn't scare me off and deter me from something that's right!" I declared ceremoniously and proudly. He didn't say another word but indicated he was ready to send off the money.

But I didn't have any luck with the subscription. I kept waiting for the paper to come. But it didn't come. Finally it turned out that the journeyman Zaruba was supposed to have taken the money to the post office. A few weeks later, however, when he had a fight with Honsa, it turned out that Zaruba still had the money order I'd filled out. He had kept the money.

Meanwhile I was trying hard to find someone who got the paper himself and was a socialist, so that I could learn from him what I so much wanted to know: what socialism was! The shoe-

---

*It's unclear why Holek doesn't go to the post office himself.

maker Honsa couldn't enlighten me as much as I wanted because, as I realized, he didn't understand much more about it than I did. The one issue of the paper that he had lent me had not even been his. Generally, it seemed to me that he only went along with socialism a little bit, and it was only a business matter for him. Soon I considered him a coward on account of the great fear he always showed when we got to talking about socialism. And just because of this I was prompted to find someone else to enlighten me. In Wenzel Nowotny, a mason who lived in the Nonnengasse not far from me, I finally found the sort of man who could satisfy my yearning. He'd been committed to socialism for several years and was well acquainted with its principles and final goals. He'd been a subscriber to the very first workers' papers in Austria, and he still had them, nicely bound. He was also cofounder of several workers' education associations that had been dissolved by the authorities. His library showed that he was a very ambitious man. Getting to know him was not very much trouble after he'd heard that I was the author of that long article in the *Narodni Listy*. He had even sensed my interest previously.

He received me amiably the very first time that I called at his house one evening after work. After a few casual questions and answers he skillfully guided the conversation to my article, and he gently reproached me for having published all that in a paper that was an enemy of the workers. I was very glad when he rescued me from my embarrassment with the excuse that I probably hadn't known any other newspaper. These people, he continued, merely intended, by this and other means, to exploit the workers for their own party purposes; but their interests were completely different from those of the workers. Then he inveighed against the Old- and Young-Czech parties and criticized their positions on economic, political, and legal questions. And then he got to talking about the nationality question in general. He said flatly that we workers, without distinction of nationality, had to be international-minded. For modern capitalism also knew no boundaries; it was drawing together the workers in the industrial areas of all nations and exploiting them without regard to their language or religion. Industrial capitalism pursued this principle everywhere it appeared in the entire world.

He ended his lecture after about two hours, without having stirred from the old trunk that he was sitting on. And for the whole time I sat opposite him on an old-fashioned chair and listened reverently and with great excitement to every word that came from his mouth; and I didn't doubt that it was the pure truth. I was happy and felt greatly satisfied that I'd finally found a man who could, with such understanding, make everything clear to me. I hadn't heard anything like it in my whole life. To me the man seemed incomparable! And I secretly envied him for his wisdom! Oh, if I could only get so far! Such passionate thoughts, stirred by ambition, welled up in me. My face glowed with bliss and my eyes beamed with joy. Nowotny's look too, and the smile that flew over his lips from time to time, revealed that he shared my joy. He was definitely pleased that he'd recruited another follower for the socialist idea.

Before we parted that evening I asked him if he might lend me something to read. He didn't hesitate for a moment but told me to sit down for a little while, and he left the room. Soon after that I heard a noise up over the ceiling. That made me a bit uneasy. I suspected that he too had hidden the books and was now guardedly getting them from the hiding place. All sorts of thoughts sprang into my head: police, house searches, courts, prison. And yet I yearned so eagerly for these books! My worries vanished in an instant when he came back into the room and handed me two books, saying, "Here, the lighter one is an almanac that contains mostly stories that are all easy to understand. But the other one is scholarship, it's *The Quintessence of Socialism* [*Quintessenz des Sozialismus*];* it has to be studied if you want to understand it. Take your time with the reading. If you don't understand something, I'll be happy to explain it to you."

The next evening I greedily flung myself into the book *The Quintessence of Socialism* and ignored the almanac, for I was driven

*The author of this book, which appeared in 1874, was the well-known economist and sociologist Albert Schäffle (1831–1903).

by an irresistible curiosity to finally learn something right about socialism. I read the first pages right through; but it seemed to me that I was groping around in the dark, and I didn't know what I had read. My unpracticed and untempered brain was not capable of taking in and digesting this lofty intellectual fare. My keenness to read went down and down. But in spite of this I didn't give up. Again and again I forced the lazy organ to new attempts until the last page was read. Then I began again from the beginning; but I also went to Nowotny and confessed my inability to him. He began a discussion of the book and explained what was unclear to me. When I'd finished reading it a second time, I started in still a third time, and then I noticed that more and more from the book was sticking in my head. If Nowotny's help hadn't been there at my side, I surely would have thrown the book aside in disgust. It went easier right from the beginning with the almanac and the other books that I borrowed from time to time from the man. First, because they were written in a more popular style, and second, because my formerly lazy brain was already more used to the hard work.

With every new work that Nowotny gave me, he did as he had the first time—he always disappeared from the room for a while and rummaged around in the attic. I didn't really know what he was doing and I didn't dare ask. My suspicion was that he had his library somewhere up in the attic. And this was correct; later after I'd associated with him for a long time and he was convinced that he could trust me, he told me that he always kept his books in the attic hidden under the floorboards. Aside from this main hiding place he had another one in the living room where he hid little things like brochures and newspapers so he didn't have to climb up the ladder to the attic every time. This hiding place was under the coal box next to the stove where the floor was a little hollowed out. And I did the same thing later when I occasionally bought books or didn't want to leave borrowed ones lying around the room all day. But my hiding place wasn't as favorable as Nowotny's. There weren't any floorboards over my attic apartment anymore, and so I had no choice but to shove the books between the sloping ceiling of the living room and the roof. This hiding place was very inconvenient because every time I wanted to get the books out or hide other ones I had to lie on my stomach in the dust up in the loft in order to reach my hand under the roof. I kept the books wrapped individually in newspaper, and sometimes they would slip down too far so that I had to get a poker to help get them out. The worst was when I moved out of this place. Even with the poker I didn't get all the books out and had to leave them there. And perhaps they're still stuck in there today at Antoniegasse 7. The other supporters of the party, whom I got to know later, all did what we did. Even though the books were not forbidden, anyone who was found with them was arrested for conspiracy. And so everyone was very careful not to let anything fall into the hands of the police. The reading material was fetched from the hiding place in the evening, read, and then rehidden.

Unlike Nowotny's more accessible hiding place, mine consisted of a chair. I'd nailed a thin board under its seat and every time I finished reading the book or newspaper I stuck it under there. I thought it was safe there from the eyes of the police in case of a search. The shoemaker Fiala had a very unusual hiding place for his newspapers. One time when I was visiting him and we got to talking about police harassment, he laughed and said, "Well, they can come here and they certainly won't find the *Duch Casu!*" He pointed to the roller blind on the windows. I didn't understand right off what he meant. He didn't leave me guessing for long; jumping up from his stool, he let the blind down with a rattle and out fell several newspapers one after another. "Practical, eh? No police spy will get them in there!" he exclaimed happily. I smiled and nodded and praised his good idea. He pulled on the cord again and rolled the papers back up into the blind. The whole thing amused both of us greatly, and at the same time it gave us a chance to think we were much cleverer than the police.

Gradually I was introduced to the rest of the supporters— tried and true comrades and socialists. Including Nowotny there were nine men in all: Rericha, Beran, Duschek, Kulic, Fiala, Kolar, Krutak, and Nejedli. That was everyone whom I got to know in Aussig, and for a long time they *were* the socialist party in the city. We were all Czechs, except for Krutak, who was a German but spoke very good Czech. Among the Germans the only socialists I ever knew were the two Liebichs, father and son, whom I got to know only later, because in those days they kept their distance from the movement. They were probably afraid of losing their jobs. Old Liebich was hoping for a pension because he'd been employed for many years in the chemical plant.

We usually met at the "Neptune," whose proprietor was a Czech and which only Czechs frequented. Beseda, the Young Czech Association, also had its meeting room there. We felt safer there than anywhere else because the place was despised by the petty bourgeois and bureaucrats, and so it wasn't visited very often by the police and other spies. There we debated, as we did at home, economic and political questions. Sometimes there was an argument with the Young Czechs, because our socialism didn't agree with their idea of "Bohemian constitutionalism." A debate like this was always something special for Nowotny, because he was a better debater and knew more than any of us, and he could always give the other guys a piece of his mind. On the whole Nowotny was the most mature in every respect, and he adhered to his principles most strictly and consistently. He was very cautious but never showed any fear; he agitated wherever and whenever he could, both by word of mouth and in writing, so as to win new supporters; and if anyone insulted or disparaged his cause, he always advocated and defended it openly and honestly. He never held back; whoever it was, he thoroughly explained his point of view, courageously and clearly. And he demanded the same consistency from each one of the others who wanted to be considered true Social Democrats. Whoever was ambivalent or thought differently than he acted was in his view not worthy of the socialists. Such wavering contradicted the new idea that demanded genuine conviction.

But obviously not everyone was as strict in every respect as

Nowotny demanded. Most of them took life as it came. They just left their principles at home and kept their mouths shut even when their own cause was being insulted. Most of them didn't have much desire for education either. They were too lazy to acquire the knowledge necessary to enlighten others and win new converts. They had become adherents out of necessity. But they lacked a strong inner conviction. And it was just this that enraged old Nowotny the most. He often unleashed his tongue and lashed out mercilessly at such behavior. But he only made personal enemies for himself. "You can't always act the way Nowotny wants you to!" the others usually protested when they were alone. And I soon saw that I was deceived in my belief that I'd find angelic brotherly love among these people. The ones who came closest to knowing as much as Nowotny were Rericha and Krutak. The latter had something Stirner-like about him; I don't mean by that that he was an anarchist.* No, he was an honest socialist and had served five months in prison for it at St. Wenzel's Prison in Prague. When he returned, the liberal city government of Aussig was so liberal that it threw him out of town. But the head of the whole district at that time was so illiberal that he suspended the expulsion decree and permitted Krutak to live in the city.

As long as the evenings were still warm and the weather was nice, we would meet and debate behind the Elbstrasse at the edge of the woods. Of course sometimes we debated things that seem totally childish to me today. Most of the time was wasted with arguments about the future state. Each of us had his own particular views on this matter and wanted to get them across. Oh, sometimes it was a bitter battle of words! Of course when Nowotny was there, these debates didn't happen too often because he quickly put an end to them. "Better to worry about the present! What the future state will be like can only be discussed in the future!" He'd always break into our favorite topic with these or similar words and spoil our fun.

*Max Stirner (1806–56) was best known for the radical individualism he professed in his major work, *The Ego and His Own* (1845).

One time there was a very vehement argument about the future between Kolar and Paletschek, a new comrade who was particularly interested in the future state. He asked us many questions that we just weren't able to answer to his satisfaction. He went from one detail to another. Finally the talk got around to eating habits and food. "OK, what's going to happen to potatoes?" Paletschek demanded, and in his great curiosity he rapidly continued, "If everyone can choose whatever suits his appetite, then of course no one will want to eat potatoes. And champagne, which only the rich drink today, will be in short supply." We philosophized the whole evening this way, just because Nowotny wasn't there. And on the way home Kolar and Paletschek still kept up the debate, which finally degenerated into more of a fight.

One time we sat around with a comrade who had come to town looking for work; he was a carpenter by trade, but I've forgotten his name. He was a nice-looking man with a pointed beard, and his speech revealed intelligence. He told us all the troubles he'd been through on account of his convictions and his participation in the workers' movement. How he'd often been reprimanded by his employers; how he'd been arrested and what he'd experienced in jail during his pretrial detention and a four-month sentence. Now he'd been fired from his last position and thrown out of town; and there he stood with no money and no work. He'd left a wife and three children at home, and he'd wandered around now for weeks looking for work, up to now without success. And he still didn't have a single shred of hope of finding work anywhere and being able to reestablish himself. Even today I am moved when I think of that tormented man. How he sat among us on the grass at the edge of the woods, sad, depressed, his head down; how pitiful his voice sounded, how heavy the words were on his lips. Only now and then, when someone asked him something, did he raise his head, and then every time you could see tears in his eyes. A hideous fate! A heartrending picture!

"But comrades," he said at the end of his story, "this can't possibly go on for long. People can't stand much longer the oppression and the burdens that get greater every year, and then they will rise up against the tyranny." Oh, his prophecy still hasn't fulfilled itself today.

I felt the greatest possible sympathy for this tormented man. My breast swelled with rage at such a great injustice. My hatred doubled for everything that was rich or seemed connected with the name of the state. I clenched my fists; I thirsted for revenge! But how to take it?

At that time one of our comrades, the master shoemaker Weiz, was let out of St. Wenzel's Prison in Prague. He'd had to serve a full two years there for conspiracy. This man too was tormented by blows of fate. He was in jail, and at home his journeyman, named Tyle, not only ran the business and took care of the customers, but also took his master's place in the marriage bed. And before Weiz came home in two years, he had one more family member! This weighed on Weiz the heaviest. He soon disappeared with his whole family, without telling anyone where he was going. Later we found out that he lived in South Germany. And still later I was pleased to learn that he was doing well again.

Because of all this, I became a raving zealot, if not actually a fanatic. I agitated everywhere I could—on the street, at the inn, and even in the factory, regardless of the possible consequences. Based on my own enthusiasm for the cause, I believed that every worker would have to recognize the socialist cause as easily as I had and would have to stand up for it no matter how much he had to suffer for it. Because he was, after all, the exploited one like all of us. I was so hotheaded that I just forced onto everyone both the knowledge I'd acquired and my written materials. I had glowing hopes that everyone I knew and worked with would immediately come over to my side. But oh, how quickly these hopes were dashed! There were some who were too afraid that they might lose their jobs and therefore wanted nothing to do with the matter. Others countered that it was all in vain, that conditions would never be different. And there were usually sharp disagreements between us. If one or another of them stuck to his viewpoint and didn't want to be persuaded, then I lost my patience and reproached him for his apathy and stupidity. For this I had to put up with the label "muddlehead." Yes, it sometimes got to the point where I was ignored at work and where what I said was taken as a joke or scorned. No wonder that I even hated my own class comrades; and when from time to time they suffered some injustice, I even enjoyed it. I rarely met anyone who agreed with my opinions and approved of the cause.

Luis and her mother finally began to fear for me, and they went to great pains to try to get me to desert the cause and its adherents, the socialists. Their pleadings and crying got nothing for them; I always remained firm and my answer was: Never!

At the baptismal ceremony of our firstborn son (I'd now reached the ripe old age of almost twenty-two!), whom we christened Heinrich, everyone set upon me—the godparents, Luis, her mother, her brother, and the rest of the guests. They painted in the darkest colors a picture of the dangers that threatened me. How many had already gone to prison for such things. How their families had been destroyed. Finally they said they could get along without me. This arguing and fear-mongering filled the whole evening. Everyone had something new to say about it because the beer gave them courage and understanding. But they troubled themselves in vain! I didn't yield. And I declared, "Jesus suffered on the cross for the truth! Why can't we too?" When Luis saw that all the urging did no good, she threw down her last trump, "If you don't give the thing up, then I'm reporting you to the police; let them do what they want with you!" Admittedly that surprised me, but I didn't take her words seriously. I just said, "That would be very good of you, because then I would at least know what I have in you."

Then I joined the workers' education association, "Koruna Nychodu," which means Crown of the East. It was a Czech club whose members were recruited mostly from among artisans, shoemakers, and tailors. The official purpose of the club, to spread education among the members, was only incidental. They were all radical Czech nationalists and the greatest enemies of socialism. They were satisfied with just meeting once a week to bellow their national songs. They understood nothing of politics and things like that. In fact, they understood nothing of true nationalism. If they ever did get into a long discussion, the occasion was usually a newspaper article saying that a German student somewhere had beaten up a Czech student or vice versa. I knew this was the way things were in the club when I joined, because Nowotny, who had been a member but was kicked out, told me all about it. He called my attention especially to a former socialist, the master spinner Schafarschik, who was the club's chief firebrand. Nonetheless I wanted to try to change the tone of the whole club. Right in the very first monthly meeting I made a motion that we subscribe to the *Duch Casu;* I argued that the club was made up exclusively of workers, who should see it as a matter of honor to have the paper on display. It would be better to stop taking one of the nationalist rags. I really got into a hornet's nest! Many asked for the floor at the same time. Of course Schafarschik was the very first to speak. Like a state's attorney, he demonstrated what a danger my proposal would be to the club. If the club took papers like that, it would be disbanded by the authorities, and the members, especially the officers, would be taken into preventive detention or even sent to jail. It had already happened to hundreds. "I warn every one of you about voting for this proposal!" he said in conclusion in a loud voice. Everyone applauded except for Schlastny. In spite of all, I took the floor once again to give better reasons for my proposal and to try to save it. I turned sharply to my opponent and lashed out at his cowardly attitude. "Don't let yourself be driven by fear, don't be led astray into a betrayal of the workers' cause; be men, vote for the proposal!" I demanded of those present. Then the vote was taken on my motion, and only one hand went up in favor of it. At the next board meeting I was kicked out.

I told the story to my fellow worker Havlas, and he advised me to join the German workers' club, "Unity," of which he was also a member. I wasn't in such a hurry now, and I wanted to see the club life first as just a guest. One Monday (that was the day they always had their evening at the pub) I went along with Havlas to the club. Now for the first time I really saw the sad picture of a workers' association. The members were mostly workers at the chemical plant. The room was filled with people, men and women, young and old. In one corner sat four musicians, and right next to them the club officers. On the tables were double liters of beer. The president kept ringing his bell and imposing fines on first one person and then another. The occasions for this were if someone addressed another with *Sie,* or if he called him something different than was written on his club cap, or even if he went out of the room with his club cap on. There were songs, recitations, and witty couplets—some of them lewd and coarse, but they took all the more pleasure in those. The pauses were taken up with music. Thick clouds of tobacco smoke filled the room. The waiters scurried to and fro; they really had their hands full. The hum and noise of people's voices got louder and louder. Oh, so that was the noble club life! Finally I thought of home. I left without entering my name in the members' list, a guilder poorer and more foolish than I'd come. But the next day Havlas was full of praise for the great fun. After a few years, however, the innkeeper Thomas bought himself a nice house. He'd been the founder and the guiding spirit of the club.

Not long after my failure in the "Koruna Nychodu," about twenty of us were excavating for a new alkali works. One morning Schindler came running up, and when he was still a ways off, he yelled out, "Going to meetings and giving speeches, eh!?" Then he moved off, like a madman.

"Who's he talking about?" we all asked each other when he'd disappeared behind the copper sulphate building.

"You, Holek," was the answer. I thought it over for a long time; who could have told Schindler that I was at a meeting and had spoken there? Finally I thought of the carpenter Rinda, who was also a member of the "Koruna Nychodu" and was on good terms with Schafarschik. Maybe he'd been the one? In any case I was soon transferred to the alkali sludge heap, which was outside the factory. That was considered the last post that you got at the factory; from there you were usually forced out completely. The six of us who worked out there were in a certain sense a penal colony. You worked right under Schindler's eyes. Whoever couldn't do the work, so that the others had to complain about him, had to go, without fail. And the work really was not easy; the sludge, which consisted of ground-up and flushed stones, had to be dragged up six meters high in a wheelbarrow and dumped out. But the weekly wage was only eight to nine guilders. Nonetheless I held out there for a year. I even liked having the hated man in sight.

Nowotny and I became the closest of friends. I valued him more and more as my master because he was well informed on everything. And he in turn enjoyed my enthusiasm. If I had even a little time in the evening or on Sundays, I went to see him. And we never put the time to bad use.

Once when I visited him, a commonly dressed man of about thirty-five was sitting with him; they were deep in conversation. They were speaking German because the man didn't know Czech. Nowotny introduced him to me as comrade Hanke. I soon heard from his own mouth what had driven him here, what misfortunes he'd had to undergo. He'd been working as a machine tender in the coal mining district, had been persecuted for his socialist convictions, had lost several jobs, and was now unemployed again. For a long time he'd gone from one mine to another, but all in vain.

It just made you cry what the man told us of all the persecutions. He stayed overnight with Nowotny. He wanted to go abroad.

One Sunday evening as we sat as usual in the Hotel Neptune, we were all very depressed as Nowotny read to us from the *Narodni Listy:* a certain Cerny had been condemned to sixteen years in prison, Paćes to twelve, and Rampas to ten—all for high treason. We all looked sadly at each other when he'd finished reading the report. I didn't know who the men were. But on the way home Nowotny told me more about what they had done to get such stiff punishments. They'd set up a secret printing press in Reichenberg in Bohemia in order to print their own paper and sell it among party comrades. But they had succeeded in producing only a single issue. Then the police had caught them. Later I got this secret paper from Nowotny and read it. It was a small four-page paper. You could see at a glance that it hadn't been produced by professionals, but for a shoemaker and a mason it certainly wasn't bad. The title was *Svoboda*—that is, *Freedom*. The content was such that even my hair stood on end and I got cold shivers.

Cerny survived his prison term but died shortly after being released. Rampas never got out of jail alive. And Paćes got an extra three years because he attacked a prison guard. I don't know whether he's still alive.

A bill proposing an emergency law was coming up for debate. We dreaded it like a storm that would bring ruin. As we read in our newspaper, it would make any freedom fighting impossible. Just how seriously the editors of the *Duch Casu* took this danger is shown by the fact that the editor Hlawacek said good-bye in one issue and then went to America. Fortunately the law was not accepted by the Imperial Council and we could breathe easier again.

Although we'd won some new supporters—it was now the fall of 1886—our small circle was not enough for us in the long run. We eventually got tired of our meetings in the forest or at the inns in remote villages. Most of us were eager for a public life— for a club. Of course founding a club was a delicate matter. The older comrades had no confidence that the authorities would recognize it. The club "Concord" and also a Workers' Education Association had already been dissolved by the police, because even the latter had promoted enlightenment from a Social Democratic perspective. Finally, after a lot of give-and-take, we hit on the idea of taking over the nationalist club, "Koruna Nychodu," by trickery, so as to get it into our hands. The first step to this end was to get membership for those of us whom the nationalists knew the least; they were to smooth the way for the rest of us. Nowotny and I were to be the last to enter. Our plan worked out for us better and better. One after another, everyone was in; just the two of us were waiting for our chance. Our people even held some seats on the board, and so we were sure of our success. The nationalists didn't seem to see through our plan, until finally Schafarschik discovered it. In a single board meeting all of our people were kicked out of the club. And so there was nothing left for us to do but continue as we had before. Today when I sometimes think back on our party activities, I have to laugh at them as though they were child's play. And yet at the time nothing else was possible. It reminds me of my childhood years when we tended the cattle in the pasture and roasted potatoes. We had to fan the fire with our caps or aprons so it wouldn't go out. But when we had enough straw or leaves on hand and laid them on the fire, then the flames shot up high.

Adelheid Popp,
Factory Worker

Adelheid Popp (1869–1939) was the fifteenth child of a family of weavers. Her father was an alcoholic who died young, leaving Popp's mother struggling to raise the family. Forced to work since childhood, Popp was a maid, a seamstress, and a worker in a variety of factories in Vienna. At sixteen she became a Social Democrat and soon after rose to prominence as founder and editor of the *Working Women's News* (*Arbeiterinnen Zeitung*) and a leader of the Austrian Social Democratic women's movement. After World War I, she was a representative in the Austrian parliament. Her autobiography, which had a preface by August Bebel, was intended to inspire other working women (as well as to inform the middle class). Aside from Karl Fischer's autobiography, which was excerpted earlier, Popp's was the only working-class autobiography to attract much public attention. It even appeared in an English translation with a preface by Ramsey MacDonald. (The translation here is new.) In this section of her autobiography, Popp shows us the Vienna of the early 1880s from the perspective of a desperate and impoverished working girl. There is no better description from a female perspective of the demoralizing search for work and the dilemmas of holding on to a job even in the face of sexual pressures from superiors.

[FINDING WORK]

It was a cold, severe winter, and the wind and snow could come unhindered into our room. In the morning when we opened the door we first had to hack away the ice on it in order to get out, because the entrance to our room was directly on the courtyard, and we had only a single glass door. My mother left the house at five-thirty because she had to start work at six. An hour later I went out to look for work. "Please, I need a job"—it had to be repeated countless times. I used to be on the street for almost the whole day. We couldn't heat our room—that would have been extravagant—so I wandered around the streets, into churches, and to the cemetery. I took along a piece of bread and a few kreuzers to buy myself something at noon. I always had to hold back the tears forcibly when my request for work was denied and I had to leave the warm room. How gladly I would have done any work, just so I wouldn't have to freeze. My clothes got wet in the snow, and my limbs were stiff from the hours of walking around. What's more, my mother was getting more and more resentful. My brother had found work; snow had fallen, so he was busy*—of course the pay was so low that he could hardly support himself. I was the only one still without work.

I couldn't even get work in the candy factories, where I had assumed they would need more help at Christmastime. Today I know that almost all of the Christmas work is done several weeks before the holidays; the factory women have to work day and

Translated from Adelheid Popp, *Die Jugendgeschichte einer Arbeiterin,* ed. Hans J. Schütz (Berlin/Bonn: J. H. W. Dietz Verlag, 1980), 48–60. Originally published with a preface by August Bebel (Munich: Ernst Reinhardt Verlag, 1909).

*Possibly shoveling snow.

night for weeks, and then right before the holidays they are dismissed without consideration. At that time I still had no idea how the production process was carried out. How piously and faithfully I used to pray for work in church. I sought out the most celebrated saints. I went from altar to altar, kneeled down on the cold stones, and prayed to the Virgin Mary, the Mother of God, the Queen of Heaven, and many other saints who were said to have special power and compassion.

I didn't give up hope, and one day I decided to put the few kreuzers I had for my lunch into the collection box for the Holy Father. On the same day I found a purse containing twelve guilders. I could scarcely contain my joy, and I thanked all the saints for this favor. It never occurred to me that some other poor devil might have been driven to despair by the loss of the purse. To me twelve guilders was such a great amount that I never thought that a poor person could have lost it. I didn't know anything about the responsibility of handing in things you found to the police. All I saw was the merciful hand of the saints in the purse lying in the way. That evening I joyously embraced my mother; I was so happy I couldn't speak; I could only get out the words "twelve guilders, twelve guilders." There was nothing but joy in our room now; and as if to crown our good luck, the next day I was summoned to report to a sandpaper and emery board factory, where I'd asked about work a few days earlier and they had taken down my name.

My new workplace was on the third floor of a building that was used exclusively for industrial purposes. Not having known the bustle of a factory, I had never felt so uncomfortable. Everything displeased me—the dirty, sticky work; the unpleasant glass dust; the crowd of people; the crude tone; and the whole way that the girls and even married women behaved.

The owner's wife—the "gracious lady," as she was called—was the actual manager of the factory, and she talked just like the girls. She was a nice-looking woman, but she drank brandy, took snuff, and made unseemly rude jokes with the workmen. The owner was very ill, and when he came himself, there was always a violent scene. I pitied him. He seemed to me to be so good and noble, and I gathered from the behavior and whole manner of his wife that he must be unhappy. At his instructions I received a different, much more pleasant job. Up to then my job had been to hang the papers, which were smeared with glue and sprinkled with glass, onto lines strung rather high across the workroom. This work exhausted me greatly, and the owner must have noticed that it wasn't suitable for me, because he instructed that from then on I was to keep count of the papers that were ready for processing. This work was clean and I liked it a lot better. Of course when there wasn't anything to count, I had to do other kinds of work.

The factory was rather far from our apartment, and I couldn't go home for lunch.* I stayed in the workroom with the other women; we fetched soup or vegetables from the restaurant, and we had coffee for the afternoon. I always sat off by myself and read a book. I was reading *The Robber Knight and his Child* [*Der Raubritter und sein Kind*], which was in one hundred parts. The others laughed at me and made fun of my innocence because I got embarrassed at their talk.

They often spoke of a Herr Berger, who was the company's traveling representative and was expected back about then. All the women raved about him, so I was curious to see the man. I had been there for two weeks when he came. Everything was in a dither, and the only talk was of the looks of the traveler they so admired. Accompanied by the owner's wife, he came into the room where I worked. I didn't like him at all. That afternoon I was called into his office; Herr Berger sent me on an errand and made a silly remark about my "beautiful hands." It was already dark when I returned; I had to pass through an empty anteroom that wasn't lighted; it was half-dark since it got light only through the glass door leading into the workroom. Herr Berger was in the anteroom when I came. He took me by the hand and inquired sympathetically about my circumstances. I answered

* Workers ate their major meal at noon, so long lunch breaks (frequently one and a half hours) with time to go home were the norm.

him truthfully and told of our poverty. He spoke a few words, taking pity on me and promising to use his influence to get me higher wages. Of course I was delighted with the prospect opening up to me, for I was getting only two and a half guilders a week, for which I had to work twelve hours a day. I stammered a few words of thanks and assured him that I would prove myself worthy of his solicitude. Before I even knew what was happening, Herr Berger had kissed me. He tried to calm my fright with the words, "It was just a fatherly kiss." He was twenty-six years old, and I was almost fifteen, so fatherliness was out of the question.

Beside myself, I hurried back to my work. I didn't know how I should interpret the incident; I thought the kiss was disgraceful, but Herr Berger had spoken so sympathetically and had held out the prospect of higher wages! At home I did tell of the promise, but I said nothing about the kiss because I was ashamed to talk about it in front of my brother. But my mother and my brother were happy that I had found such an influential protector.

The next day I was overwhelmed with reproaches from one of my coworkers, a young blond girl whom I liked most of all. She reproached me for having taken her place with the traveler; up to now, if he had something to do or an errand to run, she had done it; he loved her, she protested through tears and sobs, and now I'd put an end to everything. The other girls joined in too; they called me a hypocrite, and the gracious lady herself asked me how I'd liked the kisses of the "handsome traveler." The incident of the previous evening had been observed through the glass door, and they interpreted it in a way very insulting to me.

I was defenseless against their taunts and sneers and longed for the hour when I could go home. It was Saturday, and when I received my wages, I went home with the intention of not returning on Monday.

When I spoke of the matter at home, I was severely scolded. It was strange. My mother, who was always so intent on raising me to be a respectable girl, who always gave me instructions and warnings not to talk to men ("You should only allow yourself to be kissed by the man you're going to marry," she used to impress upon me)—in this instance my mother was against me. She said I was going too far. A kiss was nothing bad, and if I was getting more wages as a result, then it would be silly to give up my job. In the end she held my books responsible for my "overexcitement." My mother got so mad about my "pigheadedness" that all the splendid things I'd been lent—*The Book for Everyone* [*Das Buch für Alle*], *Over Land and Sea* [*Über Land und Meer*], and *Chronicle of the Times* [*Chronik der Zeit*] (that's how far advanced I was in literature)—were thrown out the door.* I collected them all again, but I didn't dare read in the evening, although I'd usually been allowed to read longer on Saturdays.

That was a sad Sunday! I was depressed, and what's more I was scolded the whole day.

On Monday my mother awakened me as usual and impressed upon me as she left for work not to do anything stupid, but rather to remember that in a few days it would be Christmas.

I went out intending to control myself and go to the factory; I got as far as the door and then I turned around. I had such a dreadful fear of unknown dangers that I preferred to go hungry than to suffer disgrace. Everything that had happened—the kiss and the reproaches of my coworkers—seemed a disgrace to me. Besides, I had been told that one of the girls always enjoyed the traveler's special favor. But he was changeable; if a new girl came who pleased him more, then she would take the place of the previous one. All indications were that I had been chosen as the new favorite. That scared me a lot. I'd read so much in books about seduction and fallen virtue that I imagined the most hideous things happening. So I didn't go in.

But what was I to do? At first I looked for work; I would have taken anything offered to me, but three days before Christmas people don't add to their work force. I wandered around the streets, and when evening came, I went home at the usual time.

* All three titles were popular periodicals with serialized novels.

I didn't have the courage to confess that I hadn't been at the factory. The next two days I did the same thing. All my efforts to find work were fruitless. I was gripped by dreadful despair; then I regained hope that some accident might help me out. I needed less than two guilders, because it hadn't even been a full workweek.

I had read so much of the omnipotence of God, of help in the hour of need, of virtue rewarded, and the like things that I convinced myself that help would come to me too. So I knelt in fervent prayer at the altar, and then, with a searching look, I went back out into the street. Maybe I'd find another purse and bring home more money than expected. I went to where the women crowded around the fish stalls to do their shopping for dinner. Although I'd always imagined fish as something very delicious, in my desperation I had no appetite for it. I just wanted money. Crazy thoughts ran through my head, but I shrank back in horror from carrying them out. It got to be afternoon. People hurried home with their packages to prepare for happy times with their loved ones. Everyone was getting off work, and I too was expected at home. But where would I get money?

Then I had a thought. I had an aunt who was in service with a countess; for us this aunt was the embodiment of refinement; her position with the countess lent her this aura. We called her the "city aunt" (that always seemed so impressive to us), and when she would occasionally visit us, we paid her the highest respect. She was considered very pious, and the church she always attended received many contributions from her. I now hoped that she would help me. I didn't find her at home; she was in church. I looked for her there, but she was already gone. I knelt at the altar, and, crying and sobbing, prayed that God and the saints would win favor for me in my aunt's heart. When I think back on it now: all I needed was two guilders and all my trouble and heartaches would have been gone. At that time I didn't yet know how much money was needlessly squandered, how many people lived in excess while others pined away in poverty. At that time I wasn't yet aware of these differences, or at least I didn't consider their injustice. I considered everything an unalterable arrangement, prescribed by God.

I have never forgotten these hours and the whole suffering of my childhood and youth. And even today, despite the many years that have passed, I can't pass by crying children without asking them the cause of their tears. At such times I always recall my own tears and how I thirsted for sympathy. Even as a poorly paid working woman, I've given many an hour's wage to strange crying children who have told me of their troubles on the street.

I found no sympathy. My pious aunt, whom I finally found, did treat me to coffee and cake, but when I finally ventured to state my request, she remained hard and pitiless. She admonished me to go right home; it was, after all, Christmas Eve, and so I would be expected. I begged and cried, but she was unmoved; with pious sayings, she refused me any help. Her last word was: everyone must humbly bear the consequences of his own deeds. So, I was back on the street. There were far fewer people to see, but the windows glittered brightly, and I could see many decorated Christmas trees.

Under no circumstances did I want to go home. What was I supposed to say? I was afraid and ashamed. My behavior of the last few days now seemed to me very wrong. I imagined the horror of my mother—my poor tormented mother, who had to count every kreuzer and who had pinned so many hopes on me. Could I cause her so much pain and disappointment? My remorse and anguish got greater and greater. If only I'd controlled myself and stayed at the factory, I said to myself. Now I too thought everything had been exaggerated—my fear of the traveler, my shame in front of my coworkers, and my worry about my respectability. All I could feel now was how wonderful it would be if only I could go home with my wages. I turned into a street leading down to the Danube, thinking that it had to be easier to jump into the water than to go home with my guilt.

As I was hurrying down one of the most fashionable streets toward my new goal, the water, I was approached by an elegant gentleman. My tears flowed uninterruptedly and my body was shaking with sobs. He asked me where I was going at such a late hour and why I was crying. This had to be my salvation; this was definitely providential! All my hopes returned, and I told him my troubles. I had to have two guilders; otherwise I couldn't go home. How agreeably and kindly the gentleman spoke. He wanted to give me ten guilders, but I would have to go with him because he didn't have any money with him. I didn't know what held me back, but in spite of my distress I didn't go into his apartment with him. When we got to the house where he wanted to take me, I asked if I might wait until he came out with the money. As he urged me and tried to lure me in, I broke loose and ran away. I had been overcome with such a dreadful fright, and the looks the man gave me had so scared me, that without thinking I raced away in the direction of home. There I met my brother, who had been looking for me for a long time and was about to go to the factory to ask about me.

Do I have to tell about what the rest of Christmas Eve was like? How neither my mother nor my brother could see what was going on inside me, how they couldn't understand my motives and couldn't forgive me? They called me naughty and lazy. Me, lazy! At an age when other children are playing with dolls and sitting in school, when they are taken care of and protected from everything—at that age I had to go out into the world and carry the heavy yoke of work. At an age when others were still savoring the bliss of childhood, I had already forgotten childlike laughter and was thoroughly imbued with the feeling that my destiny was to work.

For many years the burden of my childhood weighed on my soul and made me prematurely serious and averse to gaiety. Much had to happen, something great had to step into my life, in order to help me prevail over myself.

I found work again; I grasped at everything offered me to show my willingness to work, and I still had some hard times. But finally things got better. I was referred to a large factory that stood in the best repute. Three hundred women and about fifty men were employed there. I was put into a large room where sixty women and girls worked. There were twelve tables by the windows, and at each table sat four girls. Our job was to sort the merchandise that had been manufactured; other women counted it, and a third group branded it with the company's stamp. We worked from 7:00 A.M. to 7:00 P.M. At noon we had a one-hour break and in the afternoon a half hour off. Although there was a holiday during the week I started there, I got the full week's wages paid to beginners. That was four guilders. I'd never been paid that well. Besides, there was the prospect that if I applied myself well I'd get a fifty-kreuzer increase in a few months. I received it after only six weeks, and in half a year I was already making five guilders a week; later I got six guilders.

It seemed to me that I was almost rich. I figured out how much I'd be able to save over a few years, and I built castles in the air. Since I was used to extraordinary deprivations, I would have considered it extravagant to spend more now on food. As long as I didn't feel hungry I didn't take into account what I was eating. All I wanted was to dress nicely. When I went to church on Sunday no one should recognize me as a factory girl; I was ashamed of my work. Working in a factory always seemed to me to be degrading. When I was still an apprentice, I'd often heard it said that factory girls were bad, loose, and spoiled.* They were spoken of in the most insulting words, and I too had picked up this false notion. Now I myself was employed in a factory where there were so many girls.

The girls were friendly; they instructed me in my work in the most amiable manner, and they introduced me to the customs of the business. The girls in the sorting room were considered the elite of the personnel. The owner himself chose them, whereas the hiring for the machine room was left to the foremen. Men and women were together in the other rooms; but in my room there were only female employees. Men were used as extra help only when the heavy packages of sorted, counted, and labeled goods were moved to the courtyard. At noon we could eat our

* Popp had earlier been apprenticed to a laceworker.

lunch at the factory. In nice weather we sat or reclined on the bundles of goods in the glass-covered courtyard. In winter we were allowed into the machine room. We weren't allowed to stay in the sorting room, where it would have been much more comfortable, because the merchandise would have picked up the smell of our food.

The girls who lived near the factory went home at lunch, and they had the best of it because they could get a better, hot lunch. For a few weeks I went to lunch with acquaintances. That was true torment. I had to walk quickly for twenty-five minutes, then I gulped down my hot lunch as fast as I could and rushed back to work, arriving always breathless and harried. I couldn't take it for long, and I preferred to stay at the factory.

From the women in this factory you can judge how sad and deprived the lot of the factory women is. Here were recognizably the best working conditions. In none of the neighboring factories were the wages so high. We were envied everywhere. Parents considered themselves fortunate if they could get their fourteen-year-old daughters positions there when they left school. Everyone strove to give the most of themselves, lest they be dismissed. In fact, married women, whose husbands had spent years learning a trade, tried to get them into this factory as assistants, because then their livelihoods would be more secure. But even here in this "paradise," everyone was badly nourished. Those who stayed in the factory during lunch break bought sausage or scraps from a cheese store for a few kreuzers. Often they ate buttered bread and cheap fruit. Some drank a glass of beer and sopped bread in it. When we got disgusted by this food, we fetched our lunch from the restaurant. For five kreuzers we got either soup or vegetables. It was rarely well prepared, and the smell of the fat they used was sickening. We often felt such disgust that we threw the food away, preferring to eat dry bread and console ourselves with the thought of the coffee we'd brought for the afternoon.

The factory owner often passed through the courtyard as we were eating lunch. Sometimes he stopped to ask us what good things we had. If he was in an especially good mood, or if the woman he spoke to was pretty and knew how to complain, he'd give her money so she could buy something better. That always made me angry; it seemed humiliating to me and provoked me.

We also tried going to a cheap eatery. For eight kreuzers you got soup and vegetables. Sometimes two girls would spend another eight kreuzers to split a piece of boiled meat. I used to go to the eatery during the time I was sick, and the doctor prescribed good food as the most important thing for me. But after my condition had improved and I was stronger, I couldn't stand spending so much. I really wanted to save money for a rainy day.

In general, the only girls who ate well were those supported by their families. But there were only a few of them. More often the working girls had to support their parents or pay for baby-sitting for their children. How self-sacrificing these mothers were! They saved kreuzer after kreuzer to better the lot of their children and to enable them to make gifts to the baby-sitter so that she would take good care of the children. Many women often had to provide for their unemployed husbands; they underwent double deprivation because they had to meet the household expenses alone. I also got to know the much-maligned frivolousness of factory girls. To be sure, the girls went dancing and they had love affairs; others stood in line at a theater at three o'clock in the afternoon so that they could see an evening performance for thirty kreuzers. In the summer they went on outings and walked for hours in order to save a couple of kreuzers of tram fare. For a few breaths of country air they had to pay with days of tired feet. If you want you can call all that frivolity, or even pleasure-seeking or debauchery, but who would dare to?

I saw among my coworkers—the despised factory women— examples of the most extraordinary sacrifices for others. If there was a special emergency in one family, then they chipped in their kreuzers to help. Even though they had worked twelve hours in the factory and many still had an hour's walk home, they mended their own clothes, without ever having been taught how. They took apart their old dresses to fashion new ones from the separate pieces, which they sewed at night and on Sundays.

Nor did they rest during the lunch or afternoon breaks. Their sparse meal quickly out of the way, they would knit, crochet, or embroider stockings. And despite their diligence and thrift, every one of them was poor and trembled at the thought of losing her job. They all humbled themselves and put up with the worst injustices from their superiors, lest they lose their good jobs and go hungry.

Many girls had the misfortune of being especially favored by one of the superiors. Then suddenly he'd change his attitude. She couldn't do anything right anymore; no longer was she promoted; instead of a wage increase, she received reprimands. She was threatened with dismissal, and so the poor girl was harassed until she couldn't stand it any longer and left of her own accord.

Then there would be rumors about some of the ones to whom this happened. People would whisper, she's been seen on certain streets showily dressed or leaning out the window to entice men. She was always condemned, and I too was outraged. No one considered whether it would have turned out differently if at the outset the girl had abandoned resistance and yielded to her superior.

At the time I knew nothing of either hidden or open prostitution; I hadn't even heard the word. Later on, when I could better judge cause and effect, I began to think differently of these girls, especially when, in the course of the years I worked in the factory, I got to know a lot of older women of whom it was said they owed their privileged positions to certain relations with a superior. Or when a woman made a scene with the foreman because he suddenly began to oppress her because he'd gotten tired of her and preferred to have her out of the way so that he might, unhindered, "bless" a new girl.

At that time I didn't reflect on any of this; I just tried to do my work properly and not get in anyone's way. What's more, such things didn't happen in the room where I worked. There wasn't a friendly or kind word from our foreman. He was a tyrant of the worst sort, and he must have seen the workers as a slave gang. No one dared to complain about him. He was regarded as the most privileged employee of the company, to which he was, without doubt, truly dedicated. He had probably long since forgotten that he had once been a worker in the same factory.

I didn't want to leave my mother ever, and I wanted to arrange it so she wouldn't have to work anymore. I was just as thrifty as my coworkers, and if one day I did spend a couple of extra kreuzers, I literally went hungry on the next day. I knew even then that I could not save up a fortune for myself. But I did want to provide for my mother, and I wanted to have a nest egg to save her from going into the hospital in case she got sick. She had a great distaste for hospitals. Like the other workers, I considered myself lucky to be in this factory, and I anxiously guarded against anything that could lay me open to blame.

"A good boss"—that was the general opinion of our employer. But in the case of this very factory owner, one can see how profitable is the exploitation of human labor. He, who really did grant his workers more than most other entrepreneurs; he, who would continue for weeks to pay the wages of men and women who were sick; he, who in case of a death made a considerable contribution to the survivors; and he, who almost never rejected a request if someone turned to him in need—despite all this, he had gotten rich through the productive labor of the men and women working in his factory.

Doris Viersbeck,
Cook and House Maid

Doris Viersbeck (ca. 1869–?) worked in several wealthy Hamburg households. She says little of her background except that she came to Hamburg in 1888 from a village in Holstein. After a few years in service, she quit to get married, and we know nothing of her later life. The publication of Adelheid Popp's autobiography prompted Viersbeck to send her story to the same publisher. She may also have had encouragement from her brother, a teacher in Hamburg who occasionally wrote articles for newspapers. In the section presented here, Viersbeck describes the agonizing months between May 1889 and February 1890, when she served in the household of the tyrannical and capricious Frau Sparr. Although the conditions described here may seem extreme, Oscar Stillich's study of several hundred Berlin servant girls suggests that such overwork and abuse were quite common (see Introduction, n. 60). Viersbeck has no class consciousness, but she probably speaks for hundreds of thousands of servant girls when she says, "I just wanted to be treated as a human being, and this right is all too often denied to servants." Her lucid, straightforward story is a vital source for understanding the transition from rural to urban life for women.

[LIFE DOWNSTAIRS]

In this house they kept a manservant to attend to the master; the women had told me about that when I'd been introduced to them. I say the women—there was an old lady (the gentleman's wife) and a younger woman, her daughter-in-law. Together they ran the household. The manservant had been in the house since the previous fall, as he told me soon after my arrival; that was probably as long as he would stay, he added. "Why?" I asked, "don't you have it good here?"

"Oh, definitely," he said, "I didn't mean that, but you'll see all sorts of things here."

"A few days ago we got a new maid," he continued, "she'll be down soon and then we can eat supper together. It's about time as far as I'm concerned, because I have to put the master to bed at ten o'clock."

"Put the master to bed?" I asked.

"Yeah, didn't you know that the master is crippled, and he's not right in the head either?"

"No," I said, "nobody told me about that."

"Yeah," he went on, "and the lady's often a bit wacky, too."

"Great prospects!" I thought.

The maid, Käthe, was a small, slight, tired-looking girl with curly brown locks on her head. I pitied her and asked whether she was tired. "Oh, yes," she said, "you don't get any rest here the whole day." Exhausted, she sat down on a chair to eat her supper, but she barely had the first bite in her mouth when the bell rang. "One, two," she counted and jumped up to go upstairs. The poor thing, I felt sorry for her; she seemed to be very young and was probably anemic too. She came right back down again with a little glass in her hand; it had been left upstairs. "Yes," she complained, "that's how it always is here; you have to

Translated from Doris Viersbeck, *Erlebnisse eines Hamburger Dienstmädchens* (Munich: Ernst Reinhardt Verlag, 1910), 28–40, 42–50, 56–62, 65–69.

climb the stairs for every little thing, and that makes me so tired."

"Oh, it'll get better," said the manservant. "Just wait till the old lady has one of her spells. Then she gets an ice pack on her head, a hot pack on her body, and a hot-water bottle for her feet. I'm responsible for the ice pack, the cook for the mud pack, and the maid for the hot-water bottle. Then we'll be running into each other on the narrow stairs." We laughed at the joke and thought, "Surely it won't get that bad."

Nothing more was asked of me on this evening, but the poor little tired maid had to run upstairs several more times. I would have been happy to have done one of the trips for her, but I was a stranger and didn't know the ways of the household. Finally, at about eleven-thirty, we could go to bed. My fellow worker was not very talkative and generally not especially friendly to me. I didn't blame her for it; it was most likely due to exhaustion. I didn't ask any more questions; I'd already seen and heard enough to give me something to think about. Anyone who is or has been in service can sympathize with me about how unpleasant the first day with new employers is.

The next morning I had to prepare coffee for the household. Käthe showed me a full coffee can and said, "Just make it real strong, that's the way they're used to it." Well, I was all ready to do that, if only I could. But coffee drinking in this house wasn't as simple as you'd think. In the dining room the table was set for two people; that was Käthe's job. Then I had to prepare a tea tray for the master; Heinrich, the manservant, picked it up at seven o'clock. On the tea tray there had to be a full coffeepot, a little creamer, a little sugar bowl (of course also filled), a cup, and a plate of buttered rolls. The second, somewhat bigger, tea tray was picked up by Käthe a little later and carried upstairs for the two ladies. On this tray I had to put a coffeepot, a creamer, and a sugar bowl (all a bit larger than before), as well as two cups; instead of buttered rolls, there had to be a silver bread-basket with breakfast rolls and black bread, a butter cooler with butter, two plates, and two knives. "Well, now that takes care of the third coffee service," I thought. Things were really done differently here than at the Möllers.* I never saw or heard anything about coffee serving there.

The daughter-in-law's two daughters, a girl of eighteen and a younger one of twelve, drank coffee in the dining room. The latter had to go to school; otherwise, as Käthe told me, she would have preferred to drink her coffee in bed—comfort loving and lazy as she was. Käthe spoke with respect and admiration only of the eighteen-year-old girl. The way she came to us in the kitchen that day took my heart by storm too. Her manner was simple and elegant. She bade us a friendly good morning and said truthfully that she had just come down to see the new cook. At this she nodded to me. She had wonderful blond hair, a peaches-and-cream complexion, fresh red lips, and splendid violet eyes. I had never seen so much beauty in one face. She asked me if I minded if she helped with the cooking now and then— she so much wanted to learn to cook. I said it was OK and she left, saying, "Grandma and Mama will be right down."

And so they were. These ladies were nice to me too. The younger lady had a basket of keys, and Frau Sparr a cookbook. I could tell right off that they weren't as stingy as the Möllers. They almost always had dessert—Frau Sparr had told me about that when she'd hired me. I had told her that I didn't have any experience with desserts because the Möllers rarely had such delicacies, but that I really wanted to learn. That's why she brought along the cookbook. "There are a lot of nice recipes in this book," she told me. "When you can make all of them, you'll be a perfect cook." For today they picked a cold pudding that was easy to prepare. "Read through the recipe a few times so you know how it's done; we always like to take the cookbook right back upstairs," she said. That was too bad; I thought it would be at my disposal. I could do without it for today, but that might not always be true. Frau Sparr told me more about the meat dish and

---

* Her previous employers.

the soup and how they were supposed to be prepared. She ended almost every sentence with "Right, Gustchen?" turning to her daughter-in-law.

She would reply, "Yes, Mama, just as you say," or "That's fine with me, Mama." [. . .]

"Oh, yes, one more thing," said Frau Sparr, coming back again, "we just can't take the name Doris, it sounds so old-fashioned. We'll call you Dora; that sounds a lot nicer." I wasn't asked whether I agreed to this. [. . .]

There was plenty of good food here; in fact, eating and drinking seemed to be the main activity. They had to have a hot breakfast at eleven o'clock even though they ate dinner at three o'clock. Of course this was my responsibility, and I also had a great deal of housework to do, so that it sometimes looked impossible to get everything done. The worst thing was that they never left us in peace to do our work. Ten times or more you were called away to do this or that, and then afterward they wondered why we were so far behind in our work. For example, every morning I had to take the big twelve-year-old girl to the streetcar ten minutes away from the house, because the little miss found going by herself so "boring"; she really would have liked to have had us pick her up too, but no one could get away at that time. Käthe had actually done it at first, but she really couldn't get her work done on time and just left it. That wouldn't do either, so finally it was decided that "Hennichen" would have to come home alone. The name Little Henny really didn't fit her at all because she was very big and fat for her age. The manservant always called her "our elephant girl," and often added that it was no wonder that she was so fat because she and her Grandpa ate like "a couple of barn threshers." The old man was also very fat, much to the sorrow of the manservant because he had to put up with him. The old man could still walk if he was heavily supported. In the summer the manservant had to take him for an hour's walk every day, and in the winter push him in a wheelchair. On his return the manservant would always tell us about the master's crazy ideas. For instance, one day he didn't want to go past the post office; and another time the man-servant had to follow along with him behind a girl in light cloth-ing because the master claimed it was "our Dora," and he wanted to know where she was going; it was hard to make him give up his ideas. [. . .]

If the bell rang once, it was for me; twice was for the maid; and three short rings meant the manservant was wanted. When they rang for me, I was allowed first to ask at the speaking tube what they wanted; the maid and the manservant had to rush right upstairs, and often just for a trifle. At the speaking tube I had to say, "What do you wish?" That's what the ladies wanted. If there was no answer, I had to run upstairs. Now, frequently I had something on the stove that couldn't be left for long. At the very least I had to take it off to make sure that it wouldn't boil over or burn, because the conferences upstairs could drag on. But this took too long for the ladies, so they rang again, loud and long, and when possible a third time, before I got upstairs. I was received crossly with mean looks. "My God, where have you been?"—that was the usual beginning. My apologies were not accepted. "Empty excuses" they called them. It often happened that they'd send for me many times a day for no reason at all. Then they'd say scornfully as I left, "See how fast you can get away!" And so they drove us pointlessly to exhaustion. Little Käthe had it the worst; how they tormented her with the con-stant running upstairs and downstairs! And then they com-plained about her unfriendly mood. They didn't seem to notice that she was tired and worn-out—or they didn't want to notice.

The manservant was a cheerful twenty-three-year-old young man. The previous fall he had been discharged from the military where he'd been with the Wandsbeck hussars; he told us a lot of funny stories, and that helped get us through a lot. But he only occasionally had work downstairs because the master took up most of his time. He was with us downstairs in the evenings from nine to ten o'clock; we were supposed to eat supper together then, and he had all sorts of arrangements to make for the night. Among other things, he had to take another tea tray of food and cold coffee upstairs, because the master slept badly at night and passed the time by eating. These people didn't ask whether the manservant got any rest.

The master didn't give us any peace down in the basement either. There was a hand bell over his bed that rang downstairs; it was there for him to use when he woke up at noon in order to call the manservant if he happened to be downstairs at the time. Sometimes he'd ring the bell constantly during the night. I complained to Frau Sparr about it and asked her to disconnect the bell for the night because we needed to get some sleep. It was always late enough anyway before we could get to bed, never before twelve and often not till twelve-thirty or one o'clock. But what did she reply to me? "What are you talking about? The bell is there to be rung, not to be turned off. If the master rings he has some wishes, and they must be respected at all times." I replied that that's why he had the manservant sleeping in his room, and he had a bell on his nightstand to wake him. "Well, he can't find it sometimes," she said. "Don't make such a fuss about it."

The lady was always very crude in the way she spoke; she seemed to have no education at all, and she had an evil tongue. Her sarcastic talk and false suspicions could drive a person to despair. Shortly after this she ordered me to make a fresh cup of coffee for the master every night at two o'clock; he didn't like the cold coffee, and reheated coffee was even worse. I looked at her in astonishment and told her that I really couldn't guarantee that I'd always wake up. "Oh," she said in her usual sarcastic tone, "just let me take care of that, I'll see that you wake up." "Right, Gustchen?" she said, turning to her daughter-in-law. Gustchen agreed with a nod of her head.

I did it for two weeks and then I went on strike. When I complained that in the long run I just couldn't hold up if I got so little sleep, she replied, "You're big and fat, you'll hold up. I want it this way and the master prefers to have fresh coffee." Up to this time she'd been right about my waking up; her loud and prolonged ringing did the job beautifully, although sometimes I could barely resist the temptation just to stay in bed. I was simply too tired, having gone to bed exhausted from work an hour before and then also having to listen to the master's constant ringing. On this evening I told the manservant that I couldn't get up to bring up fresh coffee; I asked if he would be so good as to take the little alcohol stove upstairs with him so he could heat up the master's coffee. He thought I was really right in finally revolting against this abuse, as he called it. Because it really wasn't the master who'd demanded to have hot or fresh coffee; the "old lady" had just talked him into it. "You don't like that old cold coffee at night, do you, hubby? Dora can always get up and make you a fresh cup of coffee; she could gladly do that for her old sick master, Johann. I'll tell her today." The master had said that you really couldn't demand that. "Nonsense," she'd said, "what do you pay servants for?"

Herr Möller was right, she did often have the devil in her. It seemed like the devil didn't even give her any peace at night either. The manservant said that she often spooked around upstairs like a ghost, peeking into the master's room and climbing up and down the stairs. Up to now I hadn't noticed her, but on the night that I'd determined not to wake up, she suddenly appeared in our room, like a ghost in a long, flowing white nightgown, with her hair down. She shook me on the shoulder, and not very gently either. "Get up! Get up! Make coffee for the master!" she called several times; I considered whether the best thing to do would be to jump up in her face, also like a ghost, or to pretend to keep sleeping. I chose the latter. But it didn't help. I finally had to wake up, but I wasn't going to get up. I was determined I wouldn't. So I asked her what she wanted. "The girl still has to ask," she yelled. "You're supposed to get up and make coffee for the master."

"No, Frau Sparr," I said, "I told you yesterday that I couldn't do it anymore. I'm not getting up because I just got to sleep, and I have to get up tomorrow at six o'clock to work. Anyway, there is coffee up there and Heinrich will heat it up for the master."

As I said this I sat upright because I was really afraid that she would slap my face, and I wanted to be in on the fight. Well, nothing happened; she dropped her fists. She must have considered that I wasn't alone in the room, and that Käthe would have taken my side; she had no use for Frau Sparr because she tormented Käthe all day long. As Heinrich said later, Frau Sparr would certainly have gotten the worst of it "in the scrap." Of course Heinrich thought the story was pretty funny. Frau Sparr rushed out of the room, snorting that she'd never known such colossal impudence.

"Impudent again," I thought. You soon got used to being called this every time there was a difference of opinion; and I often wondered after such scenes whether I'd really behaved impudently without provocation. I could always say no with a clear conscience. I just wanted to be treated as a human being, and this right is all too often denied to servants. Like my sister, I consoled myself; she had very good employers now but had also had the opposite experience here in Hamburg. She too had been labeled with this flattering trait; and I knew for certain that she was anything but impudent. I have to mention one more incident; it's just too ridiculous. My sister's mistress had ordered her to put on a clean white apron whenever she made the bed. This order wasn't hard to carry out and so she'd followed it. But one day they were out of clean white aprons and so she had put on a clean blue apron. The lady saw it and my sister apologized; but with her hands clasped and raised, looking toward heaven, she [the lady] implored, "Dear Lord, help me to withstand the impudence of this girl!" Now, what is more impudent—appealing to God about such a trifle or putting on the blue apron?

As for me, I couldn't think about getting any sleep on this night. These scenes disturbed me more than I wanted to admit. I began to get a case of "nerves," something unknown to me before. That morning, I was awakened at five o'clock instead of six. I knew that an angry, bitter day would follow. At six o'clock the ladies ordered coffee upstairs; of course it wasn't good enough and it was sent back down; it had to be made fresher, and even then, it didn't taste much better. But, unfortunately she had a cook who couldn't make decent coffee; and so it went the whole day. I just had to swallow a lot of the insults. Did she think she was making me docile this way? If she did, she was very wrong; she would have achieved a lot more with kindness. The next night she tested my mood. She rang again at two o'clock, but I ignored it, and I'd locked the door of our room to prevent a nighttime assault. Once again I had to get up at five o'clock; that would be the last time, I thought to myself. I made up my mind to tell the lady that it wasn't necessary to go to work before six o'clock. In the morning I was greeted with abuse. "A terrible mess," "laziness," and the like rained down upon me—that is, although my name wasn't mentioned, it was all laid on me because I was the only one there. I never got in a word, but I never got up again at five o'clock, and the ladies had to get used to it. Of course I had to put up with a lot of bitter and vile words.

There were similar scenes with Käthe and Heinrich, but with each at a different time. When she was mad at one of us, then the others were her pets—that was the most disgusting thing. She seemed to expect that we would join in her malice, but she didn't have any luck with that.

I was unhappy in these surroundings and wrote to my dear mother, asking her whether she thought I should give notice on the first of August, so that I could be out of there on the first of November. Frau Sparr had prudently hired me with a three-month period of notice; and I'd let myself be persuaded. Käthe and the manservant had been smarter, they had only one month's notice. My mother wrote back to me that it would make a very bad impression if I wanted to change jobs after only half a year; anyway, it couldn't be that bad, for her sake I should hold out for a year. What did my good mother know about conditions in Hamburg and bad employers? She meant well for me, I knew that, and I didn't want to distress her, so I said nothing on the first of August. Oddly enough, it had been going very well recently. Frau Sparr was behaving tolerably, and we were breathing a lot easier. To be sure, the manservant didn't trust the peace.

"She's just that way as long as you can still give notice; afterward the war will start up again," he said to me. She had acted the same way with the previous cook, who then suddenly got sick and had to go to the hospital; she'd had her fill of the irritations. As ridiculous as that sounded, I didn't really doubt it, for no one knew better than I that it could easily happen from this vile treatment.

[*The manservant Heinrich quits.*]

Frau Sparr was often sick too. Life in the house was scarcely tolerable then. I really don't know what was the matter with her. The manservant claimed that she and her daughter-in-law had had a fight, and that it had degenerated in the same way as her kindness on good days. Everything about these people was unnatural. The twelve-year-old daughter told us once that her grandma had taken too much of the morphine that she always had to take to calm her nerves. Curiously, no doctor was consulted. The manservant just said, "The old lady is having her spells." Then we knew; it was time to get out the ice pack, hot-water bottle, and hot pack. The manservant hadn't been exaggerating when he'd told us that all three of them would be in use at the same time. It was true; and what's more, I had to provide relief for Frau Sparr with a massage twice a day; and sometimes I even had to clean her bedroom because Käthe was too noisy for her. Of course I fell behind in my work. It was up to me to get it done, for I had to get the sick one something to eat or drink almost every ten minutes. They'd say, "Make Frau Sparr a little cup of coffee and put a tasty buttered roll with it." After a while it would be: "Frau Sparr doesn't like it, fix a nice cup of tea and put a soft-boiled egg and anchovies on the roll. If there aren't any more anchovies in the cupboard, then you'll have to go get some yourself because we can't spare Käthe up here. And please hurry up!" So it went the whole day. From early morning until late in the evening the loaded trays went up and came back down empty, despite her lack of appetite. And our "healing apparatus" was never just as it was supposed to be either; the hot pack was too cold, the hot-water bottle was too hot, and the pieces of ice in the ice pack were too big, it pressed down too hard. The next time it was perhaps just the opposite; there was always something wrong. A lot of "blessings" came down the speaking tube onto my head. "You have it good," Käthe said. "You don't always have to be face-to-face with them when they scold you." She couldn't defend herself and had to listen to all kinds of abuse that she really didn't deserve; but she was resentful for days and gave short unfriendly answers; she "sulked" and so the employers labeled her "moody." How in the world could a servant girl ever feel wronged?

Fun-loving Heinrich was gone now, and in his place we'd gotten a forty-year-old bachelor in the house. He looked miserable and ill, and though he made every possible effort to appear bright and cheerful, he just wasn't up to the exertions and tensions, of which there were many here. The doctor advised him to take it easy as much as possible. But you couldn't spare yourself in this house. "Sparing and slaving both begin with the same letter of the alphabet," Georg remarked (that was the new manservant's name). The master liked to have him around but believed that Georg couldn't get him up the stairs alone, so he wanted Dora to support him on the other side—then it would work. So I had to help out again; however, the stairs turned out to be too small for the three of us, and the master ordered Georg to push him from behind and then he could get up. So I had the master firmly by the arm, and he clutched my free hand with his hand, and the manservant had his hands spread out on the master's back. A pretty picture, eh? When the ladies weren't around, it got even better, as Georg also put his hand on my back. When I told him to leave off the nonsense, he said, "Well, around here you have to take every opportunity to fool around so you don't forget how to laugh." There was something to what he said; usually we were in a bad mood and only occasionally were we ready for a laugh. There was always something new to get us down.

One day Frau Sparr had sent me to the post office; I was supposed to deliver thirty marks. When I came back, Frau Sparr was in the storeroom getting out beer and wine for the day. They

were locked behind a grate. I gave her the postal receipt, and
that was the end of the matter for me. Shortly thereafter she went
upstairs. Sometime later I was summoned to the speaking tube.
"Tell me, why didn't you give me the postal receipt?" her voice
echoed down the tube. "That sort of thing should be taken care
of right away, bring it up immediately!" I replied that I had
given her the receipt when I got back, that she'd taken it by the
wine cabinet. "Absolutely not," she replied. "I would know. I'm
not crazy." I'm not either, I thought, but I didn't say it; but I
intended to check to see whether the slip was still in the storeroom. But I looked in vain, I couldn't find it. I was about to go
up and tell Frau Sparr when she stormed downstairs, heaping
insults of the worst kind on me—of course I hadn't delivered the
money; I should own up because she would find out soon anyway;
the granddaughter had already been sent to the post office to
inquire. I stood there speechless. I didn't know what was happening to me—being accused of being a common thief, it was
frightful! The young girl soon came back from the post office and
told her mother that everything was OK. "What!" she replied.
"What's supposed to be OK? I don't have the receipt. Who
knows how the whole thing hangs together?" And still spitting
abuse, she went upstairs. The girl threw me a sympathetic look
and followed her grandma. She too suffered a lot from the moods
of her stepmother and grandmother. You often saw her going
around with teary eyes.

I had to cope with my troubles and the extra work caused by
this incident. Only a person who's always been honest his whole
life and has been so roughly accused can sympathize with how I
felt. Toward evening the girl had to fetch something else out of
the storeroom and she found the postal receipt in a locked cupboard. She came into the kitchen, obviously very pleased, and
showed me the receipt. "Dora, it's a good thing that it's been
found, isn't it? Now you can relax again. Grandma is so easily
upset, but I didn't doubt your honesty for a moment." These
words and also the fact that the receipt was found did cheer me
up, but they didn't take away my bitter feelings.

Some readers might say: Why didn't she just leave and find justice somewhere else? And today I do ask myself: Why did you stay after this incident? Yes, well today wasn't then; I was young and knew that I had to earn my living; and what would my dear old mother (who had so strictly raised her children to be respectable) say about her daughter running out on a job? Country people take a much dimmer view of such things. No, I didn't want to distress my mother. And so, the word was: stick it out. I certainly expected to be called to the speaking tube, and to be told that the error had been discovered, but nothing of the sort happened! Never before had working late into the night been so hard for me as on that day, and I went to bed with a heavy heart. I lay there for a long, long time and cried; then I began to think about how I could get out of this house as soon as possible, but in a less conspicuous way. Finally I decided to starve myself until I got ill and they had to send me to the hospital.

With this resolution, with thickly swollen eyes and a raging headache, I set to work the next morning. Secretly I still hoped that Frau Sparr would realize that she'd done me an injustice and would at least mention the fact. But in vain; she swept past me in her careless manner, not deigning to look at me. I couldn't stand it so I asked, "Don't you have something to say to me?"

"What am I supposed to have to say to you?" she replied in an offended tone.

"You could at least admit your mistake of yesterday," I said.

A contemptuous "Bah" was all she had to reply. I starved myself for two whole days, but on the third I couldn't resist. Once again I ate my coffee and bread in the usual way. If there is enough to eat around you, it's not so easy to condemn yourself to starvation and then really carry out the verdict.

Another time, when it once again seemed that it would be impossible to hold out any longer with these people, I drank a half bottle of vinegar. I felt miserable enough afterward, but still not so sick that I had to leave. I didn't want to fake being sick. I wanted the doctor really to find me sick.

Then there came a time when I resolved to do my duty completely and quietly to put up with all the trouble. But they made it very hard for us to carry out such a resolution. The more quietly and calmly we accepted the undeserved reproaches and scoldings, the more irritable Frau Sparr got. Even her daughter-in-law was incited against us; at least it looked to me as if she was not doing it out of her own conviction, when she "set us straight," as Frau Sparr called it. She was no doubt dependent on her in-laws and had to help out especially her "dear" mother-in-law in order to be on fairly good terms with her.

Sometimes things got pretty hot between them. One morning, it must have been about six-thirty, the manservant came into the kitchen to get the coffee for the master. He looked out of the window opposite the door. "Who in the world is that coming through the garden?" he said turning to me. "Come here quick, Dora!"

"Well, who could it be," I said. "It's probably the gardener; he often gets here early." But, I go over to the window anyway, and what do I see? Frau Sparr with her hair down, her feet in big soft slippers, and a gray nightgown wrapped around her body. Before we could recover from our shock, she came inside, sat down with a sigh in a chair, and asked me to give her a cup of coffee quickly; she'd had a terrible night and had spent the time since two o'clock in the chicken coop. She just couldn't stand any longer being near that ungrateful person upstairs. The "ungrateful one" was of course her daughter-in-law. She continued nonstop the abuse and reproaches against her; not a good hair was left on her. She greedily gulped down the coffee I brought her; she must have been freezing, because it was autumn. It wasn't long before her daughter-in-law came in, fell around her mother-in-law's neck, and kept on begging forgiveness. I left them alone; I didn't want to be indiscreet, and anyway, such emotional scenes offend me when they don't come from the heart. They soon went upstairs, and the whole day long the manservant and Käthe had plenty to say about how nice the two ladies were being to each other. There was no end to the kissing and embracing. "If only it lasts," said the manservant. We knew there wouldn't be peace for long. I never envied these people for their riches. They didn't have the most wonderful thing there is in this world: peace in the house.

Everything done for our benefit was so arranged that others could admire it. For instance, every noon the maid had to set our table according to a definite plan. Nothing could be missing; the manservant got a glass of beer, and every day Frau Sparr herself made us a fruit bowl of all the fruits that were in season. We ate with silver-plated forks and spoons, and the silver platters could never be forgotten; in fact there were even knife-rests. The table had to be set hours before we ate so that the delivery people could admire it—and admire it they did. How often we had to hear, "You really have it made!" Their words were accompanied by greedy looks at our elegantly set table. Usually I didn't say anything at all, but when I did, it was usually something like, "Not everything that glitters is gold." For how rarely did all three of us eat together at our beautiful table! It was normal for the bell to disturb one of us at mealtimes, often two of us were called, and sometimes all three. We'd quickly shove our plates into the oven; then, by the time we'd carried out the orders, our mealtime would be over, and we had to gulp down our food with our plate in our hand. But our beautifully set table had been admired by others, and so had served its purpose.

Käthe's and my room was also very nicely furnished; nothing was lacking that might contribute to our comfort; the manservant said the furnishings were "fit for a prince." It was too bad that we had absolutely no use for our princely room; on the contrary, you just had to spend more time cleaning it. That was time we could have better used for other things, like mending stockings and underwear. There was no free time for these things; we had to do all the most essential things at night, and our eyes regularly closed with exhaustion. One time, on her nightly rounds, Frau Sparr discovered me asleep next to a still-lit lamp. She scolded me terribly. She just couldn't understand why I'd sat up so late mending because there was just so much "free" time to do my needlework. I said, "Frau Sparr, please name me just one hour in the evening that we could dedicate to our own affairs,

I don't know of any." Backed into a corner like that, she could only defend herself with the most outrageous sorts of insults.

A few times Käthe and I used our free evening—which we weren't always supposed to take anyway—to fix our torn clothes. We didn't dare let the ladies find out; we stayed quietly in our room. If we heard steps coming from upstairs, we quickly blew out the lamp and remained quiet as a mouse until the danger was past. Actually it was ridiculous that we let ourselves be so intimidated, but we knew for sure that she would have immediately pressed us into service. What's more, Frau Sparr would have acted self-righteous and dressed us down horribly for being liars. To avoid such scenes, of which there were already enough, we preferred to receive no visitors. [. . .]

Christmas, that beautiful celebration, was approaching. People always say, "The pleasure of anticipation is the best part." But there could be no talk of pleasure here. There was an awful lot of work waiting for us, because there was going to be a party on the first day of the holidays, and the preparations were being made amidst frightful confusion. Just as we started one job, Frau Sparr would say, "There are still a few days to get that done, better do this or that." She got us thoroughly muddled. I admit that there are preparations for every holiday, and a little extra work doesn't matter; but I know from experience that things can be done quietly and with presence of mind. Already a week before the party she was constantly wailing: "If only you do a good job on the dinner! If only the meat is real juicy, and you've got to be especially careful with the pudding!" So it went every day. At night I dreamed of burned meat, failed pudding, and who knows what all. On Christmas Eve they had all been invited out, and the manservant had to go along because the master was crippled. Käthe had asked for time off to spend the special evening with her parents who lived in Hamburg. So I stayed in the house alone. On any other evening it would have been a blessing to me to be able to do my work quietly without being disturbed. But on this evening I'd have given a lot to have another human being around, not because I felt any boredom—for they'd seen

to it that no boredom would take possession of me—but celebrating Christmas Eve so alone and so piled up with work was
something I'd never experienced. I was sad, very sad. I had vi-
sions of Christmases back home. How beautiful, how wonder-
fully beautiful they had been amidst loved ones, good parents,
and brothers and sisters! How many joyous Christmas carols were
sung, and how great and genuine was the joy at the modest presents under the glowing Christmas tree! "Oh blessed, oh blessed
to be a child still!" These words fit my mood, and I cried many
tears those hours I was alone. How banal it seemed to be preparing food and drink for mouths and stomachs when the heart and
the soul starved and thirsted. We'd been told that we wouldn't
get our presents until the next day. That was OK with me, but
Käthe would have liked to have been able to tell her parents
about them; but patience was called for here.

The first day of Christmas saw us on our feet early. Today I
was supposed to prove myself as the "perfect" cook. It was the
first large party where the cooking was left solely to me. I put
my best into it and thought it came off satisfactorily in every
respect. Not that I got a word of appreciation from the ladies—
God forbid! But while they were serving, Käthe and the manservant had overheard a lot of praise about the food and its preparation and reported it to me. That was some consolation for me,
because now Frau Sparr had no occasion the next day to let loose
with a lot of talk about my inexperience, something she liked to
do whenever anything went wrong.

Our Christmas presents turned out very well; Frau Sparr
wasn't stingy—that was actually the only good thing about her.
Our plentiful presents had already been on display the day before
in a little room that the visiting ladies and gentlemen had to pass
by, and they had to admire how amply the "good" Frau Sparr was
bestowing presents on her servant staff. And later, at every little
opportunity, we were always hearing, "How ungrateful, eh,
Gustchen? They just aren't worth getting so many presents."
We'd often say among ourselves that she should save this observation; there would come a time when she could put it to better

use. That's because all three of us intended to give notice on the first of February. Käthe and the manservant could go on the first of March, but unfortunately I'd have to stay until the first of May.

In January, Henny, our "little pet," as her mother liked to call her, was to give a children's ball. The frightful preparations with their unpleasant upheavals—without which nothing was done in this household—were drawing to a close. The day before the festivities Frau Sparr charged me with bathing the white Pomeranian dog so that he too would have a festive appearance. It was only Wednesday, and Saturday was his bath day. Georg, Käthe, and I had to alternate at this job. It was my turn. Even though I still had a lot of things to do at the stove, Frau Sparr demanded that it had to be done before dinner, because I was supposed to bathe not only the Pomeranian but also the white cat, our "little puss." I remarked that I'd never heard that cats would let themselves be bathed, but she snapped, "And there's a lot more that you haven't seen or heard too." Then she said again: "So, do you understand, get going now so that puss will be partly dry by dinner, and she can enjoy her milk at the right time. And how pleased Little Henny will be when not only pup but also puss appears so nice and clean at the ball."

Now I had to step on it so that this extra work would get done too. In the laundry room there was a big wooden washtub that was used as a bathtub for the dog. He could be bathed easily, and after he was dried off, he was wrapped in an old woolen blanket where he lay quietly until he was completely dry. Not so with the cat, who was having her first bath today. As soon as I put her into warm water, she spit and scratched all around horribly, and before I could stop her, she was past me, through the open doors, and up the carpeted stairs, leaving wet footprints behind. Just then a hideous outcry broke out upstairs; the wet cat was caught, and Frau Sparr came into the laundry room with her, screaming abuse at me. I apologized and put in a good word for the frightened cat; but completely ignoring my well-intentioned warning, she yelled at me that she would show me how well cats could be bathed. I shouldn't presume that it couldn't be managed just because I didn't understand it. As she was saying this, she put the cat back into the water; but she'd barely finished the sentence before the poor animal, hissing and spitting, burst from her hands and jumped up first onto her shoulder and from there onto her head. And there she held fast in such an original pose that I had to laugh out loud, despite Frau Sparr's perilous situation. With each front paw in an ear, the back paws fixed on her forehead, and the dripping tail hanging down over her nose, puss could not be moved to let go of her victim, who of course was all the while crying loudly for help. Everyone came running; even the wet dog had freed himself from his warm covers on account of the noise and watched the comic scene with his tail between his legs. All efforts to get the cat down from its lofty perch were in vain; the poor animal of course feared that it would be put back into the water and so it clung in its uncomfortable place. Frau Sparr had no choice but to go to her room with the cat still on her head, and only there did her daughter-in-law succeed in removing the cat. Georg wanted to call the fire department as a joke, so that the story could be made public. The bath story gave us something to laugh about for a long time afterward. Frau Sparr escaped with a scare and some cat scratches on her face, but the poor cat was a long time in getting over her first trip to the bathtub. For days she lay in a basket behind the stove before she even got up the courage to have some milk. Of course she wouldn't let herself be seen at the children's ball, and her play and somersaults were never again as funny and jolly as they had been earlier.

The first of February was an uneasy day because all three of us gave notice, Käthe and Georg for the first of March and I for the first of May. Frau Sparr strained every nerve to persuade me to stay. Among other things she promised me a complete new set of choice cooking utensils if only I would stay with her until I got married. Unfortunately, I had no prospects for marriage. I also knew that I'd have to pay dearly for those choice new cooking utensils, and that I'd rather do without them. For a couple of days she was friendly and smiling and even fawning. On the third day she asked with a friendly smile, "Well, you're going to be reasonable and take my suggestion, aren't you?"

"No, I'm sorry, I can't (I lied), my mother needs my help, I'm going home on the first of May." I was afraid of her anger; that's why I needed this lie, and it seemed to work for me. The phony friendly face did disappear, its place taken by lurking, scornful glances, but for the time being I was spared her abuse. She probably wanted to talk it over with Gustchen first, and she may have thought that it would be well to be on good terms with me as long as possible. Käthe and the manservant were of no value to her now; she dealt with me fairly tolerably. She had something else on her mind now: the whole house was to be redecorated before we left. And that really would be something!

A few days after I had told Frau Sparr I couldn't stay, the grocer called at the door, as he did twice a week to see what we needed. It was the same young man who had recommended me to this house a year before. It was my duty not to forget to order anything. Frau Sparr seldom bothered with him, even if she happened to be downstairs. Today it was different. After I'd finished with the grocer, she called him back, met him in the entryway, and closed the kitchen door behind her. I didn't have to be a busybody to be curious about what she had to discuss with the man. Of course I immediately thought of the old saying: Eavesdroppers hear no good of themselves. But it might be different if I listened; I resolved to try. So I leaned my head against the door, and I could hardly believe my ears when I heard Frau Sparr say to the grocer: "Listen grocer, could you get me another cook by May? A replacement for Dora, but understand, someone just like her, because I've always been very satisfied with her; she'd certainly stay on but her mother needs her."

"Ah, yes, and you know well," she said closing her spiel, "the girls have it good with me."

"Oh, certainly, Frau Sparr," was the last thing I heard the grocer say. I didn't pay much attention to the rest. I really would have liked to have contradicted her, but I kept quiet to preserve the blessed peace. So you see, dear readers, the eavesdropper hears only nice things. I seemed like a stranger to myself. Frau Sparr satisfied with me? And the way she'd treated me! What would happen to someone she wasn't satisfied with?!

[*The decorators come, making it hard for Dora to get any time off.*]

In the first mail delivery the next morning I got a letter from my brother, inviting me to a concert with him that evening in the Hansasaal; he'd be waiting for me in front of the concert hall between eight and eight-thirty. I was very happy; after all, I hadn't talked to my brother in a long time. But I also knew it would be hard to get away. I shared my doubts with Käthe and the manservant and asked for their advice on whether I dare ask permission from Frau Sparr. They both said, "Definitely, you should do it; today would be a good day." And the manservant offered to let me in on a secret if I'd keep it quiet. I promised, and he told me that Frau Sparr intended to engage a manservant but no maid from the first of March to the first of May. She said that Dora could handle it alone for two months. "So," the manservant said, finishing his story, "see to it that you get out of here now; later it will be absolutely impossible, because we know how this household is." So now this too! When Frau Sparr came into the kitchen that morning without saying "Good morning," my heart just sank. But on the other hand, it was still very tempting to be able to spend a couple of hours in my dear brother's company, listening to a good concert and giving my weary bones some rest. I brought up my plan as amiably as possible. She planted herself in front of me, hands on her hips, and looked at me with her sea-blue eyes so disapprovingly that I understood without a word what she thought of my request. Finally she tapped her forehead with her index finger and looked up imploringly. This expressed what she'd said to me many times: I must be crazy.

My face flushed; did one have to put up with everything from this uncouth woman just because she was rich and I was poor? And again I thought, "Oh, if you could just get out of this house forever!" There was no end to her scolding and abuse, but I was able to say to her very calmly: "Fine, Frau Sparr, don't get excited on my account. I'm leaving my job today, I'll straighten up the kitchen and then I'll go."

She burst out laughing and said, "There are ways to get obstinate servants back to their work, I'll just show you how we deal with them."

"Do with me what you want, but I'm not staying," I told her.

"You'll stay because I wouldn't give you a groschen of your wages, and without money you won't get anywhere," she replied.

"OK, fine, keep my quarterly wage."

The daughter-in-law was called down, and they discussed it loudly enough that I could hear everything. She wanted to get a policeman, who could surely force me to stay, because there certainly was no law allowing servants simply to leave their employers in the lurch whenever they pleased. I couldn't hear what her daughter-in-law said. With horror I thought to myself: If they can force you to stay, what then? I didn't know the laws that well, and then suddenly it hit me: "Then you'll drown yourself! Just so you don't have to stay here any longer." The lower windows had iron bars on them, but the window on the staircase was halfway up, and I would get out through it at night, and there was a little pond in the back of the garden. Frau Sparr had a shawl sent down, put it on, and stormed out into the street. She called over a policeman and with wild gesticulations seemed to be trying to get him to come into the house with her. But he just shrugged his shoulders a couple of times and went on his way. I'd watched it from a little window in the coal room. She came back inside, snorting with anger. Then the manservant was sent to the gentleman next door. The neighbor came but soon left. In the meantime the manservant had whispered to me, "If you give up your wages, nobody can force you to stay." I got my courage back.

In a moment Frau Sparr came back down with a reasonably tolerable expression on her face and said to me: "Let's make up, OK? You're actually right, we can easily arrange for you to go out today. Go ahead, and everything will be as it was. I know you well enough to know that you wouldn't cause me so much embarrassment. You're such a good, dear girl." With these last words she even stroked my cheeks.

"Serpent!" I thought. I said aloud, "Oh, no, this time I'm not being good, I'm going." The daughter-in-law had come back in and they both worked on me together. Among other things, they pointed out to me how stupid it would be to abandon three months' wages. "I'll be glad to leave them if I can just get out of here," I said.

Seeing that her efforts were in vain, she started the abuse again and said, "You act as if you were in a hell."

"Well," I said, "it can't be much worse in hell with the devil."

Then she came at me with her fists; she'd have hit me if her daughter-in-law hadn't pulled her back. A peculiar calm had come over me; it must have been the thought that I was going to go, no matter what. I went to my room to pack my things. She screamed after me, "See that you get out of here at once, at once, and take all your things with you at once, or else I'll throw them out after you." I didn't think this scandalous outburst was worth a reply. She would see what I was doing; as a precaution I locked myself in my room; and I packed my things neatly and securely. I felt sorriest for Käthe, who said tearfully, "If you could have at least stayed until the first of March!" I comforted her that it was only a week till then. I knew the others would face some unpleasant days, but I'd had enough of them myself.

Käthe slipped back upstairs; Frau Sparr had forbidden her to speak to me. In a few moments the manservant came to the door with the request that I was to figure out exactly, down to the last pfennig, how much was owed me once the quarterly wage was deducted; Frau Sparr wanted nothing more to do with my affairs. I told the manservant that that wouldn't be necessary; I was due so many marks and so many groschen, and I'd give her the small change along with the quarterly wage. A little while later he came back to tell me that I was supposed to get the money myself upstairs. When I'd gotten all my things ready to go, I went upstairs. Oh my, what grumpy faces I saw! Even the old man, who'd always been so friendly to me, followed me with nasty looks. There was a paper lying on the table next to the money. Frau Sparr pointed to it imperiously and said, "Please, sign that!"

"I won't sign anything I haven't read," I said.

"Then, please, please," she said with cutting scorn, "if you can read at all."

"Maybe better than you," I said, not wanting her to get the better of me. I read: "The undersigned herewith acknowledges to have broken a contract." I told her, "I'll sign this scrap of paper only if you add 'for which she has given up her quarterly wage.'"

"I won't think of it," she yelled at me, "and if you don't sign it I won't give you this money either."

"Good," I replied, "I'll find justice yet."

With that I was about to go. But the daughter-in-law and the old man said, "She can ask for that, just write it so we're done with the whole thing." Cursing and scolding, she wrote it, and I put my name on this ridiculous document, pocketed what little money there was, and left the unfriendly house forever.

Nikolaus Osterroth,
Clay Miner

Nikolaus Osterroth (1875–1933), the son of a butcher, was a clay miner from the Palatinate, who in later life became a successful Social Democratic politician. Already a union and party organizer before World War I, he was elected to the National Assembly of 1919, served as a member of the Prussian Diet, and worked as a government mining consultant. His autobiography, published in 1920 by the Social Democratic Vorwärts Verlag, is an inspirational political statement; unlike most other such works, however, it is highly personal. In the parts excerpted here Osterroth tells of the rigors and dangers of working in a clay mine in the early 1890s. We then follow the devout young Catholic as he awakens to the causes of economic injustice, and, after an intense inward struggle, rejects his religion. The great value of Osterroth's autobiography is that it reveals the spiritual crisis often brought on by conversion to Social Democracy. Like many workers, Osterroth supplanted his Christianity with the evolutionary monism so popular at the end of the nineteenth century.

IN THE MINE

I began at six o'clock on a Monday morning. My heart filled with fear and curiosity, I grabbed my miner's lamp and started down the ladder, which led 120 feet straight down to the floor of the shaft. Desperately, I clung to the rungs of the ladder; just a few meters down they already got wet and very slippery. The man before me scampered down the ladder with the agility of a squirrel, whistling a popular song as he went. The song cut into my soul and made me think of all the guardian angels and saints. Behind me were a couple of older miners who teased me good-naturedly; we didn't have all day to get to the bottom, they said. They made me very ashamed and I strained myself to the utmost. I sent all my frantic prayers—with and without indulgences—up the narrow shaft to the heavens I could no longer see. The shaft was very uneven because some of the supporting props had been pilfered, causing the ground to sink; in places the ladder hung in empty space so that I was sure I would fall.

In my fear and ineptness I knocked my lamp so hard against the ladder that the wick disappeared into the oil and the lamp went out. I appealed to my patron saint and Barbara, the patron saint of the miners, promising her that I would say three paternosters in her honor on the ladder every morning if she would protect me. Finally I was down, and I sloshed around in a muck so heavy and sticky that I could hardly walk. Since my light had gone out, I groped after the man in front of me; he was only three meters ahead of me, but his lamp glimmered very red as though he were at a great foggy distance. The men behind me had arrived on the floor of the mine, and I wanted to make way for them. Bang! I received a blow on the forehead that sent me reeling senselessly. The entrance to the tunnel was only one and a half meters high and I'd hit my head so hard against the supporting beams that I cut my forehead. What a beginning! O

Translated from Nikolaus Osterroth, *Vom Beter zum Kämpfer* (Berlin: Vorwärts Verlag, 1920), 67–72, 129–51.

God, can anyone work and live in such a place the whole year long? But you had to be able to. The other miners were totally indifferent to the surroundings and joked about my misery.

Their backs bent down, the men walked through the partially collapsed tunnel. They stopped at the clay face. I saw everything indistinctly, as in a fog. My head buzzed and hummed and I was very dizzy. In front of us, between the supporting beams, lay a huge shapeless clump of bad, marly clay that had fallen from the ceiling the night before. The miners shone their lights on the four-meter-high ceiling, and said that no one had seen any pressure splits on Saturday evening. The clump, which they called a "cow," had broken four beams out of the timbering. The men estimated that it weighed about fifteen thousand pounds. One of them said that if it had fallen down at noon on Saturday they all would have been killed.

Holy Barbara, what fearful prospects! I increased my vow from three to five paternosters. Suddenly one of the miners discovered a long pressure split on the ceiling of the left side of the tunnel, next to an abandoned clay face. The oldest man was in favor of propping up the place for the time being with planks and posts, and only then breaking up the "cow," removing it, and repairing the smashed timbers. But someone else said, "Oh, don't worry, that's another five thousand pounds. Hand me up the pick." He got his way and he jammed the pick into the split and pulled. Nothing happened. The youngest of the three, the one who'd been ahead of me as we climbed down the ladder, cried out, "Wait, I'll help." He took another pick and jammed it in the same way. The old man and I stepped back among the support posts. All at once there was a violent burst of air and a smashing thud on the floor; the "cow," which was even bigger than the first one, lay on the floor.

The youngest fellow had taken a big jump back to get out of the way. But the "cow" had been faster and had struck him on the ankle. He lay there stretched out in front of the "cow" not saying a word. Suddenly he tried to get up and he let out a mighty shout, "I've broken my leg!" He was right; he'd suffered a fracture of the ankle bone.

My whole body shook as I heard that carefree twenty-year-old man cry out. Immediately, we very carefully freed his foot from the "cow." Then I had to climb up the shaft and call people to help me bring him up to the surface with a winch. In my excitement, climbing up the wet, slippery ladder was even more excruciating than coming down. I would certainly have fallen if my anxiety about the injured man (who was a relative of mine!) hadn't turned my fingers to clamps of steel.

There was no more thought of work for the morning. In the afternoon, when we were once again back at the clay face, the two others were also in a very subdued mood. The old man reproached his comrade for not following his advice, and for daring to tackle the "cow." The younger man probably saw his negligence and was very dejected. But he may well have been right in his contention that the supports would not have held the weight of the "cow," and it would probably have broken through. Then it could have smashed all of us. I was so depressed about these obvious dangers on the job that I almost would have preferred Herr von Tretmühl's factory.*

But constant danger desensitizes; soon the others were indifferent again and began to work on breaking up the "cows." These were hacked up with wet axes into small clumps that I had to stack one after the other in piles at the front of the tunnel by the shaft. The old man continually reminded his comrade, "Don't make them so big; the poor boy can't handle them like that yet." That was really true. As insignificant as the little rectangular clumps were, I was still no match for them. The wet axes had made them slippery. I couldn't get a grip on them with my hands, even when I dug my nails in until they almost broke off. With a frightful struggle, I rolled the clumps onto my knee and tried to get control of them, which by the sweat of my brow I succeeded in doing about twenty times. Then I rolled them out to the shaft because I couldn't lift them anymore.

The good-natured old man laughed and said that wrestling with the clumps would soon make me strong. Then he said I

*A brick factory where Osterroth had previously worked.

should rest, and he gave me an ax and told me to cut off a corner of the "cow." But I was supposed to take my time; there was no hurry. As my strength permitted, I was supposed to cut into the same groove and in between dip the ax into a pail of water; I'd gradually work up the confidence I needed. I followed the old man's instructions, but with every other stroke I missed the line I was supposed to be cutting on, and it was evening before I'd cut off the corner—about three hundred pounds. I hadn't even earned the salt for my soup, even though I was dripping with sweat. The old man smiled and said, "Just be patient, in a month things will go better; that's the way I started out too." When the "cows" had been removed, the overhang was timbered right up to the clay face and then we worked on the clay seam.

The seam is about sixty centimeters long and six meters wide; when it's cut down to the height of your chest, it looks like a bench. This is separated with picks from the wall behind so that all around the seam there is a twenty-centimeter-deep groove barely big enough to stick your finger in. So that the picks don't get stuck, a big ladle full of water is poured into the groove after every ten or fifteen strokes; because it's wet, the pick springs back out of the elasticlike clay. From then on, cutting these grooves was the main part of my job; and it was strenuous work requiring a lot of practice, especially up by the ceiling, which had become vaulted as a result of separating the seam. The seam is then cut with an ax into strips twenty-five centimeters wide and equally deep; these are then cut away horizontally with the ax. When the seam is down to knee high, the clumps are also cut away from underneath with the ax. Depending on the thickness of the clay layer, the tunnel may be as much as five meters high, so that the upper half of the seam has to be cut from a scaffold, a very tiring job.

The hardest work is the rough cutting with the ax and cutting away the clumps from the seam. You can't take it for more than three hours because your hands get completely exhausted. So the shift is divided into four two-hour sections separated by breakfast, lunch, and the afternoon break. In his youth a miner's arms twitch from exhaustion even when he sleeps.

The clumps that have been cut off are thrown behind the seam between the supporting pillars; they call this area the gallery. If the gallery is filled up, then the younger workers pile the clumps up on one side near the shaft so that you can still get through the tunnel. When there are a great number of people employed in a mine, then two tunnels on opposite sides of the shaft are worked, and one man works steadily at piling up the clumps. He also has to load the clumps onto wagons at the top of the shaft. The poor devil has to transport 800–1,000 wet, slippery clumps, each of which weighs 100 pounds. After years of this, his back gets all crooked and his arms get long like an ape's, so that he can scratch his knees without bending over.

For several hours every day the clumps are lifted up the shaft with a winch. In earlier days this work was usually done by women or girls. It was a really murderous job and frequently resulted in premature births or great damage to the child-bearing organs of the women workers. After protracted pressure from the miners, the Bavarian Mining Law finally put an end to this disgraceful women's work.*

Clay mining demands great skill, both in cutting the clay as well as in boring the shaft and supporting it. An apprenticeship of five or six years is required before a miner gets the skill needed for cutting. He's regarded as fully skilled after his military service.

I really worked myself to death to attain the highest level of skill. After I'd worked two more times in the winter months helping my father with the household butchering, I got strong. I'd become a young man who had respect for his own strength, for whom no work was too hard. No piece of bread or sausage was big enough for me either. If Jesus had had eaters like me when he performed his miracle with the bread, there would have been no twelve full baskets left over. In the meantime I'd gradually become an adolescent, and I made the most of these years, though without violating my vow to St. Barbara;† I still re-

---

*The Palatinate is on the left bank of the Rhine, but it was part of Bavaria from 1816 to 1945.

†Presumably to say five paternosters on the way down the shaft each day.

mained true to that as a twenty-four-year-old man, even though my behavior was sometimes excessive. [. . .]

MY FIRST ACQUAINTANCE WITH THE SOCIAL DEMOCRATS

The process of impoverishment in the clay-mining industry had accelerated greatly in the early 1890s and reached a climax during my military service. A combination of circumstances—competition, senseless overexploitation, and an epidemic of extravagance—had combined to impoverish a succession of earlier mine owners. They couldn't acquire any more new mines because the price had risen enormously; those that were still affordable could not be successfully exploited with the primitive methods in use at the time, because the clay lay too deep and the operating costs were too high. Other mine owners could anticipate the end of their business. Their mines were still exploitable for a number of years, but they couldn't acquire new mines because of the very depressed clay prices and the fierce competition. Their existence hung by a thread that in a short time would unravel itself. Only a very few families had worked themselves up or gained possession of larger clay beds through lucky speculation. But even with these beds the possibilities for exploitation were very limited because of the depth and the resulting increasing hardness of the clay.

The downward slide of the clay-mining business was made even worse by another circumstance. In the neighboring village, which lay over the deepest clay layers, there was a poor engineer who had married into some money and set up a small clayware factory. Because of all the competition among the mine owners, he was able to obtain his raw materials, clay and luting sand, for a ridiculously low price. The man was successful, and after two years his small factory had become a big one that he added to each year. He quietly bought up fields here and there and started to drill in them. All the heads were shaking. But the new factory owner continued to buy, through his skillful agents, everything that was attainable. Eventually he went for very deep-lying beds that were little in demand. One day he even began sinking two shafts. He applied the new techniques of coal mining on one of them. Huge, meter-wide, metal rings were riveted together and driven into the second shaft. After both shafts had reached a depth of over one hundred feet and had cost an enormous sum of money, the work had to be stopped on account of water and quicksand. For several years there was no more drilling or land buying.

But soon a second clayware factory grew up next to the first, growing just as rapidly and also buying up clay beds. A short time later the two factories merged and began their own mining and clay shipping. Mostly they shipped crushed and fired clay (called *chamotte*), thereby greatly reducing their freight costs.

Such was the state of affairs when I got home from military service. Almost all the clay-mine owners had to fear that sooner or later they would be eliminated by these developments. To prevent that, they finally got together in a sales cartel that they thought would put an end to the wild competition and bring the prices back up to a profitable level. In their stupidity and alcoholic stupor the owners had taken a long time to see the light. But even after the founding of the sales cartel the competition hadn't stopped, and for the workers too things still looked bleak. The mine owners fought bitterly over their share of the business. And the workers were out of the frying pan and into the fire, because the new director of the cartel had made several suggestions to the lame-brained mine owners about how they could lower production costs at the expense of the workers.

Up to this time the mine workers had enjoyed rather free, almost patriarchal working conditions and were driven to harder work only by low piecework pay. But now they were to come under strict work rules with a sophisticated penalty system. Moreover, the piecework rates were to be made uniform, which in reality meant reducing them to the lowest level. And finally the miners were not permitted to burn the scrap wood and the old lumber that they got during the essential, but time-consuming, retimbering in the tunnels. This was a traditional right of the workers and saved them having to buy wood and coal. The attempt to introduce these work rules created bad blood among the miners and stirred them to resistance, which at first found an outlet only in tavern debates.

When the mine owners stood by their plan, which they intended to introduce on 1 May, the miners turned to the priest, so that he might help them fight against this obvious injustice. But instead of standing by them, the priest preached that the employer was an authority appointed by God whom one had to obey. Humble obedience was the greatest virtue of subordinates. There had always been master and servant, and God had given the master the right to command his servant.

The workers could see what the priest was driving at, and they streamed from the church over to the tavern. There they reviled the priest in most unchristian language as one who, in exchange for the gift of a new church window from a mine owner, would preach patience to the workers instead of instilling humanity and righteousness in the mine owners.

This was in the middle of April, just at the time that I was in inner ferment and on the lookout for new political goals because of the malicious policies that the Center party was pursuing in the Bavarian Diet. Up to this point the fight about the work rules hadn't aroused me very much; I didn't know any way to stop them. But now, when I heard with my own ears how the priest unambiguously sided against the workers instead of speaking to the conscience of the mine owners, I was angry and saw the priest above all as a Center party man. His was the correct Center party policy of just the sort Dr. Siegl* had always condemned: groveling to the upper classes and ready for any betrayal of the people; leading the people by the nose with religion; and always representing the "heretics" as the only danger.

*Dr. Johannes Siegl was a member of the Bavarian Diet and the editor of the Bavarian particularist newspaper, *Bavarian Fatherland* (*Bayerisches Vaterland*).

But now where was the threat coming from? It came only from the Catholic mine owners, who hypocritically donated painted church windows, altars, bells, etc., and oddly enough, just in recent times. Who had influence on these people? Undoubtedly it was only the priest, who asserted that he was God's appointed adviser on all questions of life. And how did the priest use his influence? Instead of defending the rights of the oppressed, whose leadership he regarded as his monopoly, he preached submission and patience to the workers. He sat at the table of the rich and accepted the gifts that they had wrung from the poor, instead of reminding them that their actions were hardhearted and unchristian. Instead of saying to the mine owners, "Thou shalt love thy neighbor as thyself," he said to the exploited and raped workers, "You are servants, and servants you must remain; God wills it for your salvation."

A terrible storm raged through me. I doubted everything that up until then I had held as noble and good. What? Did the priests treat the religion they taught us as a petty business matter not only in politics but also in daily life? It was totally impossible to harmonize the offensive behavior that the priests were manifesting here with the religious truths and Christian moral law that were so vehemently defended by the same men. Didn't all actions of any self-respecting person, not to speak of a priest, have to be a mirror of his convictions?

In the midst of my crisis of conscience I sat down and wrote a fiery letter to the local priest. I illuminated the present social problem, criticized his behavior, and described my tormenting doubts. I asked for help for the workers, even if it was only an attempt. For me and many others, even a fruitless attempt to help would have been an act of deliverance that would have once again placed firm ground under our stumbling feet. I signed the letter "One for Many" and nervously awaited the consequences. Surely the results of my cry for help would show up in the sermon on Sunday. Surely I was not deceived! The priest had dedicated his first sermon to the workers, so now on the second Sunday he would certainly aim his warning at the other side. He would raise his voice in warning against an act of violence that would bring to the mine owners, not the blessing of the community, but rather only curses, quarrels, and embittered struggles. Surely the priest would justify my hope and determinedly tell the truth to both sides!

My disappointment was boundless. I heard not a word in the sermon that could have justified my fervent hopes. Instead there was an unctuous litany about the ruses of the devil, "who runs around like a roaring lion trying to devour whomever he can." And then there were some rumblings against the "anticlerical" newspapers, which awaken the spirit of conflict and dissatisfaction and estrange the flock from its shepherds. I went home with an empty head and a dying heart. I was incapable of thinking, and after supper I ran to the tavern where I got drunk in order to numb myself. The whole week I was in a hopeless mood and wasn't even interested in my *Bavarian Fatherland [Bayerisches Vaterland]*.

On the last Sunday in April a leaflet was thrown through the open window while we were eating lunch. For a while it went unnoticed. After lunch I picked up the sheet of paper and glanced at the front and back sides, without reading the text. It was labeled, "To the Voters for the Reichstag!" and on the bottom of the back side it said, "The Social Democratic Reichstag Members." Now some life came into me. That was what I was looking for: a program, an authentic pronouncement of Social Democracy!

I began to read. Sentence by sentence there was an indictment against the government and the bourgeois parties, against armaments expenditures that had been driven to unbearable heights, against the insanely increasing debt burden of the Empire, against the excess of the new naval appropriations that oppressed the people, and against the plundering of the masses by tariffs and indirect taxes. And there was more: The stagnation of social welfare; the misery and lack of rights of the working class; the prison terms that the Emperor threatened, which would destroy the workers' right to organize! All that made an enormous, totally new impression on me.

Suddenly I saw the world from the other side, from a side that up to now had been dark for me. I was especially aroused by the criticism of the tariff system and the indirect taxes. I'd never heard a word about them before! In all the Center party speeches they kept completely quiet about them. And why? Wasn't their silence an admission that they'd committed an injustice, a clear sign of a guilty conscience? I didn't believe my eyes—a six-pfennig tax on a pound of salt! I was seized by a feeling of wild fury about the obvious injustice of a tax system that spared the ones who could best pay and plundered those who already despaired of life in their bitter misery.

But then I found something new that really gripped me: The Social Democratic leaflet not only criticized, it not only put its finger on the festering wounds and showed that the class character of society was the cause of the wrongs—no, it also produced a series of highly illuminating suggestions for the abolition of these wrongs. Numerous demands for the betterment of the condition of the people were made to the state. And then the leaflet turned to the voters, with a flaming appeal to them to make use of the universal suffrage, the greatest right of a citizen, in order to retaliate in the name of the people against a hostile government and treacherous parties.

The leaflet affected me like a revelation. But who had brought it? I had to speak to the man. I had to find out more about this mysterious party. I ran through the village, asking everyone I met about the leaflet distributor. I heard that it was a whole column of bicyclists from Ludwigshafen, who'd flooded into the village after church and who had stopped at the last inn to regroup before going on to the next village to distribute their leaflets. I ran through the streets and met the red bicyclists* just as they were about to move on.

Quickly I told these strange people what was on my mind, how the leaflet had affected me; and then I asked them whether I could get some more publications from them. I must have made a very odd face during my hasty confession, because the red mes-

*Red in this context means socialist.

sengers looked at me in astonishment the way the discoverers of America had stared at the natives. And then it was obvious that a feeling of joyful satisfaction overcame all of them, and they sat down again and for a whole hour they told me about the aspirations of Social Democracy and the growth of the young union movement. How heartily they laughed at the hopes I'd placed in the priest, and how convincingly and plainly they described how above all we workers lacked union organization. A union would bring together the weak uninfluential workers in order to counter the employers with the power of united action.

God, how clear and simple it all was! This new world of thought that gave the worker the weapons of self-awareness and self-consciousness was very different from the old world of priestly and economic authority where the worker was merely an object of domination and exploitation!

Once I'd gotten hold of these bringers of enlightenment I wouldn't let them go; I didn't have to be invited twice to help distribute leaflets in the remaining two villages of the county. With the winged zeal of the newly converted, I leaped from house to house, taking three steps at a time and feeling lighter and happier than ever before in my life. My new friends liked my zeal. When we parted late in the evening, they gave me an "Erfurt Program"* and some newspapers, and promised that they would soon send me a package of pamphlets and newspapers. I spent almost the whole night studying the program, and I had the feeling that all these thoughts were etched into my brain with flamed writing.

The next day was the first of May. After a short, feverish sleep I awoke—for the first time as a Social Democrat. This was the day that the new work rules were to go into effect. A good third of the workers didn't show up on other Mondays, but today almost all stayed at home. Everyone was afraid to report to the mine inspectors' shed in order to receive the "dog tags," the newly introduced control tickets. From nine o'clock on, they filled the taverns, and there were lively disputes about the new

*Adopted in 1891, this was the official, Marxist-oriented, program of the SPD.

situation. Someone threatened to tear everything to shreds; another wanted to set fire to the straw roofs of the mining huts; and a third suggested organizing a revenge campaign against every mine owner and smashing windows. Everyone swore that he'd rather starve than recognize the new work rules by getting the "dog tags." I sat quietly in the corner and thought about the happy enthusiasm with which my new friends from yesterday had spoken of their May Day festival planned for today.

OUR FIRST MAY DAY FESTIVAL

"May Day festival! Worldwide holiday from work! We demand the eight-hour day! We're demonstrating for international peace and the protection of labor!"* That's what I'd read in the May issue of the *Palatinate Post* [*Pfälzischer Post*], which the socialist messengers had given me the day before.

The idea flashed through my brain: If the workers of all the great cities in the civilized countries are celebrating this liberating festival today, why shouldn't these hollering and aimlessly groping miners also catch the enthusiasm of the idea of the First of May? They didn't want to go to work anyway. Wouldn't it be a crime if I kept to myself the knowledge that I'd fought so hard to gain and considered the seeds growing in my heart as my private possession? Why shouldn't I lift the others into the new world of freedom? All at once I jumped up onto my chair and clapped my hands for quiet.

"Fellow sufferers!" I said to the astonished listeners. "You're all skipping work today because you won't give in to the pressure of the mine owners. We can't find anyone who will free us from the unjust yoke that they wish to place on us. So we'll help ourselves! We're strong enough if only we're united. We're not the only ones not working today. It's the First of May and hundreds of thousands of workers throughout the world are taking

*In 1889, the Second International had proclaimed the first day of each May as an international workers' holiday in defiance of capitalism.

off work and protesting the tyrannical yoke that they suffer under. It's true that all of these celebrating workers are Social Democrats, but they're exploited and oppressed people like us. And if no one else will help us, let's give it a try with Social Democratic help. The drowning man doesn't ask who's helping him, he grabs the first rescuing hand. That's what we'll do. I propose that we celebrate May Day this afternoon with a huge party in the woods. When our employers see our numbers and our unity, they'll understand that we don't give a damn about their work rules. So unite! Up with May Day, the world festival of the workers!"

It was an electrifying thought, and evoked joyous enthusiasm from people who had been at a loss about what to do. In no time all the preparations had been made and the innkeeper agreed to bring a wagon of beer and food to a nearby corner of the woods. The excited people ran from one tavern to another and announced the plan to general jubilant agreement.

An hour later everyone was in his Sunday best and patrolling the streets and the taverns. I reread my leaflet and the May Day article in the *Palatinate Post,* took my shiny trumpet, and blew out the window the signal to gather. As in a procession, everyone gathered behind me in the street while I marched out in front, proud as can be, and blowing the trumpet marches I'd learned in the military. Some of the women leaned out the windows and laughed, and some of them ran to the door after their husbands, scolding them for their "laziness," only to stop and gape in astonishment at the parade of festively dressed people. The mine owners, city councilmen, and the mayor peeked timidly and fearfully from their windows, making no attempt to stop the unapproved "parade with musical accompaniment."

At a sunny corner of the woods near the meadow we stopped and sat down on the cool grassy ground, like the apostles at the Sermon on the Mount. Before us in the valley the mines looked dead, while here at the forest's edge three hundred proletarians who still knew nothing of Social Democracy celebrated a Social Democratic May Day.

Everyone was in a good mood and beamed with enthusiasm over the improvised party. After the first refreshments my close friends pressed me to give a speech. They had all heard my speeches in the Peasants' League and they knew I had a facile tongue. Of course I intended to give a speech and struggled with my shyness, the novice's stage fright. But I let myself be guided by my friends and my feelings, and I gave the speech.

At first I stammered and got confused when I saw the many curious people hanging on my every word. But soon the joyous shouts of agreement made me overcome all obstacles. I was amazed at myself, at how fast the new ideas from the article and the leaflet popped, one after another, into my mouth. And they were as new to my audience as to me. I discussed the purpose of our festival; I spoke of how our helplessness and powerlessness had emboldened our enemies, the mine owners, to impose the oppressive measures, the wage cuts, and the work rules, and to curtail our rights. I showed my comrades how impressive our unity was, and how it would help us further if we recognized the misery of our situation and got to know and value the means of improvement. I described how the workers were politically and economically exploited, deprived of their rights, duped, and deceived, and how deliverance from economic and political misery had to come from the working class itself. I described how the workers had to be unified and could not be allowed to fight among themselves for religious or political reasons. There were only two opposing sides that affected the workers very deeply and they were not "here the Catholics, there the non-Catholics"; rather, they were "here capital, there labor"—"here masters, there slaves"! If we wanted to prevent the deterioration of our working conditions and fight for improvements, then we needed an organization that included all of us; and if we wanted to protest against political injustice and strive for healthier political conditions, then we had to vote for the Social Democratic candidate in the upcoming Reichstag election. Only the Social Democratic party dealt fairly with the workers, for it was the only workers' party that the upper classes fought against.

I worked myself up into an ecstasy like the apostle at Pentecost, and I was dazzled by the perspectives of the new world of thought that I had absorbed myself in. My seeds of thought were mixed with a lot of chaff, and they fared about as well as those grain seeds in the Gospels: Some fell among the thorns, some on rocky soil, and some were tread upon. But a respectable portion grew up and bore fruits that richly rewarded the efforts of the young sower.

In the excitement the clothes were almost torn from my body, and everyone was happy that for the first time in human memory all were united and acting in concert. Only a small number of grumblers or religiously fanatic workers remained aloof—some of them directly hostile, some of them uncomprehending. In the short run, most of them were all fired up; but groveling and the force of habit soon reduced them to their old mental slavery.

It was decided at the May Day festival to simply ignore the new work rules and to go to work without the "dog tags"; further, we decided to meet every Saturday evening to discuss our job concerns. I was charged with making the arrangements to join a union organization and with seeing to it that we obtained the *Palatinate Post*. It was more than I could have hoped for. The Social Democrats who had distributed the leaflets gave me the address of a union functionary in Ludwigshafen; at my invitation he appeared on the very next Saturday and was able to sign up 140 people for the Factory Workers' Union. Unfortunately we knew nothing about any organization of mine workers; and the functionary we'd called upon apparently acted according to the proverb: "Charity begins at home." It took nine years before the clay-mine workers found their way to the German Mine Workers' Union. After running a few critical discussions of mining conditions in our village, the Social Democratic press was able to muster over one hundred readers; and at the Reichstag elections that were held six weeks later the Social Democrat Ehrhardt, the jolly "Count Palatine,"* got over half the votes cast.

* The reference is to Franz Josef Ehrhardt, a wallpaperer, who was elected to the Reichstag in 1898.

There was no more talk of the work rules or the wage cuts; the plans of the mine owners were shattered.

The clergy were beside themselves at this unexpected awakening of the mine slaves. It took the priest and his assistant two weeks to get over their amazement. In the third week the priest announced a discussion meeting for the Reichstag voters in which the "most worthy Herr Chaplain" would give a speech on "Social Democracy as an Enemy of Religion." There were a large number of priests at the overflowing meeting, and of course the mine owners and their followers. The priest answered my discreet request to say a word in the discussion by saying that only the local people entitled to vote could ask questions. The sly old fox! I wasn't yet twenty-four years old and so I couldn't vote; but his assistant, who was going to revile Social Democracy, was even younger than I. Most of those attending the meeting were so angered by the way that I was muzzled that they walked out, leaving the most worthy brethren, as well as the mine owners and their relatives and lackeys, to their own devices. So the whole tirade on the part of the overzealous Center party chaplain was rendered superfluous; and all the other attempts to lure the workers into Center party meetings were a failure.

The most worthy gentlemen then tried other means. Up to now the priest had preached on Sunday; but since he wasn't an especially good speaker, he turned the job over to his assistant, who, instead of preaching, gave a pure Center party speech. He even dragged the satirical paper, *The True Jacob* [*Der wahre Jakob*],* up to the pulpit in order to scare the churchgoers away from Social Democracy. Any person who contradicted him he reviled by name from the pulpit. The firebrand servant of God was zealously at work fighting the red dragon in the confession booths, at sick beds, and even in the schools.

Before the impromptu May Day festival the clergy hadn't cared much about the workers' situation. Indeed they'd even openly taken sides with the mine owners; but now they racked

* This was an extremely popular Social Democratic humor magazine that lampooned established institutions.

their brains in their tonsured heads for ways they could help the workers and at least alienate them from Social Democracy. The upright Center party chaplain could not do enough to his opponents with ordinary verbal abuse, so, on the principle of "divide and conquer," he founded a local chapter of the Christian Miners' Trade Union. At first it flourished fairly well because all the pious people and the fawning lackeys joined it. There now began a period of the most savage self-destruction among the workers, while the mine owners steadily forced down the piecework rates. The more active Social Democrats were defamed, reprimanded, and some, who didn't have the necessary willpower, were hounded into submission. Soon the unscrupulous servant of God even succeeded in inciting the wives against their husbands, and the parents against their sons. What did it hurt if the methods of these gentlemen were not particularly Christian? The ends of the Center party and mining capital sanctified any means!

In any event, after a few years the violent fraternal battle calmed down a bit. The Christian splinter group went under almost completely, and there were large breaches on our side too. With the workers' internal squabbles, no improvements in the working conditions could be brought about; rather, conditions got worse and worse until many of the shortsighted workers doubted the purpose and value of union organization. But the clergy couldn't win back one inch of the lost terrain!

FROM MOSES TO PROMETHEUS

"Declaration of religion as a private matter," I'd read in the second part of the "Erfurt Program." If freedom of opinion and the equality of all its members are requirements of every moral community, then it follows that in matters of belief everyone has the right to guide himself solely according to his own convictions and to profess the faith that he considers best. The community therefore must guarantee complete freedom of conscience.

Whoever has left behind the evolutionary stage of religious consciousness must enjoy the same legal protection as the believers. This principle of tolerance must be carried out as strictly as possible. Rule by priests is equally intolerable, whether the priests are atheists or believers. What a citizen believes, or whether he believes anything at all, is his business. The state must refrain from any interference in this private affair; it must neither exercise nor tolerate the oppression of conscience. The social, economic, and political tasks of the community must not be mixed up with things about which the individual himself must decide in his own conscience. To prescribe an official state religion that occupies a dominant position over those with other beliefs and over nonbelievers is an absurdity. Every method of so-called Kulturkampf must therefore be decisively rejected. Behind the mystical wall of the state religion there always lurks the struggle for dominance and possession, the intention of economic oppression.

Right from the beginning I had a bad conscience about the consequences that my joining the Social Democratic movement would necessarily have on my religious convictions. Of course the clergy's one-sided partisanship in favor of the mine owners had already been a blow to the fundamentals of my religion; but I separated the person of the priest from the cause of religion. To my relief I didn't find a single sentence in the Social Democratic program that would have offended my religious feelings. I became convinced that socialist economic theory and the class struggle of the workers could move on a base of complete religious neutrality, and for the time being I was reassured. But soon I found sharp attacks in the Social Democratic press against clerical institutions and even an occasional word of scorn against things that were holy to me. That made me very uneasy.

In any event I wanted to remain true to my religious convictions, even if the ugly, unchristian manner of fighting on the part of the servants of my religion made this difficult. And so I fought through many a bitter battle between my political and my religious convictions; I wanted my politics to fit harmoniously into my religion. Of course the malicious campaign that the clergy conducted against me brought about a gradual chilling of my religious feeling.

My poor old father was even offered money by a priest if he would throw me out of the house; and my bigoted mother made life hell for me. As long as I stayed home she never stopped yelling at me to mend my ways, and when I stepped out into the street, she continued yelling at me from the window, much to the glee of my political enemies; she threatened me with the devil and every earthly and eternal punishment. I thought the same thing that Huss did when he was at the stake and a little old woman dragged up a bundle of wood to burn up the "Godless one": "Oh, you holy innocent!" But when I observed repeatedly how the priest's assistant incited my mother to expose me as the "Antichrist," I felt a repugnance to hear the teachings of the Gospel coming out of such a mouth, and to see God's deputy in the person of the slanderer. But my father refused to do my enemies the favor of breaking with me; in fact, reading my newspaper reawakened the old democratic ideas in him.

While my religious doubts were being awakened by the behavior of the clergy that so damaged religion, the Social Democratic press made me aware of philosophic and scientific questions. I read pamphlets on the relations between Social Democracy and Christianity, church and socialism; and the hunger for knowledge drove me ever further. This kindled in me a passionate desire for clarity on all the questions of religious doubt that tormented me. Some of the priest-baiting writings that fell into my hands did more to strengthen my religious convictions than to shake them. But in the socialist literature catalogues they recommended some purely scientific works, which I eagerly seized upon.

Like those of all pupils from the Catholic grammar schools, my religious convictions were based on the Mosaic story of creation. God's six-day work was for me the point of departure for everything that happened. God created the universe with the earth as its centerpiece. For the earth is inhabited by men, and they are the real purpose of God's creation. The great sun serves solely as the heat and light for the human home. The loving God's intention to create for man an eternal, immortal paradise on earth was thwarted by man's regrettable original sin. As a punishment he drove men out of paradise, revealed to them their nakedness, and sent them disease, suffering, and death. As atonement he imposed on them the curse of having to earn their bread laboriously by the sweat of their brows. In a moment of regret at his creation that had gone awry, he promised man redemption through his only-begotten son, who, four thousand years later, became a man in a stable in Bethlehem. He led a wretched earthly existence of poverty and self-denial and suffered death on the cross for the atonement of our ancestral original sin and for all our sins. And so by his physical death he overcame our death in sin; and he left behind for man his body and his blood as a guarantee of our redemption, an eternal sacrifice for our failings. He gave his apostles the power to absolve or bind, and to Peter he gave the power to tend his lambs and sheep. And this power carried over to every successor of St. Peter, the bishop of Rome. Appointed by God and armed with the insight and wisdom of the Holy Spirit, he is the infallible teacher of mankind and the protector of the faith and the treasury of grace of the church.

Is this doctrine not grand and consistent? It admits no bargains; it makes no concessions. And with all its miracles and legends, which represent a striking proof of its truth and divine origin, it anchors itself firmly in the child's soul. Yes, it roots itself in the heart and bewitches the intellect, which renounces sovereignty over itself and takes refuge under the wings of faith.

And only one thing can be dangerous to this faith, only one thing can shake it: and that is this very intellect that now and then is so vain that it wants to be independent and actually misses applying the measuring stick of criticism to the beautiful faith in miracles. But the intellect will not fall into this trap if it has no contact with the "serpent"; for it's only the serpent that whispers the evil doubts into your ear. So the devilish whisperings of the serpent must be kept away from the worthy intellect.

Unfortunately the trees of knowledge are no longer as isolated as they were in paradise. Oh, no. The serpent lurks seductively everywhere—in the liberal, in the Social Democratic, and even in the so-called nonpartisan newspapers. It lurks on the chairs of the universities and in the laboratories of the scholars; it sits on the huge telescopes of our observatories and on the machines of the factories; it sticks its head out of hundreds of thousands of books and pamphlets. And even if the infallible highest teacher and protector of the old divine truth emphatically declares that the results of human research, these whisperings of the serpent, are pernicious errors; and even if he puts all the "godless" books, journals, and sciences on the Index and forbids the believers to taste the forbidden fruit on penalty of losing eternal salvation— it is still all in vain. With a smile, the serpent calls out to the unflexible dogmatic faith: "And yet it moves!"*

What can they do in an age of tolerance and humanity in which there are unfortunately no more torture chambers or burnings at the stake? Yes, if only they could drag the whole development of human thought since the heretic Copernicus before the forum of the holy Inquisition; if only they could burn up on a huge fire this whole vain science and all its followers . . . ! But, unfortunately, "And yet it moves!" In fact, the foundation of the religion preached to the common people is the six-day work of God, the Mosaic story of creation. For eight, even ten, years the whole religious instruction in the schools revolves around this wise story of creation. It's tied by thousands of threads to every human emotion. And these threads, which are tied up year after year at precisely the most impressionable time of a person's development, these threads do not break easily! Indeed they are the lifework of hundreds of thousands of "God's servants" who have created in the schools, the churches, and the family the most useful looms with which to tie the threads and to knot them all into each other.

---

*Galileo is said to have muttered this phrase under his breath after the Inquisition had forced him to recant his teaching that the earth moves. The Catholic church's attacks on Galileo were frequently denounced in the popular scientific literature of the sort Osterroth was reading.

The only possible way to hold people in this old fantastic children's faith is to keep away from them everything distressing that could destroy their childish faith. Already in school the church instills the little ones with a loathing for "heretics" and tries to keep the children away from them. In adolescence the church catches the young person in a confessional youth club; in adulthood, they have for him Catholic workers' clubs, Catholic trade associations, and Catholic social clubs. The professional defenders of the faith smell danger even in membership in an "interconfessional Christian" union.

The reading of any newspapers and books that breathe the spirit of the new era and represent the results of free research is prohibited for the believers, on the threat of excommunication, the expulsion from the churchly community. A censorship, unmatched by the absolutist pre-March state, protects the believers from the influence of the serpent reason. There is only one science: theology; only one source of knowledge: faith, the "divine revelation" and the writings of the church fathers; only one purpose of existence: eternal salvation.

Whoever wants to free himself from the spell of these ideas can only accomplish it with the most severe inner struggles. Anyone who succeeds without such struggles has religious ideas of only a very superficial nature. For me, liberation from this spell was enormously difficult. I'd already been a Social Democrat for a whole year and I still clung fast to my religious convictions; the socialist literature that I was steeped in could scarcely have torn me away from my convictions. So I experienced in my own mind how serious Social Democracy is in its proposal to make religion a private matter. When I had convinced myself that socialism did not contradict my religious ideas, I passed on from the study of socialist literature to philosophic and scientific works.

The first thing I read in order to master my doubts was *The Essence of Religion* [*Das Wesen der Religion*] by Ludwig Feuerbach.* There I found much that was strange and a lot that fed my

* Feuerbach (1804–72) was a widely read philosophical materialist; *The Essence of Religion* appeared in 1846.

doubts. Feuerbach saw the main task of his work as the conversion of his readers from friends of God to friends of man, from believers to thinkers, from prayers to workers, from candidates for the beyond to students of the here and now, and from Christians who feel themselves half-animal and half-angel to whole human beings. But with me he failed in this goal. The depth of his thought surpassed my power to understand. His philosophy did increase my doubts, but it gave me no certainty, and just as I had before, I prayed with the same fervor to the Holy Spirit to give me a holy bandage for my wounded soul.

I felt I could not go on living like this. Either I had to renounce all independent thinking and take refuge back in the legendary world of the creation story, or else I had to find certainty about the origin of the world, that great inconceivable wonder, and about the purpose of human existence.

Socialism gave me a thorough answer about how we ought to arrange things most conveniently on this earth. But it did not answer the great questions of where we came from and where we're going, of the origin and purpose of the world. The story of creation no longer sufficed for me; I'd had my nose rubbed in too many things that directly contradicted the Mosaic account.

The worst thing was that I was totally isolated. It was impossible for me to discuss such questions with my friends; they weren't tormented by these things. They were cut out to be "happier" and they didn't worry about lofty speculation. Religiously they were completely indifferent; they went to church because it was the custom, and they believed because they had learned to believe. If their fathers and their environment had been Mohammedan, they would have prayed to Allah just as indifferently as they now pray to the Christian God and his heavenly household. My party friends in Ludwigshafen thought well enough of me, but I didn't dare confide in them either. I knew that they were nonbelievers and I didn't want to expose myself as a person who was unclear about such "simple questions."

So I turned completely in on myself and devoured voraciously all possible books, but without finding satisfaction. This was understandable because there was no plan to my study. I was like a superstitious treasure-hunter who first has to dream of the treasure that he seeks. So I let myself be guided by the titles of works and did not find the truths I sought. But what good does it do the hungry youngster to serve him ham and roast when his stomach doesn't yet produce the juices to digest these nourishing morsels? For him they are no substitute for mother's milk. But finally I succeeded in getting the mother's milk that I could manage without teeth, and that I could digest because it contained just the nutrients I needed.

The book was called *Moses or Darwin?* and was written by the well-known Professor A. Dodel.* Written in a very popular style, it compared the Mosaic story of creation with the natural evolutionary history, illuminated the contradictions of the biblical story, and gave a concise description of the evolution of organic and inorganic nature, interwoven with plenty of striking proofs.

What particularly impressed me was a fact that now became clear to me: that evolutionary natural history was monopolized by the institutions of higher learning; that Newton, Laplace, Kant, Darwin, and Haeckel brought enlightenment only to the students of the upper social classes; and that for the common people in the grammar school the old Moses with his six-day creation of the world still was the authoritative world view. For the upper classes there was evolution, for us creation; for them productive liberating knowledge, for us rigid faith; bread for those favored by fate, stones for those who hungered for truth!

Why do the people need science? Why do they need a so-called Weltanschauung? The people must keep Moses, must keep religion; religion is the poor man's philosophy. Where would we end up if every miner and every farmhand had the opportunity to stick his nose into astronomy, geology, biology, and anatomy? Does it serve any purpose for the divine world order of the possessing and privileged classes to tell the worker that the Ptole-

* Arnold Dodel (1843–1908) was a professor of botany at the University of Zurich. *Moses or Darwin?* (1889) was his most popular book.

maic heavens have long since collapsed; that out there in the universe there is an eternal process of creation and destruction; that in the universe at large, as on our tiny earth, everything is in the grip of eternal evolution; that this evolution takes place according to inalterable natural laws that defy even the omnipotence of the old Mosaic Jehovah; that everything that lives in the organic world is related by blood; that there's no difference between matter and spirit; that spirit is simply the result of the movement of matter? Why tell the dumb people that Copernicus and his followers have overturned the old Mosaic creator, and that Darwin and modern science have dug the very ground out from under his feet of clay?

That would be suicide! Yes, the old religion is so convenient for the divine world order of the ruling class! As long as the worker hopes faithfully for the beyond, he won't think of plucking the blooming roses in this world. But once he's acquired the ideal goods of knowledge, then he'll also crave a bigger piece of the pie of material goods, as well as the nectar of every attainable pleasure of life.

The possessing classes of all civilized nations need servants to make possible their godlike existence. So they cannot allow the servant to eat from the tree of knowledge. "For in the day ye eat thereof, then your eyes shall be opened, and ye shall be as gods"—or at least as the earthly gods of the ruling class. So religion must be retained for the people!

The basis of my faith was shattered by the reading of this splendid book. An oppressive weight was lifted from my breast, the scales fell from my eyes, and I became a different person. Yes, Feuerbach turned out to be right: I changed from a candidate for the beyond to a student of this world, from a prayer to a capable worker.

Here on the beautiful earth, which one needs only to turn over in order to harvest the heavenly fruits, I found a full replacement for the lost heaven of the Mosaic cuckoo house in the clouds. I didn't lose my God; he just got other features and characteristics. The dark, vengeful, and punishing God in whose name the priests had dragged millions of poor, struggling people to the torture rack and the stake, now showed me his nicer face. I saw the yearning for God in the spirit of practical human charity, which is spit upon and crucified every day by the high priests and learned theologians, by the rich and the mighty of this world. And yet every day it celebrates its resurrection in the hearts of millions of those with toils and burdens who seek and find redemption in the recognition of their human dignity. It was the year of the Goethe anniversary. Along with the new God I also got to know Faust and Prometheus, the great poet's god-men who embody the deepest yearnings of our race.

A new trinity revealed itself to me: the solidarity of all mankind summarized by the word charity; man's Faustian struggle through error toward truth and self-conscious creative power; and the titanic battle of the human mind with the hidden secrets of nature.

Now I understood that the individual cannot and should not be an end in himself without losing his humanity. No, higher than the brutal ego stands the right of the whole, its right to knowledge and the pleasures of life.

Franz Rehbein,
Farm Worker

Franz Rehbein (1867–1909), from rural Pomerania, was the son of a tailor and a washerwoman. He spent his youth and young manhood hiring himself out for various kinds of farm work throughout northern Germany. In 1895, he lost a hand in a threshing machine accident and was forced to give up farm work. He spent his later years eking out a living as a minor socialist journalist and trade union functionary. This autobiography was written at his own initiative as an extension of his journalistic work and somehow found its way into Paul Göhre's hands. The chapter presented here covers Rehbein's life in the early 1890s as an agricultural day laborer in the Ditmarsch, the lowland along the North Sea north of the Elbe estuary. Rehbein's work takes on added importance because it is the only account (except for childhood memories) of farm labor by an actual rural laborer. To be sure, Rehbein had moved to the city when he wrote his autobiography, and as a Social Democrat from age nineteen, he had never really been a typical rural man. Nonetheless, he provides a uniquely valuable view, not only of the limited options of the landless rural proletariat, but also of the effects of machinery and the industrial work mentality on the German countryside.

IN THE YOKE OF DAY LABOR

I was going to use my time as best I could to put away a little money for my intended marriage; but my days as an unmarried, free, day laborer were cut short. My girlfriend told me confidentially that we would be getting married soon—that in fact we had to. There was no way to put it off. In the fall my "carefree bachelor days" came to an end. But what did it matter? Hadn't the same thing happened to hundreds and thousands of others before me? They had to see to it that they would get by—and get by they did, though at times they had it rough. What did I have my healthy bones for? Why had I learned to work anyway? Couldn't I support a wife and child? And just as well as all the other poor devils who eked out their existence here as day laborers? Neither my girlfriend nor I were pampered; besides, we'd never dreamed that we could be allotted anything but the typical day laborer's fate. We knew nothing of life except work, and we didn't expect anything more. If we could earn enough by our own labor to fill our bellies, then we didn't want any more, because that is all the others had.

That summer we got married. My bride and I had agreed that she would continue to work as long after our marriage as her condition permitted. Meantime I would work around in different places as an "unattached married man," until we could move in together in the fall. There was nothing unusual about this setup; many young people who "had to get married" did the same thing.

We didn't take many pains with the wedding ceremony. I took the day off from work, and my bride got the necessary time off from the farm where she worked. Two day laborers we knew accompanied us to the ceremony—and then we were married. Afterward one of them turned to us in a philosophical mood and remarked: "You know, what's happening to you is the same thing

Translated from Franz Rehbein, *Das Leben eines Landarbeiters* (Darmstadt/ Neuwied: Hermann Leuchterhand Verlag, 1973), 249–67. Originally edited by Paul Göhre (Jena: Eugen Diederichs Verlag, 1911).

that always happens to people like us when we get hitched. To us it means, he has a wife and she has a husband—and the good Lord has a couple of poor people!"

At noon the next day we were both back at work.

After this I worked for several weeks on the construction of a dyke that was being put up to protect some reclaimed land along the coast. Then it was harvest time. Because of the slow ripening of the grain and the large supply of labor, the wages for reaping and binding fell to just over half the usual rate for piecework. As a result my harvest earnings were only so-so; this was all the more unpleasant since I'd counted on making a tidy sum from the harvest so that in the fall we could fix up our little place decently. And then when the harvest was barely half over, I unexpectedly got into a very bitter fight with the farmer my wife worked for—a fight that led to a sudden and violent solution to her poor working conditions.

Up to then my wife had had no cause to complain about bad treatment at this place. She did the work she was supposed to do and didn't get into any trouble. And the farmer and his wife had always recognized this. But recently her condition was, understandably, making certain kinds of work too heavy for her; for instance, she could no longer carry the big full milk cans in from the pasture without help. This gave the farmer's wife an excuse to make all kinds of open and veiled reproaches and nasty remarks. Now the farmer's wife would have been entirely within her rights to pay off my wife what was coming to her and release her from service; there was no way she could serve out the rest of her contract, and they were going to have to get another maid eventually anyway. But instead she scolded and picked on my wife at every opportunity and made life absolutely miserable for her.

Of course, when I heard of this irritating behavior, I had a word with the farmer and told him that if my wife was not treated with the simple human decency owed to her, I'd have to demand her immediate release from service; under no circumstances would I tolerate her being tormented by verbal abuse or overexertion. That was too much for the mighty marshland farmer. Who was I to rebuke him in his own house? He knew how to treat a "sweetheart servant girl" even if she was my wife ten times over. She had to do her duty as was demanded of her, and only then, when it no longer suited him to have her around, could she leave. With all his abusing, he worked himself up into a rage. Of course I was ready with an answer, and before I knew it, we had come to blows. There on the fine, soft ground of the farmyard, we really had it out. The whole thing ended with my wife leaving their service at once and the farmer quite willingly (though with a rather puffed-up face) paying my wife's wages.

On the first of October we finally got our things together. Earlier I had rented a place in the village for sixty marks a year. The cottage belonged to a landless cottager who lived in the front end himself and rented out the little back apartment.

The house was very old and tumbledown; on one side it even had to be propped up so the wind wouldn't suddenly blow it in. Naturally we had only one room, as long as a jail cell and not quite twice as wide, though by far not as high; I could easily reach the ceiling planks without even stretching my arm up completely. Still, it was good enough for us for the time being; most of the other day laborers didn't have anything bigger—and then too, a small place didn't cost so much to heat in the winter. Fuel was very expensive in all of the Ditmarsch because there is no wood or peat there; you have to get them from the upland areas or else burn coal.

Besides the living room, our apartment had a little stone-floored front room with a chimney and some loft space. The cottager also let us use a little garden plot to grow a few vegetables. There was no barn; if you wanted to get a pig or goat from one of the tenant farmers, you had to build your own little shed on the garden plot. For the time being I didn't need a barn anyway, because it cost too much to feed a pig over the winter, and it was still a long time until the next summer.

Of course we young people tried to make our lodgings as livable as possible. Yet it was remarkable—though the little room couldn't hold much, we never seemed to have enough to fill it. We always lacked something that we really needed, and it always looked awfully bare both in the living room and the front room. I just wouldn't have believed everything you had to get to furnish an ordinary day laborer's place. With the buying of all the household furnishings our savings melted away like snow in the sun. Finally I had gotten together the necessary furniture—both new and used—as well as kitchen utensils and work equipment. A few hundred pounds of potatoes were stored, carefully covered with straw, under our somewhat decaying bedstead; and there was a stockpile of fuel that looked like enough to keep the place comfortably warm at least until Christmas.

In the meantime the stork arrived. It was a robust baby boy that my wife now rocked on her lap, and I mean actually on her lap, because we didn't have a cradle. We usually put the little fellow into a laundry basket propped up on two chairs.

Soon the winter came, bitter and hard.

Previously the walls of the house had been just wet, but now the windy sides were covered with glistening ice; and when the northwest wind howled, the cotton curtains on the windows blew all over the place. What was worse, on one of the windy sides some of the stones in the wall had worked loose so that an icy draft cut through the room. And to top it all off, the wind ripped a big hole in the already damaged roof, and in no time the floor was covered with blowing snow. So I had to spend the Christmas season fixing up the old place as best I could. The cottager helped to rethatch the roof; and I stopped up the holes and cracks in the wall with anything I could get my hands on— rags, rope, straw—anything to keep the bitter cold out. Even so, we could barely get the room warm. Usually we huddled up close to the little iron stove; so we always felt like one side of our body was sweating, while the other had icicles growing on it. My wife had her hands full just protecting our baby from the cold.

To make matters worse, the winter unemployment was spreading. For the first time I learned what it meant to have to struggle along as a "free" and married day laborer in the "blessed marsh."

None of the farmers had anything for us day laborers to do. There was nothing happening on the farms. The final threshing of the grain was done by machine, and there was no chaff to separate either. The rest of the work was taken care of by a couple of farmhands or young boys. So there we day laborers sat and stared out the window. Gradually I was overcome by a feeling of uneasy depression that got worse every day, the longer I had to sit around. You can stand staying at home for a few days, at most a few weeks, then you start seeking out others to chat or play cards with, and hope that better times will come soon. If you're used to regular work, and the unemployment goes on and on, it gets damned uncomfortable just stuck between four walls. Damn! What a feeling to be young and strong and sitting around at home without any work while you want so much to work! You feel really ashamed just to be seen on the street.

It's as though every shrub and dung heap grins at you with malicious pleasure. All the while, the few groschen you've saved up are fast disappearing; you can already count off on your fingers when you're going to have to touch the last taler; and then what? Oh, how beautiful and heavy every taler looks when you've earned it, and how light it becomes when you have to spend it!

With pent-up rage you see the prosperous farmers driving to their visits and amusements, unconcerned about the increasing misery of the day laborers. There's so much fat on their steaming horses that you can't count any of the ribs on their bodies, and all the while you're tightening your belt from one day to the next. It's strange the kind of thoughts that you have then. There you sit, a poor wretch who would gladly work; but the people for whom you've worked yourself to death for low wages in the summer are now shrugging their broad shoulders indifferently— how can they help it that they don't need any workers?

Many day laborers began to go into debt; they got credit with the village merchants or else they received a little cash advance from farmers they knew, which they intended to work off in the summer. The same thing happened to most of them every winter; and many, especially those with large families, had to exhaust themselves the entire summer just to pay off the debts of the previous winter. Then when the next winter came, they were broke once again, and the whole business began anew. Those who couldn't get any more credit had no choice but to turn to the parish relief fund. In fact it wasn't at all uncommon for the day laborers' children to be sent from farm to farm with a begging basket.

By this time, the situation caused by the unemployment had become unbearable to me. Should I too go into debt? No, better that I leave my wife and child for a while and see if I could get work elsewhere. So, with a few other day laborers I made the eight-hour trek to the Kiel Canal,* which was under construction at that time, and there I got a job as an excavator. I stayed there until the spring, when there was once again farm work in the marshlands. But in early summer there was another stretch of unemployment, so I preferred working in a brickyard until the harvest. There I worked as a finisher for twenty marks a week. The hours were from four in the morning to eight in the evening with a break of two hours—in other words, a fourteen-hour day. I went home only on Sundays. During the week I ate in the firm's canteen with the brickworkers from Lippe who worked there. I should say that I ate, God willing: it was peas, always nothing but peas! Even today I get a sick feeling in my stomach when I think back on it.

A few weeks earlier, Peiter Pink, the farmer I had worked for before, had agreed to take me on for the harvest. My wife worked faithfully alongside me. Up to then I'd never wanted her to work with me because it hurt me to yoke her up too; in my opinion the man alone should be able to earn enough to support the family, especially with a small family like ours. But my wife said there was no way of knowing what it was going to be like next winter, and she insisted on working with me at harvesting. We took our little boy with us to the fields in an old, used baby buggy and left him behind a haystack where he could sleep, or play, or cry as much as he wanted. Sometime he'd have to get used to the fact that he was just a day laborer's child.

*The Kiel (or Kaiser Wilhelm) Canal was constructed between 1887 and 1895; it connected the North Sea with the Baltic Sea.

Soon the sickles were heard in the wheat fields and the stalks fell. My brother-in-law and I worked together at the reaping, while my wife sheaved behind us both. As far as the eye could see, it was the same picture: Wheat field upon wheat field; men, women, and children hard at work—the men in shirts and trousers, the women with their skirts tucked up and their sun hats pressed down on the backs of their necks. All hands were hard at work because the harvest earnings were the main source of income for the whole year. If the varieties of wheat ripen in quick succession, the reapers' wages reach an acceptable level of twenty to twenty-five marks for each Ditmarsch morgen.* The binders' wages are half as much, because one binder can bind and stack as much as two reapers can cut. Since a reaper can do an average of two to two and a half morgens per week, and a binder about twice as much, a husband and wife can sometimes actually make a few hundred marks at harvest time—though under the pressure of piecework. If the wheat varieties ripen slowly, one after the other, so that there is a lot of slack time, the reapers' wages are only sixteen, fourteen, or even twelve marks per morgen, and the binders' half as much. Then, despite the greatest possible effort, it's not possible to save up even a few extra groschen, and many day laborers' families look forward to the winter with even greater anxiety. So the harvest time always seems too short; it's scarcely begun when it's already over. But as long as the harvest lasts, the day laborer has only one principle: Work, work hard, work yourself to death. Here it's literally true: Piecework is murderous work! You push yourself so hard that you wish the day was forty-eight hours long instead of twenty-four.

I left the house by 3:00 A.M., and after a half-hour walk, I was in the fields. At about six o'clock we ate the first breakfast, which my wife had in the meantime brought from home. We supplied our own food, as did most of the day laborers who took their families to work. This way you get a few more marks per morgen, and since the family has to cook anyway, it's better for a married man to get cash rather than food from the farmer.

* The size of a morgen varied from about 0.6 to 0.9 acre, depending on local custom.

When the weather is good, the work goes fairly well. Of course up to eight or nine o'clock the reapers are almost always soaked with dew from the knee down; after that things go more smoothly. But the binder has it much worse because the dew soaks his clothes all over the front of his body as he ties up the sheaves. His hands suffer the most; the dew makes them tender and sensitive so they look like a washerwoman's hands that have been in a tub of water all day long. His fingernails work loose painfully and the fingertips get raw. Frequently he injures his hands on the sharp stubble or slices a finger on a flat pressed stalk. As soon as the dew dries, the ends of the grain get hard, and the higher the sun climbs the sharper they stab. During the first few days the binder's hands burn so that he can hardly stand it, but after they are filled with prickles and little cuts, they get more and more numb. I often secretly pitied my wife. But what good did it do? If you wanted to earn anything in the country, you couldn't be sensitive; you had to take advantage of the harvest weeks.

The rainy days are among the worst things about the harvest. You come to work, but you don't get anything done no matter how hard you try. As long as there is just a little sprinkle, it's OK; you don't think anything of it. But if there's a heavy shower or thunderstorm that soaks you to the skin, then you have to knock off work. You sit behind the haystacks, your clothes dripping, and wait for it to clear up; but one rainstorm is barely over when another one, if anything more violent, comes along. A horrible discomfort racks your body; you half sweat and half freeze. When the sun finally comes out again, it means back to work with twice the exertion, because, as much as possible, you have to make up for lost time. You hardly allow yourself time out to eat. Your arm swings the sharp sickle even harder than before. You cut swath upon swath, covering everything with your sweat. The women binders tie up sheaf after sheaf with their nimble hands, pausing hardly at all to stand up and take a deeper breath. And how often the sickle has to fall, and how many sheaves must be bound before a single morgen of wheat is stacked up!

Finally, late, late in the evening when your exhausted limbs can do no more, the workday ends. Only after the sun has long set and the fields are shrouded in the misty darkness of evening, do you get off work. Nature finally takes its toll; your body must collect new strength. About an hour before we men stopped work, my wife took the baby buggy and went home in order to have supper ready when I got home at nine or ten o'clock. Of course often I worked through the whole night, catching only one or two hours of sleep in a haystack. Especially when the wheat was heavy, one woman was usually not strong enough to stack up all the wheat that two reapers could cut, so I had to take time in the evening to finish the stacking that had been too much for my wife. And after rainy days, I had to use the night in order to keep in step with my work partner whose wife was sick and couldn't help out.

Bringing the harvest into the barn was done for a daily wage rate, with food provided by the farm. All available wagon and horse teams were pressed into service to bring the rich harvest in. The word went out to all: Give it all you've got! We work like bees; wagon after wagon is loaded and unloaded, and even with a full load the horses trot so that no time is wasted. There is no respite for the horses, and the people don't spare themselves either; but at least the people know how much depends on their hard work and persistence. If the landowner comes out and says, "People, the barometer's fallen, there's rain on the way," then no one even pauses to say a word during the work. In the barns all you can hear is the sound of the pitchforks and the gasping breath of the unloaders and stackers. One wagon is barely unloaded and rolled out when another full one is pushed up to the loft, for out in the fields also the loaders are doing their utmost to clear acre after acre. So it goes, right on into the night. Ah! At night after a day like that (sometimes a day and a half!) you can really feel it in your limbs; you know what you've done. My wife was often so overcome with exhaustion that she fell asleep while she nursed our baby.

After so much hard work it was a great comfort to receive our harvest wages. On the way home on payday, as we filed past the fields of stubble that we had soaked with our own sweat, it gave us a certain satisfaction to press the beautiful hard talers in our pockets.

Right after the harvest weeks I worked with a threshing machine crew. [. . .]

[In the Ditmarsch] not every farm has its own threshing machine as they do on the large estates; nor are there any cooperatively owned machines as elsewhere. The owners of a threshing machine are independent businessmen who purchase their own machine either for cash or on installment payments. They hire the necessary crew and travel from farm to farm to work for the various farmers with whom they've contracted. [. . .]

The threshing machine work itself is among the most exhausting and grinding imaginable. You have to slave away, hour after hour. The more hours in the day, the sooner the farmer can be rid of the machine, and the fewer the meals he has to provide for the crew. The more hours the machine master can rack up, the more grain he can thresh, and the higher his profit. And the more hours that the crew works, the higher their weekly earnings. Work begins at the latest at 4:00 A.M. and often as early as 3:00 A.M.; and then you run the whole livelong day without a rest until at least eight o'clock, and frequently to nine, ten, or even eleven or twelve o'clock at night. The breaks last no longer than it takes to eat your food; including the pauses to lubricate the machine, there is no more than an hour off during the whole day. Even supper is no occasion for a break, because that is eaten only at the end of the workday, no matter how late it gets.

The work goes as fast as the "sweat box" can swallow the grain. Man has to keep pace with the machine; he becomes its slave, himself a part of the machine. Picture to yourself the uninterrupted howling and rumbling of the thresher and the almost impenetrable dust that envelops it, and you can imagine what this sort of machine threshing means for the worker. Dust, almost a centimeter thick, sticks to the crew, especially if the grain has been rained upon; often the crew's eyes are swollen and burning so that they can barely see out of them. Likewise, your nose is completely stopped up from breathing in huge amounts of dust; and whole globs of black slime come out of your throat when you spit. Your skin is covered with sweat from the heavy work, and the dust sticks fast, causing an unpleasant itching and burning; it's as though your whole body were covered with ants.

If you've put in fifteen, sixteen, or eighteen hours under these conditions, you're dead tired in the true sense of the word. You're so tired you can hardly get your supper down; you'd most like just to stretch out and go to sleep at once. But you can sleep right after you get off work only if the machine is going to stay at one farm for several days. Frequently you have to travel from one farm to another late in the evening or even in the middle of the night. Sometimes you go to a village hours away, and, as luck would have it, in the pouring rain. What's more, if the machine gets stuck in the wet and muddy marsh lanes, then you can't even think of a rest. The engine and threshing casing have to be raised with levers, and the whole crew has to put their shoulders to the wheels or pull on ropes and chains in order to help the horses. When you finally get there, the machine is put in shape by lantern light, and only then can everyone try to find a place to get a couple hours of rest.

Since there aren't enough beds on one farm for so many people, only the machine master, the fireman, and the two packers get beds. The rest of the crew has to crawl into the straw, the hay, or the chaff, whatever they can find. Imagine what it felt like for us poor devils with soaking-wet clothes to have to camp out in straw on chilly fall nights. You can hear your teeth chattering in your mouth before you get settled in and halfway warm; and then just when you're having your best sleep, the steam whistle sounds, calling you back to work. So that we won't sleep the night away, the water carrier has the night watch, and he also sees to it that the engine is fired up in time. Once the crew has managed to crawl out of their straw beds, they rub their half-closed eyes with their sleeves and then go right to the threshing. Nobody thinks of washing or combing up; it would be pointless because in a few minutes you'd be just as you were before; at most you would just irritate your eyes even more because the dust settles thickly on moist eyelids and starts to burn.

The machine master's first task in the morning is to give all his men a shot of schnapps. Because of the short night's rest, a little bad liquor has to revive your flagging energy. And really, the booze does wonders. Once everyone has downed a bit of schnapps on an empty stomach, the sluggish life-spirits renew noticeably; and with the rumbling of the thresher, everyone does his work completely mechanically, just as on the day before: The throwers toss the sheaves up to the machine; the swath cutters cut the cords around the sheaves; the packers guide the loose sheaves into the drum; the binders tie up the threshed straw into bundles; the porters drag, like automatons, sack after sack to the ground; the "chaff major" wends his way through the tumult with a full tarpaulin; and the bundles pile up in regular rows. Finally the dawn comes, the gloomy oil lanterns are extinguished, and a whistle calls the crew to breakfast. The first two hours of the new day are behind you.

After twenty minutes everyone is back at his post, and the work goes continuously, with at most one short pause for lubrication, until noon. Then we quickly wolf down lunch; we've barely swallowed the last bite when the back-to-work whistle sounds. You don't even have time to wash your spoon; you can only lick it off, or, if you really have to, wipe it on the corner of your dusty smock. At four o'clock there is a snack break, and as for quitting time, well, only the machine master knows when that will be.

So it goes day after day. Since they usually work on Sunday too, it can happen that you put in three weeks at a stretch in the dust and filth without once washing properly or sleeping in a bed. Even if you once risk sticking your head into a pail of water, you usually have to dry off on your own smock or an old grain sack, because the farmers don't give out any towels; they think that's too good for the crew. Eventually you find yourself in such a state that the lowest gypsy looks like a nobleman in comparison.

As long as you're at places with good food, you can stand it, and it's easier to stay ahead of your exhaustion. But after several farms in a row with bad food, even the most patient workers get sullen. Many farmers give the crew the worst possible food so that they can get rid of the machine quickly. They reckon that where there is bad food the crews will work as fast as they can in order to get away from there fast. So it can happen that every noon for a whole week or at least five days, you get the notorious dumplings with gravy. When you consider that breakfast and supper are always the same anyway—milk and bread or beer and bread—then it's understandable how this miserable slop finally makes your whole body feel sick. After so many meals of slop we considered it a real blessing when we came to a farm where there was something else on the lunch table.

I already mentioned the schnapps that every threshing-machine worker drinks on an empty stomach first thing in the morning. But this isn't the only time. Rather, schnapps is given out at regular two-hour intervals, except during the three meals. It is, so to speak, the life elixir of the machine personnel.

It would be very easy for thoughtless observers to turn up their noses in disgust at this practice; but that would be totally wrong. No one who really tries to imagine himself in the dog's life of the threshing-machine worker can condemn his use of alcohol. The expression "dog's life" doesn't even come close to describing his existence, because even the most badly treated dog has it better. Think of the unspeakably long working hours, the lack of rest and the intensity of the work itself, the cloud of dust and dirt, the miserable straw beds at night, the all-too-often perfectly wretched food, and the fact that sometimes you are so tired due to the endless overexertion that you can barely keep on your feet—think of all this, and then it's understandable that most of the workers regard the schnapps as an indispensable means of reviving their flagging spirits and breathing fresh energy into their exhausted bodies. If afterward the exhaustion is even greater, then another shot of liquor can help.

Besides, what else were we supposed to drink? Granted, for

the usual thirst, the landlords handed out flat thin beer or buttermilk. As long as the buttermilk is halfway fresh, it agrees well with your stomach. But if it's old and sour, or even bubbly like pig swill, then you can feel the effects right away when the seat of your pants billows out violently like a balloon. Then there are continuous explosions of such vehemence that you can successfully compete with a flatulent old horse. You also get an evil slimy aftertaste in the mouth that not even chewing tobacco can get rid of. Then you really long for a drink that can clear out your throat from time to time; and unfortunately, the only thing available for this is schnapps.

Now it certainly would be better if at least in the morning when they got up, the crew got hot coffee instead of schnapps. This could easily be done since the water carrier (who doubled as night watchman) could put on a pot of coffee without even troubling the farmer's wife. Coffee at the afternoon break would also limit the desire for schnapps. But, as the well-known rhyme by Fritz Reuter has it: "Roast beef and plums make a nice meal, it's just that you don't get it."* It's just too much trouble for the landowners to make any little extra effort "for the people." For God's sake, "these people" must not be pampered.

The only pleasant changes during the threshing campaign are the paydays. These come irregularly, following the work schedule, sometimes weekly, sometimes every two weeks, or even every three weeks. Everyone is always curious about the number of hours put in. If you've reached 100 hours, then you speak with satisfaction of a good week; an 80–100 hour week is considered average; less than 80 hours is bad. I personally have worked on three threshing campaigns, and I remember well, as if it happened yesterday, what a feeling of satisfaction we had when the machine master proudly told us one payday that in the previous week we had worked 124 hours. That was certainly a record; almost 18 hours a day, seven days a week! Actually it was a good

---

*Fritz Reuter (1810–74) was a popular novelist and poet who wrote in Low German.

deal more than 18 hours, because as mentioned, you don't get paid for moving between farms or for setting up or dismantling the machinery—not to speak of the hours that the machine master customarily cheated us out of.

Certainly the result was a relatively good weekly wage that we brought home; but, in any case, it was best not to think about how hideously tortured you had been.

A City Man on
a Farm

In his massive study of agricultural labor in eastern Germany, Max
Weber wrote of the difficulty of keeping young people on the estates
in Mecklenburg (and elsewhere). With so many children off to the city,
the estate owners were forced to rely for their hardest work on contract
laborers from outside—"down-and-out artisans" or "dubious characters displaced from Berlin." One such character we meet here. Identified only as "Otto," he is an unemployed (though surely not "dubious")
Berlin factory worker, who has served twelve days in jail for being
"work-shy." Upon his release, he finds himself in the hands of Herr
Puhlmann, an unscrupulous agent who signs him up for a year of "easy
work" on an estate near Neustrelitz, about sixty miles north of Berlin.
As Otto quickly learns, life as a "foreign" (i.e., from Berlin!) contract
laborer in the early 1890s is one long humiliation and drudgery. This
is, to be sure, a city man's view of the country, but it is notable that
Otto's perceptions are similar to those of Franz Rehbein, a rural man.
What is perhaps most striking here is the mixture of ignorance and
fear so deeply embedded in the petty hierarchies of rural life. It is no
wonder that Social Democrats were so often frustrated in rural areas.
Otto believed that the workhouse would have been preferable, and his

experiences invite comparison with Ernst Schuchardt's account of life in the workhouse.

Otto is a *Hofgänger,* a word for which there is no equivalent in English. I have translated it as "contract laborer" to distinguish it from "day laborer" (*Tagelöhner*). The importance of this distinction is evident in what follows.

This short account (the majority of which appears here) was published by the Social Democratic Vorwärts Verlag in 1896 and contained a preface by August Bebel. It's unclear what prompted Otto to write or how he came in contact with the publisher.

WINTER TRAVEL

Three other men, who were bound for the same place, got off the train with me. When we asked at the station how to get to the estate, no one could tell us anything. Only a rural postman would know, and from him we learned that we still had another 6 hours to go. A 5- to 6-hour walk in this cold and snow! In many places the snow had blown in meter-deep drifts, over which there were no more than footpaths, which you had to follow with the greatest care. Despite all our caution, we often missed the path and went in over our knees in snow. Of the four of us only one had socks, and even those were full of holes. The rest of us just had cloths wrapped around our feet. Our shoes were split open in the sides or toes. Snow came through these openings, first thawing and then freezing in little balls. And then our hunger! I can't even describe how we suffered on that day! We cried! I got frostbite on my feet on this march. If we'd only had some money, we could have gone in somewhere to get warm. A constable, who followed us, kept us from begging. We would have done it. Finally, after a 5½-hour hike, we reached our destination.

Translated from *Hofgängerleben in Mecklenburg. Selbsterlebtes und Selbsterschautes von einem Berliner Arbeitslosen,* with preface by A. Bebel (Berlin: Vorwärts Verlag, 1896), 13–31, 33–35.

AT THE ESTATE: THE SERVANTS' QUARTERS

The estate was deserted. There wasn't a person to be seen anywhere. We went up to the house, assuming that people might be
living there. A maid met us and we asked her for the overseer.
She answered us in Low German, which we didn't understand.
Finally she put down her pots and led us to the overseer. We
couldn't help but wince at the gruff "Come in!" that answered
our knock. We opened the door and found the overseer sitting at
a desk, smoking a pipe. We greeted him, but instead of returning our greeting, he asked at once, "Well, you must be from
Puhlmann?!" He said it with a voice that sounded as if he could
never be friendly. But I heard later that he could talk in a very
friendly way with the Mecklenburg day laborers and contract
laborers. Dealing with slaves had made plantation owners in
South America hard and unfeeling, and many overseers were the
same way in their relations with contract laborers from other
regions of Germany. In general, contract laborers who are outsiders are treated as barely human. The idea in Mecklenburg is that
outsiders who come to Mecklenburg as contract laborers aren't
good for anything else.

We said "yes" to the overseer's question and handed him our
letters. When he'd read our letters, he asked the first one of us,
"What are you?" "Mason!" was the reply. "Well, you must be an
apprentice?!" The mason, who must have been about twenty-two
years old, didn't answer him at all. And so it went with the rest
of us. "Go into the servants' room." We went, but we couldn't
find it and instead wandered from one room to another until we
ran into the housekeeper, just as we were about to go into her
room. She exploded. We couldn't understand what she said, but
we could tell that she was cursing. When she'd finally calmed
down, she led us to the servants' room.

This servants' room, in which the farmhands and maids spent
evenings and Sundays, was wretched. It was filthy, smoke-
blackened with broken windows, and it made a very unpleasant

impression. There was a rickety table that must have been as old as the estate itself, two benches in similar shape, and along the walls there were cupboards where the servants kept their bread and lard. Then, for every farmhand there was a pair of oiled boots, which filled the whole room with the smell of boot oil. That's what it's like inside a servants' room, and it's like that on almost all estates. We sat down on one of the benches and waited to see what would happen. We were keeling over with hunger. After a long time one of the maidservants brought coffee and two slices of bread smeared with lard for each of us. Even though the estates have so many cows, the servants get butter only on the rarest occasions—only on holidays. And the lard is from America, so it's not too expensive. The "distress" of the great landowners just doesn't permit them to feed their servants decently.

RAFFLING OFF THE CONTRACT LABORERS

The farmhands returned from work shortly after five o'clock, their quitting time. First they looked us over and asked this and that, but we could see that they were looking down on us. Soon after they entered, they got their supper, which consisted of leftovers from their midday meal, since they cook only once a day on the estate. They do get meat at noon but not in the evening. The day laborers got off work later, and at that time the overseer came in with three of them who were to draw lots for us. Each drew a piece of straw, and it had been decided in advance who would go with the one who drew the longest piece. As soon as each of us had his "lord," we had to follow him home.* This was agreeable to us because we were still freezing, in spite of the fact that the servants' room was heated.

* It's unclear how four contract laborers were raffled off to only three day laborers.

THE DAY LABORER'S LIFE

And so we followed our day laborers, under whom we were to
serve, to the village. The whole village consisted of about twelve
houses, in each of which lived three or four families. Each family
usually had a main room, small bedroom, kitchen, and cellar, or
where there was no cellar, another small bedroom. There was also
an attached animal stall. The main room we entered was very
simple but fairly clean, which isn't always the case. On the rectangular table there was a little kitchen lamp of the kind used by
most of the families. At the table sat two children and an old
man, the husband's father-in-law; he was part of the "old folks
crew" and still had to work, despite his great frailty. The wife
came in just as we entered. I wished them all a good evening and
received a friendly reply from each of them. After a while the
wife got out the food and gave everyone a spoon. There were no
plates. Everyone took his spoon and reached into the bowl that
was sitting in the middle of the table. Of course I did the same.
I couldn't recall ever having eaten anything like this. Later I
learned the name of the dish; it was called "vegetable stew" in
Low German. Well, this stew was quite something: some so-
called fodder beans, some peas, whole or half carrots and parsley
roots, celery, leeks, and a whole lot of potatoes. In Berlin I'd
often heard that you were supposed to have big pieces of bacon
or ham in the country, but no matter how I strained my eyes I
couldn't see any. The next day I learned that there was never any
meat in the evening, and in many places only a little at noon.
After we'd eaten, we all began to peel potatoes together. It's the
custom for the whole family except the wife to peel potatoes in
the winter—starting 24 October or even earlier, until the beginning of May. The ice on my feet had thawed by now and they
were beginning to freeze horribly. I had no other socks and wasn't
given any. Finally the work was done and it was time to go to
sleep.

And so it goes the whole winter—as soon as the potatoes are
peeled you go to bed. Usually it's about seven o'clock, but some-

times earlier. These people have no amusements. Only a few of the day laborers get newspapers, and not one of them owns any books. Of course, with their wretched pay, the contract laborers can't subscribe to a paper, and even if several wanted to go in together, they still couldn't subscribe because they don't have any money. During the first part of his contract—at least for the first quarter—the contract laborer gets no money at all. The only literary entertainment you have—if you don't prefer to ignore it altogether—is the *Mecklenburg Sunday Paper* [*Mecklenburgischer Sonntagsblatt*] and books that the pastor loans out for twenty pfennigs between 24 October and Easter! The books are perhaps fine for children, but for someone who doesn't find pious children's stories exciting they aren't much.

Before going to bed I was given a fresh shirt because many contract laborers bring vermin with them; otherwise we certainly wouldn't get one. Despite the fact that it was probably the husband's oldest and worst shirt, I had to pay dearly for it at my departure. Then they showed me the room where my bed was. This room was very damp; in fact, some clothing that I once had hanging there for a long time got so thoroughly mildewed that it split completely in two when I put it on. The bed was very thin. Nonetheless, after the exertions I'd been through, I slept very well. The next day was a Sunday so I had a day of rest before starting work.

It was already pretty light when I awoke on Monday morning.* I got dressed quickly because it was pretty cold. When I came into the main room, an odd sight met my eyes. The whole room was filled with sticks; and in the midst of them sat the day laborer and his father-in-law making stick brooms. I wished them good morning and went into the kitchen to wash. There I met the wife who gave me everything I needed for washing, except soap. When I asked for soap, the woman looked at me in astonishment and said, "Soap? We don't have any for ourselves, if you want some, you'll have to buy it for yourself." It was only

---

*Given what follows, Otto must mean *Sunday* morning.

after a few moments that I got the drift of what she was saying, and then I had to laugh. In the meantime the woman had nothing better to do than tell her husband and the neighbors how I had demanded soap. "That's a real fine one who asks for soap when he hasn't done anything yet." By that she meant that I hadn't done any work yet.

When I was done washing, I went into the main room, where everybody looked at me. Somewhat self-consciously, I sat down at the table where the coffee was waiting; there was also a plate with fresh cow's butter and a few pieces of bread. There are certain times when the day laborers have butter, but it's only when there's a lot of extra. There's very rarely butter in the summertime because the reapers buy it up. Unless you're used to it, you can't tolerate too much of this bread, because the grain hasn't been cleaned and has all sorts of things in it which to my mind don't belong in bread. There are little stones, vetches, peas, chaff, and straw. This bread is called "coarse bread." However, at the three festivals there is "fine bread." When I was done drinking my coffee, the wife asked me to get water from the fountain. I got up willingly and followed her into the kitchen, where she gave me a carrying frame, called a "yoke," and hung two buckets on it. The fountain was at the other end of the village, and I had to pass by almost all of the houses. When I went by, people ran to the window and looked at me with curiosity. This staring was very distressing to me. They weren't in the least embarrassed to display their curiosity. I had to run this gauntlet four or five times. Incidentally, fetching water is exclusively the contract laborer's job. Every day he has to go four or five times—morning, noon, and evening. It takes about ten minutes to fetch a load. So you can see how much time is spent just on this. But there was even more in store. As soon as I was done fetching water, I was given other work. First I had to get a whole kettle full of potatoes out of the cellar for pig food; then, once again I went down to the cellar to fetch beet roots and stomp them into little pieces.

Now I thought I was done but found myself profoundly de-

ceived, for I'd scarcely walked into the main room in order to sit
down, when my housemaster told me to help him bind brooms.
I replied that I didn't know how. "You'll learn soon! Come here!"
So I bound brooms. After a while I asked what all the brooms
were for. "They go to the estate!" And I learned further, to my
greatest astonishment, that every day laborer was obligated to
deliver sixteen brooms, for all of which he received the grand
sum of fifty pfennigs as compensation. My astonishment was
even greater when I heard of the further duties imposed on the
day laborer. I'll put these at the end in the sample contract,
which, though not applicable to the estate I'm talking about
now, does give a general picture of rural conditions in Mecklenburg; with a few alterations this contract is generally valid.*

I soon got pretty skillful at broom binding, so that my day
laborer even praised me; this was all the more extraordinary since
the Mecklenburg day laborers seldom utter a word of praise to
"foreign" contract laborers, whom they call "Prussian." When we
were finally done, there was breakfast: a bowl of scrambled eggs.
Of course they weren't the kind of scrambled eggs we're used to
eating; they had flour in them so that not so much egg would be
used. Of course the unused eggs had to be sold! Along with the
eggs there was a little piece of bread smeared with lard. For the
rest of the morning there were a variety of little jobs to do—
cleaning the dung out of the pigstys, etc. For lunch we had the
Mecklenburg national dish: plain potatoes and bacon. Here's the
recipe: "Boil peeled potatoes until done, drain and serve." It's
served with bacon. They showed me my bacon, which was put
out separately. I couldn't complain about the size of the portion.
After lunch I had nothing more to do, and so I asked for something to read. "We have only the Bible and a calendar." I took
the calendar; it was filled with the silliest nonsense, but my

---

*The contract (omitted in this selection) obliges the day laborer, his whole
family, and any contract laborers who may serve under him to be "faithful,
industrious, and obedient." It also specifies the day laborer's duties and privileges, as well as the payments he receives in both money and kind. There are
no restrictions on hours or working conditions.

people just couldn't praise enough one of the stories in there. The previous contract laborer had read it aloud to them, and they wanted me to also. When I was done reading, they burst out in astonishment: "You can read better than we can say the Lord's Prayer. Not a one of us can read like that." I said nothing, quietly absorbing this extraordinary praise. I was about to continue reading when almost all the "foreign" contract laborers on the estate arrived to visit me.

HOW THE CONTRACT LABORERS
ARE TREATED

We exchanged greetings, and I answered as best I could the question each had on his mind. All the contract laborers were from Puhlmann—freed convicts, that is. And yet there wasn't a one of them whom you could label an ex-convict in the usual sense of the word. It was the bad times that had put them out of work and impoverished them. They were either men who had begged in order to satisfy their gnawing hunger and had gotten caught at it, or else they had been kicked out of the "Palme."* Masons, painters, glaziers, and almost all kinds of craftsmen were represented, for on the estate there were twenty-one such contract laborers from outside Mecklenburg. There were perhaps six natives, almost all girls. Eighteen of the twenty-one men came to see me. After the greetings were over, they all casually sat down wherever they pleased. The Mecklenburgers are used to this; they do the same thing. The day laborer and his wife sat among us and listened with open mouths as we talked of Berlin.

All the contract laborers were undaunted and hoped later to be able to work at their crafts again. And yet how many of them had deceived themselves. In the time I was there over half of

* The "Palme" was the shelter for the homeless in Berlin. As Otto had discovered, a homeless, unemployed man could stay there only five days before being turned over to the police.

them decamped; some, who wouldn't put up with anything, were driven away. Only one of them remained for his full year. The reason people left was that most contract laborers weren't even treated as human beings but rather as work animals. They're easy to replace; Puhlmann can deliver enough, at least in the winter. Also, there are many unscrupulous people, who, for a quarter or half year, treat the contract laborer so badly that it's simply impossible for him to stand it any longer. Only a very determined laborer responds in kind to the brutality, and it's not long before he's driven away. He has at least rescued a part of his wages, even though they take almost everything. They deduct the travel money, insurance coupons, and compensation for all the things ever loaned to the contract laborer—they take out almost as much as if he'd gotten everything new. The day laborer tries to squeeze as much as he can from his contract laborer. If a contract laborer decamps, the day laborer gets all the hard-earned money due to the contract laborer. It's always the very worst for the contract laborers who work for people who have ingratiated themselves with the overseer or owner. Many of them told me that on Sundays they got no breakfast or lunch at all. Many wept as they complained of their troubles to me. Almost all the ones who decamped were forced to take another contract-labor position; and they often fell into even worse hands, or right into the power of the police. Of course they were then punished for being work-shy, and if they had a previous conviction, it was very possible that they went to the workhouse. Some of those I know claimed it would actually be better to go to the workhouse than be a contract laborer. It's just that then you'd be a convict and have no freedom. Well, when it comes to freedom, the contract laborer doesn't have very much of that anyway. First he has to work on or for the estate, and then when he comes home to the day laborer, there are so many things to do that he's glad to go to bed when he's done them. Only some of the winter months are an exception. But then you just have to go to bed earlier. Where are you supposed to go? It's cold outside and you can't stay up in the main room, so you have to go to bed! Only on these Sundays did we stay together until ten o'clock. We would have liked to stay up longer if the people hadn't complained so much that it cost "too much oil."

THE CONTRACT LABORER'S WORK

The next morning I was supposed to begin work with them for the first time. But my comrades had already told me so much about the "easy work" that Puhlmann had promised that I dreaded the next day. That night in my room I slept somewhat worse. I was freezing terribly and it took a long time before I got warm in my bed. When I woke up the next morning at about five o'clock, I already heard my day laborer outside stirring about, feeding the pigs, and doing other jobs. The wife had gone milking. Whether it's Sunday or a workday, they get no rest in bed. In the summer you get out of bed long before four o'clock.

It wasn't long before the head of the house called to me, "Otto, you have to get up, it's time!" I stood up, got dressed quickly, and washed; this time I didn't ask about soap. My people had already drunk their coffee when I came. While I was drinking, my day laborer said to me, "You have to clean up the dung." This was the very job that yesterday the contract laborers had described as being one of the worst; and here it was the first thing I had to try my luck on. He got me a fork and a rake, as well as a handbarrow (called a "bier") that we were supposed to carry the dung out with. You don't start work until seven o'clock, so I had plenty of time before that to fetch a few pails of water. A day laborer's wife rarely fetches water. That is the contract laborer's work.

Finally the estate clock sounded the signal to come and now we set off to work. One of the contract laborers with whom I was to work started to laugh when he saw me. "Child, doesn't your old man have any knee boots he can lend you? You can't do anything in those shoes!" I looked at him. He had on blue linen trousers tucked into a pair of huge knee boots. We didn't have much time to talk because everyone was already off to the estate, and we had to hurry if we didn't want to get there late. When we came to the cow barn, I saw a peculiar sight. In each of fourteen stone and cement cribs there stood two rows of cows, with fifteen cows in every row. In all there were over two hundred cows and about forty to fifty calves.* Six of us had to clean out the dung for all of these cows, and to top it off, we were supposed to do it before noon. The ones who don't finish have to come back in the afternoon, and can go home only when they're done; but then they don't get paid. The contract laborer gets twenty pfennigs from the day laborer, but the amount paid by the estate to the day laborer is deducted. The contract laborer is completely powerless in the face of this. If you have a weak build, you have all you can do to clean half the barn by noon. If, instead of the contract laborers, the day laborers come to clean the barn, there are just as many working and they work just as long; but the contract laborer's wages just don't compare to the day laborer's. Generally the dung is cleaned out every day but Sunday. Then on Monday two extra contract laborers come for the work. But even so, the work is hated even more than usual on Monday. If you're not familiar with a cow barn like this you don't understand what this work means. Even the Mecklenburgers shy away from it. As I said, it's the worst after a day off. Just as soon as we started my shoes were full of dung water; and worse still, my hands, face, and clothes were totally splattered. The Mecklenburgers put on their oldest clothes for this work. But us? We had to work in the clothes we wore every day. Often you slipped or dropped the barrow because it was heavy, and then you stumbled over it. The cow dung was hard to handle, and the barrow was often so heavy that you could scarcely lift it.

Some time later I got a rupture doing this work; not only did I get no compensation at all, my day laborer actually wanted to dock me for the time I was confined to the house. Of course I

---

* Either an arithmetic error or a poor description.

didn't stand for that but insisted on my full wages. With the greatest exertion we were finished by noon. But did we ever sweat! The stench didn't get out of my clothes for a week, and it didn't come off of my hands so easily either. The twenty-pfennig pay wasn't worth the filth.

At lunch I told my day laborer that I couldn't go to work in my socks and shoes. He grumbled something unintelligible to himself but got out some old worn-out clothing and boots and gave them to me—on the condition that he could deduct three marks from my wages for the boots and four marks for the rest. After lunch (vegetable stew again) I wanted to rest a bit, but that idea got a nice reception! First I had to fetch water again. It's absolutely incomprehensible to me what these people do with so much water. It's impossible that the pigs get that much water, and there aren't many dishes to wash: only a bowl and meat plate, and, when they have vegetable stew, the spoons. When they have plain potatoes, everyone uses his pocketknife, the same one you use for all other work—for example, scraping off hardened cow dung from the pitchfork; that's what my house head did with my pitchfork, since I'd neglected to do it.

After fetching the water, I still had some small household chores to do, so that the clock had already sounded before we were finished. For the afternoon I had to go to the threshing machine. All in all this is the best wintertime work because you're at least sheltered while doing it. But the work itself is not easy. First the machine is started up with a head of steam. Bringing the sheaves to the machine is very exhausting work and is done exclusively by the contract laborers. Day laborers are usually paid by the amount they thresh. They can scarcely get enough grain brought to them, so you're really taxed to bring as much as the feeder (the man who throws the grain into the thresher) needs. The man who unties and loosens the sheaves has plenty to do also; and the grain seeds often fly into his face—not a pleasant feeling. Those inside the barn, as well as the man who unties, suffer terribly from the dust. All the day laborers have to do is carry off the threshed straw, and they find plenty of time to rest. Overall the contract laborers have it much rougher than the day laborers in spite of the fact that the latter earn at least double (and for threshing four times as much) as the former. For threshing, the day laborers usually get to keep every twentieth bushel. But there are estates where they get only every twenty-fifth. [. . .]

A TYPICAL ESTATE OWNER

This gentleman had purchased a new threshing machine. It took eight horses to run it, whereas the old one had needed only four. Since the workers could earn more with it than with the old one, he immediately changed the payments from one bushel in twenty to one in twenty-five. I've hardly met anyone who understood how to exploit and torment his people as well as this forester. And on this very estate the workers are so pious and God-fearing that it must be a real joy to the forester. On many estates the day laborers have heard something about the Social Democrats and agree with them, but they just don't dare to declare themselves openly for fear of being dismissed. But on this forester's estate the day laborers want nothing to do with the Social Democrats. After all, the forester, the pastor, and the beloved *Mecklenburg Sunday Paper* preach zealously against the Social Democrats, so people have to hate and detest Social Democrats. These gentle-men maintain that the Social Democrats want to take away the day laborers' few hard-earned pfennigs and distribute them to do-nothings and vagrants.

From childhood, the Mecklenburg worker is raised and kept in ignorance. Religion is the main subject in school. There are many, very many, workers who can barely read and do arithmetic, but they know by heart pious songs and sayings, as well as the fairly long Mecklenburg Catechism. They can relate whole Bible passages, which must give their betters a hearty laugh. And their fear of the police is scarcely believable. For the country people the constable is the ultimate.

I'll take this opportunity to describe how voting for the Reichstag is frequently done in Mecklenburg. The overseer or the owner has the day laborers who are eligible to vote come to the servants' room. The gentleman gives a little speech and hands out buttered bread and brandy. Then everyone gets his ballot (of course the name of the employer's candidate is on it) and goes into the overseer's room where the wheelwright and the governor* sit as poll watchers by the ballot box. Everyone puts his ballot into the box. The overseer even opens the ballots of those who don't look too certain. I've heard from many people that this procedure is the general practice.

CONFLICTS OF INTEREST BETWEEN DAY LABORERS AND CONTRACT LABORERS

I'll now return to the main theme after this little digression. As mentioned, the day laborers can't get enough to thresh, so that the contract laborer has to work beyond his capacity. When the contract laborer says he can't work anymore, the day laborer replies, "Then we'll help you!" Often the contract laborer is beaten. He can't defend himself either. He is alone and there are many against him. If the contract laborers don't help themselves, then they don't get any justice anywhere. If they complain to the overseer, he just says, "You probably deserved it!" or "It serves you right!" The view that the Mecklenburger is very hard-working and the contract laborer is the opposite is absolutely untrue. Most day laborers work hard only when the overseer or owner is standing behind them, or when they have to do some work alone, or if it's for their own profit. For the day laborer, the main thing is that his master thinks he's hard-working. The contract laborer, on the other hand, works at the same pace whether the boss is there or whether he's alone. Nonetheless they are considered lazy. And yet every overseer or owner must say to himself

* A supervisor of the mowers; see the section "Springtime Work" below.

that it's impossible for the day laborers to work as hard for the whole day as they do when they're being watched. When the overseer is gone, they go back to their old pace, and the contract laborer has soon overtaken the day laborer. Of course the contract laborers taunt the day laborers a good deal, especially when there are many contract laborers present. This angers the day laborers mightily, but they know that the contract laborers are right, and that makes the contract laborers even more hated than they already are. If they could get along without outside contract laborers, there soon wouldn't be a single one in all Mecklenburg. But, much to the chagrin of the estate owners, that just doesn't work. On many estates they've urged the day laborers to hire Mecklenburg contract laborers. But Mecklenburg children of fourteen years, just out of school, demand such a high wage that the day laborers would rather take "foreigners." Giving a contract laborer six more talers is a big outlay for them. Mecklenburgers will hire themselves out as contract laborers only up to their seventeenth year at the latest, then they take a position as a farmhand or a maid. In this position they have it a lot easier than as a contract laborer, and they get twice the pay. If a "foreign" contract laborer is working alone with a day laborer, he always has it very bad. But if all the contract laborers on the estate are together, then no day laborer will dare provoke a contract laborer.

A SMALL-SCALE REVOLT

The first day I worked with the machine, the sheaf untier and the thresher feeder got into an argument that would have ended in blows if they hadn't been in such a dangerous place. "Touch me and I'll throw you into the machine and you'll come out chopped straw!" yelled the contract laborer to the day laborer. The latter got scared because at the sound of the argument all of us contract laborers came running over. The day laborers stood below and looked up. Since the machine was running, they couldn't help their fellow worker. "Stop it! Stop the engine! I'm not staying up here. I won't work with these people!" yelled the day laborer. The engine driver turned off the steam engine. The contract laborer was told to come down and do something else. "Not a chance, I'm staying up here!" The day laborer wanted to climb down when the overseer came to find out why the machine had been shut off at an unaccustomed time. When he discovered the reason, he had the contract laborer come down and told him to go home. Of course we were one man short now, but we were supposed to accomplish as much as we had with the help of the man who'd been dismissed. We were on our guard against that and continued working just as we had before. The day laborers got furious and screamed that we were lazy. We just laughed at them. Then they came up and were going to "shut our loose mouths," as they liked to put it. We gathered in a group and raised our pitchforks as though we were going to attack. When they saw that we were serious, they turned around and one of them ran for the overseer. He couldn't do anything either, but he just calmly gave us another man. Then we continued our work.

Such scenes occur frequently. But they don't always turn out so well as this one. If the contract laborers are in the minority, they frequently receive beatings.

From 24 October to Shrove Tuesday there are no afternoon breaks; we work through from noon to the evening quitting time. The day laborers take bread with them that they eat on the go. The Mecklenburg contract laborers also receive bread to take with them, but only rarely does a "foreign" contract laborer get a piece. With the hard work, it's no wonder that you get terribly hungry. We got off work at about five-thirty and went home. Shortly after we got home we had the plain potatoes left over from lunch but without bacon. But it tastes good when you're hungry. In fact, I was still hungry when the potatoes were all gone. After eating we peeled potatoes again and then went to bed. Barn cleaning alternated with threshing, and so all the days passed until the snow melted and the ground thawed so that the fields could be tilled for summer wheat.

SPRINGTIME WORK

Working with the horses is the best work of all. Each day you plow or harrow you get ten pfennigs extra. And you don't have to exert yourself. But usually the locals are given preference in this work; even the girls have to work with the horses, which they gladly do. Generally the Mecklenburgers are given preference with every kind of work. There's only one kind of harrowing for which outside contract laborers are used almost exclusively; this is the so-called "scotching." With this method one strip is harrowed at a fast walk and another at a trot. There are estates where the harrowers sit on horseback. But many estate owners feel sorry for the horses, so the people have to walk. The head farmhand is present, but he sits on a horse; the others are all "foreigners" and they run even if they finally drop. The overseer rides on a horse alongside and urges you on. Since there are almost always four to six men harrowing, it can happen that you get hit with the riding whip, which puts you in a bad mood. It's not easy work. The horses stir up dust so that you can hardly see, and you sink over your ankles in dust; the sweat just keeps dripping from your brow and your shirt sticks fast to your body. By noon you look as though you've been rolling in sand. If by mistake a Mecklenburg contract laborer is assigned to this work, the women say, "My boy can't take it; he can't do it; if he can't get other work he'll stay home today!"

But the contract laborer from outside can't stay at home; he has to work and if he should collapse, he can go if he has to. There are more where he came from, but Mecklenburg contract laborers are scarce.

The days get longer and longer, and now we work until eight o'clock; and if sometimes it's a bit later, then that doesn't hurt anything. The work keeps getting harder until it reaches a high point at harvest time. But it's already very hard at haying time. Even if the haying is not as hard as it could be, the workday is very long, especially when a meadow has to be finished. As a rule, the contract laborers and the women do the haying. A so-called "man" does the mowing. One "man" supervises the contract laborers and has the high-sounding title "governor." They are very conscious of their high rank, but they are so afraid of the overseer that they hardly dare come home on time with the contract laborers. Usually you work fifteen minutes past quitting time at noon and even longer in the evening. If a Mecklenburg farmhand has a position as a governor, he holds onto it because it wouldn't be easy to get another.

When the hay is dry enough, it's loaded and driven in. Sometimes we were still loading at nine o'clock in a meadow three-quarters of an hour away from home. Often enough it was going on ten o'clock when we got home. When you'd eaten, you were usually glad to be able to go to sleep.

When I was out in the meadow for the first time loading wagons, I didn't think that bringing in the hay would be too hard work. Only when I got to the unloading in the barn did I feel how hard the work was. The hay was stacked up stepwise from the front; each of these steps is called a "foot." Two day laborers and two contract laborers stand alternately on these steps. Actually there were supposed to be one day laborer and one contract laborer on each step, but since the former system is more efficient, that is the way the day laborers stood; also, with this system they didn't have to work as hard, since they are more skillful than contract laborers at this work. It was fairly hot outside, but in the barn there was such an oppressive heat that we were sweating just standing still, even though we were wearing just trousers and a shirt. Up until breakfast time it was fairly tolerable, but as the sun climbed higher it got worse and worse. Wagon after wagon was unloaded. We were in constant motion; there wasn't even enough time to wipe off the sweat. We had to keep hoisting the hay with our pitchforks. Woe to us if we didn't quickly get hold of the hay passed up to us or if we didn't reach high enough for those standing above us to get hold of it and it fell back down. We were really trapped. They hit us with forks from above and stabbed us with forks from below. The other contract laborers couldn't come to help us, and we couldn't help them because the day laborers wouldn't let us by. Complaining

to the overseer doesn't help either because the day laborers just
say that they didn't strike us, and besides we were lazy.

It was the worst after eight o'clock. You think it's quitting
time after every wagon that's unloaded. But then another wagon
rolls up. Your knees are really shaking, and the sweat drips heavily into the hay. We're tormented horribly by thirst. What
you've been allowed to bring along to drink is gone by afternoon,
and you can't get down to drink water. When you hoist the hay,
the hay seeds fall down your neck and cause constant itching and
burning on your sweaty skin. The Mecklenburg contract laborers—if they're not loading out in the meadow—were clever
enough to climb way up to the top where all they need to do is
to push the hay to the side, and they stand so close together that
they can easily do it. After we saw that, the next day we also
climbed up on top but were brought back down by the day laborers.

On our first day at this work it got so dark that you couldn't
see anyone; still we had to stay up there. But so much hay was
falling down that the overseer finally realized that it wasn't working. You had to be as careful as possible climbing down so that
you didn't knock down one of the feet. They'd rather have a man
hurt than have that happen. Each of those feet cost a quarter of a
day's work. I couldn't think about eating after this first day of
unloading work; I was sick to the point of vomiting. The evening
air refreshed us some. Of course, when I got home I had to fetch
water again. You can't get out of it no matter how tired you are.
The next morning my bones felt like they'd been battered; I
could barely move.

WHEAT HARVEST: A SECOND REVOLT—
THE WORKERS' MARSEILLAISE, AN
"IMPROPER SONG"

So it went for days and weeks, and at the wheat harvest it got
even worse. The "men" go in advance and reap; the contract

laborer, working behind his day laborer, must immediately bind up the cut wheat. Since on many estates the day laborers get paid by how much they reap, the contract laborer has to bind as fast as he can. Your hands are all filled with thistles so you can grasp something only with the most extreme pain; your hands usually get festered with sores too, but you still have to work. "We used to have that too!" the day laborers say, and you have no choice but to keep going and bear the pain. But one time it got too bad. Even the local contract laborers, who could really handle the work very well, were grumbling. We didn't want to torture ourselves half to death, so we agreed among ourselves to work a little slower—even though it was still fast enough—when all of a sudden the overseer came. The local contract laborers had stuck with us until then, but when they saw the overseer coming they got scared. Now they really started to work, but they hadn't gotten much further when the overseer arrived. When he saw that we were so far behind, he got angry and began to curse us. We said nothing, but kept on binding at the same pace. When he saw that we weren't binding any faster, he called to the governor, "They will stay here until everything that's cut is bound up!"

We didn't do it; when the day laborers quit for the day, we stopped binding, packed up our things, and followed the day laborers. When we entered the estate yard, the overseer came up to the governor and asked:

"Have they finished all the binding?"

Of course the governor had to answer "No."

"Why did you let them go home? Didn't I tell you that they had to stay there until everything was done?"

The governor said that all his orders and threats hadn't worked. Then the overseer came up to us.

"Why didn't you stay there?"

"When it's quitting time we stop!" one of us said.

"Shut up! I didn't ask you! Go back at once and finish your section!"

"Not a chance!" our spokesman spoke up again.

"Will you shut up, you scoundrel?"

"Am I a bigger scoundrel than you?" asked our comrade calmly.

That was too much for the overseer. He raised his riding whip and would certainly have struck the cheeky spokesman if the latter hadn't moved first. He tore the whip out of his hand and tried to break it, but he couldn't. Now the overseer jumped on him with his fists ready. But he'd made a big mistake about the strength of our comrade, for the latter grabbed him, lifted him up, and in front of everybody, threw him into the sand. The overseer jumped up sputtering with rage.

"Get off this estate and don't let yourself be seen here ever again!"

"No, Herr Overseer, first I'll get my wages and my papers!"

"And I'm telling you that you're not going to get anything!"

"Well, we'll just see about that!"

Now the overseer ordered the day laborers, who had just been looking on silently, to get the man off the estate. When the day laborers tried to carry out the order, we crowded around our comrade. As soon as they saw that we were in earnest, they stayed where they were and we left the yard singing the Workers' Marseillaise.*

This incident, however, had legal consequences. The next morning a policeman took our friend away from work. I learned later that he'd gotten three months for assault and there was a further penalty for refusal to work. The rest of us were also fined five marks for refusal to work. We petitioned for a judge's decision with the result that we were acquitted, but we got a reprimand for singing "improper songs," and to top it off, we had to pay the court costs. The prosecutor's speech contained, among other things the following lines: "In order to prevent the corrupting influence that foreign contract laborers exercise on the

---

* The unofficial anthem of Social Democracy.

rural inhabitants of Mecklenburg by these and similar actions, the defendants must be severely punished so that they lose the desire for such things."

POETRY AND PROSE IN AGRICULTURE

To us, agriculture didn't appear as poetic as it's depicted in poems. How often we drank mud water from ditches! We often got such headaches from all the stooping in the burning sun that we thought our heads would split in two. If grain binding was no easy work, driving the grain into the barn was even more tiring—actually worse than bringing the hay in, if that's possible. Each man alone had to pass on the heavy sheaves. And it took some practice to pass on the sheaves as fast as they were handed to you. The barley was the worst; the prickly hairs got all over you: in your socks, your trousers, down your neck—in short, you couldn't get away from them.

Some of the grain was threshed out in the open field. Since this was the heaviest work time, the day laborers' wives had to help. In order to use as few women as possible, the contract laborers had to take the most difficult posts and do the work of two. The worst post was at the grain elevator, called the "stoker." One contract laborer had to stand there and remove as much as two men, using all their strength, could put into the machine. This was overall the hardest work I had done, especially when the sun was burning down hot from the sky. On a grain rick perhaps seventy-five feet in diameter stood two contract laborers, two women, and an old day laborer who had to stake up the edge. With all the real work, we two contract laborers hardly opened our mouths—at most for a curse. But the women and the day laborer just couldn't talk enough. What's more, they were standing so close together that they only moved the straw a little further on. When my partner came closer to me and didn't throw the straw as far as he had at first, the women began to cry bloody murder. "No, no! Come back here! Let the other man do some work!" We explained to them that they were the ones who weren't doing anything and who could do something. The woman's husband came up and grabbed my friend by the neck, and it was only thanks to the fact that I came at him with a raised pitchfork that he let my friend go. But we had to retreat fast because the rest of the day laborers were already coming up; we ran over to the other contract laborers and so the fight ended. The only thing was that now that we were down, we could get a drink. You're not allowed to leave your post and bring everything to a halt, even if you're collapsing from thirst.

[*After the grain harvest they work digging potatoes.*]

FALL AND WINTER WORK AND THE HARVEST FESTIVAL

After the potato digging it was sugar-beet time. It was already noticeably cold when we left each morning at daybreak for the sugar-beet fields. With a lot of work, a shuttle line had been set up bordering on our field. Two cars were filled almost every day. We weren't allowed to leave the field before they were full. Then it was quitting time. Of course there were no rest breaks during the work. What's more, we were so soaked through by snow or rain that we had to take off every piece of clothing on our bodies when we got home. When this work is over, the hardest part of the contract laborer's work is done. What's left to do isn't so bad, but then, from 24 October on there is no more afternoon meal break.

When everything has been brought in from the fields, they celebrate a harvest festival, where there was free dance music, brown beer, and diluted whiskey. There are also cigars at this occasion, but they're distributed according to your rank. The day laborers and farmhands each get four cigars. The contract laborers, being the lowest, get only two. So even on this occasion the contract laborer doesn't get his due. There's dancing either in the barn, the granary, or the milk house. The festival begins about three o'clock in the afternoon, and at five o'clock most of the farmhands are drunk, shouting for joy and kicking up their legs like horses. It ends about two or three o'clock in the morning. On some estates there is dance music four times a year; on others only once; it could end up costing too much and making the workers greedy for pleasure.

Right after New Year's there are two or three cartloads of wood that have to be sawed and split. In the evening we stood there by lamplight or moonlight and sawed and sawed. On Sundays we split wood. When this work is done (it takes several weeks), you start carrying dung to the garden. Sometimes the garden is more than a quarter hour away from the house. Several more weeks go by with this work. Then it's time to turn over the soil in the garden, plant the potatoes, cut weeds, etc. If you're not busy at the estate, you have to work for your day laborer, day after day. Only on a few Sundays a year are you free from work, and then only for a few hours.

CONTRACT LABORER'S CHRISTMAS

Winter had come to the country and with it Christmas. Generally on the twenty-fourth of December they skip lunch break and quit work at two o'clock. After eating and all sorts of preparations, it's time to decorate the Christmas tree, a fir tree about a half meter tall. The entire decoration consists of a few apples, nuts, some pastries, and three or four lights. The children's presents (colorful kerchiefs and other useful little trifles) are laid between the branches, and the whole thing is hung from a hook in the ceiling in the middle of the main room. The children are already thoroughly familiar with the presents and so don't get much pleasure from them. At five o'clock the service in the local church begins, and everyone who can still walk goes. Even we were invited to come along, but we declined with a thank-you. We heated up the mowers' shed and celebrated our own Christmas. When the people got back from church they had supper. To celebrate the day there were cold meats—for the first time all year. A pig had been slaughtered shortly before, so everyone could feast on ham, bacon, etc. Some of the neighbors are there; the talk is of pigs and cows until the farmhands come from the estate. One of them is dressed as St. Nicholas and now the talk gets dirty. The children howl and scream and the adults laugh. Then the house head gets out the brandy bottle from which everybody takes a big swig. "Drink up, Otto! Today is Christmas! Take a lot!" Aside from a few apples, that was my entire Christmas present. The local contract laborer gets one taler, even if he's not with his parents; but we outsiders were like children, we would just spend the taler. But we thought we deserved at least something from the day laborer; after all we'd worked a whole year for him.

THE CONTRACT LABORER'S WAGES

How much pay does the contract laborer really receive at the year's end for all this work? When I left I received 16.32 marks. The rest was deducted for expenses and things that were now long worn to tatters. I couldn't take anything with me except two old shirts and two old pairs of socks!

What was I supposed to do now? I had to go be a contract laborer again because with what I'd earned I was in the same position I'd been in before. And many contract laborers have it much worse—they get paid only a few pfennigs.

Sixteen marks and thirty-two pfennigs! That was the pay I got for such long and hard work! I could have earned as much at the workhouse without having to do such exhausting work—and I would have been less despised than I was here as a "free" man doing honest work.

Picking through a dump. Sketch by C. Koch, 1883. (Archiv für Kunst und Geschichte, Berlin)

"The blessing of old-age and disability insurance." Picking up pensions, about 1890. (Archiv für Kunst und Geschichte, Berlin)

Berlin workers celebrating the first official May Day (1 May 1890). Sketch by E. Hosang. (Archiv für Kunst und Geschichte, Berlin)

Carrying breakfast beer to workers at a construction site in Munich, about 1900.
(Ullstein Bilderdienst, Berlin)

A dormitory for working women in Berlin, 1906; the rent is twelve marks per month, with coffee included. (Ullstein Bilderdienst, Berlin)

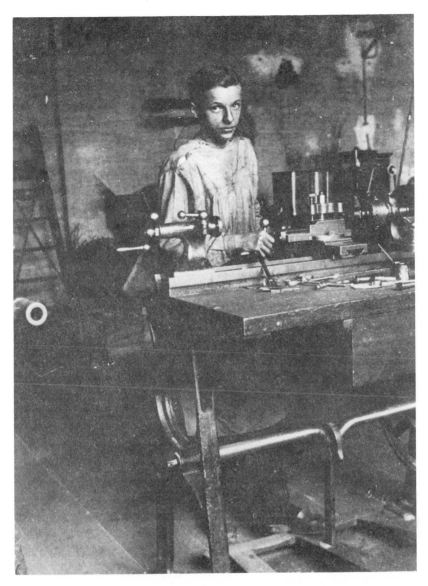

An apprentice turner at the lathe in a metal shop, about 1900. (Archiv
für Kunst und Geschichte, Berlin)

In the wood shop of a Berlin colony for the unemployed, 1897. (Ullstein Bilderdienst, Berlin)

Mealtime at the workers' colony Hoffnungsthal at Bernau near Berlin, 1907.
(Ullstein Bilderdienst, Berlin)

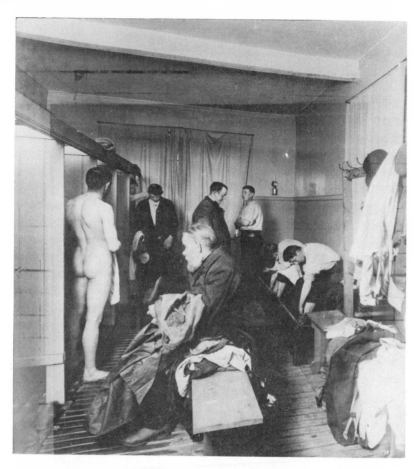

In the shower room of the workers' colony Hoffnungsthal at Bernau near Berlin, 1907. (Ullstein Bilderdienst, Berlin)

Migrant farm workers on their way through Berlin, about 1900. (Ullstein Bilderdienst, Berlin)

A laundress picking up laundry from her customers in Munich, about 1900. (Ullstein Bilderdienst, Berlin)

Women making candles, about 1900. (Ullstein Bilderdienst, Berlin)

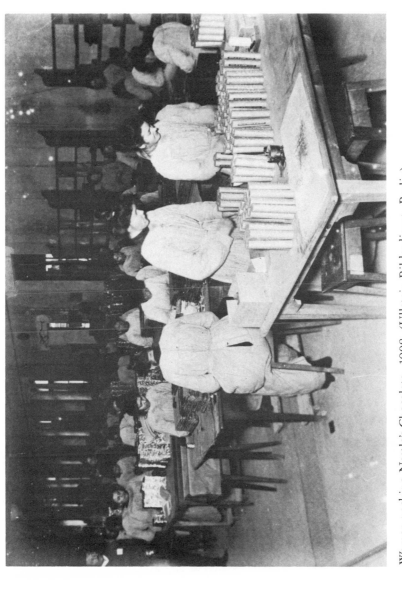

Women packing Nestlé's Chocolate, 1908. (Ullstein Bilderdienst, Berlin)

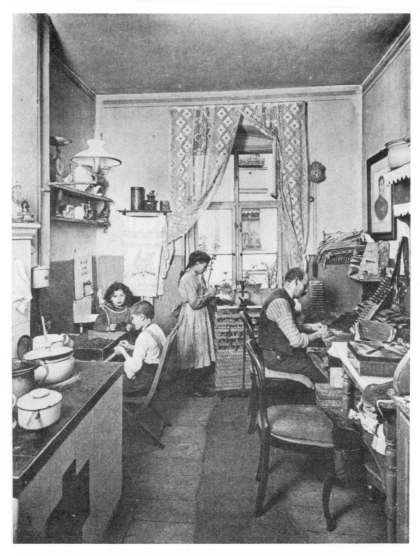

A family making cigars in their Berlin kitchen, 1910. (Archiv für Kunst und Geschichte, Berlin)

Inside a Berlin tenement house, about 1910. (Ullstein Bilderdienst, Berlin)

A family of nine in a Berlin cellar apartment that doubles as a workroom for making clothing, 1912. (Archiv für Kunst und Geschichte, Berlin)

Cutting wood for delivery in a fancy neighborhood in Munich, about 1900.
(Ullstein Bilderdienst, Berlin)

Moritz Bromme,
Woodworker and Metalworker

Moritz Bromme (1873–1926), who worked in the wood and metal industries in Thuringia, wrote his autobiography while recovering from tuberculosis in a sanatorium in 1903. He had come to the attention of Paul Göhre, his editor, through articles in various socialist publications. If ever anyone had Social Democracy in his blood, it was Bromme. His father, a railroad worker, was an avid Social Democrat and had been imprisoned during the Socialist Law era (1878 to 1890), during which much socialist activity was illegal. As is clear in this selection on Bromme's personal life in the late 1890s, Social Democracy was more than just politics for the young Bromme; rather, it was a whole way of life for the self-consciously "modern" worker. The story of his conflicts with his conservative wife at home and with his boss on the job are among the best examples of how political perceptions are entangled with specific work and family situations. In the years following the writing of his autobiography, Bromme achieved modest distinction as a Social Democratic journalist; after World War I he was a senator in Lübeck.

MARRIED

During the whole winter my fiancée seemed to me to be acting very suspiciously. In the spring I was sure that I was the cause of her distress. I kept waiting for an explanation, but she kept quiet until one evening I raised the matter myself. She admitted it but hadn't wanted to say anything about it to me before my final military physical exam. If I'd gone into the army, she would have committed suicide, she said, because she could not have gone home in such a condition. Of course, at my physical exam I called attention to all my defects, and because of my left ear— which had a badly punctured drum—I was assigned to the untrained reserve infantry. Nothing now stood in the way of my marriage, but one thing is sure: if I hadn't gotten my bride pregnant, I would not have gotten married for a long time and perhaps would have joined the army.

So, in July 1895, we moved into a spare alcove room in my father-in-law's little house. Even on the first day the expenditures for our own household were completely new to me. What could you get for a mark? I hadn't saved up anything; all I had was enough to pay the tailor for my wedding suit. Since I couldn't get anything from my house, it was lucky that my wife at least had the bare necessities: a bed, a dresser, and just enough linens. She bought a sofa for cash and got a table with four chairs from her parents. I got a wall clock from my father. And then, from Müller, the carpenter—an old friend who later moved to South Germany—we bought on installment an end table, a wardrobe, a kitchen cupboard, a mirror, a washstand, and a bedstead.

Our wedding took place on the tenth of August with a rather nice celebration. Things really got started the night before. My friends Robert and the carpenter made things very lively; and that evening we drank up a small keg of beer. The next day my

Translated from Moritz Th. W. Bromme, *Lebensgeschichte eines modernen Fabrikarbeiters,* ed. Bernd Neumann (Frankfurt: Athenäum Verlag, 1971), 219–42. Originally edited by Paul Göhre (Jena: Eugen Diederichs Verlag, 1905).

parents, three brothers and sisters, the two witnesses, two friends from the "Society for the Protection of the Interests of the Workers," and my wife's three sisters (one with her fiancé) were all there, and then we had a full house. It was a beautiful summer day; thanks to my in-laws there was plenty to eat and everyone had a fine time. The old women had warned us about getting married during the dog days of summer. But we had to anyway, for on the 28th of the same month my first daughter arrived; I named her Hedwig. My wife had gone with me to work early in the morning; about ten o'clock she had to leave work; and when I got home at noon it was all over. I was very pleased that she didn't have to send for me. We had the baptism at the Workers' Society Ball on the twentieth of October. For my daughter's godparents I had gotten my friends, Wilhelm Kuhl, Müller the carpenter, and Robert's wife. To the baptismal certificate Kuhl attached a beautiful dedication written in elegant round script. It went like this: "You were born as a child of the proletariat—a people dispossessed and oppressed—so when you grow up—you'll stand up for freedom, truth, and justice." This first baptism was a genuinely happy family celebration. We enjoyed ourselves in a way that we didn't on later occasions. I've arranged only three baptisms; for the other three the midwife went to church alone with the baby, and the names of the godparents were just filled in.

My wife went right back to work, and my mother-in-law took care of the baby—for four marks a week if I'm not mistaken. Now my wife had previously had a child by a salesman who worked as a bookkeeper in a store where she was a maid. But soon afterward the man drowned during a boating party on the Unstrut River near Rossleben, and she was left with neither a husband nor alimony. This little boy, whom my parents-in-law had taken in, was sickly because when he was very little his first foster mother had always put him by the bare stone wall where he had to spend the whole day, even in bad weather. So he had always been catching colds and from them he got a kidney infection, which was especially acute during that autumn. My in-laws, who were very fond of the little boy, did everything possible to get him cured, and he had cost them several hundred marks; still, nothing helped, neither medicines nor natural treatments. The poor little fellow lasted four years before death put him out of his misery. He, unfortunately, was the cause of the first storms in our marriage, because my in-laws, who had to work hard and were without means, sometimes asked my wife for contributions for the boy. Usually it was ten marks. But my wife never said anything to me about it. She apparently wanted to avoid any cause for a quarrel. However there was no cash available because we had to pay off our furniture and things. I earned only thirteen marks a week and my wife nine. So my wife frequently brought home some sewing in the evening—cashmere or coating, which she sometimes worked on through half the night. The breaks in the yarn and threads in these fabrics had to be sewn up with the same yarn, and in this way she earned an extra two to five marks; but there was still no extra cash. When her parents came and made financial demands on her, she sometimes borrowed money, one time fifteen marks from the butcher. She'd paid it off down to ten marks, but then another expense came up and the butcher—not wanting to wait—told me about it. This brought on our first quarrel because she hadn't told me anything about it.

So we really had to struggle to get by, and when the year was over, we were almost finished ourselves. Then too, we were both still young and expected something from life. I especially didn't want to give up my socializing and that provoked another row. My father-in-law did hard forestry work—like felling trees, pruning, planting, and stump digging—all for very low wages, and he didn't go out for any amusements; so I was supposed to limit myself too. What's more, he earned a lot less than I did! The only advantage of his work was that every woodsman got to take home a handcart full of waste wood every evening. But what a drudgery that was, dragging a fully loaded cart down frequently soggy paths from deep in the forest and then another half, three-quarters, or even an hour and a half to the house! You can't find a more exhausting work than that. I'd be half-dead in the evening if I had to do such heavy work. And then at home the wood had to be sawed up, split, and dried before you could sell it. You usually get nine marks for a cord and there is a lot of wood in a cord. You can barely collect ten cords in a year. Besides, they wanted to provide their own fuel; so they bought tree stumps and dug them out. That is even worse drudgery. A skinny factory worker can't even begin to do it. Yet my father-in-law is in his late sixties and still does it. Of course he's worked his whole life outside, first in agriculture and now this forestry drudgery. In the summertime when there's nothing to do in the local forest he works on the harvest with farmers or on the nobles' estates.

As I said, I couldn't do his work. He doesn't even have any desire to go out on Sundays. He rests then. But when people like us have put in a whole week in a stuffy factory, we want to get some fresh air on Sunday and chat with our friends and probably have some fun. The old rural generation asks nothing more of life than to eat, sleep, and work; or at most to leaf through the local paper—that's their entire intellectual nourishment. The modern worker, however, demands more. He demands, at the very least, to take part in the pleasures of life. He wants to educate himself. From my school days, I had especially loved and valued books, and I still have today almost all the books from my last three school years. I constantly wanted to know more. But whenever I bought another book I was scolded. Book buying, amusements, going out on Sundays—that took money! My wife joined in preaching the same line; and later when I worked in the metal industry in Gera and occasionally bought another book because I made more money, I was still scolded. But they still couldn't stop me from building up a sizable library over a period of time. I was also given a large number of good books by my old school friend Dietzmann.[. . .]

So, as I said, because I wanted more out of life, my wife's family kept telling me: It's better to knuckle under; you should be satisfied with your fate. Why all this party and union business? It's OK to vote for the Social Democrats, but otherwise you should keep quiet. There have to be rich and poor. Oh, the intellectual horizon of these poor old country workers extends no farther than this! But I stuck to my opinions; and I had countless arguments with my wife about them. She would often say, the workers would certainly give us nothing if the factory owners don't even give us anything. Remarkable! No factory owner ever gave me anything but my scanty wages; and that was a lot less than what I actually would have earned. And I always told my wife my frank opinion about it. In the beginning all the instruction helped not a bit, but eventually she became shrewder. Now she's even gotten organized—all without my doing and in spite of the fact that she only works at home. She's become a member of the Textile Workers' Union. But in the first years of our marriage she hadn't reached such understanding.

In March 1897, my wife gave birth to another daughter. We named this one Erna. Now we really had to screw up our courage. Should we pay seven or eight marks for the care of both of our children? That would have been crazy. So my wife had to stay home now. She continued to take in sewing. At first her earnings were OK. But then they got a new supervisor who knew nothing of her earlier work in the factory. The pieces of material she received started to get worse and her earnings went down. Now we had to be even more careful because the children cost more and more money. Sometimes my wife got snappish! Often at lunchtime she was in a bad mood, and she'd hit the little one on the hands because she was grabbing the cups and knocking one over. Finally she would just hit her little fingers with the spoon. The first time I just watched quietly and forbade her doing it again, because I knew well why she did it: simply out of frustration about the wretched money that just wouldn't go far enough. To pay off one debt we had to borrow somewhere else. Were there going to be still more children? I got very worried when I even thought about it. One day our boss brought some Parisian articles into the workroom. It was the first time I'd heard of them; before I'd known nothing about contraception. The boss talked me into buying a box of pessaries for 1.20 marks. Later I even got a second box. Afterward the married workers talked frequently of such "protections." Some of the things you heard you can't repeat in writing. Aside from complete abstinence, the surest method was said to be the "suburban business." "Coitus interruptus" is the medical term for it. Only later did I learn that it was very harmful for both the man and the woman. Despite the fact that I used the pessaries and the last mentioned method, I found myself with a son, Ernst, a year later. Unfortunately he is very sickly, very weak, and has a pale complexion. I wonder if those cursed things are to blame. My wife's great fertility appears to run in her family because all of her sisters have proved to be equally fertile.

My family situation became more and more difficult. I wanted to go off to look for a better-paying job. I'd found a position in a harmonica factory in the Gera suburb of Leumnitz, where I could earn seventeen marks a week. There I would help in the making of wooden slippers,* a skill I had acquired to perfection. But once again I had difficulties with my papers. The boss insisted on two weeks' notice; and at the same time he offered me a one-mark raise. And my wife was more against it than for it on account of how far it was—every day three hours walking to work in addition to the eleven-hour workday; that was too much. But countless others have to do it too. So I stayed where I was and worked for fourteen marks a week. But what's a one-mark raise? It's like a drop of water on a hot stone. There were five of us now. Hedwig slept with my father-in-law in his bed, another child with me, and the third with my wife. At least this way we didn't have to get a new bed. But that had to happen sometime, so the prospects for the future were blacker and blacker and my wife's mood always worse. After barely two years I already cursed the marriage.

Added to this, I became ill as a result of an accident. I'd been

---

*Bromme does not explain why he would be making slippers in a harmonica factory.

working with a young fellow cutting red beech boards. These were almost too heavy for two men, being about five meters long and a half to three-quarters meters wide. One day this fellow was behind me, chatting away, his mind not on his work, and as we tried to lift the board up to the circular saw, he simply threw it down. I couldn't get out of the way in time, and the board suddenly shot up in the air and came down onto my left foot. I was wearing wooden shoes and my big toe was badly crushed. "Tui-tam" carried me home on his back. The doctor didn't come until the next day and he prescribed Lysol baths. I can't describe the pain I experienced the first night. It was so bad that I could hear the angels singing. Still, during these days I read through a whole year of the *Book for Everyone* [*Buch für Alle*].* I especially liked the novel by Zobeltitz, *Healing Poison* [*Heilendes Gift*],† which tells about a Javanese plant poison that cures epilepsy. I lay at home for three weeks; then I put on a primitive wooden sandal that my father fashioned for me and limped back to work. It was still another two weeks before I could put on a shoe again. I was barely healthy when my daughter Erna, who had been growing up strong, got sick from a vaccination. Before the vaccination she was jolly and blossoming and plump; after the vaccination she was so sick that we had to put ice-cold compresses on her every half hour. Then she got thin as a rake, pale-faced, and quiet. After that she had pneumonia twice, and her little brother Ernst has had it six times in just two years. Once again a large part of our scanty wages went to the druggist! How much, depended on the doctor. One doctor usually prescribed only compresses and baths; while the other just gave medicine. Our finances were now all the worse, and my wife's mood was getting worse, not better. If I had worried as much as she did, things would have been sad indeed. We were already long past being able to afford butter, it had to be margarine. But still, if

---

*A popular magazine with many serialized novels.
† Fedor von Zobeltitz (1857–1934) was the author of many popular novels. *Heilendes Gift* appeared in 1898.

the [Workers'] Association was having some entertainment, we joined in anyway because my wife was, and still is today, very fond of dancing, though I no longer have any interest in it. Then her parents and her unmarried sister, Selma, would scold us. "Stay home and first pay off your debts!" they said. This made my wife angry, and I got sulky and started to spend more time with my friends. Sometimes we got to fighting, which really made life bitter for me; one night the fighting actually drove me out to the swimming hole. I really wanted to drown myself. But then I thought of the children. What would become of them? And so, for the sake of the children I took up my joyless life again; but the cares and the miseries remained, as we will see later.

Our bosses, that is the new ones, had gradually expanded the slipper and wooden shoe business. We couldn't get enough wood so we had to bring it in from Lucka and Stettin. We had an annual commission to deliver several thousand pairs of wooden shoes to Kapstadt. Because of this we even had to work overtime to make the necessary wooden soles. The small workroom was filled with a tremendous amount of dust that made me fear the worst for my lungs. My mother had died of tuberculosis. And I always had a secret fear of it. When there was dry wood with a light dust that didn't fall to the floor, or when I worked the sander myself, I wore a respirator mask over my mouth and nose. I'd gotten it from an apothecary shop in Frankenstein in Silesia. Of course the ignorant rural workers laughed at me and mocked me. When you're young you don't like that, so I used the thing only when absolutely necessary. Still, I'd frequently discussed with my fellow workers the necessity of having a proper ventilation system in the place. But how to get it? A small window fan was already in use in front of the sanding table, but it was in no respect enough. What was needed was an exhaust duct system that would take the dust directly away from the machine. Two years earlier I had tried to found a local chapter of the Woodworkers' Union with my friend Wilhelm Kahl, who was then Association president in Gera. Our own shoemakers' local had long since passed away. My father and I had been the last two members. Although I'd tried repeatedly several times since then, nothing had come of it. At a founders'-day celebration for the Textile Workers' Union in the summer of 1897 I met with the carpenter Rössel, and together with him I wanted to make a final effort to organize the Ronneburg woodworkers. We went from house to house to the carpenters and basket makers. I myself agitated in the factory, as much as I could. But only the majority of the nailers, the sawer Barofski, and some of the mousetrap makers, among them Karl Brüger, were willing to join. So we were finally ready for the founding. After a lecture by Franz Meusch, leader of the Leipzig woodworkers, thirty-two workers joined the union. Among them were almost all the carpenters in Ronneburg. Unfortunately they didn't stick it out for very long: the dues provoked reprimands and abuse from the members' wives. And since in financial matters the wives usually "wore the pants," their wishes had to be heeded. Soon we were down to fifteen to twenty members, but they at least remained steadfast and true to the organization. In one of the new union's membership meetings dealing with grievances at individual workplaces, I brought up my old complaint about the heavy dust in our shop and demanded unconditionally the installation of an exhaust system. We decided to inform the Altenburg Factory Inspector Böhnisch so that he could take care of the abuse on an upcoming inspection of the factory.

On a Thursday, just when both bosses were away, the factory inspector appeared and checked thoroughly not only the boiler but the whole factory. He asked Barofski, who was busy at the bandsaw, about everything, and then he came to us in the sanding room. I had to turn on the sander. He pronounced the ventilation totally inadequate and ordered an exhaust system. The next morning one of the bosses went up to Barofski and asked him about the inspector's orders. "And where does this ape of an inspector live?" he asked. Then he ran all around town, cross-examining all the workers and trying to find out, at any price, who the discontented elements were. At his orders the sanding was moved into the main building, but the exhaust system really was installed.

During these days in the year 1898 the elections for our state parliament took place. Of course I'd been agitating unceasingly among the rural workers in our factory, so that they'd get out and vote. I myself voted for the first time in my life; I had just turned twenty-five. The polls closed at six o'clock, and from our area only two "bumpkins" (as the local country people were called) had gone to the polls. At 5:10 my father and I succeeded in getting three men to go home and vote. They must have tipped the scales because our comrade Schüler was elected with only a one-vote majority. We were delighted that we had contributed so directly to the victory. Of course, the government men wanted to declare the election void because one ballot had Schiller (not Schüler) written on it. But the parliament said it was valid because the ballot need show only the intention of the voter. Since then the Altenburger peasants have gotten more modern; since 1904 they have voted with printed rather than handwritten ballots, although it was an effort to get them to agree to the change. Among other arguments against the change was the fear that the voters would completely forget how to write. A few weeks after the state election came the Reichstag election, and once again I put a great deal of work into agitation. Unfortunately we lost to von Blödau, a big landowner who got fifteen thousand votes, while our Buchwald got only thirteen thousand. I can still see today both our bosses laughing. Of course they were happy that the representative of big money went to the Reichstag. Still, later we had our laughs too.

On a Saturday morning, some four weeks after the election, and when the exhaust system was about finished, one of the bosses called me into his office. Even before this there had been tension between us; one day, as I stood for a minute with another worker, the boss shouted at us about our supposed laziness; it was as though we were in a military barracks. Maybe a newspaper article had caused his anger. The *Elector* [*Der Wähler*], then the party [SPD] newspaper, had carried a story from Ronneburg according to which a shoe factory owner had gotten the druggist up in the middle of the night and asked for five pfennigs worth of louse lotion. So, as I mentioned, the owner called me in and gave me a real dressing down. "Look, Bromme," he began, "you're the one who got us in the soup with the inspector. You need to worry about your family instead of the party and union activities. Naturally you're through in two weeks and it hurts you more than me. We don't want to employ thankless people like you who get a raise and then turn around and send the inspectors after us. See that you get out of here; in two weeks it's all over. Smear me all you want in the *Elector*. I don't give a hoot."

So I was going to be out of work, something that hadn't happened in seven years; and now I was married and the father of three children. I was really depressed. But there was one consolation—and I couldn't praise it too highly—the union. Werner, the district head from Gera to whom I immediately reported my case, definitely promised me the appropriate financial support. After all I'd been thrown out of work on account of union activity. He advised me, however, to make one more try to get my firing rescinded. The next Sunday our union local met and discussed my situation. Someone suggested that we write a letter to the firm asking them to keep me on. He wrote it and then told me to recopy it neatly, because I had the best handwriting of anyone present. I did it, even though it bothered me to take action on my own behalf; but my family's support was at stake. In the letter the firm was asked to cancel my termination for the following reasons: First, because I was married and the father of three children; second, because I was only very slightly to blame, the real guilty one being the union proxy, Rössel the carpenter, who didn't even work for our firm; third, because the social understanding between management and workers had been good up to now and ought to remain so in the future; and fourth, because a possible proclamation of a boycott would cause great harm to both the owners and the remaining workers. The letter was signed by Rössel; and comrade Schüler, the Social Democratic diet representative, had also given us permission to add his name. He got his supply of wooden shoes and slippers from the firm, and so he thought he might influence the owners to take back my dismissal. However it turned out differently and the letter was a disaster for us. The owners were offended by it and saw it as a threat to their existence. After consulting with their lawyers, they brought suit against us for attempted extortion, claiming that the letter was designed to gain "financial advantage" for me. Of course the union provided us with a lawyer; the fears of my excited and foolish wife that I would spend three to six months behind bars were premature. Nonetheless she caused me a lot of grief at the time. She used to say to the children at every opportunity, "It won't be much longer before you won't be able to see your old man because he's going to jail for three to six months." Or else, "Other people, like the village bumpkins, are laughing that they now have a healthy workplace and don't have to breathe in any more dust, and you have to go to jail."

In the meantime the union's governing board had approved my request for financial support and set my allowance at twelve marks a week. I couldn't get work in the wood business in Ronneburg; I had to go to Gera and look for work there. But nothing worked out. In neither the harmonica factories nor in construction or furniture making could I find work. In answer to an ad, I applied to a master glazier in Grimma who needed someone to tend the woodworking machines. I would have gotten eighteen to twenty marks a week, but my wife didn't want me to take such an uncertain and distant job because she thought moving there might not be a good thing. I could have gotten work as a mason's assistant right away; but because of my weak constitution I wouldn't have been able to do it for very long; and anyway, I wanted, if possible, to look for work in the wood industry. One day, after three weeks had gone by, the union proxy came to me and said: "Listen, we don't want you to just lounge around at union expense. You could have had a job with Lange, the master mason, why didn't you take it?" That was just too much for me. I replied that I hadn't organized just so I could slave away as a helper. The next day I went to the district head in Gera and he agreed to come to our next membership meeting. There it was clearly determined that nobody had the right to force me to take just any work, and in the same meeting enough light was shed on my case to reveal that our secretary was the one who had informed on me. He had told the sawer, Kranzritter, who the complainer had been, and Kranzritter told the machinist, Schnabel, and he, of course, couldn't rest until he'd informed the owners. One of the owners was against letting me go because of my practical knowledge, but the other one replied, "If he had died, we'd also have to get somebody else." At the meeting the bigmouthed informer was kicked out of the union, and it was decided that I could have support until I got work.

A few days later Master Sergeant Prager sent for me and interrogated me. He wanted to know who had written the letter because, while Rössel and Schüler had their names at the bottom, the letter was not in their handwriting. So there must have been a third person in on it. Without any ceremony I admitted my involvement but stressed that my colleagues had dictated the letter to me. Further, I observed that I had not wanted to take up the pen in my own defense, but that in the interest of my own livelihood I'd finally agreed to write the letter. The constable tried to represent party and union activity as pointless, and confided to me that one of the owners had told him that I was one of their best workers. The matter seemed to be pressing because it was only a few days before we were summoned before the judge magistrate. As mentioned, the words "possible proclamation of a boycott" were seen as an extortion attempt. Schüler testified that he would have struck the words if he'd been present at the writing of the letter. As a result of his testimony, the charges against him were dropped and only Rössel and I were to come to trial. Schüler was just to be a witness.

In the meantime I had gotten work in the tool factory, Wesselmann Drills and Co., Inc., in Gera. At that time this firm was engaged exclusively in the production of the double-spiral drill and the special casing that went with it, which were patented in all countries. I heard about it through a friend who worked for the company. There was no more work for me in the wood business and so I transferred to metals. The foreman Beeger, who took me on, was a very friendly man of about thirty. He put me to work at a mortising machine that I adjusted to very easily. I also had to file off blisters and to center drill. This last involved drilling into the pieces of steel so that they would fit on the lathe where they were shaped into drill bits.

At first, working far away from home seemed very strange. Up to this time I'd always been home at breakfast and the afternoon break, and now I scarcely saw the family for the whole day. I took the workers' train to Gera at five-thirty in the morning, and I didn't get back until eight in the evening. In the morning the children were still asleep, and when I came home in the evening, they were so tired that they couldn't keep their eyes open at supper. They fell asleep over their food and had to be carried to bed. At noon I ate only bread and sausage and drank a glass of beer with it. A midday meal in the evening before you go to bed doesn't agree with you the way it does at noon. In short, from then on there was no order in my daily life. In the beginning I got an hourly wage of twenty-five pfennigs; at Christmas I got a two-pfennig raise. From this, one mark went for the fare that the railroad collected every week. So my wife now had to work hard along with me. She often sat up the whole night and sewed. It really cut me to the heart that I couldn't offer her a happy and carefree life. But what could you do if you wanted to live? It was fortunate that my wife was healthy and strong. This gave me special consolation later when I frequently found myself in the TB sanatorium. In my wife I had a strong, hardy person to look after the children. Admittedly she was often embittered because she was denied any rest or relaxation. Other women who had no children could take part in every festivity, and she, who would have liked so much to have danced away her cares for a few hours, had to sit at home and sew and sew or mend the children's clothing or darn socks.

My trial in the boycott case took place before the Altenburg provincial court on my brother's birthday, the twenty-eighth of November. For our defense we had retained the Altenburg attorney, Dr. Höfer, who called Factory Inspector Böhnisch as a defense witness. Böhnisch was also the court-appointed expert. In order to establish exactly how I was informed upon, the machinist Schnabel was also called for the defense. Herr Beeger gave me the day off without any trouble. Of course I told a white lie and said I was a witness rather than the defendant. In the early morning, with my heart pounding, I said good-bye to my wife. She predicted a heavy punishment because she'd read in the newspaper a few days before that a mason in Dresden had been sentenced to six months imprisonment for the same offense under similar circumstances!

At the train station I met my fellow sufferer, Rössel, and the prosecution witnesses, among them one of my former bosses; we all took the same train. Schüler was already in Altenburg because the state parliament had just begun a new session. After arriving in the capital, we dropped in on the editorial offices of the party newspaper. A month earlier it had changed its name to the *Altenburg People's Paper* [*Altenburger Volkszeitung*]. The editors impressed on us the need to tell the exact truth and promised to attend the proceedings themselves. After drinking a cup of coffee, we went to the hall of justice. Another trial was still going on; Rössel and the others listened to it. But I just couldn't. My heart was pounding so much and I was so nervous that all I could do was pace back and forth in the corridor. Finally the factory inspector came in. I greeted him, and he studied me and saw how nervous I was. He asked if I were Rössel and I corrected him. Then he said, "You're pretty nervous, aren't you?" I said I was and told him that I was naturally that way. He reassured me and said: "Just tell everything that you know. It's the owners we're going to get. You certainly don't have anything to fear." Gradually I relaxed and looked forward with composure to what was about to happen.

"The case against Rössel and confederate," the court usher called out. We two defendants had to sit in the notorious dock.

Our lawyer sat down in front of us and reminded us a final time to explain that it would not have been at all within our power to organize a boycott. My ex-boss sat down next to the factory inspector, smiled at him, and apparently tried to start a conversation. But he had the wrong man because the official just turned his back on him. The charges were read out, and then we defendants were asked for our version. While Rössel related the course of events, I observed our judges. I breathed a noticeable sigh of relief when I spotted two familiar faces among them—namely, the stepson of the innkeeper of our former union meeting place, and the Ronneburg magistrate Dr. Schubert from my cherry trial.*

When Rössel was finished, it was my turn to speak; I didn't have much to add. Mostly I described the behavior of the boss after the inspector had inspected the factory. The court expert, Böhnisch, turned very red when I related that the boss had asked Barofski, the man who had informed on me, "Where does the ape live?" And further, how he'd said to Schnabel, "What if that inspector fellow comes back and torments us?" Of course the owners didn't want to remember. The boss, whose huge mass of fat aroused laughter among the spectators and provoked calls of "He doesn't feed on wood dust," even claimed that he considered the inspector a fine man of the sort you would like to socialize with. Schnabel didn't want to remember anything except that he'd heard from the sawer Kranzritter that I had made the complaint in the membership meeting and he'd told the owner about it. "Now, sir," the court president asked the boss, "in other respects wasn't Bromme always a diligent and competent worker?"

The witness replied, "He was never diligent; I won't say anything against his competence, but he was a big agitator; especially at the time of the local diet and Reichstag elections he was always reading newspapers and constantly agitating among my workers for the elections, for the Social Democratic party, and

---

*Bromme had previously been in trouble for taking some cherries from an orchard.

for the union." That's what the man said in front of the court, and I'd been assured by Master Sergeant Prager that I was considered a diligent and competent person! Then Schüler was called, and after his testimony he asked to be excused because he had to attend an important committee meeting in the diet. "Oh, you're the diet deputy Schüler?" the court president said. He asked the defense lawyer and the expert whether they had any more questions of the witness. They said they didn't and Schüler was excused with a bow and "many thanks" from the president.

After this, Factory Inspector Böhnisch was asked to give his testimony and expert opinions. He said something like the following: "The complaints of these workers were entirely justified. I was pleased that they turned to me. I myself can't be everywhere, so the workers should come to me. That was their perfect right. I've had my eye on this factory even under the earlier owner, but he had no money; and where there's no money even the factory inspector has to keep quiet. But just when the ownership changed, I'd made it a matter of principle to bring about changes in the hygienic conditions; that would have happened without the instigation of these workers. At my last inspection I went into the shed, a wretched room with machine after machine. Everything was enveloped in a frightful cloud of dust, so that it would not have taken long for these workers to catch consumption. All I can say is that the defendants didn't exaggerate in any respect. They were completely within their rights." Then it was our lawyer's turn for his speech for the defense. Basing his argument on the expert's testimony, he tore the whole case to pieces, and pointed out that we had absolutely no power to proclaim a boycott. He demanded the acquittal of both defendants and the assumption of expenses by the state.

Now all eyes were riveted on the first state's attorney. In his speech he said that there were all the signs of an attempted extortion, and he moved that both defendants be sentenced to a week in jail plus assumption of the expenses. The judges withdrew to consult. Anxious minutes followed. A half hour must have gone by and the judges still didn't come back. There was an eerie silence in the courtroom. I looked questioningly over to the editors who were sitting among the spectators. Then I turned to my codefendant Rössel and whispered in his ear that we'd probably have to be prepared for a three-day sentence. Fifteen minutes later the state's attorneys came over and whispered to our lawyers, "Your chances are getting better." How endlessly long the time was! The clock hands crawled ahead like snails. I thought of the proverb: "Better a frightful end than a fright without end." What was my wife thinking about at home now?

Finally, after an hour and ten minutes the judges reappeared. "In the name of the Duke"—What would this mouth pronounce now?—"the court dismisses the charges and the state assumes the court costs." What a feeling of joy there was in me! The president continued, "Nevertheless the court was not convinced of the complete innocence of the defendants; therefore they must pay their own expenses." "You're acquitted, you can go," the president called to us. Then we went into the witness room where the boss was already putting on his coat. Just then our newspaper publisher appeared at the door and called out, "Hey, come on, let's go and see the ape now." The boss turned red but didn't say anything. We said heartfelt good-byes to the factory inspector and our lawyer. Then we had lunch and drank a few glasses of beer together. Toward evening we took the train home; I'd already sent a telegram to my wife at noon: "Both let off free." The union reimbursed us for every pfennig of our expenses and every hour of lost work time, even those during the pretrial hearing. Only someone who's been in a similar situation can imagine our joy. The owner had gone back on the earlier train. When he got to his office, he sent for my father and told him of the acquittal, which he'd already heard about from my wife. He would have been sorry if I'd been convicted, the owner added.

Then came quieter times again. My brother returned, after long travels as a mason, in order to take winter work nailing slippers. Later he always worked during the summer as a mason in Leipzig until he got married a few years ago. His wife owns a little house and a nice fruit and vegetable plot that she inherited from her grandfather. So he is not badly off and lives happily, especially because, unlike me, he has no children. As for me, my wife presented me with another daughter in the last days of the previous century, on Christmas Eve to be exact. It was our fourth child and we named her Elisabeth. It was a sad Christmas holiday, and it still makes me sad when I think about it. The other three children needed to be looked after and my wife lay in confinement. If my mother-in-law hadn't done the most urgent housework for me, I would have been desperate. Still I didn't consider myself completely unhappy because we had several pounds of flour to make potato cakes and fruitcake, and we had a roast rabbit for the holiday too. The rabbit was supplied by my father-in-law.

Of course, during her many confinements my wife never had "childbed soup" or any such hearty nourishment. The strongest thing I could offer her was a cup of chocolate; otherwise she had to make do with coffee and rolls. She shunned pastry and cookies because these contained a lot of yeast, and one of her friends had died in her childbed after enjoying pastries. My wife always crawled out of bed on the second day after her delivery and on the third, or at the latest fourth, day she was up and taking care of the house as usual. After a week she was back to her sewing. Unfortunately, after her second child she no longer had health insurance, even though I'd always pressured her to have it. Only recently has she become a member of the health plan at her factory. What good luck that she was never bedridden in the meantime, as has happened to me so often! For although she's had to live a worse, more wretched life than I, she's healthier and stronger than I am. Her weight always stays at seventy-five kilos or more. Her total abstinence from any alcohol certainly helps; she even scorns light beer. When the youngest children were babies, she always slept badly at night. They'd sleep during the day and cry for hours during the night, which of course made their mother angry, upset, and nervous, and likely to get carried away with harsh language, abuse, and curses against the children. It's too bad that she could only nurse the children for six to eight weeks; then her milk would run out.

How often she complained to me of the suffering that having

so many children had caused her. It broke my heart whenever she read in the paper that such and such a family with no children had lost another baby. Then she'd cry out: "No, these people are lucky, they have it great; now they've lost another baby, that would have been the sixth if they'd all lived. They can have all the fun they want and people like us are tormented; we have to spend everything on the children and can't give ourselves anything. You can't even justify putting a ragged skirt on your body, the children take too much. Just last week I spent two marks at the shoemaker's, this week Heddel's shoes are being resoled, Ernst's are worn out again and have to be fixed, and Walter doesn't have any shoes at all. Then they all need felt slippers and we badly need a bed; I'd rather go without eating; sleeping three to a bed is no sleep at all." Amidst all this, abuses and harsh language against the children, curses, and finally tears. She grew up among peasants, uneducated; all she shared with her sisters were harsh words and bad food, mostly potatoes, bread, and chicory broth. Any view of a higher life of the mind was foreign to her. She considered all of my books a useless extravagance. I forgave her because she was still good-hearted and bore a lot of suffering. I compared her to a mater dolorosa when she used to sit on the coal box and complain bitterly of our sad plight.

So it continued, year in and year out. And still more children came. True, I did earn somewhat more in the factory, and I got some outside income as a fire insurance agent, but that yielded hardly anything. Then I was a correspondent for the *Chemnitz People's Voice* [*Chemnitzer Volksstimme*] because the *Altenburger People's Paper* was a regional subsidiary of a Leipzig paper and couldn't always use everything. I also contributed frequently to the *Berlin People's Paper* [*Berliner Volkszeitung*]. By this work, and later activity as an agent for a dry goods firm in Thun, I at least earned enough to pay the rent and have some pocket money; and I could occasionally satisfy my intellectual hunger by buying a book, magazine, or such. I also tried my hand at writing fiction, but mostly without much success; but my first story did succeed and was accepted by the *True Jacob* [*Wahrer Jakob*] with a fifteen-mark royalty. My wife had grumbled that I'd sat up half the night writing. But even she laughed when I brought home the three blue five-mark notes. She'd just gotten up from her childbed and was happy that I could use some of the money to get her cocoa and a pigeon. *Postilion, Forward,* and *The New World* [*Postillon, Vorwärts,* and *Die Neue Welt*] have also published articles by me. On the whole my writings leave a lot to be desired. But they have at least brought me a few marks extra income. Later, when I was often lying at home sick, these things became my main income. Except for a few pfennigs of health insurance there was then no other income and we really had to do without. We went deeper into debt that way.

In July 1901, my wife gave birth to a second son, our fifth child. My wife wanted to name him Walter, so naturally I agreed. He too was taken to church alone by the midwife. No baptismal ceremony was organized for him since there was of course no money. I had my cousin, the engineer Oswald Böttger; my old boyhood friend, the teacher Ernst Dietzmann in Meuselwitz; and Richard Grau, a fellow worker I'd grown fond of, all registered as godparents. They gave me permission to do it, and the whole thing was taken care of. But now there was still another mouth to feed in the family and once more we had to cut back. Naturally I didn't get any fatter. Shakespeare says somewhere in his works, "The leanness that afflicts us, the object of our misery, is an inventory to particularize their [the patricians'] abundance."* If that's so, our employers must be raking in huge riches, while on our side an immense mass of misery, misfortune, care, and worry is generated anew.

Coriolanus, act 1, scene 1. Bromme paraphrases as, "Die Magerkeit des Plebejers ist der Gradmesser, an dem der Patrizier sein Kapital misst."

A Barmaid

This anonymous author (ca. 1882–?) tried all the usual work open to working-class women: a variety of unskilled factory jobs and domestic service positions. Dissatisfied with the harsh conditions and low pay, she finally settles into the relatively well-paid job of barmaid. We know little of the author's background, and why she wrote an autobiography is a matter of speculation. She may have met the editor during the period of her life when she traveled in middle-class circles as the mistress of a man she had met in a tavern. In any case, her account affords a unique look into the semirespectable world of turn-of-the-century taverns, where the barmaid was considered "fair game" for any man with money. This extraordinary autobiography is a mine of information on sexual mores and the part they play in the subjection of working-class women. The setting for the two chapters presented here is a large north German city (possibly Hamburg), probably about 1900.

IN THE FACTORY

My work in the factory consisted of folding letter paper, counting it off, and packing it along with envelopes into boxes. The workday was from six o'clock in the morning to six o'clock in the evening or from seven o'clock in the morning to seven o'clock in the evening, depending on the time of year; there was a one-hour lunch break. My wages amounted to six marks a week, which I turned over to my mother in return for room and board. I couldn't even get myself a pair of boots with the paltry wages; and what's more, I had a foreman who was very strict with me, especially because my jokes often made my coworkers laugh and kept them from their work—or so he said; it wasn't at all the case. So I soon quit the job and went to work in a cardboard box factory. I had to stand at a large machine and finish making the cut boxes.

My wages were eight marks a week, and I would have been happy to have stayed there, but I was frail and I couldn't tolerate the prolonged standing that the work demanded. I was sent away in two weeks, but I didn't get upset about it because, as I said, standing up was so hard for me that I was often thinking of some pretext just to be able to sit down for a while. The difference between the two jobs was just too great! In the paper factory I had to sit the whole day, and now I had to stand the whole day; it was just too much for me.

For a change, and in order to recover, I took a position as a governess—in a family with no fewer than eight children! I most enjoyed being with the wet nurse, who slipped me all kinds of tidbits to eat in return for favors I was happy to do for her. I was exceptionally well off here, though the work was hard. But they say the grass is always greener on the other side of the hill, and so I couldn't hold out long in this job either. My boss had a

Translated from *Im Kampf ums Dasein! Wahrheitsgetreue Lebenserinnerungen eines Mädchens aus dem Volke als Fabrikarbeiterin, Dienstmädchen und Kellnerin,* ed. Dr. G. Braun (Stuttgart: Verlag von Karl Weber & Co., n.d. [ca. 1908]), 67–109.

suspenders factory in the yard of his house, and when I saw the factory girls at work, I longed to sit among them instead of tending children. So I approached my boss in his office and asked him to take me on in his factory, which he did, after he'd gotten over his astonishment. There was an emotional departure from the many little ones. It really hurt me to have to leave the little ones; but my yearning for the factory and the higher wages (seven marks a week!) must have been stronger.

My work was easy and I liked it. But my fondness for change quickly drove me away to a competitor's factory which paid one mark more a week. Things were much harder there because the directress supervised very closely; still I was in good standing with her. I was soon well liked because of my singing of witty refrains and songs that I knew from my earlier days. When the other factory girls heard these songs, they quickly took them up and it really sounded like a music hall. It probably would have gone on like this for a long time if the factory owner hadn't noticed that less work was being done now than before.

Once when we thought he was in his private apartment in the front building, he listened at the door and heard what was actually going on. Right at that moment I was standing at a sewing machine and singing a crude verse that the workers found terribly funny. It was a Monday, just when there was usually a lot to do because the material from Sunday had to be processed. The boss listened quietly to my recital, then he came in and signaled me to come to the office. I knew already what was in store for me. I was reproached for corrupting his whole personnel; I received my wages, and I was out. Still, I tried to get back in favor with the man by having his wife, who lived in the house in front, intercede for me, but it did no good.

There began now a very tough period for me. Everywhere I looked for work everything was always taken, so that I was really getting desperate.

We had a lodger who worked at a glassworks and she took an interest in me. She succeeded in getting me a job there at nine marks a week, without overtime. Now unfortunately, the work shift there was from four o'clock at night until four o'clock in the afternoon and in alternate weeks just the opposite. This was extremely exhausting considering the heat. Actually, our work was of a kind that should have been done by men, because we had to take the red-hot bottles to the cooling room using special shovels with long handles, and we suffered excessively from the heat. Of course this work made us very thirsty—all the more because the bottles planted all sorts of ideas in our heads—and so our tin coffee jugs were empty before we knew it. Fortunately we could buy a light brown beer cheaply from the workers' wives, who fetched the beer in buckets from a brewery and then put it into bottles.

In the long run the work in this place didn't suit me because it was also rather in disrepute with the other factory girls. The work was very dirty too; and we looked like Negroes when we went home. That didn't matter when we came home at night; but in the afternoon we were very ashamed to walk down the street like this, but we couldn't wash up at the factory. Along the way there was a good deal of teasing from people we knew.

Also, I felt like a convict because at the glassworks everyone had a control number at the entrance and exit.

After I'd earned enough so that I could buy some clothing, I got out of this factory.

I then went to a shoe factory, where I had to pack shoes. My partner in this work was very much in the family way. It was known that one of the higher functionaries in the factory had gotten her into this condition, but that he didn't intend to marry her; she was very unhappy about all this.

Since the man in question had to stop bothering her, he was looking for another victim for his lust; his eyes fell on me, but he didn't have much luck because I bluntly brushed him off. The result of this was that after two weeks I was back out on the street again, which was unpleasant for me mostly because the work had been easy and the pay relatively good.

I then worked in a candy factory, where I assembled so-called "good luck packets." But I soon got out of there because I was eating more candy myself than I was putting into the bags. Then I got a job feeding paper into the press in a print shop, a position I soon gave up because the prolonged standing was too tiring for me.

My mother advised me now to learn straw-hat making, and I went to a large hat factory where I was taken on as an apprentice. I was assigned to an older spinster lady who was supposed to teach me the machine weaving of straw hats.

Of course at first I wasn't very skillful at it; and since my mistress was a very easily irritated and excitable person, the whole day long she kept hitting me on the hands whenever she saw me doing so nething wrong. That didn't bother me too much though, because I was used to totally different beatings at home,* and so sometimes I even intentionally provoked her in order to make her angry. My fellow workers knew what was going on and laughed every time the woman got mad, which of course only made matters worse.

All of us here were subject to the foreman, who tormented us a great deal. For example, he made us wait for hours, often totally ignoring us, in the office where we had to pick up our work. When we would ask him politely to take care of us, he'd say roughly, "Don't have time," and off he'd go. This situation was particularly bad for us because we were doing piecework; so, if we weren't given any work, we didn't earn anything. As it was, straw weaving was already very badly paid; the processing of one bundle of straw, from which three to five hats could be made, took us a good half-day and paid thirty-five pfennigs. We even had to pay the factory for the yarn at seventy pfennigs a roll, and also buy machine oil and other utensils (which they always overcharged for), so that on payday there wasn't much left for us. When we delivered the hats, it often happened that the directress would throw back at us the ones she thought weren't well made; this happened many times, depending on her mood.

This directress was an especially beautiful woman whom I

---

* An apparent reference to beatings by her father.

quite frequently stared at and admired for her beauty, in spite of the bad treatment she meted out to me.

Because she had us completely in her power, we couldn't allow ourselves any grumbling, lest we be thrown out.

We worked in the loft of the factory, which was called the "straw floor." Women who cleaned men's hats worked beneath us on the third floor; they thought they were a lot better than we poor straw-hat weavers, which is why they wouldn't even say hello to us. During the time we had to wait for our work, we busied ourselves with all kinds of needlework, played cards, and so on; of course we didn't earn anything then.

Because my highest wages amounted to no more than five to six marks per week, I got fed up and stopped going.

For a change, I took another day position in a private home, where two days later the wife went into labor and gave birth to a child in my presence. Despite my tender years, I assisted her bravely, although the mother's screams of pain broke my heart.

Now that I'd had a taste of factory life, I no longer had any desire to deal with the many little children here, especially because the diapers didn't agree with me, for obvious reasons. So I took a job in a fish smokehouse where I took fish off the spits and put new ones on. There I was among nothing but older women, who teased me as an innocent young thing and tried to disgust me into leaving. I felt very uncomfortable there and I just gave up my wages and didn't return the next day.

Next I went to a cigar factory, where I had to strip tobacco leaves. I was the only girl there among nothing but men, and one can imagine that the talk I heard there was often very "salty." Like all cigar workers, these men were fanatic Social Democrats, so I was introduced to politics, in which I gradually acquired an interest.

The air in the workplace was not exactly the best because all the workers smoked as they worked, so heavily, in fact, that you often couldn't recognize the person sitting right across from you. I suffered greatly from the smoke and asked for something to take for my headache; one of the workers advised me to smoke along with everyone else and my headache would go away. Of course I followed the advice and my headache really did get better. Before it did though, I showed all the symptoms that beginning smokers suffer from, which greatly amused my coworkers.

I smoked small cigars that were made especially for me, and gradually I found pleasure in it.

I had to put up with a lot of pestering—often carried too far—from my male coworkers; but since they didn't appeal to me, they didn't get anywhere with me. After a few weeks, when I realized that in the long run I couldn't take working in the smoke, I quit my job. I was actually fairly sick, so I stayed home for some time, which got me back into debt. And when I finally looked for another job, I couldn't find one for a long time.

I then went to a hiring agent to see if she had anything for me; what I wanted was something easy because with my weak constitution I couldn't take on any hard physical work. As fate would have it, I fell into the hands of an agent whose specialty it was to recruit very young girls as barmaids, for which she was very well paid by the barkeepers. After I told her my troubles, how I couldn't find work because of my physical weakness, she told me I'd come to just the right person; she knew of a job for me where I wouldn't have to do any more than serve the customers, and where I could still earn up to fifty marks a week.

That was just what I wanted to hear because I had a lot of debts and also wanted to get myself some nice clothes, which I hadn't been able to do up to then.

I ran straight to my mother to tell her of my lucky prospects, and delighted, she went with me to the agent. It didn't occur to either of us that it really wasn't right for someone so young to become a barmaid. We didn't know that this position had a bad reputation; rather, we thought that you could become a barmaid just as well as a housemaid.

The tavern owner liked me as soon as he saw me. He hired me, and all I had to do was buy an apron, get a coin purse to tie on it, and cut off a couple forelocks—and there I was, a barmaid. And so began a new period of my life.

MY FIRST EXPERIENCES AS A BARMAID

My first position was in a very small tavern with only four tables, served by two barmaids. My colleague was a divorced woman who had run away from her husband because he had mistreated her. I was young and (so I was told) pretty; and my full head of hair was often admired by the customers. So this woman was jealous of me and tried to damage me in every way. But nothing worked for her; I was preferred by the customers because they were put off by my coworker's insolence, whereas my modest and shy manner really attracted them. The owner's wife had me approach a customer as he came in the door; and as soon as I'd gotten him his drink I was to ask him, "May I have a drink with you?"

At first I did it very shyly and I was frequently offended by the crude behavior of the customers, because they usually didn't take me up on my offer right off, but rather made all sorts of filthy comments before agreeing. Often I cried bitterly after the customers were all gone because I had to put up with so much. The customers' first question was usually, "Where do you live? Can I come and visit you?" And then they would try to kiss me or otherwise fondle me, which I always vigorously forbade. I usually heard in reply, "This is no cloister, my child!" or, "That's only your first reaction, you'll like it better!"

My coworker, who was of course more easily accessible, always called me the "Virgin" or the "Hypocrite," because she just couldn't understand why I didn't willingly agree to the customers' propositions, as she did. We got a cut of ten pfennigs from every fifty-pfennig grog we were treated to; we had to consume great quantities of this wretched hooch, made out of nothing but bilberries mixed with cherry juice. We also got a fifty-pfennig cut from every bottle of so-called "red wine," which cost fifty to sixty pfennigs wholesale but was sold for five marks. In this little tavern, where the owner's wife was always on watch, the customers couldn't get too fresh without this corpulent lady calling them to order, or if that didn't work, kicking them out. She didn't want to have anything to do with the police. If, in spite of all this, the customers often spent a lot of money in the tavern, it was usually in the hope of being allowed to accompany us home after work—usually at three or four o'clock in the morning. But by that time they were usually so loaded that they were happy if we packed them into a taxi that drove them home.

One time it even happened that a sailor who had signed on to a crew forgot all about his ship in his stupor of love and wine and didn't get there until it had already left. He got into a lot of trouble.

It didn't bother him though; he simply came back to us and kept on drinking. Sometimes a very respectable type would stray into the tavern; for example, I remember a young man who came frequently and fell in love with me. He not only behaved very respectfully toward me, he also accompanied me to my door early in the morning so I wouldn't be molested on the way home.

The long walk was nothing to him so long as he knew that I'd gotten home safely.

Since I wasn't at all accustomed to drinking alcoholic beverages in my youth, at first I couldn't tolerate too much, and I often went home drunk. I was glad to get into bed, where I went to sleep immediately. We took turns waiting on the customers, which often led to quarrels between us about whose turn it was. One time my coworker thought she could claim a customer whom I was supposed to wait on; she got so mad that she smashed a full beer bottle on my skull and knocked me unconscious. But she didn't escape punishment, because just then my friend came into the tavern (as he did every evening), and when he saw what had happened, he gave her a good thrashing. Of course I knew nothing about it; I lay on the sofa in the tavern until the next morning and then was taken home in a taxi by the young man; there I was packed immediately into bed and given ice compresses.

It took a week for me to get the cobwebs out of my head. Of course I didn't go back to my old position but rather took a new job that the young man had arranged for in the meantime.

This was a larger establishment, where I had seven coworkers.

Since there was already someone there with my name, I was immediately rechristened by the owner—of course with the accompaniment of generous toasts by all the customers present. I served in a little alcove in the rear where there were two tables, while out front each girl had to wait on only one table. Like all newcomers, I was teased by my older coworkers and used as an errand girl.

This tavern was also relatively respectable, since the owner didn't leave his place at the bar and constantly saw to it that nothing indecent happened. Because my section was in the rear, my customers thought they had a right to be more venturesome than in the front room. But they were mistaken, because even here you were constantly under the eye of the owner, who could keep close watch on the whole room through a little window behind the bar; not to mention the fact that I didn't put up with anything. Though the customers were prevented from touching you, they took revenge by being all the more filthy in their talk, so that I had ample opportunities to learn what I still didn't know along this line.

If the customers came into the tavern and bought a grog or even a bottle of wine for us, they considered us fair game with which they could do everything they wanted; of course they got very angry when they saw that they couldn't get what they wanted, so there were a lot of nasty scenes, and often even physical violence on their part. Almost all of them wanted to accompany us home. Since that was out of the question, we arranged things so that when we got off work at about three o'clock in the morning we would go with them to a neighboring coffeehouse that was known as a gathering place of the "demimonde." We then quickly disappeared on some pretext and left our "admirers" sitting in the coffeehouse while we slipped out through another exit we knew about.

We were all the happier to get into bed since we usually had to be at work at one o'clock in the afternoon and thus had a sixteen-hour workday behind us.* So, being a barmaid is not as

---

* Perhaps a misprint; the workday described is only fourteen hours.

rosy as certain people imagine, since the excessive drinking of bad wine and other alcoholic beverages can't be called a pleasure and debilitates your whole body.

You might think that our behavior would keep the customers from coming back, but you'd be wrong. The next day they tried to make us jealous by bragging about their "successes" with the ladies at the coffeehouse; of course they didn't suspect that that was exactly why we had dragged them there.

Every girl in our tavern had a "fiancé" to whom she was faithful, so other men had no luck with her no matter how much they spent on her. Of course there were occasional exceptions, but if the owner found out that the girl was having anything to do with customers outside the tavern she was fired immediately, because the owner naturally wanted to string the customers along as much as possible without letting any of them reach his goal.

The owner also didn't want the customers to see the barmaids' engagement rings, since the customers would have stayed away had they known they couldn't do anything with the girls. So the rings were always carried in your purse and put on only when your "fiancé" was around. You could usually tell exactly when this would be since most of them were sailors, whose arrival could be learned from the ship's register. The barmaids were also frequently engaged for business reasons, and since there was also an engagement ring in these cases, they had to be careful not to get the rings switched.

The "business" engagements were made only to get the customers to come back and drink a lot. These engagement parties were especially lively, so that the engaged gentlemen often left the tavern without a groschen in their purses. Each "business" fiancé wanted a picture of his chosen one to carry on his travels, so each of us girls had a whole bunch of photographs that we'd gotten cheaply; this was particularly nice for me because in my girlhood I'd never been photographed.

One evening there came into the tavern a sailor of the better sort, whom I had to wait on. He was wearing a gray hat and overcoat that I found particularly attractive and striking since I wasn't used to seeing such fine clothes. I took an instant liking to the man, all the more so because he behaved in such a quiet, reserved manner, which was usually not the case with the other customers. He noticed from my shy manner that I probably hadn't been a barmaid for long, which I confirmed. When I told him a lot about my childhood, he began to get still more interested in me.

I told my sweetheart of my paternal grandfather who lived in a town in what was then Denmark, how he was frivolous and inclined to drinking. It's said that once when he was drunk he'd given my pregnant grandmother such a kick that she later died as a result during the birth of a son—my future father. It affected my grandfather so deeply that he gave himself up completely to drink and later died in a lunatic asylum.

My father was a cigar worker in a suburb of a big city, and joined the socialist movement at an early age; he was a zealous agitator among his fellow workers.

Since the Socialist Law was in effect at that time, he soon came into conflict with the law, and, along with eight comrades, he was sentenced to prison for distributing socialist literature.

The nine months that he spent there were the very darkest days of his life and prompted him to spend a lot of time in pubs in order to politicize. He would spend the better part of his earnings there, so that his affairs went quickly downhill.

As one of the oldest children of my grandparents, my mother had to go to the country and do heavy housework; and in her fourteenth year she had to leave her parents' house with a little bundle in her hand and support herself, because there wasn't any more bread in the house for her.

She took a variety of positions as a maid, where she had to work very hard. But that didn't hurt her because when she was only a seven-year-old child she had had to work in the sack factory in her hometown during the winter when there was no farm work to do; she got a starvation wage of six pfennigs per thousand sacks. At the same age she'd also worked in a match factory when there wasn't much to do in the other factory.

In her hometown she'd had a boyfriend from a well-to-do family; they had already had a love affair (and not without consequences), so she persuaded him to come to her later in order to get married. However the young man's parents would hear nothing of it; by threatening to disinherit him if he married such a poor girl, they forced him to drop her and make a wealthy marriage—in which he was very unhappy because he couldn't get over the loss of his young lover, who was considered very beautiful.

While my mother was working in the sack factory, she gave birth to a pretty girl; but the baby lived only a year and even today my mother grieves for her.

During this time my mother boarded at the same house with the man who would later be my father; that's how they got acquainted. They were soon sleeping together since my father promised to marry my mother, which he did only after my mother had given birth to three children. He had persuaded her to move to a larger city, where he got employment as a cigar worker while my mother entered a sack factory there.

After the marriage he got secretly engaged to a cook whom he often spent time with and went out with. This affair lasted eighteen months, and my mother knew nothing of it because my father had told her that the doctor had ordered him to take daily walks for his consumption.

My mother might not have found out about it for a long time if she hadn't been using her lunch break at the factory to wash dishes for a woman she knew who ran a lunch counter; in return she got a free meal for the whole family. One day this woman told her that an acquaintance of hers had gotten engaged to a man who was also a cigar worker and who had the same name as my mother's husband. She became suspicious, connected it with the frequent walks, and, in order to find out, persuaded the woman to accompany her to a dance hall which the pair frequented.

The day after this woman learned the true situation, she told my father's "bride" that if she wanted to see her "bridegroom" she only had to go two houses further and there she could see him sitting together with his wife and four children.

The girl actually did go and found my father while he was with his family; I've been told that he had me on his lap just at that moment. When she saw what the situation was, she went up to my father (who turned chalk white), spit in his face, told him to go to the devil, threw the ring at his feet, and walked out. And that was the end of the matter.

As far as my parents' wedding goes, my mother told me that for the civil ceremony my father had to borrow a suit, cylinder hat, and coat from a master joiner she knew, because he himself didn't own such "precious" items. As usual, there wasn't much money in the house, so my father intended to sell a box of cigars that he'd saved up at work and use the proceeds to show my mother a good time on the wedding night. But he stayed in a tavern with his friends drinking up everything in celebration so that my mother sat at home alone with the children and didn't even get supper. The next morning my father showed up in an undescribable state in his borrowed suit!

A promising beginning to a marriage!

My friend listened attentively as I related this, sympathized with me, and was probably thinking that I was a chip off the old block. You can do what you want to with her! And I believed his deceitful words and loved him all the more for his sympathy and interest in me. We kissed to our heart's content and I often forgot where I really was, so that the owner, who was watching us, had to knock to remind me of business.

I thought that this man had honest intentions with me because he often spoke to me of marriage. But he kept mentioning that I'd of course have to give up my job and be a maid again if I wanted to be his bride. I took this to heart and went back to being a maid right away so that he would find me "worthy of him" when he came back from his voyage. It's obvious from this that I truly loved him, so that it wasn't hard for him to do what he wanted with me after he'd lured me to his ship and gotten me drunk on a strong Malaga he'd given me.

I found out afterward that he just wanted to have me out of the tavern because he had his eye on an especially pretty coworker of mine and I stood in his way. I found out about it by accident and was so unhappy from jealousy that I resolved to throw myself into the water right at the place where his ship was docked. I carried out this decision but was pulled from the water by the sailors, who had observed me without my knowing it; they quickly dressed me in dry men's clothing—there being no other kind on the ship—and took me to my friend's cabin. I stayed there until one o'clock in the morning to surprise him with his new lover, and, sure enough, about that time he did appear with her. However, I didn't get to see her because when my friend came on board and heard about what had happened, he sent her away and came to me saying, "Look how you've disgraced me! What will people think!"

That was his first thought, not a word of love for me, so that I saw how things stood, and I was cured of my love from then on. The next morning, when my clothes were dry, I got dressed so I could go home to my mother and have a good cry. She comforted me and gave me new courage to live; she also advised me to give up my maid's job and go back to my old position since I was better off there.

When I went back to my old tavern, I was met with "Hello" from my former coworkers. My competitor had since been fired because she didn't know the difference between "mine" and "thine." I later heard that she'd ended up in a bordello, which was where she belonged anyway. She was the only barmaid in the whole region who had come down so in the world, for in those days the barmaids were not as disreputable and tainted as in later times; rather, they were careful not to do anything wrong.

Misfortune never strikes but once. I got to know a man who spent something on me in the tavern and persuaded himself that he could go home with me; he had no success, but I had to pay dearly for that. Of course I accompanied him to a café in order to "dump" him, just like the other customers; but he saw my intention and took my umbrella, which I didn't want to lose, as a "hostage."

I wanted to go with him to still another café where I might have better luck getting rid of him; on the way there we passed his apartment and he tried to get me to go up with him. When he saw that I wouldn't, he got mad and ran off with my umbrella with me in pursuit shouting, "Help! My umbrella!"

The man stopped at a policeman and I saw how he said a few words to him and then went on, leaving my umbrella with the policeman. When I came up to the policeman, I got my umbrella back but at the same time the policeman said to me, "Come with me!"

"Where to?" I asked naively.

"You'll see," he replied. We went into the station, where a policeman received me and took me to a back room where a variety of the lowest class of prostitutes were already sitting.

Of course I immediately started to cry and complain, because I had no idea why I was really here since I was the victim of the theft and had done nothing wrong.

I spent the whole night crying despite the comforting of the policemen; I couldn't think of sleeping because the benches were much too hard; I couldn't understand how the other women and girls could sleep. The next morning the police van, called "Green Gus," pulled up and took me, along with every imaginable sort of character, to the town hall. I was to have a physical exam here; but since that wasn't possible because I was having my monthly period, I was taken in the same van to the hospital. I had to stay there until the end of my period so that I could be examined then. We were all stripped for the exam and first weighed; then, one after another, we had to lie on a specially designed table, called the "Tiroler," which made the exam easier. During the exam the young doctors stood around and helped the head doctor, and made comments that were not always very delicate.

I thought I'd die of shame because I'd fallen into this company very unjustly. When my turn came, the doctor found nothing wrong with me; he just remarked that I had a bad tooth, which he immediately pulled out, although I asked him to leave it because I could have kept it for a long time.

Of course I was then released and I went back to my job again, where I blamed my absence on illness because I was embarrassed to tell the truth, although I was completely blameless for my stay at the hospital.

The way I make out the thing now was that this man wanted to take revenge on me because he couldn't get his way with me despite spending money on me for drinks. But what I can't understand even today is why this man, who had certainly slandered me, was not brought face-to-face with me, but rather simply believed!

Otto Krille,
Factory Worker

Otto Krille (1878–1954) was the son of a mason killed in an accident before Otto's birth. In 1895, he was discharged as "unfit" from a military school, where he had studied to become a noncommissioned officer. For the next five years he struggled to make his living as an unskilled factory worker in Dresden. His ambition was to become a free-lance writer. After a stint in the army, he was befriended by a bourgeois patroness, who helped him to establish himself as an editor, poet, playwright, and eventually, a youth leader. In 1933, he emigrated to Switzerland, where he lived until his death in 1954. Unlike the other authors in this book, Krille writes from the perspective of someone who has "arrived," albeit in a modest sort of way. Like those of Franz Rehbein and Franz Bergg, Krille's autobiography has a self-conscious literary quality about it. Nonetheless, Krille has certainly not lost touch with what it feels like to be unemployed and struggling for dignity. And his atmospheric evocation of Social Democratic politics is unsurpassed in the autobiographical literature.

FACTORY WORKER

It was humiliating to have to run from factory to factory and from business to business to offer myself as a scribe, a packer, an errand boy, and a work boy. But what else could I do since my knowledge of practical workaday life was very small, and my mother was unable to pay for me to learn a profitable trade. The first times were the worst for me. The false sense of shame that I had from the military school made me hesitate at the doors or even turn around. When I had gotten up the courage and shyly and blushingly stammered out my request and softly answered all questions, the end result would kill all my hopes for the rest of the day. Except for my discharge certificate from the noncommissioned officers' school, I had neither testimony of work performed nor anything else that could speak for me. All I had was my honest seventeen-year-old face. But on my discharge certificate was written in fine neat letters: Discharged as unsuitable to be a noncommissioned officer. You could make everything or nothing out of that, and my dear fellow citizens (in all their humanity) probably thought the very worst. The searching looks that they gave my face revealed their thoughts. I secretly clenched my fist during this silent inquisition; and my shame was even more oppressive when I still didn't get the position or was sent away with the remark that they would write if I got it.

I'd had such a colorful, glowing vision of life and had yearned so greatly for my freedom, but after these secret tortures there wasn't a glimmer of all my dreams left. Any thoughts of a career as an actor were obliterated, and I even missed out on the sense of regret that often gives consolation to weak-willed people. What did I know about life anyway? It looked so different than in books. Like a Kaspar Hauser who'd been in an underground

Translated from Otto Krille, *Unter dem Joch: Die Geschichte einer Jugend,* ed. Ursula Münchow (Berlin: Akademie Verlag, 1975), 89–97, 103–6, 108–14. Originally published by Egon Fleischel & Co., Berlin, 1914.

prison,* I was suddenly confronted with the mystery of life, whose stony indifferent face could only preach: Work so that you don't go under. I was a slender, pale, and shy boy, and must have offered to the world a conflicting picture. Although my mother didn't reproach me, I could tell from her anxious looks how much my fate and my continued unemployment worried her. But not for a minute did I have any remorse or secret yearning to go back to the military school. Even as a simple worker I had the freedom to think and do as I pleased outside the factory, and I had control over my own fate. Or so it seemed to me.

Finally one day I returned home with a happy face. I'd found a position as a scribe. I was a little anxious about the demands that would be put on me, but my joy overcame all. Of course my handwriting was not exactly beautiful. I'd been told before that a hen chased through the ink would leave tracks just as neat as my writing. The next morning I started my job with my heart pounding. The business was called the "Office of Real Estate Sales" and was owned by two older bachelor gentlemen. Besides me, there was a man of about twenty-seven who was a kind of bookkeeper. The two of us comprised the staff. The work was easy; mostly I had to make two copies of contracts. The signing by both parties usually took place in the single-room office. Usually one or more bottles of wine were drunk and I always got at least a glassful. Then the men would exchange views on all sorts of subjects; they talked a little about politics but more about pleasures, especially women. The conversation would always become cynical. All this was a new world for me, but I didn't like it. I soon noticed that the business was not always conducted cleanly, and the wine was only there to put the buyer in a good mood for the fleecing. I soon found it deeply repulsive. One time they sent me to see a widow who had a little grocery store. I was supposed to warn her about a debt; but I quickly saw that she

---

* Kaspar Hauser, a mysterious youth who appeared suddenly in Nuremberg in 1828, was popularly thought to have been raised in total isolation.

was very badly off, and when she made promises with tears in her eyes, I returned to the office empty-handed. There they told me that tears were cheaper than money and we would have to make short work of her. The bookkeeper advised me that on such a fool's errand I should at least have had her serve me a bottle of wine. The next time he went with me and was quite hard on her until she gave us cigars and wine so that he would promise to put in a good word for her with his boss. Of course he never did. I had to drink along with them; and never has wine had such a bitter taste. After a few weeks the widow's store was closed.

The "Office of Real Estate Sales" also soon ceased to exist, and I was quite satisfied since I'd never had a happy hour there. But now I was unemployed again, and I had to run to the newspapers every day in order to get the want ads as soon as they came out and, if possible, be the first one to show up for an advertised position. This time I did it with different feelings than before, and also with more skill. I'd seen something of real life and its hideous struggles. Since there was an economic crisis, it was once again several weeks before I had work; my mother's melancholy face often cut me to the quick. There were hundreds in the same situation as I was in, or even worse off. Before, I had considered it a disgrace to stand around at the newspaper printer's and fight for a paper, and I would sneak off like a beaten dog. This remnant of my military school education disappeared fast. And I learned to see and to feel.

One thing was certain: I had to look for work in order to be able to live; I had an honest desire to work, but I couldn't get any. My will to live was fading; I seemed to be pushed to one side, delivered to an uncertain fate, perhaps destruction; and there was no place where I could complain about it. Somewhere there had to be a gap in the order of the world. And the thought that perhaps thousands of others were in the same predicament made it even more horrible. It was a pitiful sight when everyone raced to get there before the others who were just as hungry. You tried to trick everyone else, and those who had money took the streetcar. They were like animals fighting for the prey. They were enemies in their hearts. Their positions made them both comrades and competitors.

For the first time I had a feeling of powerlessness toward life. My mother worked for the big Dresden Lace and Curtain Factory. She worked at home, removing the superfluous threads that the machine production left in the pieces of cloth. She succeeded in getting me work at the factory. So I started work—for the first few days fetching spools, shuttles, and other things that were needed for the power looms. Then I got my own winding machine. It transferred the thread from big wooden spools onto the little spools, made out of two connected metal plates, which could be used at the looms. You had to pay some attention while threading the spools, and then while the machine was going you had to see that any breaks in the thread were immediately retied. As soon as I had the necessary dexterity, I occupied my mind by examining the completely unfamiliar surroundings. Only a few of the men and women workers were organized. My desire to learn something of socialism and Social Democracy wasn't satisfied here. With respect to all social life there was a general stupor of the sort that we associate with a virtually extinct generation of workers. During the breaks the talk was of personal experiences and pleasures, or else there was erotic banter or dirty jokes, directed especially at the younger women. I was completely isolated.

The fate of an entire class of people was soon frighteningly clear to me. Day after day, week after week, year after year, always this monotonous life with no variety. For centuries, thousands of lives had just been unwinding, like the threads on my machine. The thought oppressed me and demanded some kind of release. This was the origin of my poems "The Winder" and others. The heavier that all this lay on me, the more urgent was my desire to get to know the new doctrine that promised an ascent from the misery.

My religious views had fallen away piece by piece. What was left, the machine unwound from my soul. No matter how much I racked my brains, I could find no sense in the order of the world, least of all in a divine order. That millions have to do without and sacrifice their humanity to a wretched existence, while, on the other hand, fantastic wealth arises and brings with it new cultural wonders every day—the very thought was torture. But I could no longer believe that it was all necessary, in principle necessary, and that there was divine purpose in this principle. That was not a life-affirming but rather a murderous belief, and doubting it was a blessing. It seemed to me even more horrible that millions embraced this faith and that philosophers wrote about life without choking on this question.

The little time that remained to me between work and rest was taken up by reading the Social Democratic *Saxon Workers' Paper* [*Sächsischer Arbeiterzeitung*] and some current political pamphlets. That wasn't enough for me; I yearned for support. My eldest brother brought me a ticket to the founders' day festival of the Social Democratic club and I decided to go.

On the evening of the festival I sat alone at a table in the hall of the "Golden Meadow" and watched with curiosity the gestures and faces of the workers streaming in. My romantic fears made me feel ill at ease. But there was absolutely nothing conspiratorial in anyone's behavior. I was still affected by the ideas from the military school. All the people around me were conspirators against law and order, and yet I couldn't see anything that made them different from anyone else. I didn't dare to speak. A man of about thirty had sat down at my table, and I looked him over mistrustfully with a few stolen glances. My brother had warned me about police spies since I wasn't a member of the club. I took it for granted that the man across from me was one of those whom the government hired to snoop around everywhere and bring misfortune to honest people.

All around the hall, in the gallery and down below, there were shields and placards with sayings on them: "Through the night to the light"; "Undeterred by our enemies"; "Light our minds and fire our hearts"; and a lot more things like that. These heightened my tension to an almost unbearable level. I could feel my heart beating in my throat. Up in front next to the podium there were several large potted plants and behind them you could see two plaster heads. As I learned later these were busts of Marx and Lassalle.

Then the music started up. For a while it was just like any other harmless festival. The strangeness, the rebelliousness that would stir me up so much was a long time in coming. Then a man of average height with black hair and a thin mustache and beard stepped up to the podium. His voice had something weak about it, with nothing of the power of a field marshall's or a leader's voice. He almost whispered the word "comrade." You could tell it was hard for him to talk. He stood there, bent forward as though he wanted to say his words specially to each individual. He had consumption. But I only learned that later.

At first his words made no sense to me. But then something came into his voice that made me listen. Something in his voice flickered, grew, and came nearer and nearer, and finally became a huge flame that lit me up totally. And then I began to understand.

He condemned the social conditions that I'd gotten to know myself. Then he spoke of the growth of Social Democracy, and he said that the founding of the smallest workers' club was more significant to culture than a battle victory. That was all new and strange to me. In the history lessons in military school they placed the greatest significance on the wars and battles that had been fought between individual rulers. Sometimes we even had to learn the uniforms and the colors of the collars and the facings of the fighting regiments. But now here was a worker (at least judging by his simple clothes) standing up there turning this view of the world upside down. How was it possible? Either he was lying or my teachers had lied.

And yet everything that the man said gave the impression of truth and moved you by its simplicity. The speech ended with a salute to Social Democracy. Everyone stood up and joined in. I did too and then sat there with peculiar feelings and thoughts for the whole evening, so that everything that followed went right by me.

The speaker, whose name was Eichhorn, was the president of the club. He was an old and revered Social Democrat, as was his wife who had accomplished fine and brave things for the party and the socialist women's movement. Both had been severely persecuted by the police. Both of them died, tragically, of consumption, which they had gotten as a result of the deprivations and persecutions under the Socialist Law.

The feelings that I took home with me from the festival were almost religious. Here was a way out of the despair. But this was soon followed by sober reflection, and I asked myself if it wasn't all deception and consolation in a never-never land. In the end, the future state seemed to be like the heaven of the religious. There was so much in the newspapers about the lies and troublemaking of Social Democracy that it was possible to be very wrong about it. But in spite of myself I felt deep down that the victory belonged to socialism. The heart is a funny thing; it allows the head to reason but still rules almost unrestrictedly. Often we take pride in our reasonable actions and don't even notice that it is actually the heart that has decided for us. I grabbed at the new gospel as a thirsty man grabs for a drink. I had to have faith in order to bear life. And of the millions who adhere to socialism today only a tiny fraction are socialists from scientific conviction; most come to socialism from a vast internal and external wasteland like the people of Israel out of the wilderness. They have to believe in order not to despair. They are socialists because socialism is their cause, material and spiritual. The worker needs it as he needs air and bread. I soon observed also that the more intellectually alive workers were generally Social Democrats.

After this I often attended mass meetings, and I slowly became familiar with Social Democratic ideas. In the past the idea of the state had seemed to me to have a kind of medieval crudity that was embodied in barracks and prisons. This attitude changed imperceptibly, because I learned to see myself as a citizen of this state who, though oppressed, still had an interest in it because I hoped to take it over for my own class. And the strangest thing was—and this revealed itself only later—that I, the despiser of unconditional military discipline, willingly submitted to party discipline. As contradictory as it may seem, socialist ideology reconciled me to a certain extent with my proletarian existence, and taught me to respect common manual labor. I no longer shied away from the name "worker." [. . .]

In the long run I didn't like it at the curtain factory, even though the work suited me OK. It was more the surroundings that caused me to quit. I missed a spirit of brotherhood among the workers.

A week after I left, I found work as a helper in a straw and felt hat factory. However, I didn't have much to do with the other workers and was used more as a packer and porter. I stayed there for three months. I can no longer remember what my wages were; they must have been about ten to twelve marks a week. Then for a while I was employed at the Precision Instrument Workshops. Despite the fancy name, this was no more than a little hole in a basement where the owner had machine parts cleaned for other factories. So I'd now risen in my workbook to the position of scourer. I then looked unsuccessfully for work for almost a month; finally on 21 August 1896, I was hired as a packer and finisher by the Welsch Straw Hat Factory. My daily task was to stiffen with sizing and shellac and to sulphurate the hats before they were shaped. It wasn't very difficult; you only needed to know how stiff or flexible each hat style was supposed to be. In a few days I learned to test the strength of the hot sizing with my fingertips. After a few weeks I was very skillful. The only thing was that the pay of twelve marks a week was too low. If I'd been all alone, I probably would have had to live in constant poverty. But I had a home with my mother and stepfather where I could save a few groschen, though it's true I just spent them on books. I rarely granted myself any pleasures, and carousing in bars was not at all my style. The workday lasted from seven in the morning to seven in the evening with an hour and a half lunch break. The hot air by the boiler and the smell of the sizing made me very tired at first, so that I fell asleep soon after supper, often right at the table; I had no interest in anything except a quick look at the newspaper. At work I was used only occasionally as a packer.

The hat workers were badly organized—that is, a large proportion of them were not unionized. A lost strike had disorganized them. The companies had brought in and trained a large number of younger workers. There were many who were straw-hat makers only during the busy season, working the rest of the time in other businesses. All this contributed to the bad conditions. Of course there were times when the earnings were relatively good, but after the busy season was over, there were many lean weeks when it hardly paid to be at the factory at all. Most of the work was piecework; the only ones who got a weekly wage were those whom they could employ the whole year round. Aside from the grievances that were inherent in the business and its labor system, the heavy drinking certainly contributed to the disunity of the workers. They drank often and to excess, even schnapps. They teased me because I drank a lot of milk. On Saturday evening, one of the workers was frequently fetched at the factory by his wife so that he wouldn't get drunk on the way home. There was a saying about him: "Good night, Mathilde, there's money on the window sill." Here's how that came about: One evening he escaped the clutches of his wife, got very drunk, and timed his arrival at home for when she was out of the house. When he wanted to leave again, she appeared suddenly, and he said those words as he slipped out the door. Two pfennigs of household money were lying on the window sill.

The taverns encouraged drinking by issuing metal tokens worth a particular amount. For example, a worker was given ten marks in tokens with which he could get drinks, sausage, or bread; and then on Saturday he paid off the debt with his wages. It frequently happened that some workers spent all their wages in the tavern, especially since they always had to drink some more when they paid off their debt. People would sit down, friends would come in, there was more drinking, and everyone stayed in the tavern until midnight. By the time they went home some of them would have only tokens in their pocket. Sober workers would also use this horrible system because they sometimes needed it to get the simplest breakfast. For weak and frivolous people it was a perfect temptation to ruin. For a long time it was part of my job to fetch the workers' breakfasts, and that's how I got to know this system so well.

"You shouldn't talk about other people's drinking if you don't know their thirst," one worker said to me when I reproached him. It's certainly true that some workers, including this man, were driven to drink by family and personal problems. But it was the piecework system that was mostly to blame because it drove the workers to find some stimulant to increase their performance. And it also generated and promoted disunity and envy among them. There was a certain ill-defined tension between the workers trained during the strike and the organized workers. The former were often very arrogant. Here again I observed that the organized worker was generally a much more likable person. Only their strong convictions kept many of them from losing control completely. The fellow with the drinking philosophy was an example; despite all his cares, he never let himself become a slave to a drinking habit, if only because he, as an organized worker, was sensitive about his honor.

Considering my youth, I was overly bold, and talked politics with the older workers. They liked that a lot. Only when I started to criticize their personal behavior was I told that I was just a green boy. This was sure to happen whenever I mocked their spirit of guild cliquishness—a spirit that deemed inferior all those workers who made hats without several years of training. Such views always made me very angry.

Later on, the business hired one, sometimes two, workers who were under me. One of them was a very intellectually aware person, even though he was rather sluggish physically. He read not only the Social Democratic daily press but also *The New Times* [*Die Neue Zeit*], the scholarly central organ of Social Democracy. I was often astonished by his sharp and sure judgment. We two hooked onto each other and talked politics a great deal, much to the displeasure of the foreman. I succeeded in getting off work on the first of May, the world workers' holiday. The thought of May Day had something overwhelming about it for me. On one day the workers in all the civilized countries were to rest their hands and loudly and clearly demand equality for all humanity. Such a community of ideas that transcended nations and races was something new in the history of the world. The thought was great and powerful, almost too great for the mass of workers whose lives had for centuries been a chain of the most trivial cares. This worker's helper had a fine feel and enthusiasm for the cultural greatness of the idea of workers' emancipation. And his sense of justice was equally well developed. I can also remember another helper who later worked for some time as a stoker in the factory. He sticks in my mind because, after he was let go, he broke into the factory office.

I worked in the hat factory for three years. After many petitions my wages had increased to eighteen marks. [. . .]

Saxony was a land of political experiments at that time. The government had succeeded in abolishing the general and equal voting rights for the provincial diet—rights that had made possible the gains of the Social Democrats.* Of course there were protest meetings against this violent curtailment of the people's rights, but I had imagined that genuine turmoil would break out. That didn't happen; but an extraordinary meeting of Saxon Social Democrats did take place where there was a great deal of debate and argument about whether they should still take part in elections for the provincial diet now that the three-class voting system had been introduced. I had trouble understanding that. I had pictured the people as an armed guard, ready at any moment to defend its rights; and now I had to watch as a single parliamentary vote created hundreds of thousands of second-class citizens. And now they were debating whether they ought to stay

*In March 1896, the diet of Saxony approved a new election law, which attempted to curb the growth of Social Democracy; under the new law, diet elections were indirect, with the voters divided into three classes, depending on the amount of direct taxes paid.

away from the polls as a protest against the new law. The real condition of things was in such stark contrast to my imaginings and dreams that I couldn't avoid a deep depression. I got over it when the 1898 Reichstag elections came around. I got to know a young worker by the name of Paul Matthes, the son of a party comrade from back during the Socialist Law days. His father had once been full of fire and had stood up for the socialist cause, and now he too knew nothing but passionate commitment to political life, even though he was no older than I. In the evenings I joined him to fold and deliver leaflets and attend meetings.

I had already admired the splendid figure of Wilhelm Liebknecht on several occasions. Now I had a chance to hear Bebel, the man always mentioned in the same breath. They were the Siamese twins of Social Democracy, though they had very different kinds of talent. Bebel was supposed to speak at the "Golden Meadow" at a meeting beginning at eight o'clock. I left the factory at seven o'clock and hurried home to change into better clothes; when I got to the "Golden Meadow" at seven-fifteen the hall was supposedly already overfilled and had been barricaded by the police. There were about a hundred people there with me; some of them left, but, like me, others stayed so they could at least get a look at Bebel. But the police drove us back from the entrance—to a fence on the other side of the street by some empty construction sites. This was to clear the way for traffic even though few people used the lonely half-built-up street.

The evening air was warm. The hall was right at ground level and the windows were open. People inside kept leaning out and making nasty remarks to the police who were standing to the right and left of the windows, through which some of the latecomers had gotten into the hall.

The porter from the hat factory, a twenty-two-year-old fellow full of all kinds of tricks, was standing next to me. "Just watch!" he said. In a few steps he was across the street; then, jumping up, he was through the window in no time. A roar of approval greeted him in the hall and he disappeared into the crowd.

The police lieutenant was furious and cursed both the policemen. One of them had to turn around in order to hide his laughing.

Now we were driven from the other side of the street. A few moments later you could hear: trot, trot. Mounted police were moving in fast. No one was now permitted in the area of the meeting hall. We were pushed back step by step. Apparently they thought things were moving too slowly. The mounted police rode into the crowd and pursued individuals until each disappeared. There was an older man standing next to me. He was overrun and fell to the pavement, while I received such a violent shove from the croup of the ambling steed that I tumbled off to one side. I was seized by a wild anger, and I kicked the horse in the side. It reared and almost threw its rider. The curse that I yelled at him made him notice me again. Other policemen were running up on foot. "If the guy in the gray jacket says another word, arrest him!" yelled the mounted policeman. The police were rushing at everyone like frightened bulls.

In the meantime Bebel had appeared and been led into the hall by the police. While he was inside giving his speech, the big mopping-up operation continued outside. The police were riding back and forth along the sidewalks. People standing in their doorways had to go inside and close the doors. You could hear cursing, and from the upper floors of the houses there were astonished and angry shouts. The surrounding streets were soon cleared of all the people. When the people at the meeting went home, there wasn't a trace of the earlier wild scene. I got to see Bebel anyway because I came back to the area at the right time with some of my friends.

What had been the point of the attack? The result was that the Social Democrats took a big lead in the main election and won in the runoff election. After I'd let off some of my anger with that kick, I was once again oppressed by that feeling that I knew so well from the detention cell at the military school. It was a vague but deep hatred of brutal power. During the following sleepless night this feeling was fused with the sense of powerlessness I had felt as I went up and down stairs vainly looking for work. I was becoming aware that the present social order had a horrible as well as a beneficial side. The smallest harmless offense brought on the full power of the state. The state was indifferent to the undeserved misery of many thousands of its citizens. And now, what happens when hunger and power collide? The whole society and culture, which have produced such infinite beauty and wonders, rest on a hideous foundation. From the beginning of man's history they have rested on blood, murder, oppression, and suffering! No, when you are aware of this, the belief in a divine order no longer evokes any joy for life. When I had such thoughts, I wished that I'd never been born. I'd been stepped on enough. Only the thought that all this was man's doing and was changeable by man's will kept me going.

Somewhere in the fog a bell strikes five o'clock with long, damp, melancholy tones. The river is steaming so much that the few lights at the steamboat landing barely cut through the fog. Behind the silhouettes of the towers and chimneys the young morning fights with growing brightness against the shards of the night, which creep slowly through the streets like birds afraid of the light. The dark arches of the bridges seem to hang in the air like ghostly paths to Valhalla. Lights sometimes move silently across them. It's the wagons of the milk, fruit, and meat dealers on the way to the market or customers. Lone pedestrians also emerge for a few moments in the middle and then disappear to the right or left into the fog. Gradually the picture becomes more definite, clearer.

I was standing on the bank and letting the mood of the morning possess me. I felt very festive. It was the runoff election day for the Reichstag and the question was: Would it be a conservative or a Social Democrat? Even though I wasn't old enough to vote, I could still canvass for votes. For weeks now my few free hours had been filled by leaflet folding and distributing. Now a final appeal was important. My friend Matthes and I stood at the end of the Albert's Bridge on the left bank of the Elbe River. We had bundles of paper under our arms. They weren't the usual kind of leaflets: there were no statistics about taxes or the burden of the army and navy, no criticism of Saxony's pernicious conservative politics. There was only a poem—poetry as an aid in the campaign:

> You men of labor, you children of need,
> For one last time with you we plead;
> For the final charge in the fierce fight,
> To take our share of our country's might.

That was how it began. The worker-poet, Ernst Klaar, had written the poem.* It was effective, especially among the workers, because there was a drumlike sound in the stanzas.

There was a happy, confident mood among the workers; only the older ones, the veterans of the Socialist Law, were more cautious and thoughtful. Along with the beautiful victories, they had already experienced too many defeats. I stood at the bridge until seven o'clock and handed out the poems, which were generally well received. Then I ran to my own work. But I didn't get much done the whole day because I had the excitement of the election in my bones. The outlook for the candidates was being discussed in the factory, and I didn't neglect to remind everyone of his duty to vote. That angered the foreman and he said, "It would probably be best if they voted you in."

I'd carried the leaflets and poems with much pride and also a little touch of romanticism, and I'd handed them out not only at the regularly prescribed times but also in the evenings on the street. Of course election fever infected the bourgeoisie as well as the working class. So I wasn't always well received. Sometimes people snarled and slammed the door in my face without taking the leaflet. There were encouraging words from people friendly to socialism; sometimes we even got into short conversations. The attitude of the shopkeepers was often amusing; they didn't want to be on bad terms with anyone so they quietly accepted the handout in their stores. I had fun trying to discover their real

*Klaar (1861–1920) was one of the poets represented in the collection *From the Class Struggle: Social Poems* (*Aus dem Klassenkampf: Soziale Gedichte*) (1894).

feelings in their eyes and gestures; for there are very few people who are good enough actors so that a twitch of their facial muscles or an angry or friendly light in their eyes does not betray their true feelings. Of course some of the shopkeepers had fanatical political beliefs. When I put a leaflet on the counter of a meat market, said "Good-bye," and walked out the door, a big bone whizzed right past my head and into the street. I didn't hear the words that accompanied it, but they certainly contained no blessing. As I came out of the next house, I saw a hungry dog devouring the bone. So here again fate turned an evil deed to a good use for some creature. I remember one other thing from these days. In one house where there were certainly no well-to-do tenants I was set upon by an angry woman on the third floor. She'd barely set eyes on the leaflet when she shouted angrily, "If only all you Social Democrats would drop dead." She wadded up the leaflet and threw it onto the floor in front of me. I stood there dumbfounded and didn't know what to reply. Only after the door had slammed shut was I conscious of my rage, and I spit after her. Afterward I realized that what I'd done was ugly and I was ashamed. I realized that being good means not doing wrong; while being noble means also resisting the temptation to wrongdoing that stems from injustices suffered. And I can honestly say that from then on I never viewed a person as bad just because he thought or felt differently than I. But today that happens to a large extent, and a great deal of private and public harm and injustice stem from it. It reminds me of a saying that I once saw on an old farmhouse:

> If every man was pure of heart,
> Then Satan's seeds could get no start.
> If every man a good seed would sow,
> Then would all men comfort and solace know.

Unfortunately so many sow not only grain for their stomachs but also thorns and switches for their neighbor's body.

In the evening I was at the "Golden Meadow" for the announcement of the election results. My friends and I sat there for hours in nervous anticipation; then when the news of victory came, I was carried away and joined in the jubilation. Dr. Gradnauer, the representative who had been elected, gave a short speech.* Then I went home. There were still some scattered groups of people on the street. Here and there you could hear people cheering the election victor. One man said as he passed by, "It makes you cry how fast the reds are increasing!"

"Yes," I said, breaking into his group's conversation, "soon the world's going to be different!"

The answer I got sounded something like "worthless scamp, needs to have his ears boxed." But I was happy.

* Dr. Georg Gradnauer was a prominent Social Democratic journalist who sat in the Reichstag intermittently between 1898 and 1924.

Ernst Schuchardt, Workhouse Weaver

Ernst Schuchardt (1866–?), a down-and-out shoemaker, worked at a variety of industrial jobs in and around Saxony. For a time he was employed in the same machine shop as Moritz Bromme, whose auto-biography of 1905 may have stimulated Schuchardt to write of his own experiences. In 1903, Schuchardt was picked up by the police for begging and sentenced to six months in the workhouse at Gross-Salze, near Magdeburg. Prussia had twenty-four workhouses with some 10,000 inmates in the early years of the century. As Schuchardt was keenly aware, the workhouse was really a prison, which sought to inculcate the proper discipline, piety, and work habits into its inmates. Although not much of a stylist, Schuchardt manages to paint a compelling picture of broken men, colorful rogues, and unctuous bureaucrats. When reading Schuchardt's account of his first few days as an unwilling weaver, the reader will want to recall the experiences of Otto, the unemployed Berliner who chose the semislavery of estate labor over the workhouse.

ARRIVAL AND FIRST WEEK

An old man had let us in, and with a very deliberate air he relocked the door. Before us lay the institutional buildings and the church. On one of the buildings was a vine climbing up to the second floor. In front of us there were gardens with well-groomed lawns. I couldn't give much thought to this well-groomed piece of earth. An old red-nosed official ordered us with coarse words to follow him. The transport of men went to the business offices where we handed in our papers, and waited to hear whether we were "clean." If we weren't, the police jail had to pick up the tab for cleaning our clothes. The guard brought us to a wing of the building, to the house baths, where we washed our bodies once again. A barber in gray institutional garb cut our hair short, almost down to the skin, with a hair clippers, and our mustaches fell too. Then he shaved us. We'd taken off our shirts beforehand. Another man in institutional garb searched our shirts for "German Reich bugs" (lice). In the mean-time, stripped to the waist, we were shaved. Tears came into the eyes of my friend Barnack when his mustache fell. After this procedure we had to bathe in old wooden tubs, long and oval shaped like the scalding vats at a pork butcher's. An inmate stuffed our clothing into a sack, which was then tagged and tied up. Each of the newcomers received a shirt, a pair of socks, a gray work suit (all of tough gray cloth), trousers, a short jacket, and a vest, as well as a black hood. Into our arms they put black trousers and a jacket with a comb, a tin food-bowl and spoon, a pair of leather slippers, a pair of shoes, and a cleaning brush. Since it was time to eat, we got our meal in the baths. Soon after the meal a guard came and took me and Barnack to the coir* weaving mill, which was upstairs in a building across from the baths, and assigned us a common locker. My friend and I had to

Translated from Ernst Schuchardt, *Sechs Monate Arbeitshaus. Erlebnisse eines wandernden Arbeiters* (Berlin: H. Seemann Verlag, 1907), 34–55.
* The tough fibers from the husk of a coconut.

fold our trousers and jackets according to regulations and put them in the locker. We had to put our shoes on top of the locker. The spoon was put into a little leather slip inside the door. We gave the bowl to the custodian who attended this room, and he put it with the other bowls. With a few gruff words the guard showed us in what condition we had to keep our locker and our things. We received a key to our "medicine cabinet"—the locker was no bigger than that.

After this we were taken to the director, a man of medium height, who asked us, "What is your name and are you sick?"

I said my name and replied tersely, "In this place, Herr Director, you're not allowed to be sick!"

Herr von B. dismissed me with a stern look. I had to wait until the others had had their first interviews. Then an old guard brought us to the secretary who got more exact information from our papers. When this was done, all four of us had to step forward, and the workhouse rules were read to us by a scribe (who was an inmate). Of course he read with a solemnity as if he himself were director of the institution.

In Prussia the workhouse rules are exactly the same as those for the penitentiary. The penitentiary rules are just much more honest—there they say "convict"; in the workhouse rules they say "inmate." After the reading of the rules we had to go to the doctor; he examined us for venereal disease. He did it with haste as though he would be glad to be done with the business quickly.

Then, under the guard of the officials, we went back to the workroom. A foreman, also an inmate, showed me how to splice and fit the ends of spun coir. I learned with difficulty. I made slow progress winding the fibers into a ball. I worked without interruption, but I didn't get much done.

Barnack had to do the same work, and it didn't go any better for him. The foreman who was teaching me was a man of twenty-eight. He was a carpenter by trade. He was to be released four weeks from Friday. He liked to talk about it, saying that two years are a damned long time.

The afternoon didn't seem too long. From the first of April to the end of September the workday was from six o'clock in the morning until seven o'clock in the evening; from the first of October to the end of March it was from seven o'clock in the morning until seven o'clock in the evening. At four-thirty we got supper—gruel and a piece of bread. We had to line up, step up to the food vat, take our bowl, get it filled, and receive a piece of heavy black bread. After the food was dished out, the foreman said grace—something like this:

"Come, Lord Jesus, be our guest, and bless what you have given us!"

After the meal there was another prayer. There was enough to eat; we could get a second helping in our tin bowl. Only occasionally did they run short. Then we worked again until the call to prayers. The first thing we did in the evening was sing a song. The foreman would recite a part of the song, then we would sing; and so it went until the end of the song. The foreman gave the keynote, and most would sing along. I myself, and some others who felt just as I did, didn't join in. Then there was a prayer, and we lined up and climbed up a flight of stairs to our dormitory.

There were about 340 male inmates and upwards of 40 female inmates in the workhouse. A good portion of them worked outside of Schönebeck and Gross-Salze. They came on Saturday evening every other week to attend church; and on Monday morning they went away again; where they worked I don't know.

Both rooms of the dormitory were whitewashed. There were a lot of beds in each one. In the first room there were washing facilities and three urinals. The guard who was on duty that day and who showed me my bed was the same one who had guarded us in our workroom. He had spent the whole afternoon walking up and down the corridor beside where I was sitting, and he hadn't let me out of his sight. I arranged my covers on the floor and put them into a bluish-white checkered cover slip. I put the top section of the mattress into a cover of the same material. I laid my sheet on the mattress and tucked the ends smoothly underneath. Everything had to be done exactly according to regulations. The turnkey counted us off, and the dormitory was locked.

As they did with all newcomers, my fellow sufferers asked me where I was from, whether this was my first time in, and how I liked it.

The man who slept next to me was in for the second time; he was from a town near Barby. He gave me a piece of chewing tobacco. "For the first four weeks you can't receive any mail," he said.

The new life and the activities in this place had made it a very taxing day, and I fell asleep exhausted.

The next morning they awakened us at five o'clock. We straightened our beds; each one looked exactly like the others. We walked in a line to the lavatory. In the evening you had to take your hand towel with you into the dormitory and in the morning put it back into your locker. The housefather, a uniformed official with a sword, frequently watched us as we washed. Afterward we made our way to our workroom or workplace.

Some of the men had to go to the toilet; they took turns. In my department we had to line up for prayers in the workroom. We sang a Christian morning hymn, and then the foreman said grace. Then there was gruel and a piece of bread. After breakfast we worked until noon, taking time out only when it was our turn to go to the toilet. There was a toilet there where we could relieve ourselves, but there was no running water.

The higher administration of the provincial police had forgotten this convenience. It stank in the workhouse rooms where men were cramped in tightly between rows of looms.

If an inmate dared to complain, the first time he would be reprimanded that he had no right to complain. This was enough to keep him from complaining a second time. I must mention approvingly, however, that the bathroom fixtures in Gross-Salze have changed. There is now a shower. Unfortunately this wasn't finished at the time I was released. It was too late for us. Some of us had caught a skin rash. On the day of my release I took a bath in an old neighborhood in Magdeburg, and the bath master came in while I was inspecting my back. It was covered with pimples and lesions and had delayed me in the bath stall.

"Man, look at your back; you shouldn't have been allowed to bathe here!"

I told the man that I'd come from Gross-Salze, and, out of fear that I'd be detained longer, I had lied to the doctor that there was nothing wrong with me.

"Yes, when it comes to cleanliness those places are pretty negligent!" the man said. All this just in passing.

The morning passed quickly. I was watched by the guard the whole time, and I couldn't talk to anyone. Then we were called to lunch. We lined up and took our bowls. The custodian filled them up and another inmate gave us a piece of bread. The food was cooked up thick. There was either rice and potatoes with thinly cut meat—that was usually the Sunday meal—or else beans, peas, lentils, or other vegetables. Throughout the summer we had kohlrabi and carrots. In the winter, white cabbage and turnips. On two weekdays there were thin, very thin slices of meat in the vegetables.

When we got to our seats the foreman said grace. Everyone had to stand. We had an hour's break at noon and could talk to each other. An old fellow of about sixty was making coir mats on the loom; for the time being I was just supposed to splice so I'd be able to make some later. His fingers were sore from stuffing and tightening the thread and the loose fibers.

"Well, friend, how do you like the work? Yeah, you learn what work really is here! My fingers have been sore for a long time, and the quotas are jacked way up, and if you don't meet them they cut back on your food, and you can see how the others are eating. This is a regular institution of heavenly care! Make sure you learn this stuff, or else you won't get anything to chew on!"

I gave him a dumb look and said, "First I've got to learn the job—how long does it take?"

"A week," he replied.

Then along came an acquaintance of mine from Tränensberg;

he'd been in for quite a while already, and he told me a few things and gave me a piece of chewing tobacco.

I made up my mind to move my hands, but by no means to learn the job right or to meet the quota after my training period. Each day I intentionally did just a little bit more, and made it appear to the guard that I was doing a great deal. It was while doing this work that I learned to daydream.

In the afternoon I received my card, which I hung up on my locker. My name and place of birth were written on it, as well as the number 38739. A duplicate hung on my bed. My bed and laundry number was 296. I had to remember this because there was clean laundry every Saturday.

At this point I should note that every day we had a half-hour's stroll around the courtyard between the building where we slept and worked and the bathhouse. We walked in a big oval circle, hands behind our backs, one man after another. During the walk on the first day I was shocked by the clean-shaven, care-wrinkled faces; later I got used to it. You could talk if there wasn't a strict guard on duty. We had to go out into the courtyard on Sundays also; only when the weather was terrible did we stay inside. The different departments went out in turns, sometimes right after lunch in the afternoon, or else later. I used to get chewing tobacco from acquaintances on these walks. We did it just when the guard wasn't watching. In this way I strengthened my resolve not to make the quota no matter what and not to be nice to the director so I could get different work; I wanted to know definitely what was going to happen to me. In all other ways I submitted to the strict discipline.

Friday and Saturday passed with the usual monotony. The guard saw no reason to reprimand me. But I almost forgot to tell about one incident.

New arrivals had to go see the chaplain, a man of about my age, whose name I've unfortunately forgotten. We had been summoned by a guard, were made to put on our black togs, and were brought by the guard into the corridor of one of the buildings. One after the other, we had to go in to see the workhouse chaplain. He was known among the inmates as a strict, heartless man. When it was my turn, I stepped in and greeted him, not as "Reverend Sir," but with the cold words: "Good day, Herr Chaplain!"

After acknowledging me, his first words were: "Do you know the Lord's Prayer? Recite it once through!"

"Dammit all," I thought, "he wants the Lord's Prayer recited, and I haven't said this prayer for twenty years." But I recollected quickly and recited it in an expressionless singsong manner. I stumbled a bit when I got to "our daily bread." But I did recite it.

"You can still do it!" was his reply.

Of course I didn't bat an eye, so I wouldn't get any extra punishment.

Then he started in with his religious inquisition. He asked me where I had last worked and where my last residence had been.

I gave him short evasive answers. I hated this man who was playing examining magistrate in a place where I already had to suffer punishment and do time.

His entire advice consisted of telling me to behave myself and to pay close attention to the words he spoke in church on Sunday.

Of course I promised with my mouth, but I resolved not to do it. The man disgusted me, and it occurred to me: This man is just like a dog trainer. A piece of meat in one hand, in the other a dog whip. I was excused and the next man went in.

We waited until the last man was excused.

Then the guard took us back to our workplace.

THE FIRST SUNDAY

The first Sunday arrived. After the morning singing and prayers, the custodians brought the shoe-cleaning utensils and the clothing brushes. Today we'd gotten coffee and a piece of bread. We polished our shoes, and I took special care that the old patched and nailed-up clunkers really gleamed; I intended to avoid scrupulously any punishment. I brushed clean my black suit and hood. Then they laid out the hymnals, one for each man. We had to form up in two lines in the hall of the workshop; a guard checked whether our clothing was clean, our shoes polished, and our caps resting on our heads, according to regulations. After the inspection we went down the stairs two at a time, like a chain. There were already three lines of people in the courtyard. The supervisor was dressed like a guard and carried a sword. The housefather was in uniform too. The two of them lined us up in three equal rows. Between each row was a space that a person could get through easily. The director of the workhouse came. In the tone of a general the housefather commanded, "Dress in line!" We greeted the director by removing our caps. He took off his cylinder hat and exchanged a few words with the housefather and the supervisor. Then the three of them walked slowly along the front row, inspecting each man, then along the second row, and finally along the third.

I was standing in the third row. Stepping up to me, he said, "What's your name?" Coldly, I gave my name.

"You did a bad job brushing out your jacket. Do it better next time." Then he corrected himself and said to the housefather, "Give this man a better jacket, this one is faded!" I said nothing to the director, but I sent a couple of piercing looks his way, and I knew he'd caught them.

After the inspection was finished, the housefather commanded, "Right turn!" and we went to the church. In front of the church were two old tin collection boxes reminding you of almsgiving. We walked three abreast in lines and arrived looking like a three-linked chain. The guards separated us. I sat under the pulpit. To my left, in a special section, sat the poorhouse residents—men, most of whom were about seventy. Like us, they held hymnals in their shriveled hands. On the left at the very front sat the free people. They were mostly women and girls, plus two old sisters of mercy. Opposite me, not far from the place where the chaplain gave Communion, sat the director and his wife. Up by the organ in the main choir loft sat the choir members (they too were inmates) and the cantor, an old man who played the organ with virtuosity. He was the only one of our superiors who guided us with kind words. The cantor played the prelude to a hymn, and then we sang. The chaplain spoke the opening prayer, and then we sang again. I held my hymnal open in front of me, but I didn't sing. With my lips pressed hard against my teeth, I inwardly cursed this compulsory church attendance. The choir loft on the side was hidden by a curtain, behind which sat the female inmates. If it hadn't been for the occasional crying fits that afflict a woman in church, you would never have suspected that there were people behind this gray curtain.

I paid no attention to what the chaplain preached. Just submit—until my term was up—in order to get out of this hell. . . .

When the others stood up, I stood up too. If they sat down, then so did I. Everything just like an automaton, like a marionette. I brooded to myself, and when the organ sounded, my brain sang a curse on this compulsory church attendance. My face didn't betray what was going on inside me. I pressed my lips hard against my bad teeth as if I had a toothache, and I sucked on my piece of chewing tobacco.

When the religious service was over, the guards lined us up again, and we went back to our departments and handed in the hymnals. An inmate packed them into a case and locked it. We changed our clothes, putting our jackets and trousers into our lockers according to regulations, and we talked quietly among ourselves.

The foreman came up to me and said: "Schuchardt, it's your first Sunday, and you've already been reprimanded by the big boss. Pretty nice start, eh?! We don't waste much time here!"

He tried to scare me by saying that the housefather had written my name down, and that something always came of that.

My work partner was standing next to us and said to the foreman, "And the beast didn't even sing in church, he just sat there like a blockhead!"

All three of us laughed; I was smart enough not to get into a quarrel with the foreman, because last week he'd been instrumental in getting the food of three men rationed because they hadn't made their quotas. I'd seen how the poor guys watched us at meals, and it was forbidden under penalty to give them anything.

They handed out books from the workhouse's collection. There were stories, issues of the *Scherl Weekly* [*Scherlsche Woche*] from years gone by, and old issues of *The Universe* [*Universum*] and *The Wide World* [*Die Weite Welt*], as well as of the Christian-evangelical *At Home* [*Daheim*].*

In these magazines I read some articles about masters of music and drama. And I read about Rubenstein, who had died in Petersburg. He was a composer, musician, and poet and had set a variety of Heinrich Heine's poems to music. There were a whole lot of Rubenstein aphorisms in one of these issues. I also enjoyed reading descriptions of people and places. I didn't like the Christian stories; once I read a story of a prodigal son. This religious twaddle really made me sick—and people were supposed to be trained to be contented and God-fearing here. . . . I consoled myself with a part of the Ulich poem:†

> Stay on your path and let people talk!
> Your path is long, people talk a lot!
> Stay on your path and follow your goal!

As a poor devil, I hadn't gotten to know the best side of God's deputies, the clerics. But I've received real favors from workers and poor people, while the pious people either gave me nothing for the courtesies I showed them, or lectured me, as they handed over a few pfennigs, about how I was a young man and could fend for myself. These people knew nothing about the life of a

---

* All the works mentioned were popular periodicals.
† The reference is obscure; possibly a misspelling.

wandering hungry worker, or didn't want to know about it. With these reflections I passed my first Sunday.

AT WORK AND AFTER WORK

On Monday the foreman taught me how to tighten the warp on the loom; I was supposed to make doormats. As I said, I learned with difficulty because I took no pleasure in the work. I didn't like weaving, this boring work. I moved my hands, did it partly wrong, and didn't get anything accomplished.

And so the first agonizing week passed.

One day during the second week I delivered the first two mats to the supervisor, who had been engaged by the Schönebecker Firm. He was generally a good man, but he gave me a sharp reprimand and said:

"Schuchardt, you make the mats very badly, working the material wretchedly and unevenly, and your knots are too loose. The mats will be ruined in the cutting machine. And you work too slowly too; you'll have to produce more, much more."

The guard in this department, a man of about forty, also gave me a dressing down:

"You just don't want to work! If you don't work faster and fulfill your quota, then I'm going to report you. If the others can make their quotas, and usually more, then you can too!"

I answered him: "Sir, I've never been a textile worker and I can't adjust to this work. I don't care at all if you report me or not."

"Go back to your place and keep working," was his harsh answer.

We inmates didn't like this guard.

It's no wonder; he was stuck the whole day in an atmosphere of fumes and dust. Even though the rooms were swept twice a day and the windows were opened during the day, the brooms were almost without any bristles. They were trying to save money that way. The floors weren't washed with water. A guard would eventually become mentally debilitated through his contact with inmates, who were either half-deranged or faking derangement; in the end the guard would have a nervous breakdown.

Barnack also got reprimanded. He had done his work as poorly as I had and hadn't produced his quota.

As he returned to his place, making a face like a little boy who's lost the butter on his bread, the guard yelled after him: "I'm going to get you! You don't want to make your quota—I guarantee it, you'll make it yet. We've cured a lot of people, you bums!"

He meant Barnack and me.

At the noon hour, when the guard left the room, the foreman and some other inmates came in and tried to scare us.

"Watch out, Schuchardt and Barnack, if you keep on working this bad and don't make your quota, you'll have your food cut back or you'll get locked up! Then all you'll get is dried bread and water, and you'll have to sleep on bare boards!"

I was careful enough not to say anything in reply.

A carpenter from Magdeburg, a heavy-set man whom I'd gotten to know in Tränensberg, had arrived here a week before I had and was serving nine months. He had it worked out to the day how long he'd be here. "Two hundred and seventy-three days is nothing to sneeze at," he said. "They're small, but damned long." As a joke, he brought two mats and laid them on top of my loom saying, "See, you dumb dog, there you've got two mats to your account and you've made your quota!"

He'd taken the mats from someone just for fun to make a joke for himself and the others. Of course everybody laughed. Even the departmental clerk, a pimp from Halberstadt who was serving a full year, teased me and said, "Careful, if you don't make your quota and keep up the bad work, you'll get an increase!" He meant I'd get more time in the workhouse.

Otherwise they weren't mean to me; I didn't give them any opportunity.

My coworker, who sat behind me (back to back, as I've said),
said to the others: "If the filthy beast just didn't fart so much!
He must be rotten inside. I'm getting dizzy from the stench! I've
actually got to send him to the can three times a day—when this
guy cuts loose you can pass out!"

"It's not that bad," I said, "your sense of smell is just too re-
fined. You can't stand a good thing!"

I wasn't used to the thin gruel and dry black bread, and in fact
my wind did smell of rotten meat.

In spite of everything we got along well, and he demonstrated
the work for me as well as he understood it, even though he
wasn't obligated to. Although he looked sullen and morose, he
was still a good partner who cheered me up when the guard came
walking through the second and third department or got in a
conversation in the third department with the foreman and the
clerk. The guard demanded that we must get along, at least in
regard to the work.

It was soon Saturday, and, as the regulations called for, the
outside workers came home to attend church. They put their
bedclothes over the bare mattresses and headpieces. Beginning
Saturday evening there was a lot of hustle and bustle. What's
more, it was the day we got our laundry. The inmates brought
me my shirt, socks, neckerchief, handkerchief, and towel. We
were called up by number to get them. We helped each other
and the business was quickly finished. The officials counted us
off, left the dormitory, and locked up.

Among the outside workers was a carpenter from Wilhelms-
haven; he was doing his first stint for begging. When I spoke to
him, he came over to my bed and gave me a piece of sausage and
some chewing tobacco. He told me that he worked in the barge-
unloading gang, and that he couldn't complain about his assign-
ment. He received twenty pfennigs a day and enough lard and
sausage. Sometimes the bargemen would give him a sip from
their bottle too. I told him of my misfortune; he pitied me and
said: "If you were as strong as I am you could apply to the director for this job, but unfortunately you're not up to it. You see,
I'm a shipwright, but there are sacks to carry—that takes all my

strength. And then the food—it's not like you're a free man and can sing, as Herwegh said!"*

He came every two weeks and brought me sausage and chewing tobacco, and sometimes one or two issues of the Magdeburg *Voice of the People* [*Volksstimme*]. "The free workers in Schönebeck are mighty fine fellows, you can ask anything from them," he told me. "And if an inmate betrays me, well, we'll take care of him." He laughed quietly as he said it.

Denouncing a fellow worker would probably have meant trouble. Everyone was glad to find out what was going on outside the walls. The workers in the coir-rug factory outside the workhouse would secretly bring the Magdeburg *Voice of the People, The True Jacob* [*Der Wahre Jakob*], and the *South German Postilion* [*Süddeutsche Postillion*] with them to the dormitory, and so in the summer we could read from seven o'clock in the evening until it got dark. Sometimes we'd exchange a few words and tell stories—both true and made up—about our days on the tramp, of good men and rough men; and we'd criticize the sins of the people of the so-called better classes, until the call to order by the master (also an inmate) summoned us to quiet down and go to sleep. The discipline was really strict. At night when we urinated we had to sit down on the pot, and if our bowels called we had to relieve ourselves very quietly. And so the days of the second week slipped by.

In the free time on Sunday afternoon I made still another friend. He was a mechanic who was obsessed with inventing a machine; the exact nature and purpose of this machine he was unable to describe for me. He was a mental wreck; he'd gotten a year and a half and the mind-killing life had early on debilitated his nerves. He worked in the supply room splicing thread for the warp and the needle. He was a hard worker and very quiet. When he did speak, it was as though he first had to weigh every word. He had a dull and worried look, like someone who thinks he's being persecuted. He asked me how long I was in for.

"Half a year, if I don't get any extra time," I replied.

*Georg Herwegh (1817–75) was a popular radical poet.

To that he answered: "The first time I was supposed to get a half-year. It was in Glückstadt, but they made my life miserable, especially my coworkers—and I beat one of them up pretty bad. The upshot was that I got four weeks reduced food and three months extra time added on! The director in office during my time in Glückstadt was not exactly the best fellow!"

I replied, "What!? You got three months extra in that institution of heavenly care—and that during your first term?"

"Yeah, yeah, no wonder that it's hard for me to talk. All that damned time being locked up and doing work I'm not even trained for—that's what's responsible for my being here. If you've ever done time no factory owner or master wants to take you on," he said, playing with his jacket buttons. . . .

"We're pathetic; I'll probably have the same wretched experiences as you and a lot of others who find their way into this place," I answered.

He laid his hand discreetly on my shoulder, and with a half-absentminded look and an uneasy laugh, said I was right.

And so the second Sunday passed, leaving deeper impressions. I became better acquainted with the "De Profundis" in dealing with people, and I secretly wished: If only it was already the twenty-sixth Sunday! . . .

On Monday the guard reported me to the supervisor, an old official with white muttonchop whiskers à la Puttkamer.* He suffered from a colossal case of bureaucratic conceit, and he was often lost in a dream world, with one hand playing with his gilded sword handle. I was shown into his room. He spoke to me roughly from behind his desk: "The guard has reported that you're not making your quota and that your work performance is very bad. What do you have to say for yourself?"

I replied frankly: "Sir, I'm not suited for this work because I'm not a textile worker. And even if I'm punished I won't be able to make the quota."

---

* Robert von Puttkamer was Prussian Minister of the Interior from 1881 to 1888; he was a key figure in suppressing socialism.

He dismissed me, saying, "Do your work and fulfill your quota, otherwise you'll be punished!" I had received my first reprimand. And so I worried through the second week, because I wanted to keep from being punished.

On Wednesday of the third week the foreman came to me and said: "Schuchardt, you'll be making floor mats now—white with a black and red inlay, according to this pattern. Set up the warp with the right number of threads and string the upper struts horizontally in the same way. When you're done, call me. I'll get it started and show you what to do. I put in a good word for you today with the supervisor. In the course of the week you'll be assigned another job. The supervisor wants to transfer you somewhere else. In all my time as foreman, I've never come across anyone who is so dumb at this work as you are. You either have a hide like a rhinoceros or you're so stupid you can't say boo to a goose!"

He laughed and was happy that he'd be a free man again in two weeks.

I did my work, but the going was slow. The mat was finished and usable, but in the time it took me you were supposed to get at least two done.

The foreman showed the supervisor this mat and the latter said, "Schuchardt, make every mat like this one; it's good, but work faster—produce more!"

I replied: "Master, the foreman started and finished this mat for me. I'm not qualified for this work!"

"For the time being just do a good job on the mats; there's no other position open!" The supervisor laughed as he said it— though apparently not out of malice: ergo, I continued to bungle along.

The guard didn't let me out of his sight all day long, but I gave him no opportunity to be able to report me. Of course I worked, I moved my fingers—but I didn't make the quota of the hated work. My basic idea was: if you make the quota once, then you're in for it, and you won't get any different work.

We had visitors during this week. A few nuns and some young

ladies looked over the work of us inmates and saw how things were made. We were making large gymnastics mats, as well as big entrance hall and lobby rugs for hotels, usually with the name of the hotel or inn woven into the rug. On the looms we were weaving stair and corridor runners, mostly nice things, some of them even artistic.

These women came up to my loom and looked at my work, which was very colorful, but otherwise the worst work. What did people like this know about textile work? When the guard had shown them everything, they left. What do such people know about the life of an inmate? They think, "Ah, these people have it good after all." Such were my thoughts, and I envied these free people.

Otherwise, one day passed like the next, everything routinely, mechanically. This uniformity disgusted me, the endless, endless monotony the whole day long—the whole week, month after month. . . .

It was Sunday again. For several days Barnack had been gone from up in our department of the coir-weaving mill. He'd already been transferred on Wednesday. He gave me the key to the locker that we had shared. I was now the sole occupant of the locker. That was fine with me because everyone was liable for his own things. If you made more than your quota, you got beer in the afternoon. Sometimes people worked so fast that a pot was knocked over and broken. Then there were people who didn't want to buy a new one for ten pfennigs, so they stole one from somebody else. The beer came from the Allendorf Brewery, which employed inmates at 1.50 marks per day. The workhouse administration received this money, and later, during the Schönebeck brewers' strike (this was after my imprisonment), Herr Allendorf couldn't get enough inmates as brewers—even though the workhouse tried to get as many brewers as possible out of the province of Saxony. The following example confirms my point. In August they released a tailor, a skillful maker of officials' and ladies' clothes. He was a lively fellow who, on account of his flawless work, was popular with everyone from the director down to the guards, and with the wives too—he'd made excellent clothing for them all. He told me once, whether in jest or in fact:

"I'm an inmate, but when the women guards and the officials' wives try on their clothes I can still grab them by the breast! Yep, that's a ladies' tailor for you!"

Five weeks went by, and one evening the favorite of the workhouse's upper and lower officials was back with us. He told us his story: He still had twenty marks in his purse and a police stooge caught him panhandling. The court sentenced him to a second term for having the effrontery to panhandle—as if twenty marks was a kingdom. And now everyone from the director to the night watchman was glad that he was back here. Only one thing bothered him—that he hadn't spent all his money and that his very interesting trip through the Harz region had been so rudely interrupted. A few weeks later he received a fine pair of duds from the director.

Time passed; on the last day of this week the foreman and the clerk came to me and said: "Schuchardt, you'll be getting away from the loom. You'll be turning the wheels of the rug-cutting machine along with three other men. Every day you'll get cheap wine. Every week there's a quarter-pound of lard, and every day one more piece of bread! You're getting out of here all right and into the pimps' division! So why are you staring like a dumb bunny who's just been hit behind the ears? Just keep on botching up until the guard gives you the word. The company selling our coir products can be happy; a swine like you would just have bankrupted them anyway."

I recall that at this time the guard was not present in any of the three departments.

The man I'd been back to back with started in: "It's good that you're getting out of here, you miserable old creature; that will be the end of that foul stench. If you keep on farting down there with the Halberstadt and Magdeburg gentlemen you won't have too easy a time of it!" He gave me his hand and laughed. After this the official actually did come to my place and said: "Schuchardt, get your things together and hand them in. Then empty out your locker and take your stuff. You'll be stationed down one floor by the cutting machine."

Following the order and taking my things in my arms, I left the workshop, inwardly happy.

Ludwig Turek,
Child Tobacco Worker

Ludwig Turek (1898–?), a typesetter as an adult, is the youngest worker represented in this book and, so far as is known, the only one of our authors to become a communist after World War I. A revolutionary his whole life, Turek deserted during World War I, fought in the Revolution of 1918–19, visited the Soviet Union, and struggled underground against the Nazis during the Third Reich. After World War II, he settled in East Berlin, continuing the literary work that he had begun in the 1920s. Like all of his works, his autobiography, published in 1930, is a call to revolution. The following selection is the opening chapter of his book, describing his early childhood in and around Hamburg and Bremen from about 1905 to 1910. Turek is a good writer, and he makes the street life and petty criminality of proletarian children come alive, almost as though they were phenomena of nature. Unlike the older generation of moderate Social Democrats, Turek does not aspire to bourgeois culture. His judgments have an acerbic and unrelenting quality that would seem out of place in the work of Popp or Bromme.

308 *The German Worker*

SO YOUNG, AND YET SO HUNGRY

I first saw the light of day on 28 August 1898, a Sunday evening. Actually, it was the light of an old petroleum lamp. I think my mother had no time for the birth on a workday. And the fact that I wasn't born in a bed like most people in this part of the world, but rather on the bare floor next to an ancient chest of drawers, shows that my mother didn't put too much store in the event. Nor can it be assumed that out of superstition she brought me into this world on a Sunday in order to commend me to the gods of fortune as a Sunday child; that would have been blasphemy; before my birth I'd already had terribly bad luck. Five months earlier, on the thirty-first of March, my father had died, and I was the only thing he left to my mother. Mighty little for the daughter of a construction worker, who in his childhood had had to share a single herring with seven brothers and sisters. My mother didn't want me to keep her away from her work very long, and so at the end of my first week of life she was already back collecting her wages from "Bertram Wholesale Seeds" in Stendal.

My grandfather is said to have told my mother at the time that his wife had always gone back to the haying on the third day after giving birth. Of course that was humbug because at the Bismarck estate in Schönhausen, where my maternal grandparents lived, the first hay cutting is in June, the second in August or September, and then there's no haying until the next summer. And I know that an uncle of mine always celebrated his birthday with a tremendous hullabaloo on the twenty-seventh of January.

On the whole, my grandfather was not too careful with the truth. That earned him the nickname "Pastor Müller." He'd picked up another nickname too: in the last years before his death they called him "Rentier Müller." In 1916, because of the lousy

Translated from Ludwig Turek, *Ein Prolet erzählt. Lebensschilderung eines deutschen Arbeiters* (Cologne: Kiepenheuer & Witsch Verlag, 1972), 5–17. Originally published by Malik-Verlag, Berlin, 1930.

war, his health went downhill fast. He couldn't work anymore because of the constant hunger. People asked him why he didn't work, and he just told them a big lie—that he had succeeded and now wanted to live as a pensioner. I was in Magdeburg, ploughing through a field with a 10.5-cm high-angle-fire howitzer, and pouring liters of sweat through all eighteen holes in my fatigues at the command "Gunners to the fore!" And all the while, my grandfather was slowly but surely starving in Stendal, sixty kilometers to the north. In the fall he was buried.

I don't know very much to say about my father. As a metalworker he migrated from the east, worked at Gruson's in Magdeburg, got to know my mother, moved to Stendal, and made iron furniture at a piece rate for "L. C. Arnold." According to my mother, he was a very hard-working man: ten hours a day and more of drudgery at the Arnold Sanatorium for Consumptives (and those who wanted to become one); then horticulture and small-animal breeding; resoling shoes for customers, etc. It was dead sure that something had to come of all that. And indeed something did, but it wasn't the hoped-for prosperity, but rather tuberculosis.

The years up to my mother's remarriage must have been very hard for me. My mother worked, and an old woman with gout took care of me. Countless times I was reported as missing to the police. I got to know my new father when I was three. I was a savage ruffian, and I can still dimly recall his first attempts to teach me some manners. My stepfather was a cigar maker, and they are among the most enlightened workers. The struggle that the class-conscious worker carried on in those days against his narrow-minded bourgeois surroundings, against the deeply rooted cliques in the courts and the police force, was unbelievably difficult. Even today the Altmark is considered a very unenlightened region; and so, even after protracted hard work on the part of many brave fighters, the record of success there has been minimal.

Probably my father longed for a freer atmosphere; he soon resettled in Hamburg where he found a position making cigars at home for a cigar factory. Although I was only seven years old, I had to work too. That was a real torture for me because it interfered with my plans to hang around the harbor all the time. A shudder went up and down my back whenever my father spread out his fingers and reached into the tobacco box, calmly saying, as though he wanted to show the insignificance of the work, "When that's done you can go." But from experience I knew, first, that this huge pile of leaves that I had to strip (stripping meant taking the midrib out of every single tobacco leaf) left me at most two hours of playtime before dinner even if I worked very quickly; and, second, that my new father was extremely unreliable about keeping his promises. After this first task, there was usually something else to do. There was a constant struggle between us. If the pile was too big and there was no prospect of any free time even with the most intensive work, I used some tricks to attain my desired goal. When my father left the workroom for a moment, I put some of the leaves back into the box and gave my pile a good shaking so that it kept the same volume. In this way I gained an hour or more for myself. Or else I worked very sloppily and, when there was a chance, mixed my stripped leaves in with those my mother had done to make it look as though she had been the careless one.

To badly paid home workers like us, it seemed necessary to sell off some of our tobacco on the black market. Every time you succeeded in concealing the short weight when the accounts were settled, you could sell off on the black market 100 or more of the 2,500–3,000 cigars you made in a week. One day the bottom fell out of the market, the manufacturer gave us no new tobacco, and for a time my work was over.

My father and mother now went out to work. Those were fine times for me. With the house key on a string around my neck, I ran around outside after school. Almost every day my path led to the harbor. I was drawn there irresistibly, and my shoes completely fell apart because the round trip from Wandsbek is several kilometers. But it was still worth it because there was often something to catch somewhere. Of course the good Hamburgers didn't just put something in your pocket, you had to do something for it. I learned a great deal about this from others. You usually got the most from the forbidden places. This principle earned for us (we rarely operated alone in this business) the hostility of all sorts of officials.

One time our gang was sitting up by the Bismarck Monument sharing a can of prime smoked herring and some white bread. Soon a policeman appeared, drawn by the aroma of these delicacies. Despite the fact that we put the herring very neatly back into the can, we heard a thundering sharp command, "No more nonsense, and beat it." Every order is sacred, at least when it says to get out of there. Then came a further order, "Stop, and let's have the can." The policeman's mouth was watering at the sight of our fine herring; he swallowed noticeably and said in a friendly voice, "Children, be reasonable, hand over the herring."

"No, you can't eat it, it's stolen," was our answer, and off we ran in the direction of the Reeperbahn.

Almost every evening exactly at six o'clock I stood outside the "Reichard Chocolate Factory, Wandsbek." In the time it took to walk to the Volksdorfer Strasse I could easily eat the chocolate that my mother had smuggled past the guards.

It wasn't possible to get high enough wages in Hamburg, and so we moved to Geestemünde. A brother of my mother lived there. Worker. Five children: Karl, Heini, Sophie, Tilly, and Hermann in a wretched smoky kitchen, gathered around a huge pot of unpeeled potatoes; in the frying pan ten pfennigs worth of bacon; after this luxurious meal they all disappeared into three beds so that they wouldn't waste any expensive petroleum—that was the Baake family. We stayed with them the first few days and it was absolute chaos. My brother Hans had been born shortly before we left Hamburg. One of the Baakes was also very tiny, so there were two screamers there. I still remember today how starved the whole family was. Mealtimes were often dramatic. The children watched each other carefully to see that everyone got an equal portion. There were often wild fights about the bones, which had, of course, already been bare when they came into the house. One day the securely locked kitchen cupboard was violently broken open; that evening their father was unable to discover the guilty one, so he took the three eldest over his knee and gave them a sound thrashing with his belt, and as extra punishment they had no supper.

My father had rented a four-room apartment on Mainzstrasse, not too big to live in but too much to pay for. After three months we were behind in the rent and had to relocate on Grünestrasse. Then we started to work at home again. Even today I have to admire how under these conditions my father got up the energy for such protracted work. He never went to bed before twelve at night. My mother did the same, and there was no more free time for me either. The workroom was terribly small. My little brother Hans sat in the damp room all day long. It was really no wonder that he took leave of this wretched world a short time later. That was a very shrewd move, as my father said at the time.

It wasn't long before we moved out of this place. We went now to Leherheide, about ten kilometers north of Geestemünde. A village, built along one street with a lot of new houses. We moved in and set up shop in one of these. Even though it was at least a three-hour walk from there to the fisherman's harbor, I still had to go with a basket to buy waste fish for ten pfennigs. On these days I got home late in the evening, dead tired.

I still remember one unusual thing about Leherheide. There was a huge rubbish dump there. Its specialty seemed to be countless old boots lying all around; there were so many that for weeks we could collect a big sack of them every day. We used the boots for fuel in the kitchen. The catch was that you had to do a lot of work with a pick in order to pry loose one of the hidden treasures. As in a mine, there are seams and layers that are more or less valuable. Gradually you gain experience and know at first glance whether it's worth it or not to dig in. For example, there is household rubbish, which, if you're very lucky, might yield a bone. The rubbish from small businesses is definitely better. Depending on their specialties, it's possible to find iron, zinc, brass, copper wire (usually insulated), or lead. All of these things are often scarcely identifiable as such; you need a sharp, practiced eye. Even smell plays a role. Rubbish from a locksmith's smells different than rubbish from a plumber's shop. When you discover a productive vein, you work it for all it's worth; you have to be careful in your picking and scraping not to mix the valuable rubbish in with the worthless—that makes the work much harder. Then too, if there are a lot of people around, you have to hold your own against the competition. If a good place has already been picked through several times, it's pointless to go through the rubbish again even if it looks promising. There are specialists too; some overlook rags and bones, and many don't want to weigh themselves down with iron; and then there are others who take everything, even the most worthless things like barrel hoops, umbrellas, food tins, wire, sackcloth, parts of mattresses, galvanized buckets, etc. All in all, it's not very lucrative, even with a lot of hard work.

For the time being my father had given up his trade; he worked on the construction of the new Imperial Harbor in Bremerhaven. This may have been the reason for still another move. This time we went to Lehe, to an ancient barrack at Wursterstrasse 4. It was a lousy snowy day when we moved. Our few pieces of furniture—which certainly no longer looked new because of the many moves—came to a rest here.

They were working hard at the harbor, both day and night shifts. I had to bring my father his food during the day shift. This introduced me to the Imperial Harbor, just as I had gotten to know the Hamburg one.

In the meantime I'd turned eleven years old. One of my chores was getting the household fuel. Three times a week I went off with other poor people's children to "buy" twenty-five pounds of bunker coal from the North German Lloyd. The customs officers and harbor police were opposed to this trade. But we needed the coal badly and so the smuggling went on. In the evening we little ones slipped unseen across the customs border; with our sacks carefully wrapped around our bodies, we crept forward cautiously. If the enemy came into sight, we had to act decisively. Either we faked a retreat or, if the coast was otherwise clear, we just broke through. This last method always made the custodian of order extremely angry. He jumped nervously to the right and left in order to catch one of us, but that rarely happened. I myself always approached this situation with such confidence that I soon earned the greatest trust among my fellows. Our gang was really a very select one: six to eight strong, we rushed upon the startled cop. The two strongest and boldest went right at the fellow; at the last moment we stopped and then raced by on either side. There was no point in running after us, we were faster.

Now the cop knew very well what was going on, and if he felt like it, he followed us slowly over to the bunkers. There were several of them in different places. If by chance the mischief maker discovered us on the big bunkers, there wasn't much he could do about it, because we always sought out only the full bunkers. Then we sat way up on top of the coal. No cop ever dreamed of climbing up on the coal to make a useless attempt to catch somebody up there. We often sat up on the coal for hours if we were sure they were waiting for us below.

I can remember one time when several policemen were lying in wait for us below the bunker. We smelled a rat and conferred about what we ought to do. There was no way of getting away with any coal, so we poured out the already filled sacks. I slid down to reconnoiter, and determined that at least six policemen had taken it upon themselves to get rid of us once and for all. To escape on the harbor side was very risky because of the lighting. Our plan was ready. We got together some handy-sized chunks of coal and five of us opened up with murderous fire onto the darkest side, the back of the bunker. At first nothing stirred, but soon there was movement below. It was clear that this side was free for the moment. As arranged, two boys quickly slid down while the five of us on the corners of the bunker threw down a hail of coal chunks. The two got through and two matches were struck, one after the other, at the customs border. The same maneuver was repeated, and this time three got through. Only then did our besiegers see the trick, and we two remaining ones clearly heard the pursuers giving chase, cursing loudly about the impudence of the coal throwing.

To our astonishment the pursuit went on for a long time. Our friends must have been almost to the customs border. There you had to get over the barrier without delay; otherwise, unless you had a good lead on the officials, you got into a very tight spot. The customs border consisted of a three-meter-high picket fence which, because of the sharp points, was very hard to climb over. The three lit matches failed to show.

There was an eerie silence around our bunker. The "George Washington" lay across from us at the wharf; from there we could hear a dog wailing. A tugboat whistled somewhere out in the night. The two of us lay flat on the coal, not saying a word. Gradually we got the feeling we'd been left behind; we climbed down from our black mountain. Halfway down my friend stopped. "Should we take any coal with us?!"

"Yeah, Heini!"

"My mother doesn't have a single piece left at home!" Silently we filled our sacks. We got out of the harbor area hanging onto the left side of a streetcar. The driver couldn't help but discover us; he looked at our black faces; we said nothing, and yet spoke volumes. He took the curves very carefully. When we got home, we learned that everyone had gotten away. So the police's big undertaking came to nothing. But the struggle continued.

If you're not used to the work, carrying cement can injure your shoulders. My father wasn't used to the work, so he badly injured his shoulders. After reporting in sick, he was unemployed, and this just at the time of the birth of my sister Lissi.

Our "provider" tramped off to Bremen and found work there as a cigar maker. The fruits of this "livelihood" arrived at our house in the form of postal drafts for three, four, at most seven marks. That wasn't enough to get the beds back from the pawnshop without exchanging them for the worst hunger. With nothing but a handful of malt coffee in your pocket it really hurts to have to watch others eating bread and margarine. During the recess at school I collected bread crusts in a big bag "for my rabbit." Everyone had a rabbit. Dry bread makes the cheeks red (so it said in our reader); in mine I wrote "gives a pointed ass and an early death."

One day in gym class the teacher beat me with his long stick as far as he could reach as I climbed up the rope. That really galled me. He knew how good I usually was at gymnastics, and he called me mean, lazy, and unruly. There being no beds, I'd slept badly and frozen the night before, and I was also hideously hungry. The few bread crusts we'd gotten by begging were not exactly made to strengthen me. For these reasons I was as limp as a wet mouse. The beating really ate at my guts. I didn't tell my mother anything about it; she already asked me often enough whether I was hungry; that was a pretext to give me her last bites. I protested vigorously even though I had a lion's hunger that seemed like it was sawing up my stomach.

In a few days the time would run out for getting some of the beds out of hock; no more extensions were possible; the pawnshop knew only business rules, no human considerations. When could my mother ever hope to replace the lost beds with new ones? For the proletarian housewife these problems are much harder and more worrying than those that General Staff members or scholars have to brood on. Whoever doubts this should have seen my mother with the big tears in her eyes. Her baby could no longer satisfy her thirst on her dried-up breast. "If papa sends money the day after tomorrow, we'll get back the big bed, and there will definitely be two marks left over. Then we'll really get something nice!" Two marks household allowance for the whole next week! The landlord was owed two months rent, and neither the baker nor the grocer was giving any more credit.

In the meantime I had to do something. *I* did. It was up to me—to be off! I rolled up my smallest bundle, and without my pick I set off. My mother shoved a bowl of gruel in front of me. "Eat, boy."

"Oh, the old gruel," I said gruffly; but how gladly I would have gulped it down. I went on my way—past the streetcar de-pot, toward Speckenbüttel, and out of the city. At least my legs were going that way, my thoughts didn't go along; they went in the other direction toward Harbor Street, downtown, past the big shops. Both, neither my thoughts nor my legs, had any particular goal. The distance between them got bigger and bigger. I reached Speckenbütteler Park. The weather was bad and there were almost no people there.

What was I looking for on these slippery paths? These well-kept paths, strewn with red gravel, angered me enormously. One time I turned around, walked back a bit, and was alarmed by my own footprints. The small heels of my mother's shoes, which I had on, made a clear track. At once I cut across through the trees until I came out onto a meadow; the racetrack was there. Looking back into the woods again, I noticed in a tree a chain with a large spring trap attached to it. There was nothing in it but the remains of a piece of herring that had been eaten away on both sides. Carefully I closed the trap so I could get it loose from the chain. That wasn't easy, and only after a half-hour's work was I on my way back to town with the thing in my sack.

Oh, but what a shock; the junk dealer would pay me only a lousy ten pfennigs for it. The swindler answered my refusal to give it up for this price with a threat to call the police; he probably knew where the trap had come from and made the most of it. What now? My hope of getting fifty pfennigs for the haul vanished, and with it vanished the wonderful things I wanted to buy—like bread, fat, scraps of cheese, a quarter-liter of milk, and a new pen; and finally the filthy fellow reminded me that I too had to vanish. I immediately went into the nearest bakery shop, grabbed a loaf of bread from a shelf, and raced wildly out. Still running, I burst into a delicatessen, grabbed two tins of sardines, and once again fled through the crowds on the street.

This quick, determined action came just at the right time. It was four o'clock in the afternoon; except for a few bread crusts that I'd had that morning at school, the last thing my stomach had had was yesterday afternoon's gruel—twenty-seven hours before. I got as far as the Dionysius Church, then my arm dropped lamely on my body and the bread fell to the ground. With difficulty I picked it up, staggered over to the church, dropped down onto the doorstep, and tore into the bread like someone who hadn't eaten for twenty-seven hours—and for three days before that had had to read that dry, and yet so watery, word "gruel" on the menu. I felt better after just a few bites.

I took the rest of the bread home. With true devotion, my mother cut slices from the bread, laid sardines on them, and we ate.

We ate stolen bread. Herr State's Attorney, you should have intervened then, that was your duty. Everyone has his duties! The most elementary duty of every person is to give nourishment to his own body. This holiest of all duties remains even when the laws and statutes don't permit it.

For a long time my father slaved away in Bremen for a few paltry marks; and my mother was often amazed at the luck that appeared on the most critical days and brought her son a great "discovery." My mother called it luck and she never stopped believing in it. She really did a lot for the upbringing of her children. Almost always when I was about to set off with my sack and pick, she would say: "Don't ever touch someone else's property! Son, son, don't disgrace me."

Finally our landlord's patience ran out. There was no way we could pay the rent. Move out! Begin again with the same old business. My father found work in Geestemünde, and that meant an improvement in our economic situation.

The Achilles Iron Foundry, a dark filthy shop, made life hard for my father. I went there occasionally, and there was dust as thick as your fist lying all around. The workers were black like Negroes. On days when they poured iron it was like being in hell. It was no rarity to work overtime until two in the morning. And even so you had to be there on time the next morning. Anyone can imagine how brutal the exploitation was under such circumstances. I later worked in similar hellholes, and I know that nobody can stand it for too long. My father held on bravely for a long time until his union activity aroused the displeasure of one of the foremen and he had to "bite the sack." ("Biting the sack" is an old union expression, still used today, for getting fired.)

Once again everything was packed up for a long journey, and we went back to Stendal. Shortly before this my mother had another baby—my brother Artur joined us.

Max Lotz,
Coal Miner

Max Lotz (1876–?) was one of the workers with whom the sociologist Adolf Levenstein carried on an extensive correspondence (see Introduction). The illegitimate son of a Jewish tenor and a variety show actress turned prostitute, Lotz had a checkered career before he settled down to a steady job. He was repeatedly in trouble for begging, vagrancy, and petty theft, though he had used his time in jail to read the classics. The excerpts here are from a forty-nine-page letter written from Gladbeck in the Ruhr on 2 July 1908. Lotz is obviously responding to Levenstein's probing questions about his deep feelings and beliefs. His description of a day in the mine and how it affects the worker is of gripping power and reminds one of naturalist literature. In the postscript, however, Lotz gets in over his head, both philosophically and syntactically. Yet the reader will be rewarded for wading through the virtually untranslatable verbosity and nebulous theory. For in the end, Lotz must command our respect as a genuine original. Lotz probably extends himself intellectually more than any other working-class author, and there is no better example anywhere of the fate that awaits sophisticated ideology in the mind of an intelligent but exhausted worker.

[A DAY IN THE MINE]

Trrrrr. The primitive alarm clock on the little night table sounds mercilessly into the warm summer morning. Startled, my wife bolts up, still asleep, to shut off the disturbance. It's 3:45 in the morning. For a moment she's half-asleep and puts off getting up, but then the steam whistle from the nearby mine screams in her ear. I awake now too, shaken by the really horrible sound. A word from me, and my wife becomes aware that the screech means the call to the mine. Time to get out of the comfortable bed.

I sleep a little while longer until my wife has gotten together a simple breakfast with a cup of substitute coffee. Then, suddenly, with a piercing call, she startles me out of my cozy half-sleep.

"Max—Max—you have to get up."

"Yes," I yawn; and I get up at once and give my bones a stretch; they seem almost to be crushed.

"You, Max," my wife says to me as I sip the coffee suspiciously, "you wanted to leave a bit earlier because today is payday, otherwise you'll have to stand around again in the washup room before you can get up to the pay window."

"Yeah, that's right, I'll hurry, Ida," I say to her. I grab my metal coffee bottle and the wrapped bread. A quick kiss on my wife's forehead and mouth, and I'm off.

The walk to the mine takes about half an hour, and on other days I always ponder some topic on the way; but today I'm in a hurry on account of payday, and so I don't think about anything.

Translated from *Aus der Tiefe. Arbeiterbriefe. Beiträge zur Seelen-Analyse moderner Arbeiter,* ed. Adolf Levenstein (Berlin: Eberhard Frowein Verlag, 1909), 25–34, 39–41, 47, 52, 57–73.

For today it's enough for me just to suck in greedily the fresh, pure morning air. What's important today is drinking up as much as possible of this balm for my lungs. Just don't think because when I think, or brood, the length and speed of my steps automatically decreases. So, a lot of morning air now, because afterward, down below, it's so sultry, close, and oppressive. With a hearty pleasure I suck and lap up the cool, refreshing drink of nature. Every time I breathe in I feel the healing breath very clearly in my expanded lung lobes, how it strokes the septums that are infected with coal dust. How beautiful! How beautiful! I take one more deep breath, and then, arriving at the control window, I call out my number, "1064."

I've scarcely called out my number when the token flies onto the counter. Through long habit, the sure hand of the token dispenser reaches involuntarily for the number. The vast majority of the employees don't need to say their numbers because he knows almost all of them. The tokens fly one after another until the stream of men stops.

As usual it strikes me that everyone here is a number. It's just the way galley slaves are treated. Of course this procedure is essential—but you still think about it. With these thoughts in mind, I enter the washup room. It's a large hall with 3,500 pulley ropes with four-part clothes hooks on them. Every rope has a number on it, and you use the same number that's on your token. The room is always filled with clouds of dust, which gets mixed in a disgusting way with the foot and body sweat of the workers who are changing their clothes. The steam coming in from the shower rooms really doesn't make the atmosphere any healthier. Greedy, furious flies are a constant bother, and roaches run all over the walls and the floors as though they were right at home. They are really in their element here. Today a sparrow has found its way inside; it was probably curious and flew into the air pipes, which are there just like on ships, bringing air from above to the lower decks. This is always something of an event. Everyone laughs when the frightened animal flies up through the squeaking rollers, trying to get out, and hits the thick roof windows. Otherwise everyone is caught up in the rush and bustle of confusion. It's payday and everyone wants to get to the elevators as fast as possible so that he can get out as fast as possible at the end of the shift. Even the entrances and exits are controlled by number. I too am in a particular hurry today. I want to get out of this stuffy air—into still worse air for eight and a half hours.

There's a pump by the pithead. Most just pass it by. But almost every morning I drink my fill as a way of saving coffee, even though my bottle holds three liters of it. I observe things here too. I often notice how, with thoughtless haste, most of the drinkers just throw the cold water from the rusty metal cup into their hot throats. Not sensible!

On the stairs leading up to the elevator landing, I meet the apprentice hewer who's assigned to me.

"Well, Max, you're early," he says, greeting me.

"So are you, Reinhold," I reply. "Have you seen Bruno yet?"

"No, he probably won't come today."

"How come?"

"Well, you know, when he's had a fight at home he usually doesn't come for three or four days."

"Bad enough that he's like that; but we'll see. It would be a lot better if he came on account of the work."

"It sure would. Two men aren't enough. The work's set up for three. Wait a second, I'll go check the board to see how much the noon shift hauled."

"If it's too little, I don't want to hear about it," I called out, laughing as he went off; and then I got in the line of those waiting at the entrance to the shaft.

The line was fairly long today. I was standing rather far back, but it goes relatively fast. An elevator in a modern-equipped mine is a true monster. Each elevator has four levels; the lower three are 1¼ meters high, and the upper level is over 2¼ meters high. The upper part of the elevator is higher so that horses, long pieces of wood, or other large objects needed in the mine can be taken down the shaft. The total height of the elevator is 6 meters, and it's 2¼ meters wide. When a box like this is screwed up out of the depths, you'd think there was a small house hanging on the haulage rope. And there are four such huge elevators that rush up and down the shaft next to each other. They can get twelve men in a sitting position on each of the three lower levels, while fourteen men can stand on the top level. The total number of persons that can be carried in the elevator on one trip is regulated by a decree from the Head Mining Office in Dortmund, and this number may not be exceeded. In this case the number is fifty. With us, at the state-owned mine, "United Gladbeck, Möller Shafts Division," it's actually impossible to violate this decree, because even if they wanted to, they couldn't cram more than fifty men into the elevator. So you can see how "wise" the Head Mining Office is in its regulations.

With a clang, the operator closes behind me the safety door that has to be attached to each level when people are being carried. Only when the electric signal from the bottom of the elevator shaft comes on can the operator above ground signal to the engine room. Three warning bells are sounded which mean "going down." The elevator sinks slowly into the depths. Fifty men are quietly put at the mercy of the unknown strength of the steel cable. Almost as though by unconscious agreement, everyone is silent on the trips up and down. Only now and then is there a remark or a quick joke. In spite of myself I'm often overcome by a certain anxiety, though not actual fear. Being long accustomed to the ride has a salutary effect so that none of the miners is really directly afraid or worried. During the one- or two-minute trip I personally often think of the countless hideous accidents that have been specifically caused by cable breaks. Above all I think about the elevator crash of the previous year that killed twenty-two miners. It was also a state-owned mine—the "Matilde Shaft" in the Saar Region. The horror of the scene in the few seconds of the fall is proved by the hideous fact that they actually had to fish the individual body parts out of the water at the bottom of the shaft. So you don't have to be the worrying type to take these few moments of the journey very seriously.

At the bottom of the shaft, that is at the loading area, the second hewer is already waiting for me. So, he actually had come. After the usual greeting of "good luck," we sat down against the wall of the loading area to wait for the apprentice hewer to arrive. It's usual for the miners to wait for each other at the shaft in order to go all together to the place where they're working. While we're sitting there, there are hundreds of miners standing and sitting around, and the hum of the voices from hundreds of raw throats is deafening. I can still remember the time I first came down seven years ago and was puzzled by the roar of the incomprehensible sea of words in my ears; you can start to hear it thirty meters from the bottom. When I got to the bottom, I understood at once the source of the unusual sound.

We talked about nothing in particular, replying now and then to words or questions from fellow workers we knew. And we didn't notice that our buddy, whom we'd been waiting for, was standing right in front of us. We jumped up laughing when he called out good-naturedly, "Well, let's get moving."

The noon shift yesterday had recorded twelve carloads on the board. "The winch must have been broken again," said the apprentice hewer as we quietly climbed up an eighty-meter rise with a thirty-degree incline. "If it doesn't get better, I've had it. What a miserable haulage. The devil with it."

"The whole eleventh cutting (that's our area) isn't worth anything anymore. The best thing would be to get a transfer. There's no point in all this drudgery. They should seal up the whole place."

I say nothing; it's always the same old song about pointless pick work. The two fellows harp on this irritating theme for a little while. In the meantime we've reached the main hauling track along which go all the loads from our section. Right across from the entrance to the hauling road a room has been cut in the tunnel and supported with heavy beams. This is the toolroom.

"What sort of tools do you have in the room, Max?" the apprentice hewer asks me. It's usual for the apprentice to carry the tools.

"Just the little pick," I answer.

"Get my pick too, Reinhold," the second hewer calls after him. We go on slowly ahead.

"Yeah, I'll get 'em."

We continue on while the apprentice gets the proper tools, which come freshly sharpened every day from the forge. We have about two kilometers to go. Even this walk to our workplace is tiring and difficult.

First we have to pass through a tunnel about twelve hundred meters long, which is the main tramway. It's always in wretched shape due to the very bad condition of the rock. According to the mine inspector, this tramway and ventilation tunnel costs the mine 8,000 marks a month in wages, wood, and other materials. Every day during the night shift sixty to seventy timberers have to see to it that there is enough clearance for a horse to slip through unhindered. I can speak quite literally about the horses slipping through, because after years of training and going the same way shift after shift the animals are so familiar with the way that they know every prop and every beam that's broken and hanging in their way. In the flickering light of the tunnel lamps the animals very skillfully avoid these places by bowing or ducking their heads. Poor, pitiable creatures! The insatiable Moloch, gold, robs even them of sunshine, green meadows, and the airy spaces above. I'm always filled with pity when I see these sweat-covered animals snorting past, harassed and driven on in the most brutal manner. They are delivered helpless into the hands of young tormentors who are usually crude and rough fellows. A lot of pointless torture takes place down here in the dark and still loneliness of the tunnels, and the thrashing of the wire whips cracks down on their bodies. I make it my duty to report any such violations to the authorities.

Because the apprentice is taking a little longer than usual, we sit down on the pipe. On one side the pipe carries water for the spraying system, on the other it carries compressed air for the ventilation system.

"Did you read the article on the Müller Shafts in the mine workers' paper yesterday?" the second hewer asked me when we'd sat down.

"Yes," I replied. "It was unusually restrained and showed clearly that the writer was unsure in writing down his thoughts."

"This place is also a pit of misery; if I could only write such a thing, I'd show the bastards something."

"Damn, it's hot in here again today. The ventilator has probably been off for a few minutes. That mechanic is a lazy bum; he's turned the thing off so he can oil it more easily. That's not allowed."

"Yeah, all the guys with sweet jobs, they know how to look out for themselves; they don't care if we have to gasp for air like fish out of water."

Other workers pass by while we're talking.

"Want to come with us?" says one of the hewers who works on the coal face above us. He'd probably caught the words "sweet job" as he went by. "You're probably waiting for a sweet job, eh?"

"Just 'cause we're standing here doesn't mean we're any lazier than you are," I call after them as they move on laughing. "Have you seen Prüfer?" (That's the apprentice.)

"Yeah, he's coming," they call back.

Their flickering lanterns disappear.

Now Prüfer comes too. The three of us go off together.

"What took you so long?" I asked irritably, even though I know that the apprentice never wastes any time. "Did you have another fight with the guy in the toolroom?"

"I couldn't help it," he replied. "I had to look around for a reserve lamp. My regular lamp had a torn safety band."

"You really got a crummy lamp," said Bittner, the second hewer. "That thing belongs in a museum."

"You've got nothing to brag about," said Prüfer. "Yours looks like a glowworm."

"Well, neither of you have to show off," I interrupted. "Most of the time my lamp flickers like the torches Nero used when he smeared the first Christians with pitch and then used them as lights for the amphitheater."

"You really have a way of putting things," Bittner flattered me.

"That's true," Prüfer agreed. "I wish I could do it too."

"Tell us about this Nero, Max," Bittner asked me, for he always liked to listen when I held forth.

"I really don't feel like it today, Bruno," I replied. "Anyway, as a Christian you surely know the basic facts about the early history of your religion, especially about those times in the first three hundred years after Christ when the Roman emperors persecuted the Christians with hideous cruelty and bloodthirstiness." (I deliberately call Bittner a Christian because I know of his indecision about leaving the church and I want to remind him, without pressuring him, to draw the consequences of his principles.)

"I never bothered about that," said Bittner apologetically. "Poking around in books is tiresome to me."

"Why? Don't you know the important words of the late Social Democrat, Wilhelm Liebknecht: 'Power is knowledge, and knowledge is power'? And Comrade Liebknecht was right when he said that, because if you don't bother about anything, then you won't know anything. And if you don't know anything, then you have nothing to say and are without influence. . . ."

As I was about to continue in this simple vein, the apprentice pointed to an especially cracked place in the tunnel and said, "Well, it'll be a wonder if things go well today. Here's at least one break."

"How are the horses going to get past here?" the second hewer wondered.

We look at the broken railroad tracks that are used to support the ceiling. "It's at least going to mess up the tramway; if it breaks we'll have the day off," I say.

"Then what the hell, let it break. Let's hurry up, I think Gippert's coming up behind us." (Gippert is our district mine inspector.)

"Yeah, that's him; I think we're the very last ones today." I look at my watch. "Dammit, it's already five minutes to six," I say, urging my two comrades to move faster.

[*Finally the three men arrive at the coal seam that they are currently working. The temperature is 30°C (86°F).*]

The Silesian, Bittner, is in a particularly foul mood today. He's depressed about a family argument, and he takes out his anger on all of us. Now, as he comes into the sweat oven with us, he starts cursing:

"Goddammit, it's hot in this hole. If I had any say about it, the manager with his shiny nose wouldn't do anything but couple and uncouple cars down here in the mine. And if he couldn't do it because of his fat belly, then I'd dock half his shift's pay for negligence at work. What a wretched beast, oh no, I'm going crazy in the head."

The apprentice always laughs especially hard whenever Bittner really gets going like this. But today, everybody, including me, seems to be in a sad mood, and we just smile feebly in agreement. My head is burning too.

Happy finally to have reached our workplace, we throw ourselves down on the toolboxes that are standing there; we're already noticeably tired. As fast as we can, we take off our denim jackets and flannel shirts, keeping on only the thin denim trousers. If it weren't against the rules, we'd take off our trousers too and work completely naked, because every piece of clothing is a burden to us. The sweat runs under your clothes and you feel totally wiped out. Because the air from the air shaft flows a little cooler up here—about 25° [77°F]—your overheated body cools down a bit while you're sitting. Each of us eats some buttered bread, and because it's somewhat later than usual today, we go right to work after we've eaten.

[*Lotz digresses to describe the background of his fellow workers and then resumes with a description of the work routine.*]

Each of us takes a sharp pick and goes to work breaking up the coal. Extracting coal goes according to a set procedure. Since the seams in a deposit are relatively parallel, the main thing is to observe the course of the seams and keep your eye on how they're separated from each other. If you don't pay attention to this, the coal gets packed in by pressure from above. The skill of a hewer is shown mainly by how he regulates his effort according to the direction of the seams. Then, too, you've got to keep a really sharp eye out for the puckers in the seam, because the seam doesn't run uniformly horizontally, but rather (at least where we are) curves gently up and down. This situation determines automatically the direction you cut in.

I let the coal I've broken loose lie on the floor so that when the apprentice returns I can shovel it immediately into the car. Since the coal face we're working on (which is eight to ten meters wide) slants downward and must be propped up, Bittner first has to throw the coal he's gotten up to the tramway. Ten minutes pass, during which each of us works to get the necessary amount of coal so that things will go smoothly when Prüfer returns with the tramcars. (Each time we fill and haul two cars.) We're still relatively vigorous and fresh, so it isn't long before we have the amount of coal we estimate we'll need.

Every car holds fourteen bushels, so I may state that the Prussian state has the honor (along with Haniel, Stinnes, Thyssen, and accomplices) of having introduced the largest cars anywhere in the Ruhr area.* In fact, in recent weeks they have tried (and as I write this, they've almost completely accomplished it) to force on us a whole new line of cars, which, according to our calculations, hold five to six shovelfuls more than the old size. The individual is powerless against such despotic actions of the bureaucracy. Of course the piecework rate for both kinds of cars is the same, so we don't have much good to say about the new cars. If you fill the shovel about the same each time, then about thirty-six to thirty-eight shovelfuls suffice to fill a car of the old model. If the hauling is going smoothly, and you're given eight of the new cars, then during a shift you're cheated out of the earnings of one carload. Currently we get 1.20 marks for a single carload of coal. Since there are three men on every crew, if you want to earn anything, your crew has to fill and haul off fifteen or sixteen such carloads. This would give you a wage of 6.00 or 6.40 marks, assuming that no costs for explosives were deducted.

* Fritz Haniel, Matthias Stinnes, and August Thyssen were among the founders of Germany's great industrial empires. The mine where Lotz worked was one of thirty-nine nationalized mines in Prussia in 1906.

[*As the shift goes on, the crew falls further behind due to a derailed tramcar, which injures the hand of a member of another crew.*]

While the apprentice pushed the cars up to the coal face and fastened the little metal control tokens onto them, we went right to shoveling the coal in. Both cars were full in about eight minutes. "Pumping" (that's what we call shoveling) is hard work because a full shovel usually holds about one-third of a bushel; strenuous loading affects your back above all. You can see that many of the older miners have rather crooked backs, no doubt the result of a lot of shovel work. What's more, if, as is often the case, there are a lot of seams 1½–3 feet thick that are also very level, then prolonged work—picking, shoveling, or whatever—in a stooping or crouching position is very hard on the worker's chest. The incessant coal dust and the usually bad and stale air (if it has already ventilated a large number of work areas) eat away at the miners' lungs. If you add to this the mining slaves' undernourishment, which is due to the bad and cheap food usually sold in our industrial areas, then it's no wonder that the proletarian sickness, tuberculosis, has become epidemic among miners. I've always been especially interested in studying the mortality tables in the mine workers' newspaper. And every time they've appeared, the horrible statistics have proved to me anew that lung disease was by far the most common cause of death among miners. For at least 70 percent of the deceased the notice read: tuberculosis or pneumonia; and then, to give an idea of the true scope of the problem, in another 10–12 percent of the death notices the dismal table said: died as a result of severe injuries sustained in an accident. Every time I read through these tables my heart wrenched at the sight of the accumulation of frightful misery. And I too feel the blood-reeking hand of sudden death constantly hanging over me; and soon, perhaps very soon, I'll feel the slowly lethal bite of the tuberculosis bacillus in my breast.

[*Lotz goes on to detail some of the other health hazards of mining.*]

We'd broken off our description at the point where the apprentice was pushing the first two filled cars away from the coal face.

"You, Max," Bittner said to me as Prüfer disappeared with the last car behind the ventilator, "my bones are already completely exhausted, I'm beaten dead as a dog. My limbs have been like this for a couple of weeks now."

"Don't always keep pestering me, Bruno; you think I'm doing any better? I'll tell you something. Just watch when Reinhold comes back and hangs his lamp on the pillar over the car; watch how the flickering light rays fall on the naked upper part of his body, portraying him against the dark background; then he looks just like the Belgian Meunier's bronze statue, 'The Miner.'* He looks exactly like it. The naked, black, dust-covered upper body, shining as though water had been poured over it; with the pale light on him and the arm muscles strained—he reproduces Meunier's original exactly. As if you had the artist's bronze statue right in front of you. It's struck me many times."

"I've never looked, and I wouldn't even notice anything like that; I always just think about quitting time. Yeah, and this is going to go on until they nail me in my coffin? I'll go crazy yet."

"Can't you ever think about anything else, do you always have to wallow in this damned wretchedness? Can't you rise above these miserable working conditions and get in touch with your humanity? You, Bruno, can't you ever manage that?"

"I don't have any desire for such a thing, and let's face it, I couldn't do it anyway. When I come home dog-tired from the mine, I just lie down on the seat by the fire and sleep and I don't think about anything at all."

[*It's late in the shift now, and the crew struggles to fill a few more carloads of coal so that the day won't be a total loss.*]

Our labor becomes more and more mechanical now. Tired and used up, with no more incentive or haste, we go through the motions mindlessly. There was coal there, Reinhold just needed to come. My forehead burned like fire. Because of my serious anemia, I suffer from mild dizziness now and then. Bittner

---

*The Belgian sculptor, Constantin Meunier (1831–1905), was known for his realistic statues of workers, especially miners.

doesn't know about it. But my head is seething and it cripples my ability to think—I can't help it. When it gets too bad, I stop "slurring" (that's what I always call the sluggish, listless work) and sit down on the mine wall to gulp down the rest of my coffee. Because Bittner doesn't have any more coffee in his bottle, he takes Prüfer's bottle, but drinks cautiously so he doesn't take everything.

"Check to see what time it is, Bruno," I call, for Bruno is over by the toolbox where Prüfer keeps his bottle.

"Just a second, I'll look—one o'clock."

"Damn, if we're going to do another two carloads, then we're going to have to get going; either he comes now or we'll have to quit for the day."

"I don't care," Bittner mumbles, "even if I collapse."

"Me too, as far as I'm concerned, it's time to quit," I say to him with resignation.

We sit down and wait. But Reinhold comes at ten minutes after one. He's had a collision on the tramway retarder and then knocked himself dead to get more empty cars. He's at the end of his strength now too. His breathing is heavy and difficult. But he doesn't quit. I'm undecided about whether we should load again or not. But because Prüfer starts to load, we have to help him.

"We'll fill up the last car with big pieces, then it won't hold so much and will be full faster," I order in a dull voice and start to load.

"Then I'll help, Max, but let's make it quick," Bittner joked, and he set right to work.

Finally it hits me that today is payday and we'd wanted to be among the first ones up.

"The hell with all of it," I curse. "Today is payday and we've got to be at the elevator in only fifteen minutes; drop everything and run for the shaft."

"Goddamn," Bittner howled, "that's right, now we've missed the first elevator because of the stupid cars, and we'll have to wait around in the washup room for an hour to get our pay."

Bittner and I drop our shovels.

"Collect all the stuff, Bruno, while I jot down the coal we've done today. If you want, Reinhold, you can fill up the cars, if not, then come along."

Prüfer doesn't answer but keeps loading. As fast as he can, Bittner loads the tools onto his back, and drags them to the box. There he sorts out a dull, worn-out tool and lays it aside so we can take it with us. In my notebook I write down the three completed shifts, the eight carloads hauled, and the explosives we used; then I close the boxes. In the meantime Prüfer has filled both the cars and comes over gasping; without saying a word, he gets dressed. We do the same as quickly as we can.

(The wages for the eight carloads we've hauled come to 9.60 marks. From that are deducted .60 marks for explosives and 5 pfennigs per man for lamp fuel; the remaining 8.85 marks has to be divided among the three of us. So today's shift gives us a wage of 2.85* marks each. Is that any kind of wage for a man who goes down into a foul-aired, dark, dangerous mine? Is such a piecework system worthy of a modern civilized worker? From the standpoint of humanity, does such treatment contribute to the moral respect of a liberal or progressive capitalist? Etc., etc. I won't give my answer to these questions now; maybe I will at the end of my report, but now, after this short digression, I'll return to the account of our actions.)

"Let's get out of this oven now," Bittner urges us, "or shall we try to trick them again?"†

We disappear. But before we leave the little tramway retarder, Prüfer yells "Stop!" He had hung up his thermometer there so that we would be able to check the temperature again. This morning at the beginning of the shift the thermometer read 28½° [84°F] here.

"Thirty-one degrees [88°F]," he said laconically and put the instrument into his pocket.

---

*Possibly a misprint; the correct figure is, of course, 2.95 marks.

†The meaning is unclear; it's possibly a reference to past attempts at getting credit for more than the carloads actually hauled.

"Whew, we're real dogs," Bittner laughed, and he gave a sigh of relief as we all were hit by the cooling 18–19° [64°–66°F] breeze behind the ventilation door in the main haulage tunnel. We all take a good stretch, glad to be getting off work. The closer we come to the shaft, the cooler it gets. This enlivens us and cheers us up again, although our exhausted muscles cause us to stagger unsteadily, almost reeling, to the exit shaft. We are very late, and on payday too—that made it all the worse for us. We were only in time to get the sixth elevator up to the top. Blinding sunlight forces us to close our eyes for a moment. Hey, that's another kind of air, different breathing, different light. An azure atmospheric haze hovers over us in the washup room and the life-giving sun beams down upon us, smiling. In the baths we say "Good luck" to each other, and everyone goes to his clothes rope to take off his wet pit clothes, to clean up, and to get into other clothes. We hurry as fast as we can because it's payday.

This is a short and concise account of a work shift in the mine. And this torture, this inhuman haste, repeats itself day after day, the only variation being that the physical exhaustion for the individual is sometimes less, sometimes greater. [. . .]

It's well known that, among miners especially, the level of both external and internal culture is regrettably extremely low. This fact is probably largely a result of the isolation of the miner's underground occupation as well as the accompanying brutality and servility of his work. Almost all the miners are heavy and rough, but they're honest types. Due to the outstanding cultural work of the union and the party, this condition is slowly but noticeably changing; and gradually a self-aware, basically sound group of men is arising. Happily, the miners are retaining their upright character. One of the main evils that the miners suffer from is the excessive tendency to alcoholism. Of course it's understandable if one of these chain-dragging slaves of capitalism comes out of the mine into the light of day, gets his starvation wages, and converts a part of them (frequently a large part) into the stupefying haze of alcoholic poisoning. This is his chief means of forgetting his misery, a misery that sees its material powerlessness as the basic evil. Generally, these bitter social reflexes take place as in the following scene.

On such days the noise in the pithead baths is deafening. A group of men is grumbling and cursing about the cheating the officials do on the wages. (Have any of the gentlemen who often try to act so "Christian" ever considered what a shocking effect their "Christian" example has on the workers? So far as I recall, the Catholic catechism states that the withholding of the wages workers have earned is the most horrendous of the deadly sins. And how often this sin is committed. And it's just here that the worker is especially vulnerable because naturally his most basic interests are involved.) One of the miners or a friend carries schnapps with him, and in the oppressive hothouse atmosphere of the pithead baths it never fails to have its stimulating effects. The cheated man blusters and storms, and in his drunken rage he screams out his misery into everyone's face; then he staggers to the pay counter and brutally demands what's owed him. Of course he's rebutted because the cashier has nothing to do with the matter. Finally he gets obstinate and the mine police throw him out. Everyone laughs at the funny incident. But every time, my heart wrenches in agony at the brutality with which a man, maybe a family man, is trampled down simply because he picks the wrong time to explode in justifiable anger and to demand his due.

You see troubled, grieving, and bitterly downcast faces. Family men with decrepit, caved-in features; you see the secret rage, the inner resentment throbbing in the arteries of the temple; because the wages he gets are by far not enough to buy what the family urgently needs. His eyes light up spontaneously with desire; suddenly he's thinking of the firewater. Afterward he drinks until he collapses senselessly. Then he sees nothing more, he doesn't want to see anything, that's why he drinks. The horrible misery of his family is behind him, at least for a day. And his family? His wife? His children? My hand trembles when I think of the scenes I've witnessed, and I cannot and shall not record them here.

You also see a lot of growing young fellows for whom life is still pretty much a secret puzzle. They get money and whoopee, off they go to low dives for the organ music and noisy card games. Youth wants to live it up. I understand the urge because I used to have it myself. The talers roll, and the next morning the reality of a hangover and a missed shift stares them in the face. The penalty slip on the blackboard at the mine brings home to them their foolishness.

Here's another picture: the notorious drunk. He doesn't even show up at work on payday. After throwing down his wage book, he counts out his money with trembling hands. His eyes light up. And usually he doesn't come back to the mine until he's drunk up the last groschen. There are a lot of such characters in the Ruhr area. They sink unnoticed into the hurried stream of existence.

But a large portion of the miners no longer trouble themselves with such doings; and I'd be lying if I said there were only a few of them. They are mostly members of the Christian or Free Trade Unions.* You often see how a sober and thoughtful worker from this group will try to keep a fellow worker from temptation. Now and then he succeeds in doing a good deed, but sometimes the tables are turned. An otherwise sober worker is frequently unable to turn down the enticing offer of a tempter who just wants to "treat him to one." And once he's in the tavern it's usually too late. Since he usually doesn't drink, his empty stomach quickly gives him trouble; stimulated by the firewater, he starts to drink inhuman quantities in order to show off. He wants to be able to put away as much as his comrade or acquaintance.

On days like this the beast in man openly bares its fangs. Acts of violence, brutal crimes, robbery, and bloodshed are its signs. It's unsafe on the streets after dark because the drunken rage must find its outlet. And I and many others go past brooding, and we shudder when we think about it. How long does this condition

---

*The Free Trade Unions were affiliated with the SPD; most of the much smaller group of Christian Trade Unions were affiliated with the Catholic Center party; a third, even smaller group, the Hirsch-Duncker Unions, were affiliated with the Progressives.

have to continue, how long will it be until the miner too wakes up to his humanity? How long will capitalism with its vicissitudes enjoy this hideous triumph unhindered and with impunity? In the age of Marx, Haeckel, Zola, Edison, and Zeppelin, how long must the working class, the foundation of the human economy, persevere in its unworthy position?

POSTSCRIPT

I have described the external torments inflicted by a single shift (not to mention the lifelong grinding-down process of such working and living conditions) on the objective feeling of the individual. In addition, I should not omit a discussion of the subjective effects; I think, worthy friend, that this is the main point of your request, and it will give you a glimpse of the psychological structure of my thought as concerns the humiliating circumstances of my inner self. At least I'll try to give such a glimpse, for I approach this task with some fear. After all, all my thoughts and feelings about the puzzle of life are revealed in these words; and I know that I won't find enough words to be able to impress sufficiently clearly on the palette of my thoughts the internal and external slavery under which I suffer.

What does thinking mean anyway? Merely being conscious of something. And without this consciousness there is no thought. And it is just because I think that I am aware of how miserably my humanity reveals itself to me. How did I come to this awareness of my miserable, weary humanity? My present Weltanschauung is the conclusion I drew from the composite of a very long chain of external influences. And what sort of impressions are these?

It's obvious that the constellation of human society as an object of natural evolutionary stages is based on the fundamental material motive of preserving life. Naturally, this striving for a secure existence affects the individual within the ensemble of society and attests to the inevitability of the life struggle. I am firmly convinced that only someone who acts on the stage of life free from material cares can fully develop his capacity for inner human dignity. I feel the need here for a personal observation. But I ask you, please do not draw the conclusion from the thoughts that I'm going to discuss, indeed feel I absolutely must discuss, that it looks like I am asking you for something. That would be repellent to me because I want nothing from you that I could not justifiably demand. And up to this moment that is nothing. I'll permit you only one exception, the sending of some books that appear to be very important to you. But there is some cultural significance here, at least for you and me. And here I should make up for my neglect of something: I thank you from the bottom of my heart for sending me the book by Bölsche.* It's a very interesting work that's proving to be very valuable to me. I frankly admire it. There's only one thing I don't understand: How could such a perceptive scientist and amiable and charming portrayer of the most secret problems of evolution and the inner connections of the animal world—how could such a man fail to boldly draw the ultimate conclusion of his thought? Is the dualistic prejudice really such a living, breathing power? I don't think so. But enough, I'm digressing. The recognition that things are as they are and that I should merely see my deliverance in the stupidity of the masses is the scorpion of my hopelessness. You will object here that in spite of this I could penetrate into the labyrinth of knowledge of the world and feel happy in this knowledge. Relatively, yes. But knowledge is connected to thought. And what good to me is a thought, no matter how exquisite or auspicious, if it's just going to be locked up in my brain? It must escape the narrow confines of my mind, it must come alive and be transmitted to other heads, as many others as possible, if it's going to be of any practical use at all. In order to

* Wilhelm Bölsche (1861–1939) was the foremost popularizer of science in the early part of this century. Lotz evidently expected Bölsche, who believed in a pantheistic God-Nature, to draw atheistic conclusions from the theory of evolution.

achieve that I have to write books, I have to become a writer. But you know that that takes money, a lot of money, and above all a lot of time. I could do it only at the cost of my limited free time and the money I need so much for other things. And then, when the leaden hands of everyday cares press down on my shoulders, and I stand brooding at the mystery of hope, I am overcome by an irresistible exhaustion; and this aversion mercilessly tramples down everything I'm always trying to build up. – – – – – In astonishment you ask what these dashes mean. I'm perplexed for a moment. Suddenly I notice with horror that I'm still unable to think at all methodically. Although I feel, and feel strongly, what I wanted to describe to you, I can't find the right form in which I can embody the thoughts I want to communicate to you. Now I understand the feeling of fear that I wrote about at the beginning of this chapter. It's a feeling that attacks and besieges me whenever I want to change my powerful and moving thoughts into a form comprehensible to the outside world. I confess bitterly that not being able to do this is a sign of my lack of education. But what's the use, I want to be able to do it even if I have to start all over again. I find it immensely stimulating that you have so suddenly drawn me into a new stage of mental labor, and I feel instinctively that great tasks are awaiting me.

In what follows I am going to be coming back again and again to economic and historical relationships, even though I know you are familiar with all of this; I must do it because the fathoming of the threads of the natural economy is the foundation on which I build my attitude to the whole world.

When I, as a wage earner, am totally wrapped up in and overwhelmed by the tumult of the mine work, I ponder how it happens that the curse of work weighs so leadenly on me and how the struggle of life oppresses me so brutally; then I want to scream and yell wildly in anger and inner resentment. But I have to keep quiet, to silence my heart; and there, deep in my breast, my dead-tired soul groans. The men around me are so stupid, so insensitive to their general degradation, so crude. But they are not to blame for their misfortune; for the outrageous guilt for the systematic oppression of their being is borne by the men of mammon. Four or five years ago the influence of the socialist idea awakened me only to the pernicious distinction between wealth and poverty, without giving me any feeling for the spiritual basis of human grandeur; at that time my materialism was abstract and my hatred of this monstrous system of human self-laceration was still very superficial. That was only natural. Although I'd cared relatively little about its ethical values, Christianity's religious spell still hurled reflexive lightning bolts into my soul, preventing me from becoming abnormally rough or insolent with my fellow men. But it was more a dark fear, a very this-worldly warning, than an ethical conception freely born in my soul. Now and then my power of thought wanted to catch a glimpse of the light, but the leaden complex of purely metaphysical dogma covered it with a dark veil. I saw nothing but the phantom of an unreachable, incomprehensible God in the stars, whose hand always held a fearful sword, drawn and ready for the most vicious chastisement. In the long run that was untenable for me. I could no longer be a sacrificial victim caught between instinct and reason.

First with astonishment and then with increasing interest, I was overwhelmed and assailed by the fact that the theory and the practice of the realized word of religion were battling it out from diametrically opposed extremes. Ideal Christianity is based on true human brotherly love, on the principle "Thou shalt love thy neighbor as thyself," which is on the same level as the basic doctrine of divine love. But how does this revaluation of the principle of the highest brotherly love appear in reality? I refer you to the shattering fact that the 2,000-year dominance of Christianity has been enough to do unspeakable harm to the psyche of the people. Even today, at the beginning of the twentieth century, we sense the hideous mass hysteria of the religious Middle Ages; and many a would-be learned and educated head still wears the foolscap of absurdity. The proofs for my contention are the faith healing in the most fashionable circles and a thoroughgoing belief in witchcraft in the rural areas of our modern industrial state.

And it's not only the spirit of the people that has been pushed down to a miserably low level by the Christian religion's historic reduction of everything to the absurd; the entire organism of the human race has also suffered. The modern industrial proletariat, as well as the rural servant class and small peasants, groan under a pasha economy of masters and estate owners, which is sanctified by religion. I'll mention here only the well-known Prussian Servants Code of the previous century whose "legal" provisions still allow the Junker to use the riding whip and arbitrarily lock up a "disobedient" farmhand or maid in a small room. I can't imagine a more flagrant contradiction to the command to love other people as yourself under the umbrella of Christian religious bliss. And then I remind you of the blacklist system of the Ruhr Basin mining barons. The horrible misery of this system has already been felt by thousands of the best workers; and it simply annuls the constitutionally guaranteed right to form coalitions. No public prosecutor or religious official has lifted his otherwise so powerful and unctuous voice to put a stop to this shameless outrage. No, property, even if stolen under the most repulsive circumstances, is declared holy in the name of God and the law, and the incense bearers do not forget to envelop this "ideal Christian" condition in a cloud of justification. Oh, they work hand in hand, these two agents, and their system works with a sinister efficiency for the degradation of the human race. How is it possible, then, that domestic labor—to take just one scandalous example among the many hideous ones—can even be legal? Dramatic literature is full of denunciations of these disgraceful conditions. (You were good enough to send me Gerhart Hauptmann's *The Weavers,** a very incisive work of this genre.) And these miseries have so often been incorporated into social dramas on the loose boards of the stage, doubtless to heal the malignant abscesses of society through such public attention. Oh yes, many a pious and rich hypocrite has shed copious and generous crocodile tears on such evenings at the theater (Ah, it was so moving!).

* Hauptmann's *The Weavers* (1892), which dramatized the 1844 Silesian weavers' revolt, was one of the major works of German naturalism.

But everything remained, and still remains, as it was. It has to, it's the "divine order." The Junker paradise of East Elbia and Pomerania; the infamous Middle Silesian and Aachen textile domestic industry; the peculiar agate-polishing industry in Oberstein; the Middle German lignite industry; the mining industry of Upper Silesia and Saarbrücken. (In Upper Silesia, the home of the most pious mine owners, women routinely work in the mines—so appropriate to the dignity of women. And the Saarbrücken mining despot, de Wendel, especially singled out for praise by the pope, has even erected a candlelit statue of St. Barbara* at the entrance to a tunnel in one of his mines; and all the while the slaves and creators of his wealth languish in hunger and misery.) All these are typical examples of the position of the masses in the Christian state.

These examples, which were first called to my attention mainly by reading socialist literature, caused me to revise the workings of my mind. I became an observer of these conditions, if at first only a superficial one. For it's obvious that this process of becoming aware at first affected my external person insofar as I turned my attention to the unjust division of the rewards of labor that affected my own interests. It was still the purely animal impulse in me, but for me it was the first stage in the quest for human dignity. Of course egoism is the foundation of economic sensibility; and I required a tremendous mental evolution to get onto the trail of the dignity, greatness, and worth that I produce as a human being in the struggle of the universal organism, and to which I can lay claim. In my case the impulse to give direction to my morality (to the extent that I'd had any ethical conceptions beforehand) was the spiritual essence of religion with its internal contradiction of harmoniously fusing theory and practice and manifesting them outwardly; then too, it was capitalism that swept me violently along this new path. I certainly don't need to define for you the historically corrupting and expropriating developmental force of the absurd capitalistic

---

*St. Barbara is the patroness of miners.

society. *Capital* by Karl Marx characterizes this world calamity most strikingly for you. So I'll refrain from recounting it for you.

What I want to tell you about is the influence of the capitalistic system on my inner feelings. There is first of all the soul of the whole system, gold. In my opinion the corrupting characteristic of gold is acquired rather than inborn. But it is totally incomprehensible to me that gold was capable of exercising such a tremendously powerful influence on the entire human race. It's inconceivable to me in that gold was concentrated in the hands of a vanishingly small minority, instead of in the hands of the enormous mass of the majority. The egotism of the masses should have long since brought radical measures to bear. But it did not do so because the radical agent of individual wealth, religion, was in opposition. And this is just what I don't understand— why the unconscious theoretical happiness of the utopian higher world should be stronger in men's thinking than the conscious tangible wish for the worldly improvement of all humanity. If capitalism and its concubine, religion, are the cause of the degeneration of the human race, then let us annihilate, totally annihilate, these agents.

Let's consider just the direct and indirect capitalistic mass murderer of mankind. What I consider especially despicable in this system is the brazen indecency with which it corrupts a man. It robs him of all self-respect and forces him into a position of the most pitiable dependence on his "masters." It dictates his political, and even to some extent his religious, views. And thus it deprives him totally of the human quality of free self-determination. The maxim "He who pays the piper calls the tune" is a shameful principle, and humanity is eternally disgraced for making it a reality. And what results did this product of higher human activity produce? Scarcely had the physical form of man metamorphosed directly out of the animal form into the brain man—scarcely had this happened, when along came a man who happened to be smarter and murdered the less gifted man with the weapon of understanding, murdered someone who was his equal brother. Even the prehistoric brute man proceeded with a certain logic in egotism, because domination over the masses for the purpose of self-enrichment presupposes without a doubt a suspicion of the inferior intelligence of the masses. And yet in these very masses with their egotism, there is the prerequisite for uplift. However, the "revolt of the human spirit," the rebellion of the collective soul of the human race against the minority clique of gold owners (Henrik Ibsen's theory), will come only after worldwide social change, not before it, as the Norwegian said. Therefore it angers me very deeply that so much intelligence among the masses atrophies because of the pressure of the capitalistic working conditions; the cultural and artistic treasures of the latent intellects lose their meaning, or even their very life.

And as for me? I feel only too much the impotence of my person. What am I? What do I mean in the great plan of the world where the physical and psychological rule of the fist runs riot? Nothing! Absolutely nothing! A nobody. But why should I be a nobody when I don't want to be? I don't want to be a nobody, absolutely not. I want to rise high up, very high up; yes, I want to be the highest in the pantheon of the human spirit. But the present-day social order (which, ironically, is called divine, the best) beats me back brutally. In order to force my way, in order to pave the way for my upward flight, I became a Social Democrat; and I have to be one because Social Democracy's strivings give me the goals and the base of economic security to be able to attempt my flight. Therefore I adhere to socialism with every fiber of courage and idealism. But I don't want to rise alone; I want to see everyone in the illuminated circles of conscious human bliss, every person who is now starving with me so humiliatingly. Their fate also grips me bitterly because I'm going to ruin with them and they with me.

If I wanted to or were able to be servile and corruptible, I really wouldn't have to worry about my daily bread. But because I can't, I suffer. It's a wicked system that doesn't permit you to be noble and high-minded. I know that many who, like me, have tried to flee up out of the disgusting mephitis have been physically destroyed by the strangulation principle of the present economy; they have been crushed, rubbed out, and stamped on, raped in spirit, branded, and sold. But no one will poison my mind, my consciousness of being a human being in the noblest sense. Above all it won't be the false god that most of them worship and that presumes to insult all humanity so shamefully. Nothing, not even democracy, can put up barricades in front of my spirit; for by democracy I do not mean doing homage to a general spiritual indolence or psychological brutality. In the Eden of thought I want to be alone; there I can tolerate no other soothing counsel than the dialectic. I'll step up to the altar of the party program to collect my thoughts, but no one will see me kneeling there.

And now a word about my view of the world, in overall general terms from the perspective of the monistic idea. This is no grand definition of the concept of "monism" but rather a little sketch of how I conceive of the controversial words "natural religion." Because the universe is only an aggregation of connections without a beginning or an end, there must be a cause that in this case contains within it the quintessence of the power of combination. It is with amazement and wonder that I look at the guiding force, which, based on inalienable laws, affords harmony to the cosmos, albeit a harmony of the most various forms and nuances. This essence of existence, which dictates and controls all, is the highest and most complete thing I can conceive of. I have respect and trust only for the highest and most complete, only for the truth of the highest order. I consider it an abnormal manifestation of reason, a deflowering of the human brain, to consecrate the idea of speculation and inspection above and beyond the highest and most complete. This super-idea must of necessity sink to the level of a caricature. Because I see in everything only the universe formed by the law of movement, I therefore see in the causality of movement the basis of the monistic creed. In my opinion, to examine this cause dialectically in its grandiose totality is man's most worthy and eminent means to uplift himself, to ennoble himself, and generally to enrich himself spiritually; and only through the influence of the unity of the objective external world does he become personally more moral. The theory of Joseph Dietzgen, the little-known and yet much-criticized philosopher of democracy, showed me the way that I considered practical to follow.* I now feel the need to cite for you the fundamental thought of Dietzgen's monism, even though I should say in passing that I'm no particular friend of this quotation. In the chapter called "On the Beliefs of the Unbelievers" in his book *Knowledge and Truth* [*Erkenntnis und Wahrheit*], he writes: "The higher essence, which manifests itself in the connection of all things in this world, and is caught up in an amazing evolution in which stones, plants, animals and men, suns, moons, and earths are only transitory moments—this higher essence can and should uplift our spirits. But such an uplift should not go so far that it turns into a childish ecstasy and fright that shrinks back before every advance, and that regards the unexplored and the uncomprehended as monstrous inscrutability and incomprehensibility. No, our cult is precisely the exploration of the infinite essence in which we and all existence in a very prosaic sense live and move. The true cult is the culture of science. The real nature is the divine nature. The exploration of the connections is the object we enthusiastically serve and sacrifice to."

Worthy friend! What I've described for you up to now in this postscript is the outpouring of my soul on the problem of life and the world. I confess that it is impossible for me to follow you any higher. I can't go any higher. Furiously, I return to my own banality. What do I feel now when, tired and harassed, I fight the brutal economic struggle for my family? What did I feel before I'd savored the storm of a revolutionary revaluation of ideas, when I slumbered in the lazy repose and helplessness of the intellectually unassuming? I'll say it boldly: Earlier my mental consciousness was a farce. I perceived absolutely nothing at

---

*Joseph Dietzgen (1828–88) was a working man, turned popular philosopher; he advocated a monistic materialism. The book Lotz cites here is a collection of Dietzgen's essays, published in 1908 on the twentieth anniversary of his death.

all that would have been able to uplift me to my appropriate place as a man among other men and make me aware. When the power of hunger, the iron claw of misery, the hydra bite of cares, and the lead weight of work ate all too violently into my bones, then I got embittered, and the rage of the moment sucked mutely on me. But then if a short hour of sunshine laughed into my care-worn face, I was once again the playing child, the wild young fellow, the contented, happy man. Nothing reminded me then of my past cares; I was naive in my hate and love for life. That I as a worker had to be more miserable than someone who had others in my condition working under him and suffered no cares, in fact indulged in the greatest luxuries—that was not important to me because, well, because that was the way it always was everywhere. What did I understand at that time about what I'd been taught in school: that man was the image of God, immortal in soul, and on the basis of his spirit the crown of creation. It meant nothing to me, because I didn't see any trace of it in myself or my surroundings. At that time I didn't notice the screaming contradiction in the fact that the crown of creation is condemned eternally to vegetate pitifully by the sweat of his brow. In a word, I just lived for the day, stupidly and dumbly.

Then almost all at once my spiritual mood changed. In a period of five years a violent upheaval of feelings took place within me. I was roughly shaken up by a Social Democratic pamphlet that happened to come into my hands. I think it was one of those little agitation calendars that are distributed free. Like someone who had just learned to see, I groped around in astonishment; and from then on, I saw in a completely different light the smug bourgeois who so autocratically and matter-of-factly provided badly paid jobs for his fellow men. Oh, so that was why the necessity of work, especially physical work, was so solemnly set forth in school as a command of nature: it was so that the one who owned the machines, the factory, and the luxury villa could take his siesta. And that was why thousands who were essentially just like him had to be racked by hunger and deformed by work: it was so that the sensualist, the avowed egotist, wouldn't get tired. Oh this cursed state of things! The anger that possessed me grew into hate, and the shameful condition of slavery that I was subjected to became an infamous torture for me. At first I hated the one who insulted and did violence to my person; but then I saw the inner connections of this wretched economic selfishness; I recognized the system that brought it about, and with enthusiasm and passion I detested the principle of the despotic state. Then I went a step further. I felt that the beacon fire of egotism was calling on me myself to storm the Bastille of pleasure; and, though from more natural motives, I too fell into the errors of those whom I hated. If I wanted to gain ground ethically, I had first to emancipate myself from the animalistic influence of selfishness. And I did it. There awakened in me an ethical man, conscious of his position in the plan of the world. But awakening is as far as it's gone. The unfavorable conditions keep me in a drowsy dream. The rage at having to suffocate in this inhuman milieu only because a few selfish men don't want it to change, still stuns and enervates me. But why should I suffocate? Are not the preconditions for things to be changed already present? Does not socialism guarantee the birth of general happiness? Yes indeed! But when?

Practical socialism is material, it has to be because it is. And socialism means the rule of the masses over consumption and production; and only through the masses will the socialist idea become fact. Thus in the masses lies the hope to become human, the yearning for peace, my vision of the new world. But then comes the bitterness that at once condemns me to hopelessness. Will the masses really awaken to their humanity? Will they awaken at all? Will a physical democracy also promote an intellectual one? Or will the essence of individual egotism be replaced by an abstract mass selfishness? I don't dare think ahead any farther because the specter of movement in the general form of life leaves me pale. The law of evolution will – – – – – – – – – – – – – – – – – – – socialism too.

Will man's soul—that organic combination of the substances of the brain that conjures up thought as its end product—also be uplifted in its entirety? I have my doubts.

On the other hand, when I observe how insensitive the masses remain despite the skillful recruiting of socialist agitators; how they persist stupidly in their icy lethargy despite the advantages offered by communal property; how they stagnate and sleep despite the promises of a happy future—then I feel simply desperate, tired of life. I know that my hopes lie here in the vaulted grave of mass stupidity. It's a hope that can be characterized as hopeless in the fullest sense of the word.

I'll close now. If the previous sentences don't satisfy you—that is, if they don't appear sufficiently noteworthy to make public the character and ethics of a worker who is striving for higher things—then I declare myself powerless even to understand your wishes, let alone to fulfill them. I don't really feel any world-weariness or lonesome mourning for myself. What would I do with the tragedy of despair? What good is it to me? Despair means not understanding life. I know the brutality of these tyrants. And this knowledge has made me willful. I will, I will force a change for myself, or else. . . .

Frau Hoffmann,
Retired Maid

In 1909, C. Moszeik, an East Prussian village pastor, published the transcript of a seventy-hour interview with one of his parishioners, a sixty-nine-year-old ex-maid named Hoffmann. In Moszeik's judgment, Frau Hoffmann was one of his most intelligent and informed parishioners, and he sought her out in the hope of establishing better rapport with his flock. Prompted by Moszeik's questions, Frau Hoffmann talks of everything from personal hygiene to the kaiser, marriage, religion, the rich and poor, and death. The selections here cover general habits and family life, but as is evident, Frau Hoffmann construes her pastor's questions broadly and has a tendency to ramble. There is much trivia here; but Frau Hoffmann's good sense and long perspective often lift her above her ignorance and provinciality. It's a pity that Pastor Moszeik has deleted some of her "sharper remarks," lest he give offense. But what remains is enough to give us an intimate feel for village routine and how it changed over the generations.

GENERAL BEHAVIOR

In the last few decades the standard of living has changed a lot for the better, even for working people. You can see that clearly, for instance, in how nice and cleanly the elementary school children are dressed. Who would have thought it possible a few years ago that workers' children could go around so well dressed! Clothes were much more expensive forty or fifty years ago. Today, if you don't have a shirt, you're stupid and lazy. You can get nice shirt material for twenty pfennigs a yard. So why should the young people go without? Nice things are cheap today. There's bright cloth in the store window. Just stand on the corner and watch the wenches go by: they're all dressed up. And not one of the girls has a skirt made from a single piece of cloth. In a pinch they wouldn't be able to make a swaddling band from it. Around here you don't see folk costumes anymore; up in Lithuania in the isolated villages you can still see them, but not in these parts. The shoulder collars with tassels as communion coats are completely out of fashion; the same goes for head finery—the black silk kerchiefs with a bow. Today everything has to be modern. Of course the working people themselves have enough to keep them busy, what with all their children; but the girls try to copy the rich people in everything. Velvet and silk aren't so expensive anymore and are really beautiful. They rustle so nicely. As long as they're working at home or in the factory, the girls go around in a plain long dress; but as soon as they get off work, they change and come back out all spruced up. We old people don't care much about such things anymore; but still, everyone likes to get new shoes at Whitsuntide.

In the summer we get up at five o'clock in the morning; in the winter at six o'clock. Years ago in the country you had to be up at sunrise. Things are not so rough now. In the old days you had to feed the cattle at night too, now you don't have to: the em-

Translated from *Aus der Gedankenwelt einer Arbeiterfrau. Von ihr selbst erzählt,* ed. C. Moszeik (Berlin: Edwin Runge Verlag, 1909), 26–47.

ployers can't get people to do it. We get up just as early on
Sunday. We have to get up early, otherwise we wouldn't get any
milk. We go to bed at nine o'clock, nobody really before then.
In the country it was ten o'clock before they got back from the
fields. Only then did they have supper. Today it's different: generally people work from six in the morning to seven in the evening, though the pavers begin at five o'clock in the morning.
Then at seven or eight o'clock they have a half-hour break for
their breakfast. If young people have to go hungry they have only
themselves to blame. Often the women are to blame. Not only
do they like fine clothes, they also have a sweet tooth. They buy
all kinds of candy and then lack the real necessities. If I'm
troubled by hunger, I have my customers who give me food.
They just wouldn't believe what a help it is to get a real meal.
The same thing happens in the winter. One poor person helps
another. A rich person doesn't know what it's like to be poor and
hungry. Oh, I know the world and its ways. We old people are
the worst off. The old person doesn't keep pace in his wages; but
in his expenditures he doesn't get off any cheaper than the young.
Employers don't take that into account. And then they call you
"you old folk, old Auntie." Well, you'll get old someday too!
Really, an old person is just unwanted dust when you're cleaning. The old are the poorest; people think nothing of them. Not
a single person came to visit us all winter long. And yet the old
should be especially honored with loving words and all that.
Only after the young have a lot of years behind them will they
really know what's proper; before that they usually don't understand. You think we dance on roses, Reverend. But we're not
dancing on roses, we're dancing on thorns. Parents who've gotten
old are usually quickly forgotten by their children. And most of
us know nothing of our grandparents. You see, there aren't any
written records from them, and there is no property that we can
remember them by either. The worker never even makes a will
because there usually is no valuable property. Where would you
get the money for the cost of the will? And there's nothing really
to will anyway.

But there can be cleanliness even in a worker's house. Many wash every day; everyone probably rubs their eyes every day. I wash myself with soap; I often give my neck a thorough cleaning; I comb my hair every morning, I think everyone does. You don't want to go around with a messy head of hair. You look in the mirror to see if everything is neat. Every Saturday there is a clean shirt. In the summer you can be all spruced up. In the winter things are different; the laundry doesn't dry then. We usually boil the laundry in a tub. Boiled laundry gets softer. Now and then the shoes and slippers are cleaned. When we go to church, the men put on boots instead of wooden shoes. The Sunday clothes are cleaned on Monday; but the weekday clothes are brushed out only if there is dirt encrusted on them. The air has to be fresh too. I like to open the windows and let the healthy air in. I know that many people, especially in the country, nail their windows shut. People who do that are stupid. I air out our room in the winter too. Of course you don't want to let your place cool down too much. Everybody really values a warm room. Warm is warm. Your bones don't ache so much in a warm room. And you have to realize, the little people don't have much spare fuel. A hundred pounds of coal gets burned up fast. Maybe you've still got something in the pot, but no more fire under it. What then? You can't burn your fingers. I don't like closed shutters either; I have to have clear windows; I even like to pull back the curtains. After all, you've got to be able to see who's going by. In the evening we often sit in the dark—to save money. People have to make ends meet. A half liter of petro is used up fast. But later on we do light the lamp. Nowadays everyone has a petroleum lamp. And it's a great improvement over the old days. The oil that we used to burn was much more expensive. In all ways things are better now than they used to be. One thing that often bothers us is smoke. When the stove smokes, I open the door right away. Cooking oil smokes too. A lot of people don't care, they can tolerate the smoke well. They must have a strong chest. We like to pack soup, coffee, and cooked foods into straw and put it into the corner of the bed. If it's wrapped up well everything stays hot and is not in the way. When everything is tidied up, the mats laid out on the floor, and sand strewn around, then our living room is a real showplace. Poor people like to have everything clean. Cleanliness is half of life. Hat, fine gloves, and a veil are luxuries for a working woman. Expensive beautiful clothes are unnecessary. But beautiful window curtains, tablecloths, and clean laundry are really nice. I want to have them always. Fine beds and nightgowns are a luxury. You sleep twice as well on Saturday with a clean nightgown.

Now I'll talk about the working woman's entertainment and relaxation. We like to read. The Bible, prayer book, and sermon book are the most important for us; but reading them is more than entertainment. Then we get the newspaper from our landlords. That's nice. You know what's going on in the world; you hear about all the murder stories—husbands killing their wives, women killing their children. O God! You can also find all kinds of crazy things and jokes in the paper. I don't read the serialized novel. I like to hear everything that's about war or people who've died, or about the kaiser, especially everything about the kaiser. Young people really like dime novels. My son has eighty books about Indians. I don't like them, they're all silly. Not long ago my boy laughed when he was reading one of those books. The Sunday papers are also nice to read; a lot of working people have subscriptions to them today—some of the papers cost only fifteen pfennigs for three months. They have a sermon in them, and even a song. Reading makes you smarter, better, and more religious.

If you have time and there's some special occasion, you also might write a letter to your relatives. Mine go like this: "Dear Son! It's a pleasure for me to pick up my pen and write to you inquiring about your health and how you are doing." Then the answer is something like this: "I enjoyed your letter and I'm glad to hear that you're healthy." Then there is probably some news about the weather and the harvest. Sometimes I write a lot, sometimes only a little. The closing goes about like this: "Many greetings to you, and once again I wish you the best of health."

Love letters usually contain the question: "How are you? Write again soon; I am true to you. Stay true to me also."

When you meet with friends, the conversation usually starts with the weather; but you also talk about food, cooking, and household things. The young people's conversation consists mostly of silliness. People today are much too smart for their own good. In the evening when the electric streetlights are burning, the girls are out in the street. Their favorite topic is: "He's going to come tonight." Sometimes at home we just die laughing when my husband comes home drunk and starts talking about Paris and the French War, even though he wasn't there. But he's heard war stories so often from veterans that when he's drunk he thinks he himself was in the war, and then he tells his stories. We don't have many special pleasures. A poor person is tired and run-down; so what kind of amusements is he supposed to have? I don't want anything more. Women have plenty to do. They are busy enough with their children when they get home after work. Of course the men have their card playing. They get their liquor at the tavern and then go to it! They play skat and other games too. A lot of times there are tricks and cheating, but it's not considered proper. The children have their own games—ring-around-a-rosy, jump rope, robbers and soldiers. I like to watch them. Those boys can do it all. They also like playing ball, rolling hoops, tiddledy winks, throwing buttons, bean and shot throwing, pass the button, drive the pigs (a ball game), stick-pin bowling, and hide-and-seek. The girls like to sing, jump, and dance. They get along with each other well; sometimes it's a real show.

Most working people are not inclined to humor. The seriousness of life weighs them down. But that doesn't mean they don't make a joke sometimes. One time when a worker was standing in front of the post office with a wagon full of huge tree trunks, another worker called out to him, "They won't take those packages in the mail." When people want to make me mad, I answer with a joke: "I write my name 'von' Hoffmann; I've nothing to do with you." We also know about April Fools' Day. One time I pulled my husband's leg by calling out to him, "There's a mouse running around you on the bed cover, and you're not even trying to get it?" And I said to a neighbor woman, "Go outside, your pig is out there running in the street." Riddles are usually child's play, but sometimes you might say to a grown-up, "Where do pancakes taste best?" The answer: "At the edge." The annual fairs are a pleasant change in the monotony of the life of a working woman in the country and the small town. Of course it doesn't pay to buy anything there. Whatever you can get there is also available in the stores in town. It's better to use your money in town. But otherwise the fair is good, especially for young people. Oh, the booths! It's fun to go in them; anyone would be curious. Booths with pictures from the Bible, especially the Lord's Passion, are popular. I always enjoy watching a gymnastic troop if they perform outside. Otherwise nobody will pay money for somersaults. There have to be such people; the world needs them. Those with little children buy odds and ends and candy, balloons, and gingerbread at the fair; yes, all the parents do. Servants frequently spend a lot at the fair. That's not so dangerous as it used to be. Nowadays the employers pay a lot for their people. Then at least once they get out of the chains that they're always in. The quick-service photography booths get a lot of customers too. If you have some ten-pfennig pieces, they're nice. I wouldn't spend any money for that kind of nonsense. The stage performances at the fair are silly too; I don't like them. The best thing for the workers' boys is the merry-go-round. Girls with children spend a lot of money there. Others, married people, don't ride on it. Once my husband got on the steamship merry-go-round when he was drunk. He rode around three times. Then he was sober. The air on such a thing must be cooler. Dancing is the best fun. There used to be more opportunities to dance than there are now. Today there isn't much going on. Everywhere it says: "Servants not admitted." The domestic servants in the big city have it better. I was still dancing when I was sixty-eight years old. I can't anymore, my head spins. But you should have seen me when I was about twenty. I was a jolly thing.

There's a lot to be said for having a cheerful mood, because our life is tough. Just think about the gossip. People are always talking about each other, especially the women. Somebody hears something and goes to somebody else to pass it on. They're always talking about other people; they know nothing about themselves. Everybody believes the bad things but not the good. In the morning when you go for the milk, it starts up—tittle-tattle! There sure is a lot of talk. The employers gossip too; they talk over the table; the girls talk over the gutter. That's the difference. The ladies are always saying, "Mine are doing this and mine are doing that; mine are no good." Then everyone gets their face powder. Talking about people usually brings no good. If only people would at least stick to the truth! But everybody puts in their two cents worth and that often starts trouble. You have to be very careful about what you say. You have to be careful even at home because women like to listen at the door. Usually they don't mean to be malicious. It's curiosity that drives them to eavesdropping. I don't like it. The eavesdropper at the wall hears only his own shame. Often really nasty things are said about you. They even make up scornful little verses about you. If you hear about it, quarrels and fights start easily. But the worst trouble usually comes through the children. The wind isn't even allowed to blow on some women's children. Once I sent my son out to beat up a girl because she'd been naughty. Before long there's a feud with the neighbors. Frequently the results are lawsuits for slander, because working women are very touchy. With simple people you mustn't say one word too many; they get mad right away. The employers aren't at all so sensitive. Certain differences in status among working people sometimes cause fights and hostility among working women. If someone has more to eat than other people he may shout, "The old beggars." Even around here there are such people. Even when there's no more to it than that, they still fancy themselves better than their surroundings. There are such strange people. There are actually some rich people among the workers. Even if they don't have too much, they still have a few hundred. Some have saved in their youth; others have married a rich girl. Then it's easier to add more. You often hear them say, "What do I need you for? I'm set." And they are set. Outwardly they usually don't live any better than others. Some of them have gone around to one acquaintance after another eating their fill. That way they can save up for themselves. But when one child after another comes into a family, then it's hard to get anywhere. By the way, the servant girls have it much better than the working women. But while they're unmarried they don't believe that. Servants and maids can live well off of their employers, but later they have to make do with gruel. Once I sent to the store for salt brine. You can eat badly cooked food, but not food without salt.* A servant girl around here had to accept a new situation because her employer of several years was transferred to another city. After working for a high official, she now came into the home of a well-to-do merchant. Here's what she said about the change: "It's sad that a high-class girl like me has to be stuck in such a job." You can even find such pretense among women on public assistance. When they advised her that she might save on rent by moving in with another woman, one of them said, "No one who's any good lives with someone." Of course quarrels and disputes sometimes lead to real fights. You can hear the uproar on the street in the evening. Hitting, clawing, pulling, and tearing off clothes—that also occurs between husband and wife, especially on Sunday morning. In fact, it's not rare for a wife to hit her husband. Hitting people in the face, though, is pretty low. Whoever can't get along with me can go to the devil. The young fellows like to fight, often with knives. I know of one fellow who had to pay a twenty-mark fine for fighting. When women fight, they usually start with fingernails in the face; then they go for the hair, and some of the women lose a lot of hair. All this doesn't mean, though, that they won't have a friendly drink after the fight and make peace. They make up with hugs and kisses—until the next fight. But this sort of thing is really the exception. There are also many good-natured

---

*The meaning of these remarks in this context is unclear.

and helpful working women. They could ask me to climb over the roof and I would do it. I'm just as nice with others as I am to you.

Once I tried to cook on the same stove with another woman. It wasn't worth it. It's a fraud. I'm not so dumb that I'd try that again. The other woman just took whatever she pleased out of the pot. No, you've got to cook and bake by yourself. Nowadays that kind of cooperation is worthless. Brother and sister don't trust each other; today husband and wife don't trust each other. So doing things together just doesn't pay. But you can demand politeness everywhere. And we too are polite to each other. Every day I say to my husband and my boy, "Good morning, little Gustav, did you sleep well?" Oh yes, we're also very modest. Greetings are the proof of politeness. Being impolite or even rude is not nice. Working people from the country can't behave as politely as others. When you say "Good morning," the reply usually is "Thank you so much." The established forms are: Good day—Thank you so much; Good appetite—Cheers, cheers! Good night mommy dear—Good night, good night my little boy! One night Gustav forgot to say good night to me, so he got out of bed and came to me to make it up. The other children weren't so sweet.

Sometimes a certain friendship grows out of good neighborliness; but this goes more for the unmarried than for the wives. Old people's friendships usually don't last long. But all the girls have their girl friends. Whole battalions of them go dancing on Sundays. It used to be that there weren't any such friendships. What's more, the factory girls want nothing to do with the other working girls. They stick together with their own. The factory girls won't dance where the other working girls are dancing. They think they're something better. At our house we see larger numbers of family friends only on special occasions—baptisms, confirmations, weddings, and funerals. We spend the time with eating, drinking, singing, and, at festivities, with dancing too. Then you have to have music. You hunt up an accordian. We had three musicians at the wedding of one of my sons.

MARRIAGE AND FAMILY

An engagement among working people is very simple. The man says to his future wife, "I'm going to marry you. Take care of everything, we'll have the wedding on such and such a day." There's no special engagement party. How can there be for poor people? He works and she works. Also they're not called fiancés; more likely people say, "He's going with her; he's going to marry her." If you're of age, you don't have to ask your parents for permission to marry; and you don't ask. In the other case the parents are asked when children want to marry. Permission is always given. Sometimes a girl catches somebody by using tricks. I know of one woman who fed her future husband when he was in the army. He married her for it. Not all men keep their promise to marry the bride. In this case it's not unusual for the poor girl to be left sitting when the baby is already on the way. But many men are honest and still keep their word even if they've already fathered several illegitimate children. Besides, many are afraid of the expensive support payments they have to make according to the new law; so the girls are better off today; but because of that they're less careful than they used to be. The bride and groom are already sleeping together regularly. How is the man supposed to be satisfied otherwise? I've got two illegitimate children myself—two boys. I never got any kind of support; in spite of that I raised them with dignity. "That" doesn't really hurt you. There probably aren't any "honest" couples. The rich aren't any different from us. If it weren't that they'd be punished with loss of their positions, the clergy wouldn't be any different either. You don't get a wedding ring until the wedding. My ring cost four groschen. It was real shiny. I don't know where it is now. Today you pay two marks for the rings. Either the bride or the groom pays. It doesn't matter; all the money comes from the same place.

You ask why we get married? Well, every working woman marries for love. After all, you like him. If I didn't love, then how could I get married? People don't want to be alone always.

One person is nothing in this world. Two are two. So one asks another. A single man won't amount to anything. Of course now and then a girl intentionally doesn't get married. One unmarried worker told me: "I've always been afraid that things wouldn't work out for me in a marriage. That's why I haven't married. Love, the way I've always imagined it, has never come along." And when you get on in years, then it's all over. Working-class girls can get a husband easier than the high-class fräuleins; a lot of them are nuns. But even working girls sometimes have a hard time getting a husband. Today the ratio is five girls to one man. So many men have to go away or are killed! The girls are left behind. That's why today they don't ask what he looks like, if they can only get a husband. People like to get married around Martinmas, at moving time, and at Christmastime. As a rule the girls are no older than twenty-three. Men marry both early and late. Some are only eighteen or nineteen years old. Insolent bums! Then there are all those children! One in arms, one on the way, and a couple more running along behind. As far as dressing up for the wedding goes, the groom wears a black suit with a little bouquet of myrtle in the left buttonhole. The bride decks herself out in a black wool dress. Black is good for anything— weddings, christenings, or mourning. When her outfit is complete, she also has a veil, white gloves and shoes, and a white petticoat. Young people always have to have bridesmaids and a best man; even if it's three or four little girls. Two witnesses are enough for the older people. At the wedding meal everyone has cake, coffee, and a little supper of meat and meatballs, and then that's it. It's enough. You have to have beer and schnapps at a wedding. The men demand schnapps. At the wedding of one of my sons there were six kegs of beer and some schnapps. The schnapps was in sealed bottles; it was just enough. You also have to have rum for grog. If at all possible, there is music to adorn the festivities. The usual instrument is an accordian—it's a hand harmonica. In a pinch you can cover a comb with paper and blow on it. The boys are real good at that. You've got to have dancing at every wedding. It's not a wedding if there's no dancing. The bride and groom have to stay till the end and outlast all the guests. For wedding presents you get a half-dozen plates and spoons and a little coffee—things like that. What can a poor person give at a wedding! Sometimes the groom's first question to the bride is, "Do you have money?" But often the lack of a dowry isn't taken into consideration in the least. If the person is healthy and has two hands, then the couple will be able to feed themselves and take care of everyone. As I said earlier, the rent is the worst. If that's paid it seems like you've built yourself a house. One person alone can't get anywhere in the world, especially when he gets old. If she has to, a woman can always feed herself alone. But a man alone goes to wrack and ruin.

The worker doesn't pay much attention to good looks in marriage. I can tell you what good looks are, but physical beauty counts for little. A nice-looking man should be neither too big nor too small. What's the point of a long list? He needs all sorts of stuff. He has to be blond. He shouldn't be too fat or too thin. Middle-sized is the best. I like a small face; puffy cheeks are not my taste. I don't like dark eyes. Blue eyes are pretty but very deceiving, gray eyes are gray but very faithful. There are a lot more pretty faces among the servants than in the upper classes. The upper classes don't get out in the air enough and they don't eat everything. Many of them have clumpy faces. Some have a nose like a fist; a big nose is fashionable; a hook nose is no good though. Actually, a man is always good-looking. A crooked nose or similar small drawbacks don't matter. Being lame, though, is tougher. A man has to be able to work. If a girl is nicely dressed and well scrubbed, and has a clean skirt, white apron, and a kerchief, then she's pretty, then she's pert. Of course there are also sloppy women; if you throw them against the wall, they stick there. The heavyset, stout girls are the best. Some women look like they're made for footraces; but however God has made you, that's the way you are. What it comes down to is that a beautiful person is a friendly person. It doesn't matter what he's like in other ways. Some people are as sour as sourdough. A friendly person is worth a great deal. When a girl says, "He's not for me, I don't like him," she's not thinking about his appearance, but about his heart.

As far as the relationship between husband and wife goes, the husband should be the head, the wife the crown. You can't hurt the husband. I ask my husband about everything. If one is pulling one way and the other the opposite way, then it doesn't work. In a lot of marriages the woman wears the pants. That isn't right. In that case the husband is easygoing and lets himself be led around by the nose. If you want to enjoy life in this world, you won't do that. There are also marriages where you can't really tell who's the boss. But the man should be the leader. After all, everything revolves around him. For example, when a letter comes, it's always addressed to the husband. When my boys write, it is always to their father. The wife has to have her rights too, but the husband has more rights. After all he's got to earn the money. It's twice as good if the husband is boss at home, even if he sometimes pounds on the table with his fist. Of course when the husband spends his wages, the wife has to be a lot sharper. On Saturday evening I go out and grab my husband on his way home so that he doesn't drink up half his wages. Many wives get a sound beating from their husbands. If I were ill-tempered, things would get pretty hot around here too, but I'm very quiet when my dear old beast comes home. Someone once complained to my neighbor, a cottager's wife, that she had been badly beaten by her husband the day before. My neighbor said, "Well, everybody has to be able to put up with a little beating from her husband, it doesn't hurt anything." A lot in a marriage depends on the right conduct of the wife. Above all the wife has to keep things in order. That's the main thing—for both rich and poor. The man can drink some schnapps; that doesn't matter. But when a woman starts getting lax, then that's bad. A wife has to be faithful and good to her husband, honor and love him. That's what that wife whose husband had stolen and been sent to prison had in mind when she said, "Even if he has stolen and has to do time, he's still my dear little husband."

Even in this Protestant area there are some mixed marriages

between workers. If he's good, he accepts her religion; if he's not, then she has to share his. But nowadays if they can just get a husband, then nothing matters—whether he's a Jew or a Gypsy. Sometimes one is German and the other Catholic.* I think that when there are children they are raised according to the father's wishes. But I think that today nobody is baptized a Catholic anymore. The Lithuanians have died out anyway.

We working women are no strangers to jealousy in our midst. These days the men don't trust the women, and the women don't trust the men. But women are more jealous. The dumb little ones are afraid when their husband just talks to another woman. "Come on in, come on in, what are you doing with her there?"—that's how it goes. If I just sat down once with my neighbor, his wife would come after me immediately; she'd come right into my own house and slug me. The men aren't as jealous. Jealousy is wrong. We old people have overcome it. Who would look at an old woman! But with the young people, it sometimes goes as far as adultery. A young woman starts seeing a handsome fellow; she thrives on it and even makes a show of it. That's a great sin: they shouldn't have been allowed to hold out their hands to each other in the church, to exchange rings, and to kneel at the altar. Sometimes there is a separation, for these or other reasons, but you're not likely to find a formal divorce between working people. Divorce is painful. They beat each other, they run away, but they always come back. Only God himself can divorce. But with the rich there are a lot of divorces. Most wives usually suffer their husband's alcoholism—and all its evil consequences like poverty, worries, and beatings—with the greatest patience. A woman I know got fifty-four blows in one day, so that the blood was coming through her coat; yet she kissed her husband on the following day; everything was forgotten.

In some areas a man has many wives. That's crazy. Every woman wants what's hers. How can he do it? On the other hand, there are also men who stay single, especially rich men. They don't need to marry. They get what they want anyway. Or do you

* In this context, presumably a Lithuanian.

think they're following their religion? Not a one of them. He gets what he wants every time. Having a little wife is nice, you hug her. A young man has his desires; women have them too (now don't worry), some of them wilder than a man's. In God's eyes an unmarried man is worthless; he doesn't even know that there are two kinds of people. A few don't marry because they have some kind of defect. Those are pitiable people.

A real working woman shouldn't be without children. The Jew says, "The more children the better." Every child brings a blessing into the house. The poor usually have many children. What can you do against God! But a woman doesn't stay healthy when she has a lot of children. Nobody can do anything about that. Having twins is an extra torture for mothers. Serving their children—that's why mothers are born. It's a bad mother who doesn't love her children. At least I loved my children from my heart. They were smart children too. They lay in the cradle like marzipan. An elegant lady once said to me, "By thunder, that Frau Hoffmann has strong sons." If there weren't any children, where would the kaiser get his soldiers from? That's why he does so much for children, and not just for his own. That's why he has schools built, and so on. Children cause a lot of work and trouble for the workers, but that doesn't hurt. Children are a gift of God. But boys are worth more than girls. Boys take in everything. A boy is a boy; he's worth more than three girls. Having a girl is unfortunate. Once they meet a man, then they're gone. A boy just puts on his cap and leaves.

The children of the rich are rougher than the children of the poor. The children of the poor are depressed. Some poor children are idlers who don't want to obey and just do what they please. But all of them behave well in church. They have to; after all, it's a house of God. Sometimes you have to laugh at the kids. One time a husband, who was usually kind, beat his wife. Afterward the family sang the song "Lord, I have done wrong." The children heard it, and from then on, whenever they had beaten up one of their sisters, they sang the same song for fun.

Working people never have just two children. We're too stupid for that. But the tree that brings forth a lot of fruit is pleasing to God. The tree that brings forth no fruit is not pleasing to God. The tree that bears no fruit is cut down and thrown into the fire. No one wants to be childless; everyone wants to have at least one. If a woman has only one child, she doesn't go to work. If there are more children, the big one has to look after the little ones. Sometimes old women in the neighborhood will do you a favor and look after the children. But that's not free. Oh, how many groschen I've paid out for baby-sitting for my children! If you don't have your own children, you often bring up other people's, as I have done with my Gustav. I got twenty pfennigs a day for the boy. In the early years I didn't even get anything. When a lady heard that, she said to me, "I wouldn't feed and clothe a child for twenty pfennigs." I told her, "The rich don't do it, the poor do." We usually rock our children in a cradle. Some working women are starting to use baby carriages, but a cradle is better. The baby is warmer in it than in a carriage. The workingman isn't much interested in his grandchildren, but the woman surrounds them with a lot of love. Once I made some feather bedding and gave it secretly to my married son for his newborn baby. When my husband found out, he gave me a real scolding and made me feel very low. Often children are responsible for fights between neighbors. Everyone stands by his children and then people come and complain. I always send them away, because complaining is silly. Children hit each other and then make up.

It always hurts me to see how illegitimate children are rejected by the whole world. You can already see the difference in the treatment between legitimate and illegitimate children when the midwives register the births. The legitimate children are listed straight down the page. The illegitimate births are noted separately. Oh, I've seen it happen. Years ago the girls had their pregnancies aborted. That doesn't happen anymore. How could it? There aren't any such clever people around anymore. In the old days the illegitimate children were even killed by the mothers. Nobody would do that now. To kill a lovely gift of God after one has been through so much—especially since the girls today get so much support money!

Poor people too have their favorite names for children. They imitate the rich people, who look for names in the newspaper. Some have pretty French names. This love of unusual names sometimes leads to funny experiences: one working woman heard the name "Hildegard" and made a note to use it for her grandchildren. Later she had to ask whether it was a boy's or a girl's name. To us old people, the nicest names are August, Fritz, Hans, Marie, Anna, Minna, and Wilhelm. People used to like names like Görge, Joseph, Christian, and Jakob. The older the world, the smarter people are. But illegitimate children have to take the mother's name, or that of a close relative—that's the custom.

The husband's or wife's mother is often part of a worker household. Some peasants are happy if the young wife is an orphan, but working people think differently. An old woman is welcome help in housekeeping; she looks after everything so that the young woman can go out to work. The wife's mother is more valuable than the husband's mother. His mother takes his side because everyone thinks first of his own people. But the wife's mother, on the other hand, takes her daughter's side. If these old folks are in the house, there will be all sorts of conflicts. Then you often hear people say, "I've still got the old lady around my neck and she's a pain." It's not good. Even if God came down from heaven, I wouldn't want to move in with my children. The rich also have problems with young and old living together; actually you see more problems with them than with the workers.

The rest of the relatives often don't stick together either. Some people are just looking for a fight. I don't want anything to do with people who get on my nerves. I'm poor but I've got my self-respect. I won't let any mean rascals insult me. The workers don't feud about property or inheritance. That can happen with the rich who have something. The poor person has nothing to fight about; he lives from hand to mouth. When someone wants to pick a fight with me, I go inside; quarreling just makes such a bad impression, pfui! Of course some people think differently from me. But they don't belong among people, they're not even good enough for cattle.

Aside from baptisms, confirmations, weddings, Christmas, and funerals, the only family holidays we have are the children's birthdays. The parents' birthdays and anniversary are noticed but not celebrated. Silver anniversaries, and sometimes even golden anniversaries, go by without any hullabaloos in the family. But the children often get little gifts for their birthdays. For example, I once gave my boy two groschen, new slippers, handkerchiefs, a scarf, and a bag of candy for his birthday. It makes you so happy to see the children happy.

Eugen May,
Turner

Eugen May (1887–?), a native of the Stuttgart area, wrote his short autobiography (the first half of which appears here) in response to a request from the sociologist Eugen Rosenstock. What little we know about May's background is contained in this selection; we know nothing of his later years. May is no thinker and no stylist, but his wide experience in the world of work (over fifty jobs between 1900 and 1920!) makes his autobiography a rich source of working-class history. In this selection—covering roughly the years 1900–1908—we encounter every kind of boss and every variety of working and living condition. Wandering around was still a way of life for many workers. And May's autobiography reveals an important side of the traveling life: the Social Democratic and union subcultures that protect a man as he moves from town to town.

THE STORY OF MY LIFE

A gentleman who has befriended me has persuaded me to try to write my life story. Of course I make no claim that my record will be interesting; nor should it be judged for its literary value, because that is not at all the purpose of my writing. Rather, my goal is to describe openly and truly every event, as well as my thoughts and feelings about everything that happened to me at the time it happened. But I should mention in advance that my views about many of the events I describe below have changed through the years and through my experience.

I can't say anything about my early childhood up to my seventh year, either because nothing happened or I've forgotten everything. In my eighth year I went to the grammar school with other workers' children.

Beginning in my eighth year I had to contribute to the support of the family by working alongside my brothers, breaking up rock for the village and in stone quarries. These were among my happiest hours because I could work completely without supervision, and then on payday very proudly hand my earnings over to my mother. After I left school at thirteen I did very hard work in a brickyard for thirteen pfennigs an hour. I stayed there for three months, and then until I was fourteen I went back to stone breaking, where I earned more. On 2 January I was supposed to start my apprenticeship in the Esslingen Machine Factory in Cannstatt; but the factory doctor discovered that I had a weak heart so I wasn't hired. I shed many bitter tears about this because according to the doctor I was a substandard person. Then I got an apprenticeship at A. & S. under a master who believed that the boy who was beaten the most would become the best journeyman. My master vigorously beat this opinion into me, sometimes armed with a wooden stick and sometimes with his

Translated from Eugen May, "Mein Lebenslauf (1889–1920)," in *Werkstatt-aussiedlung. Untersuchungen über den Lebenslauf des Industriearbeiters*, ed. Eugen Rosenstock (Berlin: Julius Springer Verlag, 1922), 16–29.

bare hands. At first I was very ashamed of being so dumb that I had to be beaten daily, and I often cried on my way home. In order to get revenge for the unjust beatings I began to provoke my master in all sorts of ways. But I didn't botch up the work because it was very clear to me even then that I'd find a good job only if I were a good lathe operator, and then I wouldn't have to take anything from any master; rather it was just that the other apprentices and I behaved badly. As proof that I could work relatively well at A. & S., I'd like to mention that within half a year I could make screw threads, and, within a year, brass sleeves for sliding heads. Once, because of a fight between me and another apprentice, the master and the foreman beat me so much that I ran away. Afterward I had to go to the doctor because my ears were swollen; because of that I was let out of my apprentice contract without having to pay any compensation.

In my description of my apprenticeship at A. & S., I shouldn't forget an old lathe operator named Abt. He was a pastor's son but a complete unbeliever. Since I often helped him to mount big pieces in the lathe, he had an opportunity to explain to me the contradictions between today's Christian church and social order, and the teachings of Jesus of Nazareth. He admired Jesus, as I still do today, but as a noble man, not as the Son of God. It greatly disturbed my Christian mother that I refused to go to church on Sundays. I explained, "After all, old Abt is the son of a preacher and he told me that what the preacher in today's church says is no longer the doctrine of your Savior; instead the preacher is hired by today's class state to police the poor." Even today, all I can say is that God is presented to the educated man very differently than to the poor man. The hokum of the preachers to the poor people about hell, heaven, and the Last Judgment just makes me sick, now that I believe in a so-called primeval force that my intellectual superiors have explained to me. The inheritance of intelligence and the continued existence of spirit were also described in a very different and much more believable way than in today's church. I've left the church and belong to no congregation.

In order to show that the capitalists are the most to blame for the fact that they are seen as a gang of exploiters by even the youngest workers, I'd like to describe what happened to me on Easter 1903. Over the holidays the steam boiler had to be cleaned, the scales scraped from the inside, and the draft de-sooted. During the first year of my apprenticeship the desooting was taken care of by the chimney sweep; but he was too expensive, so in the second year of my apprenticeship I was assigned to the job, along with one of my coworkers named Zeyfang. The chimney sweep had taken five hours to do the desooting; it took us seven. On the Tuesday after Easter there was a big quarrel, and we were severely beaten because we'd taken two hours longer. It should be remembered that we were getting double pay for overtime. At that time my wages were four pfennigs an hour, and my friend Zeyfang (who was a year older) got six pfennigs. So with overtime that meant eight and twelve pfennigs an hour, respectively. You need to take into account too the fact that we didn't get any special clothes for the job. We had to ruin our own overalls. We didn't get our wages for seven hours but only for five. So all I got was forty pfennigs, along with a good thrashing and soot-covered blue overalls: that was my payment for seven hours of holiday work on Easter 1903. If I'd been stronger, both the foreman and the master turner would have at least ended up in the hospital. But I guess that mine was a typical apprentice's fate.

After all he'd had to go through with me as an apprentice turner, my father decided to try me out with a blacksmith; so he placed me with a master who also gave me room and board. Listening to the talk of a well-traveled journeyman had aroused a desire for freedom in me, and I tried to run away. But now my father really made it hot for me, and, beaten more cruelly than a dog, I was back swinging my hammer the next day. All the beating didn't make me more docile; I just got more obstinate.

It got so bad that my third apprentice contract was also dissolved, and I had to go to the W. Brothers' Boiler Shop in C.; at my father's request, the smith (whom I was to help) and the W.

Brothers really took me in hand. I had to hammer by the fire or do riveting until I saw green and blue before my eyes. And then they'd say, "Pay attention, you scamp, we're going to break you." Now and then there were beatings here too; still, I'd have to say today that with all their toughness they had a good streak in them. I never complained at home, but always said that I liked it a lot at the boiler shop.

After about three months in the boiler shop, when I'd learned the skills demanded of me and had gotten used to the smiths' rough behavior, I was treated better. They looked upon me as one of their own, not as a "scamp" who'd been placed there to be broken. Sometimes I experienced some nice examples of solidarity, even though the old man still gave me a rough time sometimes. I have fond memories of my work as a boilermaker. After about five months my mother pressured me to go back to a lathe shop where a friend of my father had found me a position. After he'd been informed about my past, Herr G. told me that he couldn't sign any apprentice contract with me; but I could start as a regular turner with him. If I could do what I'd told him I could, he'd pay me according to the work I performed. The words "payment for work done" awakened great joy in me; I'd be able to show that in spite of all that had happened I was a useful fellow, if I could only have my freedom and not be in a straitjacket. At first I got fifteen pfennigs an hour, whereas I'd have gotten only six pfennigs if I'd stayed with my first apprenticeship at A. & S. Herr G. treated me like a fully skilled journeyman, so I always tried to do work like a fully skilled journeyman; and within a short time I had gotten two raises I hadn't even asked for. Eight months passed and both Herr G. and I were satisfied, but then I got a new foreman. He must have been informed that I was only sixteen and a half years old and hadn't finished my apprenticeship. This man immediately tried to put me under his thumb even though I could work as well as the seventeen- and eighteen-year-old turners. Finally I told him one day, "I don't have to put up with anything from people who were fired from W. & P." I'd learned by the grapevine that he'd been let go by

W. & P., and I thought that was a disgrace and still do today. His dismissal was a disgrace because he didn't leave freely but rather was forced out by the firm. Frequent voluntary change of jobs is no disgrace in my eyes, but rather very advantageous for a young turner; but of course you should not leave as a result of a quarrel, but rather only to gain professional experience. The man wanted to box my ears, but by this time I'd gotten so strong that I was able to defend myself with the help of a file I happened to have in my hand. There was another big scene. Herr G. demanded that I yield to the foreman; but I preferred to quit. Then I went to the Sch. Firm as a turner. When the master asked for my workbook, I said I'd forgotten it; I first wanted to show what I could do as a turner before I handed over my workbook, which recorded all the positions I'd had. On the fourth day I had to give it to him. Right away the master came and said to me, "You're not a turner, just take a look in your workbook!"

"Yes," I said, "it certainly doesn't look good, but try me out and pay me for the work I do!" He agreed and I received as much as the fully trained turners, which made me very proud.

After I'd worked at Sch. in Cannstatt for about four months, I got the opportunity to enter the K. Firm, which I was glad to do because I could earn more there, and with more opportunity to learn. This was the first time I'd done piecework, and the master pulled every variety of trick that masters use to arbitrarily fix or reduce the piece rates. I had to make parts at a cheaper rate than the older turners; and because I was unaware of the rates, this rascal sometimes succeeded in getting me to do work cheaper than the thirty-five-year-olds to forty-one-year-olds had done before me. Afterward, when the rate went down and I earned nothing even working hard, the older workers were supposed to make the same parts at the low rate, and so they too wouldn't have earned anything. They complained to the master and he told them, "This young man made them at that rate and earned a lot of money too," even though that wasn't true. When I told my fellow workers, "The old man lied, I can't earn anything at the low rate," I made an enemy of the master; my fellow workers disliked me too because, even though I didn't know it, I made things at a rate at which an older turner couldn't earn anything. I kept thinking to myself, "The rate must be OK; you're probably just not yet a capable turner," and the shameless master exploited my doubts. Under these circumstances I thought it best to take off after three months of work. I'd burned my first workbook before I'd started there, and in my new one the only thing listed was the K. Firm. Now I got a job at the Daimler Motor Co. (D.M.G.) under the master Aldinger. I had no complaints either with him or with his successor, Lauster. Working conditions at D.M.G. were tolerable because the piece rates were good. If you made something that had no fixed rate, you were paid at a so-called piecework hourly wage, which was a few pfennigs less, sometimes a few pfennigs more, than the average piecework rate. (At that time the regular hourly wage was only thirty-two pfennigs an hour, while the piecework hourly wage was forty-five to fifty pfennigs an hour.) There were plenty of tools, which helped raise our output; and the wash- and dressing rooms were also good.

My recreation in these years was athletics and a good glass of beer; at that time drinking was a big part of my life. Today I regard the hours spent at the tavern as wasted; and I very much approve that drinking among young people today is no longer the matter of honor that it was fifteen years ago; in those days you were admired if you could empty a whole liter of beer in one draft. The older fellows set the example. Of course, today's craze for soccer is just as damaging to the training for a trade.

I would have been satisfied with my work now, but there was another blowup with my father. I should remark that I was not completely free of guilt myself. It was shortly after Christmas 1905 when I had this fight with my father. For a long time I'd been planning to set off on my travels in the spring of 1906, but because of the fight with my father, I moved out in mid-January and lived in Untertürkheim. But since it didn't look good with me living in Untertürkheim while my parents lived in Münster, I told my fiancée (I'd gotten engaged at seventeen) that I'd leave soon on my travels. Since she made all kinds of objections, I dreaded bidding her farewell, and so I left for Augsburg without saying good-bye. From there I wrote my parents and my fiancée. My parents didn't reproach me much for sneaking off, but my fiancée did. I thought to myself, she won't die of a broken heart; and today I'm happy that she didn't because we finally intend to get married in the near future.

In Augsburg I got work with a bicycle and sewing-machine mechanic; and I found lodgings at the home of Herr Brunold, who was head supervisor at the Bavarian State Workshop in Augsburg. I felt at home at his house since there were five or six little children there, and I always got on well with children. Brunold sheltered me from the big-city life by insisting that I go out only with him or the whole family. Frau Brunold was protective and always said, "Stay here or else wait until my husband is going out too."

I liked the work too until one day I did something wrong on the lathe. But I didn't realize it at first, and when the master pointed it out to me, I told him that he was wrong, not me. Then he got real mad and yelled, "You damned young devils just barely get trained and then you give me lip." Since I was over eighteen and away from home, I thought I could get back at the master for talking to me like that by slugging him. But, oh no! I had the wrong man, because after he'd gotten over his amazement at being struck, he beat me up. It was so bad that when I told Herr Brunold that evening that I'd beaten my master, he laughed ironically and asked, "If you look like this (I had a puffed-up face), how must your master look?" I just want to say here that two years later in 1908 I asked this same master for work once again. I thought he wouldn't recognize me, but I'd scarcely asked him when he said to me, "Well, have you wanted to whip a master again?" I told him no, that I'd had enough the first time. He forgave me for my impudence, laughed, and gave me travel money, as masters used to do for traveling journeymen.

As a result of letters from my mother and my fiancée, and also because I had no more money, and there was no prospect of work in Augsburg, I returned home on foot after a four-month absence. On the way I worked for a week at a construction firm so that I wouldn't arrive home completely broke. Then I went to work at Hesser's in Cannstatt, but I didn't hold out very long. I felt I had to be off again and left on foot for Plauen in the Vogtland (Saxony). On the way I lived by begging and support from masters; I stayed in hostels and cheap hotels for twenty to thirty pfennigs a night. In Plauen I got work in a machine factory. My friends introduced me to the big-city life; but I didn't earn very much, so when the others went out for coffee with their "fiancées" after dancing, I had to run on home quietly and sullenly; with no money, I had no "fiancée." I worked very hard and soon was well trained in the mass production of embroidery machines. I now earned good money (twenty-five to thirty marks a week). And on Sundays after dancing I could go for coffee with a "fiancée."

I saw a good deal of misery in Plauen. It was not just the schnapps drinking and the putting-out work in the embroidery industry. I also saw girls (many from Bavaria and Bohemia) who had come to Plauen to work and found themselves at the mercy of their wages. On Sundays they were glad if a fellow picked them up and bought them something to eat, because the girls earned only six to nine marks for a sixty-hour week of embroidery work. I've often seen girls, who couldn't find a "fiancé" on Sunday, stand around the dance hall all day without being able to eat anything except the mustard and bread they'd brought for their supper. Here's where my hate for the bloodsuckers of the embroidery industry originated. Instead of paying the girls a half-decent living wage, they occasionally arranged a dance for the factory girls where every girl could bring her "fiancé." There they drank a lot of toasts to the rascals. Afterward the band of bourgeois hypocrites lamented the degeneracy of the working people; although in most cases the very same bourgeois factory owner and the masters (who are probably trying to be bourgeois) have each gone off with one of their factory girls. I have evidence that there are owners elsewhere too who regard their factory girls as "fair game." In Plauen I was initiated into politics by the woodworker with whom I lodged. In my opinion he was an ideal socialist. I'd joined the metalworkers' union at D.M.G., and if it hadn't been for the notorious association law in Saxony (a special law aimed at the workers), I would have registered as a member of the Social Democratic party. Still, I joined the workers' gymnastic club in Plauen. I got along well with my master, but not with the guard. He was a sergeant who had been kicked out of the army, and couldn't give up his barracks attitude in dealing with the younger workers. His wife ran a beer, bread, and sausage concession in the factory and fleeced the workers whenever she could. Then afterward, she'd tell the master that such and such a worker had drunk so many bottles of beer that day. One day I got into an argument with the guard about my control number. When the fellow started doing his barracks act, I gave him the Götz von Berlichingen greeting* and a few slaps. I was nineteen years old. I was fined one mark for the incident, and if I hadn't been in good with the master I would have been fired. This happened shortly before Christmas 1906. It was very common for bums who'd been kicked out of the army to have jobs as guards.

So I spent my time in Plauen with work, going to the theater, cheap music, dancing, and gymnastics, until the January 1907 Reichstag elections. In spite of the association law, I took part by attending meetings and distributing Social Democratic leaflets. I heard both Bebel and Ledebour† speak, among others. Bebel made a better impression on me than Ledebour.

In the machine factory there I saw rationalized work for the first time. With my eyes I stole as many ideas as I could about procedures, special tools, and machines. My friends told me that the father of this rationalized work was Herr Director Z., a man I still respect today. I can still remember how Herr Z. would

---

*Roughly equivalent to a Bronx cheer.
†Georg Ledebour (1850–1947) was one of the leaders of the SPD's left wing in the Reichstag.

often talk to the workers about the possibility of making this or that piece better or differently; he also talked about whether a certain tool could be fashioned to produce a part. The result was usually higher earnings for both the worker and the owner. I remember one particular case where Herr Z. paid a friend of mine twenty marks for an improvement. Today I ascribe the tremendous growth of the Vogtland Machine Factory to Herr Z.'s behavior. I just wish that all directors wanted to get more in touch with their workers instead of always relying on the very questionable intelligence of their masters, etc. Because it's rare—to speak only of my own trade—that a "master in a lathe shop" is a real master lathe operator. Rather he's usually the one who toadies, tattles about his fellow workers, and always plays the model boy for his superiors. I got into a fight with my master because he didn't want to give me election day off to distribute Social Democratic ballots, even though the ballot distributors of the bourgeois parties did get the day off. So on the day before the election (26 January 1907) I quit work without giving it much thought, even though it was the middle of winter and I knew I'd have to leave Plauen and hit the road again.

On the thirtieth of January I traveled to Gera and got work there right away.

I was now twenty years old and thus subject to military service. I'd often racked my brains trying to think of ways to maintain my freedom. I'd already registered, but one week before the examination I took an afternoon off from work to report to the county office that I was about to go off on my travels because I didn't have any more work in Gera. It was a Saturday and I quit that evening even though it was too late for my master to get my papers for me right away. I hadn't told him that I intended to evade the hated military draft. My fellow workers asked me why I was quitting so suddenly. I told them the reason and they all approved, and the older ones who had served in the army gave me some good advice.

I walked by way of Fulda to Grossauheim near Frankfurt and there I got work. I liked it very much there, but after two weeks the joint went bankrupt. I had twenty-seven marks in debts and was immediately let go along with 151 other men. All I had was twenty-six marks and so, after agreeing with my landlord to pay him six marks and leave my trunk behind, I set off again. Between Easter and the beginning of May, the spring military physical exams were being held everywhere, but since I was on my travels, I could shirk them without penalty.

Now I went back to Saxony and, even though my clothes and shoes were in tatters, I got work in Meerane. I would have liked it a lot there, but the work was not very exacting (looms); so after four weeks I left and got work in a real filthy joint in Werdau. All five of us who worked there had to wash up in an ordinary pail. After a week I quit. I got other work right away, but it wasn't much better. I would have left Werdau, but there were seven girls who worked at the spinning mill living in the same boarding house, and among them was my wife-to-be (from whom I'm now divorced). So, just because I liked it so much at my lodgings, I looked for work a third time in Werdau and found a position in a lathe factory. Things were somewhat better here even though the equipment was poor and the piece rate low. But a young fellow will do anything for love. I should mention here that while I was still working in Gera my fiancée in Münster had called off the engagement because I didn't think it necessary to write to her very often, and I'd told her bluntly that for the time being I wasn't thinking of coming home soon. For a while I was lovesick—but other towns, other girls. When I finally reregistered for the military in Werdau, the end-of-the-year call-ups were already over, and so by my traveling I'd managed to put things off for a year; for the time being I gave no thought to the next year. Conditions in Werdau, where textiles were the main industry, were the same as in Plauen: a sixty-three-hour week in the spinning mills with the pay not high enough to live on but not low enough to die on. I should say a few lines here about my landlady in Werdau. She was very pious and took it upon herself to win me back to the Savior by her prayers. I often sang Württemberg church songs for her, knew the Bible well, and told her about the life of Christ (from my own standpoint); so she got her sisters and brothers from the Salvation Army to try to lead me—the unrepentant sinner—back to Christ. But it was all to no avail—despite my attendance at Salvation Army meetings and my landlady's radical cure. This latter consisted of a challenge to me to see whether I had the nerve to say aloud in the dark, "I don't believe in God, and I don't want to go to hell; heaven won't take me, so where will I go?" I got up the courage to do this without any trouble, and I told the woman, "I'll either be burned or buried." She was a good woman and meant well, and her honest Christian faith compelled my respect. She often warned me not to marry my future wife, who, she said, might be hardworking and tidy, but lacked goodness and depth. To my detriment, I paid no attention to her warnings because a pretty face and lusty blood were all I wanted then. Urged on by my mother's letters, I went home in the middle of September, but I couldn't stand it; home was too confining for me. I frittered away my money visiting with my old school chums, and then one day at the end of September I left without having looked for work and without saying good-bye. At the union hall in Stuttgart, I looked for a travel companion, but finding no one suitable, I set off by myself with two pfennigs in my pocket. I left Württemberg via Leonberg, intending to see the Rhine and its industrial cities.

I worked for a while in a foundry near Karlsruhe and then joined all the various characters in the wine harvest. Then I came to Mainz, where I found the worst union hostel I have ever encountered anywhere on my travels. Every five to ten minutes the police would come in looking for criminals. To this day I can't imagine why the Mainz union local directed its traveling comrades to such a dump. But in any case, the landlord had greased some palms somewhere so that the bums in the city could use his dump to fleece the traveling comrades (at cardplaying, etc.) for his own benefit. After several days I landed in the "holy" city of Cologne. My hunger was terrible because begging is prohibited in all the Rhineland; you have to live on support from the union and food from local charity that wouldn't fill anyone's belly. In Cologne I received some support from the union; and I used the time to see all parts of the city, even though I was always hungry. I just couldn't understand why the police were so lax about the bordellos, and why they tolerated the biggest bordello of all right by the holy cathedral. You just can't describe the gang that lived there. In my opinion the misery that children and burned-out whores sink into there should cause the servants of Christ to redirect their gaze from the heavens to the sad realities around them—to their down-and-out, ignorant, and thus pitiable neighbors. I found these conditions a ringing indictment of our contemporary social order, and of the bourgeois hypocrites who lift their eyes piously and proclaim, "I thank God that I'm not like those other people." All the while they do nothing to see that boys, who will be husbands and fathers, learn enough not to be objects of exploitation. Seldom if ever are they raised with the help of the wife and mother. She's usually too ignorant or too tired after work to give her children a decent upbringing. This bunch of bourgeois hypocrites, who often know how to exploit for their own sensuality the misery of poor girls, are the first to show their horror over the great number of "fallen girls." But the conditions of the poorest of the poor could be changed by education from an early age; in other words, by parents with more time and money to give their children a suitable upbringing. After I'd stayed a few days in Cologne and used up the support money from the union, I reported to the police as an indigent. In Cologne, as elsewhere, you couldn't go to the police station without getting a good dressing-down. After I'd been compared with the pictures in the mug-shot book, I had to wait until a few more unfortunate fellows came in, whereupon we were marched off in a troop of about ten men to the city shelter for the homeless. When we arrived, we were received by one of the employees. From his rough language I judged that he was a military guard or, as I usually put it, a down-and-out petty officer. The way he carried on and called us names is just beyond description. After our names had been taken down, we were allowed to go into the sleeping hall. But, oh God, the air that hit us stank so much of sweat and old dirty underwear and other pleasant things that at first we couldn't breathe. The "beds" consisted of a plank that ran through the whole hall like a long worktable divided down the middle; there were no sheets or covers of any kind; you had to lie directly on the boards. Finally the night was over. In the morning there was black coffee and black bread along with various curses from the fairly young attendant. I would have liked to jump for the fellow's throat. But the worst part was when we left, for factories with well-deserved reputations as hell-holes (and which couldn't get any labor locally) send their agents to the shelters to recruit people who are on the verge of desperation. This was what happened in Cologne. An agent (or "slave trader" as the workers called him) from a cement factory near Mainz (unfortunately, I've forgotten the name of the town) was there to recruit workers. You got free travel and room and board, and you had to commit yourself to work there until you had no more debts. I very much wanted to go but was warned against it by an older fellow who had once enjoyed this "good deed"; he said the room and board were very bad, the wages were miserable, and the canteen owner knew how to extract every last groschen of hard-earned wages. What was more, working in a cement factory completely destroyed your clothes so that you couldn't leave without getting new ones; of course that only happened rarely, for as they said, "A lot of tracks lead into there, but very few lead out." Having heard this description of the conditions, I said no thank you. My refusal unleashed torrents of abuse from both the agent and the attendant, but I just took off. I just wish that those of the better classes who are so astounded at the envy and class hatred of the dispossessed would visit one of these "charitable institutions" in disguise. I guarantee they would have a better understanding of the impoverished and their desire for an improvement of their lot.

I'd like to add that worker recruitment like that described here took place in every kind of charitable institution, and that the "good" families who exploited their domestics always got a steady supply of young girls from such places. In a similar manner the Firm S. in Cannstatt, which had a sad notoriety for their "humane" attitudes, brought in orphan boys from all directions, because, with conditions as they were, no father would want to send his son there.

There was no work in Cologne, so I decided to go back to genial Saxony. Without anything in particular happening to me, I walked to Kassel by way of Hagen, Iserlohn, and the Sauerland. They called the Sauerland the "Bacon Switzerland" because when you begged you usually got some bacon along with your bread. In Kassel I made my first acquaintance with lice, which I carried with me through Münden, Mühlhausen, and Langensalza, all the way to Erfurt, where I got cleaned at the city hospital. I begged at the door of a railroad-man's family; they asked to see my union book, then let me in to eat with them at their table. It often happened that families would let me eat with them; and I always thought it was very nice when people treated me as a human being and not as a vagabond. In Apolda I got work as a planer at the Firm B. But first there were a couple of very bad days; I'd been hired on Friday morning, but I couldn't start until Monday. I had no money and I didn't want to go begging again because if I had been caught and locked up for a few days, I'd have lost my new job. Since it was the middle of November, I didn't have any desire to stay outside, and I couldn't borrow anything before I'd even started work. So I just had to go hungry until about noon Sunday when a stranger who was working took an interest in me and brought me to his lodgings. It was a boardinghouse for fifteen to twenty working fellows; there I could eat and sleep on credit. Oh, but what characters there were there! Pitiful old men ruined by booze and the deprivations and burdens of tramping about; youngsters who were out from under their parents' protective wings for the first time; married men whose wives and children were God knows where; violent and rowdy fellows; and capable artisans who, unfortunately, had succumbed to drinking. There were frequent brawls when the whole bunch, including me, was drunk; and the landlord gladly urged us on, so he could

sell some of his terrible firewater. It amazes me today that I usually came away pretty much in one piece. I would have liked to
have moved out of there, but the landlord always knew how to
get everyone's last pfennig. You were always tied to him and
forced to buy his crummy stuff because without money you
couldn't get anything anywhere else. A friend of mine (named
Wilhelm Herzog) and I tried to get away from this bunch. We
got some fuel so we could heat our own room; that way we
wouldn't be forced to stay in the heated common room where
you were always provoked into spending your money. But, oh
no! Scarcely had the landlady seen what we were doing than that
dirty rat stole our wood and coal on a Sunday evening when we
wanted to heat our room. She wanted to stop us from heating
our room so we'd come back to that old quagmire where we'd
lose all our money. But the landlord had made a big mistake. My
friend Wilhelm grabbed the table and smashed it into little
pieces and I did the same thing with a chair; the old man came
running in horrified and stammered, "OK, boys, what are you
doing there?"

I replied calmly, "Getting firewood because your old lady has
stolen ours."

At that the old man disappeared without saying a word; and,
having finished our "work," we lay down for the "sleep of the
just." We must have been asleep for about an hour when the old
man came in with two constables and had us arrested, because he
no longer felt safe with us in his house. And we'd been asleep!
There was nothing we could do; we were chained together like
criminals and led off. The old rascal pointed out to the police
that we were now homeless and thus under suspicion of being
fugitives, so it would be a good idea to detain us for investiga-
tion. This rascal held several official positions including a seat on
the district council, and he was also a member of the Social Democratic party. We were released on Monday evening.

Now I got work as a turner at Stieberitz and Müller, where
they made brewery machinery. Stieberitz's son-in-law often
praised me for my good work. He discussed with me the kind of

lathe that would be most suitable for my work. I described for him the advantages of the prismatic lathe with spindle, and he decided to buy one for me. But the military still plagued me because it was time for the spring call-ups, and I had no more desire to put on a uniform than I'd had the year before. I just didn't know how I could leave after Stieberitz's son-in-law had been so good to me. I hated to offend such a humane employer, but on the other hand, I hated the military even more. So I cut work with the hope that there would be a scene at the factory the next day, which I could use as an excuse to stop work. The next day the gentleman came to check on his pet worker; he asked me where I'd been. I said, "I cut work," and that I wanted him to let me go.

But he just said, "May, I wouldn't have expected this from you; don't do it again!"

I said, "Yes, I made a mistake and I think I'll have to do it even more in the future, so please, just fire me without notice." He wouldn't agree so I had to get nasty in order to get my way. I didn't want to be surprised by the call-up in Apolda. I can still see today how the gentleman's face got longer and longer. I felt truly sorry for him, but I just couldn't tell him my reasons; since then I've often asked him for forgiveness in my thoughts. If I had a chance today I would give the good gentleman a heartfelt explanation of my rude behavior and apologize. If I could, I'd prove to him today that he didn't waste his goodwill on someone unworthy, that my behavior was dictated by hatred of the military.

So now I left town. I traveled to Munich via Gera, Plauen, Hof, Münchberg, Bayreuth, and Nuremberg.

In Munich I was in the Capuchin cloister, and I observed a woman who had brought in an offering, and was praying in front of the crucifix. Her eyes burned as though she had a high fever. Then she stood up and covered with kisses the wounds that were painted on the wooden Savior. Even today I pity this poor deluded woman; and I think that those who drive people to such things are common criminals. I wish longingly that a great light would come to mankind and drive away these black-hooded vultures.

By way of Dachau I walked to Augsburg where I stayed for a few days visiting friends and, as I've already described, my former master. There was no work there so I had no choice but to move on and to beg.

Via Ulm I returned to Stuttgart, but I didn't show myself at home because my clothes were ragged and I had no money. But I couldn't leave without seeing my hometown; so I stood on the Wilhelm's Bridge in Cannstatt and looked over at Münster for about fifteen minutes; it was 31 April 1908.* I stayed one more day in Stuttgart and then walked to Pforzheim via Leonberg. I couldn't get work there either and had to move on even though I'd had enough of tramping.

* A misprint perhaps.

Aurelia Roth,
Glass Grinder

Aurelia Roth (ca. 1874–ca. 1935) grew up in the Iser Mountains of northern Bohemia. Her short autobiographical statement (presented here in full) is part of a collection of testimonials and documents commemorating the twentieth anniversary (1912) of the Austrian Social Democratic women's movement. The collection is edited by Adelheid Popp. Despite its brevity, Roth's work stands out for its vivid description of the horrendous working conditions in the Bohemian glass industry, where the workers coped with hardship with a combination of resignation and gallows humor. The reader may note here (as elsewhere in the writings of Social Democrats) a kind of working-class analogue to the pride of the self-made bourgeois. Roth had been through everything, and she had not just survived—she had actually helped to reform the working conditions in the grinding mills. Class consciousness came easy to her, but it is fair to ask: How many really had the time and energy to heed her call to do "their duty as class-conscious workers"?

A GLASS GRINDER

Hundreds of thoughts run through my head the moment I begin to write about my experiences. I don't know how and where I should begin.

I'm thinking back on my childhood years, on my adolescence, on everything that's happened since that time.

So far as I can recall, I was always a weakling. In my tenderest years I suffered very serious illnesses. Today I understand that all of this is attributable to the bad conditions in which we lived: a wretched apartment, insufficient nourishment, etc. That my father was a drinker probably contributed a lot also. He paid very little attention to the family, so my mother had to do all the providing alone.

Even with the greatest diligence and thrift it wasn't possible for her to pay for everything the family needed. There was nothing left for her to do but to have us children go to work. My parents were glass grinders, and my mother was also a bead worker. When there was a slump at the grinding mill, she worked at home. Very often she worked in both places—at the mill during the day and at home evenings.

I was the youngest of three sisters and, like the others, as soon as I was coordinated enough I had to help in the production of black glass beads. This is admittedly easy work, but it was strenuous enough for my weak constitution. I often had to skip school to work. For me that was the greatest sacrifice I had to make. I didn't get much time to learn, and still less to play, but it hurt me the most if I had to skip school. In those days the workday in the grinding mills was sixteen to eighteen hours. When Christmas was approaching, they often worked through the whole night. We children weren't spared either. Before I even began school I knew that the story of the Christ Child was just a fairy tale.

Translated from Aurelia Roth, "Eine Glasschleiferin," in *Gedenkbuch: 20 Jahre Österreichische Arbeiterinnenbewegung*, ed. Adelheid Popp (Vienna: Kommissionsverlag der Wiener Volksbuchhandlung, "Vorwärts," 1912), 52–61.

My mother often admonished us to work very hard so that she could bring us some joy at Christmas. I used to ask for nothing but beautiful things. But on Christmas I was always very dissatisfied because I didn't get what I wanted. How my dissatisfaction must have hurt my mother! I didn't want to stay home, I preferred being in school. The teacher always liked me because I was very attentive. I was eight years old when I began to reflect on a variety of things. My father was the occasion for this because there were almost always violent scenes when he came home drunk. I would hear things then that I didn't understand. My mother reproached him very bitterly when he brought no money. He should be ashamed that the children had to work for him. Often he would smash things. Very often my mother and I were forced to spend the whole night hidden outside. There's one night I'll never forget. It was a Saturday. All three of us had worked hard with our mother. Sunday was the day we delivered. It was already midnight when we were allowed to go to bed. Then my father came staggering in, mad at my mother that we were still awake. When my mother answered him, he smashed all the beads to pieces with his walking stick. All of us children started to scream at the top of our lungs that now we wouldn't get any money for them. We'd deprived ourselves of so much sleep and now it was all in vain. What would we live on for the next week, my mother moaned.

I was secretly angry with my father on account of his alcoholism and often thought about how wonderful it could be at our house if it weren't for this evil passion, because when he was sober he was always good. I could relate a lot more about how much poverty and misery alcohol trouble brought to us. Suddenly he became seriously ill so that for two full years he was confined to bed. Those were the best times of any I can remember while my father was alive. We had to work even harder, but it was easier because there was peace in the house. Then there came a depression in the bead industry, and my mother was forced to seek other work for us. I had reached my fourteenth year and was given a position in a glass shop as a messenger and a cleaner of glass articles. I got paid four guilders every two weeks for this work. During this time my father died. Once again we were in a very difficult situation. My earnings were too low for my age, so I had to learn grinding.

I mourned for my father only because he'd been confined to his sickbed for so long. Actually, even after his death I couldn't forgive him for not caring for us like a father.

And so I entered the grinding mill.

Today, what I still can tell about this time seems even to me almost beyond belief. If I hadn't lived through this time myself, I wouldn't believe that there ever could have been such hideous conditions in the Iser Mountains—an area blessed with natural beauty.

MY FIRST DAY IN THE GRINDING MILL

It was a large workshop with a single workroom where over sixty people worked. Men, women, young girls, and boys were all mixed together; in fact, there were even school-age children working there. My uncle was the master and the foreman. As he led me in, they yelled at me from all sides: "Hey, here comes a new polisher. Come on, buy us all a beer." Someone else called, "Yeah, if you want to be a grinder you've got to pay your admission first, otherwise you won't learn anything." Beer glasses and bottles were presented to me. I can still feel today how I blushed with shame; more than anything I wanted to turn right around and leave.

My uncle led me to a polishing table where an older woman was working. I was supposed to sit on the other side and watch the woman. I was supposed to do what she was doing. There was no training period, I immediately became an independent worker.

There was so much noise in the room that I could hardly understand what my uncle was saying to me. There was total confusion—laughing, singing, whistling, and children crying. I was thoroughly frightened and dared not look around.

So I began to work. They gave me crystals to polish.

I was shaking as I picked up the first two pieces, afraid that something might happen. Then the kidding started again.

"You have to smear paste on your fingers, or else you'll cut them." Laughter erupted on all sides.

The work went much easier than I had imagined. It wasn't long before I had several pieces polished. The woman inspected them and was very satisfied with me. She said I would learn it quickly. That encouraged me. Soon I ventured to steal a few glances at my surroundings. But I was astounded at what all I saw.

The place was veiled in a hazy cloud so that the people sitting in the back couldn't be seen well. I saw children of all ages in this dust-filled place. There were even newborn babies there.

Little children were even lying on the windowsills. Most of the little ones were lying in cradles next to the polishing table and crying pitifully. The woman I was assigned to also had a two-week-old baby next to her in a cradle. When the little fellow began to cry, his mother stuck a pacifier in his mouth with her dirty fingers.

"There you go, you little lout," she said. Then she set the cradle going with her foot and kept on working. I saw filth wherever I looked; on the floor lay scraps of fruit, tobacco ashes, etc. I even noticed that the phlegm of coughing people was spit onto the floor. The children were playing in this morass, and they even had their food handed to them here. When a little bit fell on the floor, nobody considered whether it was a danger to the children. Some of the women even brought their food with them and cooked their lunch in the shop.

I'd seen enough on my first day and yearned for quitting time. At home I complained to my mother that I hated it and I'd rather do some other work. Her reply was: "It's just a matter of habit; wait till you're used to it, then you'll like it OK. The grinders are good-natured, that will cheer you up." So I would have to get used to it. It was the same in all the grinding mills: very deficient ventilation, in most of them none at all. After you'd worked in such a place for an hour you were so covered with dust that you could write on your blouse with your fingers. In addition, there was an excessively long workday and not even the most minimal sanitary facilities. Pregnant women worked up to the very last hours of their pregnancy, and as soon as they could leave their bed, they came right back to work. In most cases they brought the infant with them. I'm not exaggerating when I state that there wasn't a single shop where there weren't tuberculars working. We shouldn't wonder that the danger of infection was great, and the number of deaths rose from year to year. Nobody even paid attention when several of the workers were carried off to the cemetery each week; it was routine and nobody noticed anymore. It frequently happened that several burials would take place on a single day. Instead of mourning the loss, they made all kinds of jokes about it. They used to say frequently, "Well, we did a good job burying him; if he knew we were so happy then he'd have peace himself; he was a jolly fellow . . ." and more of the same.

I was only fifteen, but I'd already seen enough of the gravity of life. I was always very preoccupied because there was no way I'd get to like it in the grinding mill. I felt most sorry for the children. I didn't have such a rosy childhood myself, and yet it seemed to me as though I still had it better than these poor creatures in the filthy workshops. Most of this generation died between their eighteenth and twenty-fourth years, many even earlier.

My mother had remarried and as a consequence I had changed jobs. Things were different in the grinding mill where I now worked with my stepfather. Not different conditions, rather different people. They talked a lot about how it couldn't go on much longer like this. Something had to be done to put a stop to these goings-on. Wages had fallen so low that the best worker couldn't earn much more than eight to ten guilders every two weeks. Women workers usually had to make do with four to five guilders for the same period. They also used to talk about how children shouldn't be brought along to work. All of that interested me. I sometimes would put in a word at an appropriate time. New life was coming into me now. On one occasion I heard a man say that if Social Democracy didn't take a hand in making way for better conditions, it wouldn't be long before typhus and starvation would break out. Hearing this awakened in me the notion that the ideas of socialism were to create a different life and better conditions. From then on I was a Social Democrat in my thoughts; I just didn't dare say it. I'd read about socialism a few times before, but I was never clear about what it actually was. It wasn't long at all before there were meetings. I didn't miss a one. My sympathies for these efforts rose and rose. People were working on the establishment of a trade union; they also wanted to put out a trade newspaper to enlighten people about how necessary it was to organize. In 1889 the *Glass Worker [Glasarbeiter]* first appeared. In the same year the health insurance law went into effect in our industry. Among other things it dictated that insured women could not return to work earlier than four weeks after giving birth. Then ventilators were installed in the workshops, and other healthful provisions made. Things began to get some better. The statutes for the founding of a union local were worked out, and we worked for the fixing of a minimum wage. When everything was ready all along the line, these minimum wage schedules were to be placed before the owners. All this was in the year 1889.

The minimum wages were to go into effect in 1890. The owners hadn't taken our demands too seriously and didn't at all expect what was to come. The strike began on the third of January. Within half an hour the machines stopped all over town. The strikers marched from one workshop to the next, and everyone joined the parade. We marched to neighboring towns. In one grinding mill where the workers refused to stop work, everything was smashed. Whole cases of glass articles lay in pieces. So it went for a few days, always one town after another. The strike was supposed to be general. When the owners saw that the people would no longer work under the old conditions, they began to negotiate and they agreed to almost all of our demands.

The first of May came. For the first time this was observed in a dignified manner as a workers' holiday.

The fourteenth of May saw the establishment of the glass workers' union local. Both my mother and I were among the first members. My enthusiasm was rising all the time. I liked the meetings best of all. I now even dared to ask questions once in a while, and sometimes I said a few words. The number of members rose and rose; it wasn't long before our local had over 350 members. Being in the union was compulsory. No master was permitted to employ a worker who wasn't organized.

And so it continued for a few years, and over time, completely different conditions resulted from the ceaseless work. Workshop regulations went into effect dictating that the place must be kept spotlessly clean, no alcoholic beverages could be used in the workshops, there must be sufficient ventilation, suitable spittoons must be provided, etc. And children could no longer be brought along to work. A downright revolution had occurred. The women too took a vital part in the organization; they were even active in the leadership. When the first Social Democratic Women's Conference took place in Vienna in 1898, I was elected as the representative of the Iser Mountain District. In the wake of this conference there was a great deal of activity among women everywhere. We succeeded in founding local groups in sixteen smaller towns. That was admittedly very exhausting work because there are a lot of difficulties associated with agitation in a mountainous area. However this difficult work was extremely unrewarding. In the long run it wasn't possible for a single person to carry out all the agitation in such a large area. Illness intervened. So, gradually, everything was ruined. It still hurts me today that these difficult gains came to naught. By today we could have progressed much further in both the union and political sphere.

And today, after more than twenty years, I look back on the

activities that did develop. Much good was accomplished, but much more could have been done if all of the glassworkers had done their duty as class-conscious workers.

Many of the finest and bravest comrades, both men and women, have been martyred in the decades-long struggle for better working conditions. Many, who were well intentioned toward the organization and worked capably with us, have not lived to share its accomplishments. Last year, when we celebrated our twentieth anniversary and honored our founders, there were, besides my mother and me, only thirteen of the original comrades still living. The tuberculosis of the nineties had raged hideously among the others.

Since the year 1899, no fewer than 263 members of the health insurance fund, 158 men and 105 women, have fallen victim to this malignant, proletarian disease. In the years from 1899 to 1908, there were 234 victims—136 men and 88 women.* In the last two years the number was 29—12 men and 17 women. The mortality rate has fallen considerably thanks to the better conditions.

However, these figures are only for the members of the health insurance fund. If you quoted the figures for all of the deaths, the numbers would be about double.

The child mortality is the highest. But I am convinced that when another report is written in twenty years, the figures will be much lower here too.

Things may change slowly, but nonetheless there is progress! Our descendents will probably not be able to report such horrible conditions as I have described here.

All our efforts are concentrated on creating a better future for our children. It's just wrong when people say: I had to suffer, my children will have to do it again.

After all, the only wealth the proletariat can leave to their children is the provision of better living conditions for them.

Even though the number of members has fallen for several

---

* Possibly a misprint; Roth's figures do not add up.

years, our activities have not slackened. I want to say freely and openly that it's often been very difficult for me to continue working. All that I've been through in my nineteen years of marriage is too much to write down. I was often afflicted by heavy blows of fate. Of my five children only a single son is still living, and I've passed on my convictions to him. As an abstainer from alcohol and a promoter of the youth movement, he is working for the same ideal to which I dedicated all of my strength. So I think I can say that I've done my duty. In the future I will continue to do it, and I will assist in strengthening women's political organization and in fighting for the political equality of women.

I believe that these details will suffice to give the readers a picture of what joys of life a glassworker has. Throughout the thirty-eight years of my life, worries about my mother have never left me. Just now, as I write of my experiences, I have been struck by a new blow of fate: my sixty-year-old mother took such a bad fall as a result of a fainting spell that her right eye was completely smashed. She is the oldest member of our local and also the oldest woman glass grinder in the town. With all her diligence and thrift she was unable to manage it so that she could rest from all her efforts in her old age. Such occurrences must spur one on anew to more work. Because if we had old-age and disability assistance, a lot could be better.*

*These benefits had not been a part of the Austrian social legislation of the 1880s.

Fritz Pauk,
Cigar Maker

Fritz Pauk (1888–?) requires little introduction, for his entire autobiography is presented here. Pauk's motives for writing and his relationship to his editor are obscure; nor is it clear why he ended his story in
1914. In any case Pauk's extensive travels and work experience provide
a wealth of information, not only about an important industry, but
also about the sometimes terrible life on the road—the dingy labor
exchanges, the men's shelters, and the hostile police, always on guard
against "vagrants." This short autobiography is no masterpiece, but it
gives a vivid panorama of a whole era and is a fitting close to this
volume.

MY HOMETOWN

I was born in a little market village in Lippe. It was December
1888. The country was covered with deep snow.

Translated from Fritz Pauk, *Jugendjahre eines Tabakarbeiters*, ed. Roamer
(Jena: Karl Zwing Verlag, 1930).

The inhabitants of the village did not have an easy life. In spring the young people who had finished school and many family men, including some gray-haired ones, left the village carrying big, gray-white sacks on their backs. They had to leave their hometown to earn their livings in the brickyards. The women were left behind to cultivate the poor, stony soil. The good fields belonged to the prosperous peasants in the valley.

My mother was not married. She lived with her elderly father and kept house for him. He was a shoemaker. He drank a good deal. My mother had many cares and worries. When I was two years old, my grandfather died.

I never knew my father. Later my mother told me that he was a cabinetmaker by trade. When he found out that my mother was pregnant by him, he disappeared and she never heard from him again.

Both of my mother's parents died of tuberculosis. Even in the last years of his life my grandfather drank a liter of brandy a day.

After he died there was a period of hardship for us. My mother rented a little room. We lived there in the winter. In the summer she went off to work in the turnip fields on far-off estates. I boarded with an aunt who had several children herself. That cost my mother thirty pfennigs a day.

I still recall clearly how I always cried a lot when my mother went off every spring with other women, bound for the turnip fields. I ran after the wagon until my little legs could carry me no further. Then I turned around and went back to the village crying. My mother didn't return until November. Then there was great joy. In the winter my mother took in flax to spin. In the evening other women came to our room with their distaffs. I listened to their ghost stories and my flesh crept.

My mother also told me that I'd once had a brother whom she'd had to board with other people. In the filth and bad care he died.

I had to suffer through many childhood diseases. I had sores on my eyes and a rash on my whole body, but I got over everything OK.

When we were bad, my aunt would just say, "The Social Democrats are coming!" Then we ran away like rabbits. Once when we were playing in the village, a man said, "Better go home, the Social Democrats are coming!" And some strange men came and went from house to house distributing leaflets. We ran off crying until we'd locked the door behind us and hidden on the floor; and we didn't come out until the men had left.

And so the years passed; summers I spent with my aunt, and winters with my good mother. Then when I went to school my life took a new twist.

In 1895, I went proudly off to school with my primer and slate under my arm. The first thing the teacher did was give us a big sweet roll. That was a happy beginning.

A year later my mother married a widowed worker with no children. So now I had a stepfather, who came from East Prussia. At first we got along very well. Then one time when I pulled a childish prank, he beat me and told me angrily, "I'm not your father, I'm just your uncle." Later I was supposed to call him father again, but I could never bring myself to do it.

During the summer months my stepfather left home to work as a brick worker. During this time he had to earn his whole year's income. Then in the winter we carried the whole year's supply of firewood out of the forest on our backs.

As an eight-year-old boy I had to leave my parents' house. On 1 April 1897, I went to work for a neighboring farmer. I had to tend the cows until St. Martin's Day (11 November). My wages were only eleven marks plus room and board. The farmer and his housekeeper were very nice and were good to me. It was a long way to school.

The next spring we moved to an estate where my stepfather had a job as a groom. The estate was high up on a hill surrounded by forests. The manager ruled it. You got a good thrashing for misbehaving even a little. Once I smeared broken eggs all over a toilet seat. The manager beat me with a riding whip so badly that my whole body was covered with streaks of blood blisters. It was torture sitting on the hard bench at school. My stepfather took no action against the manager because he feared for his job. He too was generally unjust and hot-tempered. My mother had gotten a lot of beatings from him. We frequently had to run away from him and seek refuge in the farmhouse.

When my two half-sisters were born, I had to stay at home and watch them while my mother worked in the fields.

IN SERVICE

In my tenth year we moved again. Once again I had to leave home to go into service for a farmer. This time I got eight talers in wages for the summer. That was a lot of money for a schoolboy in those days.

I'll never forget this farmer. He was responsible for my physical deformity. I still remember well how my mother brought me there. When she left, I cried for a long time. During the first weeks I was well treated, but this didn't last. Later the farmer's wife beat me for the smallest faults, even for not coming home from school on time. During the summer I had to get up at three-thirty in the morning. First there were twenty-five to thirty pigs to be fed, and afterward fifty sheep to be taken care of.

It was six o'clock by the time all that was done, and time for breakfast. Every morning there were coarse ground oats with milk and bread crumbs. You ate with a wooden spoon. School began at eight o'clock, but I had an hour-and-a-half's walk to get there. Still I was happy to go because it meant a relief from the heavy work at the farm. School was already over at ten o'clock. Everyone ran back home. If the farmer had something for me to do, I didn't go to school at all. If the teacher asked why you hadn't come, you only needed to say that the farmer had work for you. That took care of it. There wasn't really much to learn in the little village school. Most of the time was devoted to the catechism and innumerable Bible passages.

In the afternoons I usually tended the sheep and pigs. Every two weeks I had Sunday afternoon free to visit my parents. One time I didn't go home but instead roamed the woods and fields with my friends. Later I lied about it at home, saying that I hadn't come because I'd had to work for my farmer. But my stepfather checked up on me and told me that I could never darken his door again. From then on I was left to my own devices. There was no guardian to look after me. The farmer could do as he pleased with me. At harvesttime I had to slave away just like a grown-up. St. Martin's Day came, but where was I to go? Finally the farmer agreed to keep me for the winter. He promised me a pair of linen trousers and a pair of shoes as wages.

Winter set in and I froze in my ragged clothes. I didn't have any decent socks anymore. All I had was a crummy pair of shoes given to me by one of the farmhands.

No one had to go to school when there was a lot of snow. But at ten o'clock I had to take the pigs out to the woods, an hour's walk away, where they could root under the snow for acorns and beechnuts.

I knew a little spot under a bush where there was no snow. I'd fall asleep there from sheer exhaustion while the faithful dog stood watch. When it began to get dark in the afternoon, the dog would bark and wake me up. Of course I was always chilled through to the bone. But until February it went OK. Then one day my left foot got badly swollen. After a few days the swelling switched over to my right leg. I couldn't walk and had to stay in bed.

You could hardly call the hole where I slept a bedroom. Right next to the stalls for the horses and cows there was a niche for all sorts of old junk; it was filled with damp, fetid air—that was my sickroom. Every day the farmer came and cursed me for being so lazy and not getting up; the cattle had to be fed. But I just couldn't do anything; I was crying with pain, but the farmer didn't send for the doctor or help me himself. When I cried at night, the farmhand was the only one who cared for me; and he also helped me with my bodily functions.

However, after four weeks the farmer got scared because my leg got worse and worse. He sent word to my guardian* that someone should come and get me immediately. The guardian spoke to my stepfather, and he agreed that under these awful circumstances he'd take me back again. So one day a wagon came to take me home. My good mother came along. She was very shocked when she saw me—lousy, dirty, sick, and in rags.

At home I first had to clean myself up before I looked human again. The next day the doctor came; he was a friendly Jew. He was enraged at the farmer for letting me get into such a state, and he advised my stepfather to sue the negligent man for damages and compensation. My stepfather did bring suit against the farmer, but before the court date, the farmer's wife came around and persuaded him to drop the suit. I thought to myself that she must have given him something; he didn't care about my future; the main thing was his own advantage. The poor-relief fund had to pay for everything.

The doctor slit open my leg, and that gave me great relief. For months I lay at home. The doctor came and went. All sorts of old women came too, and they often treated my leg. When, after exhaustive treatment, the doctor realized he could do no more under these circumstances, I was taken to the county hospital in Detmold. There was a horrible journey to the train station, over bumpy lanes in a farm wagon with no springs. It was my first train trip. I'd never seen houses as big as the ones in Detmold.

After I'd been signed in, I got a bed in the boys' ward. It was the best possible location. Through the big window I could see the nearby Grotenburg with the famous Hermann Monument.

I was operated on twice, but it didn't help. The doctors concluded that my foot had to be amputated to save my life. And so it happened. I'd imagined that the amputation would be worse than it was. The terrible, persistent pains came only when I awoke from the powerful anesthetic. Ten days later it was healed and I could stand up. But that didn't last long. I now had to try

---

* Given what Pauk said earlier, it's unclear who this person might be.

to get along on crutches. A few days later I slipped on my crutches and fell down fifteen steps of the stone stairs, landing on my barely healed stump and breaking it open. It got infected again and filled with pus. It wasn't until late August that I was healed and released from the hospital.

I hobbled to school on crutches until a few months later I got an artificial foot. My first attempts at walking were helpless and laborious like those of a little child. With time it went better. But for a long time my heart broke when I watched my chums playing, without being able to join in.

In one year we moved twice. I had to go to school in a nearby town. That was a big difference! We had many different subjects that they didn't have in the village school. So I learned all sorts of things that I hadn't heard about previously.

In the summer of 1902, my mother got very sick, and I had to stay home from school to take care of the housework. I now had three half-siblings who needed my help. My stepfather was at work from morning until night. The summer was coming to an end, and I was supposed to be confirmed on Michaelmas (29 September). Toward autumn, my mother got somewhat better, and for the final three weeks I could go to school again. The pastor hadn't given me the confirmation lessons during the summer.

My parents discussed what sort of trade I should learn. Several of my friends had already been accepted as apprentices at the cigar factory. They asked me whether I didn't want to do that also. Because of my leg injury I had to consider a sedentary occupation; I couldn't do any other kind of work. I told my stepfather what the boys had said. He went off to the factory. I was accepted, but I first had to come by and introduce myself. I did, with my school books under my arm and my heart pounding wildly.

The factory owner looked me over from head to foot, gave me a few school exercises to do, asked about my circumstances, and then patted me on the shoulder and said in Low German something like the following: "Yes, my boy, you're pretty small but you certainly can learn to make cigars; you can sit down doing it. Come back when you're out of school!" Overjoyed, I went home and told my parents the good news.

One day in school the teacher asked everyone what he was going to do. I told him, of course, that I was going into the cigar factory.

The teacher wished all the other boys all the best in their trades; but afterward he told those of us who were going into the cigar factory that we were all good candidates to get consumption. This put a considerable damper on my enthusiasm.

My stepfather didn't want to buy me a new suit for my confirmation. I got one as a present. I proudly displayed myself that day, dressed just like my friends. We played hard for one last time. And with that I had taken the hard step into life. Behind me lay a time that I don't like to think about even today.

CANDIDATE FOR CONSUMPTION

My stepfather didn't go to church; that's why he had refused to get me a new suit. I never learned what he thought about religion or why he never went to church.

For the last few days before the start of my apprenticeship (which was to last three and a half years) my head was all in a tizzy. I was happy and hopeful and indescribably excited. The day drew near. The night before, my mother prepared all the buttered bread I'd need for the next day, because I wouldn't be able to go home for lunch during the break. I couldn't sleep the whole night because of my anticipation and excitement. I had to get up at five-thirty to be at the factory by seven o'clock.

It was 1 October 1902. I was already in the factory yard at 6:40. After a little while the older boys arrived and began to rebuke me because I was standing under the little porch. The greenhorns were supposed to stand outside. I made way for the older boys right away. We new boys stayed outside, exposed to the rain. Then the tower clock struck, and we went into the factory. The oldest of the wrapper makers showed me my coat hook and the master's room. I went in but had to go right out again because I hadn't knocked. Then the master went into the factory with me, where all eyes were on me, and he showed me my place.

My teacher was an older woman cigar maker from whom I never heard a bad word during all my apprenticeship. The first days in the factory had a very exhausting and stupefying effect on my spirits. There were probably sixty workers in the room. I wasn't used to the noise and commotion. We new apprentices were not allowed to say a word unless we were first spoken to. We always had to keep our eyes on our work; and we also had to put up with a lot from the older apprentices. You could ask them this or that about how something was done, and right away they would curse you in the worst way. The cigar makers were very taciturn to us. They had certain guild customs and traditions. We had to greet them on the street, and if they caught us smoking cigars, they beat us.

At first the worst thing for me was that they teased me about my bad leg. I shed a lot of tears about that. Later I got more used to the conditions. Despite the fact that we worked from seven in the morning to seven in the evening with only two hours of breaks, we still had to go to night school twice a week from eight to ten o'clock. I learned all sorts of things, even though we were so tired we nearly dropped.

When I got my first wages, I had to treat the older apprentices to a little schnapps. With this I moved up a small rung on the ladder and was able to move about more freely in the factory.

I lied to my stepfather regularly. I told him that I received only ten marks for two weeks' work. Actually I got somewhat more, which I used to buy sausage from the butcher. Although I committed other little sins too, I later was always a very clean-living person. Others were not so lucky and didn't make the grade. I'll give one short example. One year after I did, another boy with a wooden leg started in the factory. He was assigned to a big tough cigar maker. He was beaten for the smallest mistakes. Finally he became apathetic, and he got more insolent every day. He had no parents. When he'd finished his apprenticeship, he went away. I heard later that he was in jail most of the time and in time was ruined. And before this he had been a very shy boy.

In our first year we weren't allowed to say a word; in our second year we made wrappers and snarled at the younger boys.

As long as you hadn't finished your apprenticeship you were not allowed to join in the singing. As early as your third year you were granted some of the privileges of the guild. After two years of work as a wrapper maker, I switched to the rolling department. This made me more independent. The best hours in the workroom were in the winter between four and seven o'clock when the workers sang. That was our joy in the numbing, long workday. The years went by without anything unusual happening.

In the spring of 1905, my good mother died after a long illness. With her death our family life fell apart. My little half-brothers and half-sisters were put in the care of strangers. All the household goods were sold. My stepfather moved to an estate to be a farmhand. And I got room and board with a pious carpenter family.

They persuaded me to join the church's trumpet band. I did because some of the cigar makers from our plant were in it also. After a short time, however, an opposition formed within the band; we cigar workers wanted to play, not just hymns, but also marches and other secular pieces. We finally founded our own music club. Many of the cigar makers were trained musicians and were part of the local city band. They made cigars on the side because you can't make a living from music alone.

I liked to listen to the visiting cigar makers who worked at our plant from time to time. Before he left, one of these visitors gave me an admission certificate for the German Tobacco Workers' Union and said I should join right away. I promised him that I would, but a friend warned me, "If the old man finds out, he'll throw you out!" So I let it drop. You couldn't conduct a political discussion because everything was always blabbed to the factory owner. Everyone wanted to be the best in the old man's eyes. Alcohol had greatly reduced the self-respect of some of the visiting cigar makers. After skipping work on Mondays, they often begged on their knees to be taken on again.

This reminds me of how I got acquainted with my first Social Democrats. A visiting worker from Saxony worked in the sorting department. He was a very able fellow and the boss even liked to talk to him, now and then asking his advice about things in his department.

One day there was a big scandal at the plant. The old man ran around the yard like a crazy man, screaming no, no, he never could have dreamed that there would be a Social Democrat in his business! Then he ran through the plant, exclaiming with breathless surprise: "Just listen to the advice that this Saxon gave me. I went up to him and asked why our good Kaiser Wilhelm Cigar was not doing well anymore. And he had the nerve to say that I should try it with a picture of Bebel on the label. No more being nice to him, he can't stay in my business, he has to go at once!"

The Saxon had to stop work at once. I can still see him proudly leaving the factory yard.

This event did not fail to leave its trace on my young mind. My thoughts began to stir. I was seeking enlightenment. It was clear to me that the boss had done this man a great injustice. If the old man would throw out an obviously good worker just because he was a Social Democrat, then he must have had some reasons that I didn't understand. I wanted to know what those reasons were, because I could no longer believe that all Social Democrats were criminals and vagabonds, which is what the newspapers and leaflets said.

During the last winter of my apprenticeship I moved away from my pious landlords because other people were teasing me about their piety and calling me "Bible Fritz." My new lodgings were actually three marks cheaper than the old ones. That was fine with me. I wanted to go off traveling as soon as I finished my apprenticeship, all the more so because two plumbers I knew had described the sunny side of the traveling life to me. The dark side I had to discover bitterly for myself later.

After I'd worked two weeks as a full-fledged new cigar maker, I got together with my friends for a drinking spree that lasted several days and ended in a murderous hangover. I didn't even care about the severe lecture I got from the master when I returned to the factory. My head buzzed in every possible way. I needed some wrapping leaves and went to the master to fetch some. But he said I should first clean out the remnants from my crate. When I came back into the workroom without the wrapping leaves again and had to work with the little Brazil cigars, the cigar makers began to tease me. In my misery I lost my temper. I thought to myself: enough, just leave! I packed my things, went to the master's room, and told him my intention. His eyes got big and he said coolly, "I can't stop you, go ahead and be a bum!" He wrote out a slip for me, and I took it to the clerk to get my papers. Then the old boss asked me in astonishment why I was leaving. I told him that I hadn't liked those Mexican wrapper-leaves for a long time. He said that if he had it to do the wrapper-leaves would be better. It was a terrible weed. You needed twenty pounds to make a thousand cigars, and the cigar workers had often cursed them. Then I got my papers. "In six weeks you'll be back," said the old man a bit sarcastically. But the "six weeks" turned into a long time. I walked proudly out of the factory yard while everyone watched me from the window of the old workroom. I wanted to make my fortune, and I would do it.

UNDERWAY

My dreams for the future evaporated very quickly. The annual fair took place on the day I quit. Everything was jolly and put you in a good mood. But afterward I started to get worried, and would have liked most to go back to the plant. Then I thought of the cigar makers' teasing, and I bit the bullet and started to think about my departure. I wouldn't have gotten far on foot. With a cigar maker who was passing through town I traveled to Bünde in Westphalia. There was definitely supposed to be work there.

I said farewell to my aunt. She gave me an ironic wish of good luck, saying I would become a bum.

We left early in the morning. On the way we had to pass by the plant, where there was someone I wanted to see again before I left. But he wasn't there so I went angrily off to the railroad station. As the train left I was overcome by a vague feeling of melancholy. I looked out the window for a long time until we began to pass through unfamiliar territory.

There was a two-hour stopover in Herford. With all the crowds of people I didn't think I'd get along too well; I thought I'd probably get lost. For the first time I was seeing a fair-sized city with all its bustling life. A traveling journeyman asked me for a handout. I wanted to be nice so I gave him a groschen and a cigar, wondering as I did whether I would ever ply that trade myself. I waited for the rest of the time in the waiting room. There was a worker sitting and reading a newspaper at my table. He was about to leave and was folding up the paper. I wanted something to read and asked him if he wouldn't sell me the paper. He looked at me suspiciously, wondering who I was. In a few words I told him my story; then he became friendlier, and as he left, he gave me a comradely pat on the shoulder and said, "*The Bielefeld People's Guardian* [*Die Bielefelder Volkswacht*] is a gift; read it with understanding and act accordingly!" On the train between Herford and Bünde I read the first Social Democratic paper of my life. I kept it for years. I was so absorbed in reading that I barely noticed when we arrived in Bünde.

I asked a small boy which inn the working fellows usually stayed in. He knew and led me right to the place. When I gave the boy a tip, he went off smiling. In the restaurant I ordered a glass of beer and began to chat with the innkeeper. He said I could certainly get work on the outskirts of town where there were a whole lot of branch businesses. I set out right away, walking across the whole town. The huge stone buildings of the cigar factories made a big impression on me. Right outside the residential area you could see tobacco everywhere. Tobacco-leaf ribs and cigar boxes were in every window. Suddenly, at the edge of town, where there were single buildings scattered all around, someone called out to me. I kept going; no one could possibly know me here. But when I looked around, I noticed someone calling from a tiny attic window. I went back a few steps and saw someone in a white apron standing in front of the door. It was one of my friends and companions-in-suffering from home. He wanted to help me right away and led me to a business where they needed help. I went in while he waited outside. At first the master didn't want to believe that a little fellow like me could be a trained cigar maker. When he'd seen my workbook, he said I could start work. My friend could see from my satisfied face that things had gone well. He helped me find lodgings; and soon I was moved in with a worker who took work at home on commission. I was supposed to work with him at home for a week in order to save paying the work registration fee. We could drink up the money we saved.

The lodgings were bad. I could see that at supper. Six children came in—thin, ragged, and greasy. A big pan of fried potatoes was put on the table. I'd been given a fork, but the children all reached right into the pan with their filthy fingers. I lost my appetite right away. I excused myself by saying that I was still a little nervous from my trip. After supper the bigger children had to strip their apportioned quantity of tobacco leaves. That went smoothly at first, but then they would fall asleep, and their father had to prod them with a long stick. When things were going well, the family—husband, wife, and children—earned a total of sixty marks a month. I could see now that it was no wonder that the children looked so neglected and the family lived so miserably.

The very next day I looked for other lodgings. I gave the first landlord two marks; he was satisfied and I moved.

The working conditions were bad. There were always plenty of schoolchildren to strip the leaves; they poured in to try to earn a little money. The workers had to do every kind of additional work too. You got paid only once a month. There was no exact limit to the work hours. You started at four o'clock in the morning and went home at nine or ten o'clock at night. With this drudgery it's no wonder that the enjoyment of brandy played a very large role.

At first I heard nothing about a union. But one day a stranger on the street handed me a collection list, and told me there was going to be a new tobacco tax; and we had to get organized to fight it. Collections had to be taken at every business. The women workers said the whole thing was a swindle, and they never gave anything; the others didn't want to either. But we didn't give up right away.

When one of our fellow workers celebrated his birthday, we refused to drink along with him. As always at such affairs there was a good deal to drink, schnapps and beer. The others got mad and got drunk even faster. When they were in the right mood, we explained that we did want to drink with them, but that they first ought to subscribe to our collection drive. So they did and then we made up for lost time in our drinking. I was able to hand over nearly six marks to the worker who'd organized the collection; he hadn't at all expected so much.

We still wanted to join the Tobacco Workers' Union. But there was no opportunity. Then one day we went to Bünde and stopped in at N.'s Inn where the Social Democrats also had their meeting place. We were quietly asked whether we wanted to join the party. We didn't want to do that but said that for a long time we had wanted to join the union. The man wrote down our names and addresses and said he would take care of everything. I stayed at my old place of work for three more months, but we never heard any more about the union.

In August 1906, I started work in a neighboring town at a

branch of a Bremen-based firm. The working conditions here were, if possible, even worse than the previous ones. You could work as long as you wanted. It was almost all women workers, and no one was in the union.

If smokers could have seen how the pure tobacco was treated here, they probably would have lost their appetite for cigars forever. The place was almost never cleaned. In the evening the tobacco on the floor was pushed into the corner. At the end of the week all the plants were simply laid out again on screens and reworked. This system was due entirely to low wages. In fact, low wages was the very reason why the Hamburg and Bremen factory owners had transferred their operations to Westphalia.

As a rule the masters in the branches were not very bright. A lawyer from Bünde had to come in to settle the monthly accounts. They couldn't make cigars either; many had learned only how to make wrappers.

In summer the work in the branches outside town was tolerable. In the winter the soft clay lanes were soggy and wooden clogs were better than shoes.

Our passionate, though forbidden, pleasure was lying by a small river and fishing. We were never caught, though we did it frequently.

In late fall we took in work from one of the branches for home processing. Our landlady had advised us to do this. At the same time she wanted to get her son out of the plant. You went to the dogs there rather fast. My friend and I were already well on our way.

Our landlady did everything for us. But the apartment was just too small. It consisted of an alcove room that was used as a living room and workroom, two small attic rooms, and a little nook in the attic. This space had to suffice for five adults. We ate and drank at the same table where we processed tobacco. It was a sad state of affairs but very typical of the hygienic and social conditions of the home tobacco industry.

THE NOBLE TRADE BACK HOME

An acquaintance of mine had set up a branch in my hometown, and he wrote to ask me whether I wanted to work there. Since I wanted to get away from the cursed existence of the home worker, I said yes. My aunt was a bit surprised that I was apparently still a respectable person. She was happy that I was home. The earnings were fairly good; all we had to do was roll. But nowhere have I ever seen such a forced breeding of apprentices. They accepted any and all who wanted to become cigar makers. The master taught them for two weeks; then they were turned over to a cigar maker where they learned to wrap; after that they learned rolling, and then that was it. They were cigar makers.

In 1907, I had the opportunity to help the SPD during the "Hottentot"* election for the Reichstag. A onetime master who'd been forced out of business by capitalistic developments belonged to the party. He worked at the factory. Election Day was of course a work holiday. From early morning on I went from house to house handing out leaflets for the party that was so hated by the petty bourgeoisie. Afterward I stood by the polling place and distributed ballots.

The party got eighty votes in our little town. That was quite an accomplishment, and in the evening we celebrated with some beer.

A few days later I decided I was finally going to order the *Bielefeld People's Guardian*. The clerk at the window in the post office made difficulties for me. He said the paper was not on the list. Finally he was forced to see it. Then he said that I was much too young and that the paper was Social Democratic. I told him that that was exactly why I wanted it. He grumbled to himself, wrote it up, and took my money. And I went happily on my way.

During Pentecost of that year I went to visit my stepfather, who was now working in a brickyard. I was very glad to get that

---

* Revolts in Southwest Africa had focussed the campaign on Germany's "world policy," which the SPD was accused of undermining.

over with because his wages and living conditions were horrendously bad.

After the holidays I returned to find my wrapper maker sick. I had to do all the wrapping work myself now. But since the wrapping leaves at this place were very bad, I definitely would have earned less. I thought about whether it would be better to leave. I had a friend who would go with me. But before we left we wanted to make a wage demand. The master approved and encouraged us. My friend and I telephoned the boss and told him that all the workers demanded a raise of twenty-five pfennigs per thousand cigars. The answer was to come in the afternoon. We already suspected something. We two scapegoats didn't even start work in the afternoon. When we went to get our papers, the master came up to us and told us that the raise was approved but that we two ringleaders were fired. That didn't bother us much.

I found my next job in L. The factory owner ran an inn on the same premises. We worked on his dance floor and slept in little cubicles in the attic. Everything was carefully arranged so that no money left the premises. Of course he saw to it that on payday all the money was used for alcohol and that nothing was ever saved.

The place was known for its high turnover rate; almost every week there were new people on the work force. The man I worked next to asked me right off whether I was organized. No, I said. He said I should come to a meeting that very evening and join up. On 10 June 1907, I joined the German Tobacco Workers' Union. I noticed that everyone restricted his drinking during the meeting. But afterward they made up for it, continuing all the way to dawn.

In the morning there was an incident. I was lying in bed when a fellow worker came up with a bottle of schnapps and wanted me to drink right from the bottle. I didn't want to and he got rough, cussed me out violently, and tried to beat me up. The owner's son tried to intervene and quiet things down. But the other fellow then got mad at him and made even more of a row. Finally the drunk fled out into the street and we didn't see him again for a long time.

In October I changed jobs again, and this time my aunt put me up again. But the piecework rates were terrible. You had to work yourself to death if you wanted to earn enough. By really killing myself I made sixteen marks in the first week. Then the master said that I was making more than he was. And in fact he did get only twelve marks, though he had free housing and fuel.

You always got time off for the fall fair in the village. At the factory there were also workers from other parts of Germany, and we celebrated heartily together with them. In the evening I had a run-in with the constable, who dispatched me back home rather roughly. To add to my terrible hangover the next morning I was also worried about what the constable might do. He'd come to the factory before me and told them that I'd been abusive and had to be reprimanded. We workers discussed what we ought to do. Finally we all decided to leave immediately. After a short dispute I received my papers; then I ran home and quickly packed my things. My aunt cried, "Boy, Boy, what's going to become of you!" I left. My two friends who were going with me were already waiting at the edge of town.

We picked fine ripe apples from the trees along the road, sang, and were in the best of moods. But after a few hours my boot was full of blood and I could go no further. We'd just barely gotten to Rinteln.

Our first stop was to see the local union head. He referred us to a place where we could get work, but we were not supposed to accept a rate of less than nine marks per thousand cigars. The local rate was said to be eight. We promised to start anyway. But the next morning, after a good night's sleep and a big breakfast, we'd completely forgotten our promise.

Our travels went better. The scenery was interesting. The sun was shining and there were plenty of fruit trees along the way. Everywhere, in all the towns we passed through, we found a strong union organization. They asked to see our union card everywhere. There was work at the factories but a shortage of lodgings. We kept moving.

That evening at the hostel we unpacked our large stock of cigars that we'd picked up in the factories and from fellow workers. When the pious hostel owner saw them, he wanted to buy some. That was fine with us since you can't carry so many in your pocket while traveling. He picked out the best kinds, and to our astonishment paid us the "generous" sum of seventy pfennigs per hundred. We were richer for the experience, knowing now that even pious Christians regarded us merely as objects of exploitation.

They were looking for a lot of tobacco workers in R., a day's journey further. We were happy about that. But then at every factory we heard that they didn't hire outsiders. When we asked the hostel owner the reason for this, he said we could have gotten a job if he'd vouched for us. But we didn't want to look for work that way.

The hostel was overfilled, mostly with those who got credit against their workbooks. Many others were turned away because of them. We were lucky and could stay, because we'd handed in our papers at the right time. All around us sat all the miserable types who wander the country roads. Tomorrow we'd have to beg too, because we were completely out of money.

I got breakfast the next morning by begging at a lonely house along the way. The people gave me soup and bread and it tasted splendid.

My friends wanted to go to the area around Bünde where I'd worked the year before. So we set off. The three of us got work in the same factory where I'd worked before. But my healthy foot was inflamed and useless from the exertions of tramping around. I had to be under a doctor's treatment for four weeks.

There still wasn't a single person in the whole plant who belonged to the union. I went to see the local union head in Bünde and was at least able to get the *German Tobacco Worker* [*Deutscher Tabakarbeiter*] regularly.

There were a lot of schoolchildren working at this branch. That was forbidden without a special permit, but it happened anyway. When the inspectors came, they hid the children in the big wrapper crates. The children looked miserable.

The year before, the drinking had not been half as bad as it was this year. Now it was out of control, and the master set the pace. When we didn't have any money, he would just write out a little slip, send the apprentice for the booze, and then deduct it from our pay at the end of the month. I got dissolute along with all the others. With all this business, we couldn't buy anything anymore, and finally all we had were the rags on our backs. This dissolute life came to a sudden end in June 1908 when the news came from the parent company that this branch was being moved. For the final few days we were supposed to work day and night. But I refused, and collected what little pay was coming to me. Then I went to the union, paid my dues, got my union book in order, and the next morning I set off all alone.

Wearing one slipper and one shoe, I tried my luck again on the road. Wherever I went, the workers teased me a lot. But what was even more disheartening was that in some places no one was in the union. When I got work in L. once again, I found that in the meantime everyone had joined up again. I started work right away and even enjoyed it. Even my apprentice joined the union. Then I was elected shop steward of my union local. But after this I was no longer in good with the factory owner.

I had many bitter experiences with traveling workers. When they arrived drunk at the union office and demanded support, I always had to tell them that they couldn't get any support in that condition, and that they should come back the next morning if they were sober. That advice was never received too well. They cussed and called me a lout and attracted a crowd on the street, which was of course damaging to the union. They always wanted to complain to the executive committee in Bremen. Of course they couldn't, but that didn't make things any easier for me.

A memorable cigar worker's prank from those days has stuck in my mind. One of the older workers who had worked for several years at the factory always used to say that he had several hundred marks in a savings account in Burgsteinfurt. He often used to brag about it. We all believed him, a belief that was strengthened when he asked me to write a letter to the bank for him requesting that the money be sent. I told him he would have to send his bankbook in too. But he said they had it at the bank. When he got the money, he was going to take us all out on the town.

Weeks passed and no money came. We started to tease him; but he insisted it would come. And, indeed one morning he came to the factory and told us that they had sent for him at the post office. He was gone for a long time. We thought that he'd started his planned spree all alone. Finally, in a cheery mood he came up to the factory owner in the restaurant. With a grin on his face, the owner came into the factory and told us that the man had just received his money.

Then he himself came in, went to his workplace, reached into his pocket, and threw a handful of silver on the table. Our astonishment was great. The apprentice was sent right down to fetch a large number of bottles of beer and wine. When we felt like it, we stopped work, went into town, and then drank some more. The old fellow paid for everything. Late at night the money was gone, and a lot of us had trouble staggering home.

A few days later the owner's son came into the factory very excited and said to the fellow who'd had the money, "What do you think you're doing, borrowing money in town on my name?!" There was no reply, and in a louder voice the son continued: "Now people are coming to me and asking for their money back; what am I supposed to do with you? I should turn you over to the police!"

The old man said dryly: "No, Herr S., it's already happened, don't turn me in. I'll work very hard and you can deduct everything over my lodging expenses." This was agreed to. The man did work hard and he didn't drink anymore, but there was no end to the teasing from his fellow workers.

One morning six weeks later he was not at his usual place.

Someone went up to his room to see whether anything was wrong. He said he didn't feel good and wanted to stay in bed a little longer. Just before noon he came into the factory himself and said he was going into town to the doctor.

Three hours later someone came running in and said that the old fellow had hanged himself in the woods. We were all shocked and all of us went out into the woods. There he was, hanging from an old pine tree. He had leaned his empty schnapps bottle against the tree.

The next morning the newspaper ran a strange death notice in which the factory owner described the dead man as a faithful and honest worker whose memory he would cherish. As was usual after a burial we had an extensive celebration. Many half-liters were drunk in honor of this curious prank.

The working conditions in the factory were very bad for us workers. I'd called the owner's attention to it several times. But he turned a deaf ear to all such complaints. So I wrote a letter to the union's district leader, and he prompted the inspector to drop in unannounced one day. The owner had to pay a sizable fine.

From then on I was a thorn in his side. Soon I got into a fight with him over a very trivial issue and had to quit.

It was 1 February 1909, and bitter cold. The wind was blowing powdery snow into every nook and cranny. I had only three pfennigs in my pocket and no other possessions except my gallows humor. So equipped, I started off the next morning on my walk out of town. I stopped in at the last houses, and the people took pity on me because the weather was so bad. In Herford I already had quite a bit of money. The shelter there was overfilled because the terrible weather had driven everyone inside.

Some would sell their good clothes for a few groschen and continue on in rags. Many bundles had been emptied of everything useful in order to make a few pfennigs. I really saw the unpleasant side of the tramp life. For fifty pfennigs I bought myself a good pair of shoes.

The shelter had a labor exchange. I asked whether there was work for a cigar maker. I was in luck. They were looking for a good cigar maker in Lübbecke. If I wanted the position I had to move fast; there was no time to think it over. With the terrible weather it was definitely better to have a roof over my head. I accepted and they took my papers. I got a ticket good for food and a place to sleep for the night. The next morning I got money for my fare and left immediately.

At noon I was there. A boy pointed out the place to me. It looked more like a poorhouse than a factory. I walked in the door. There was a little old woman sitting in the room knitting. I asked whether I was in the right place, saying that I'd come from the labor exchange in Herford and wanted a position as a cigar maker. When she heard that, she clapped her hands over her head with pleasure and said, "How wonderful that the dear God has sent us a cigar maker."

I had to drink coffee, and then I was off to the factory. A visiting worker and a young girl were working there. The man turned out to be from near my hometown. He asked me right off whether I had enough money to have a drink later. I still had enough for a few bottles of beer. In the evening the owner came, looked at me, and said nothing. I was told that he always did that, but that in the evening he always came home in a cheerful mood. I slept in the attic room with my new friend. The room at least had a window. Next to it was another little room for a cigar maker; it had no window and was full of junk.

The next morning I was awakened by a tremendous noise in the house. The old man was in pain and was cussing everything. My friend reassured me, saying that it was like that every morning. Right then I would have most liked to leave, but the terrible weather outside scared me. I could probably hold out for a few weeks.

Our lodgings were right in the owner's home. We had to pay eight marks a week. Never in my life have I eaten so much cured horse meat and old beef sausage. The pay was wretched. That was due mostly to the bad materials. But still we were happy not to have to tramp around outside like beasts the way many others did. The police forced them into the stone quarries where they had to work in the cold until noon to pay for their wretched shelter.

We were paid our few groschen on Saturdays. We then took a sled and slid down the hill to the tavern, which catered to outsiders and also housed our union local. Afterward we had to crawl up the hill on all fours.

Four weeks later the sun laughed in the window, tempting us and awakening the desire to travel. Our present position just wasn't very nice.

My friend told me a lot about Soltau. He had worked there, and the owner had often written to him that he was welcome to come back. And if possible he should bring someone with him. I didn't even know where Soltau was, but my friend had nothing but good to say about it, and I trusted what he said. If I'd known that Soltau was in the middle of the Heath,* I certainly would not have gone with him. In the shelters I'd heard only bad things about the Heath.

TRAVELING AGAIN

I remember Soltau for the good food and lodgings but also for the beauty of the nearby Heath; we couldn't get enough of outings and walks on it. But most of all I remember Soltau because it was here, on 1 August 1909, that I became a member of the party. There weren't many of us, but it's still a pleasant memory for me. For a long time I collected contributions for the party in Soltau.

In Soltau my life finally became somewhat more congenial and quiet. I now got a little of what I'd missed in my childhood. I had no worries, the wages were pretty good, the workers decent, and I liked the landscape and the friendliness of the people.

Among my comrades at my lodgings was a somewhat older mason who kept away from the younger fellows and so was often

* The reference is to the Lüneburger Heath of northern Germany.

scorned by them. He liked me a lot because I was reserved. I soon understood his unusual behavior. He was always buying beauty creams and going through all kinds of expensive procedures to remove the deep folds and worry lines from his face. He was overly eager to find a girl to marry. But he was too shy to approach one. So he tried to make himself handsome but didn't get very far. Finally I promised to help him meet a girl.

During the spring fair we went to the dance hall and had a look at the pretty girls. The mason was willing to spend quite a bit. We both screwed up our courage by drinking beer.

Finally I discovered an older girl sitting alone at a table. I pointed her out to my friend, and he hesitatingly decided to ask her to dance. She was happy to. After a few dances she asked him to come over to her table. He did, and when I saw the quiet smiles on their faces, I disappeared and let nature take its course.

The next day the usually laconic mason was whistling one song after another. He was delighted with the girl. And toward the end of summer their happiness was made complete in the lovely brown heath.

The girl's parents ran a little farm not far from Soltau. We often rode out there on our bicycles, first out the main road and then a "pipe-full long" across the Heath. It was beautiful and each of us was absorbed in his own thoughts.

I also attended the wedding, and it's among my fondest remembrances. We danced under the trees to accordion music until late in the night. And then the rest of the night we slept dead-tired on the straw in the barn. We didn't notice until morning that we'd been lying all tangled up with the girls.

It wasn't long before the mason was a happy father. With a quiet smile on his face he rocked a robust little boy in his arms and on his knee.

I was happy that I'd helped him to get all this.

During this time I often went on short trips. By chance I was able to take a longer trip to Holland. It was the spring of 1912. A cigar maker from Holland worked with me. His father was a native German who'd fled over the border at the beginning of the war of 1870. My fellow worker had already done his military service in Holland. But for the last five years he hadn't shown up for the annual registration check. Every year his family wrote him that there was still a warrant out for him.

He was very homesick and wanted very much to visit Holland. After discussing things thoroughly, we decided to go to Holland together over Christmas. As far as I was concerned we could go anywhere.

We left while it was still dark on the morning of Christmas Eve. At first we could see only shadowy outlines of the landscape as it flew by us. As it got light we looked out eagerly and watched the whole countryside with its fields and pastures, villages, forests, towers and railroad stations, names, and people. Just before the border some very friendly people came in and asked us where we were going. They changed a good part of our money into guilders. As we discovered when we got to Holland, these were people who made it their business to cheat their inexperienced countrymen.

On the other side of the border I was astonished by the politeness and neatness of the train personnel. Every traveler was shown to his seat by a friendly conductor.

The baggage inspection went smoothly. My quiet comrade slowly became more talkative. We fell to talking with all kinds of people; I didn't understand a word of the language. But I was always given my share from the schnapps bottles and snuffboxes that were offered to us. The people made a very friendly impression. Toward evening we left the train at Deventer. My friend was met at the station. There were many tears at the reunion. But finally everyone became joyful. His people lived in a workers' quarter where all the houses had been built by cooperatives.

I made a lot of acquaintances in the days we were there. When I got a look at the big union hall, I got some idea of the size of the free trade unions in Holland. Deventer was not a big city. Once again one of my countrymen cheated us in a money exchange, deducting 3 percent, while the bank took only ½ percent. At a party one evening one of the visitors stuck a plaque with a picture of the queen of Holland onto me. I tried to protest. My friend said that that would offend them, so I put on a good face. The congeniality was extraordinary. We couldn't keep up with all the invitations; besides, my friend had to stay at home, otherwise they wouldn't get to see him. The beer was bad. Schnapps was the big thing.

Like all good things, our wonderful days in Holland came to an end. We returned to Soltau, richer with many experiences. For a few weeks my friend continued to work beside me; then one day he left, leaving no clue as to where he was going. I heard nothing from him until shortly before the outbreak of the War. Then he was told that the Dutch government would no longer prosecute him. He returned home joyfully and thus escaped the whole gruesome business of war.

May 1914 was like any other May. There was a married man who worked with me at my old place in Soltau. The owner's storehouse was filled with cigars and he wanted to let the older fellow go. I couldn't agree to that, so I offered to leave myself for a time and go on a long trip. I had quite a bit of money saved up. I wouldn't have to go begging from door to door.

I traveled to Achim, the big cigar maker's town; I got my union book and stayed at the inn that the cigar makers frequented. It was a Monday and many of the home tobacco workers were playing hooky. There was lots of laughter and hubbub in the tavern. Someone was standing on the counter and keeping time with a big cooking spoon. Cigar makers enjoy singing and usually do it well, so the mood became more and more riotous.

The next day I had a terrible hangover. Despite that I started the day with lots of schnapps. On my way in the blistering heat I got terribly thirsty and I looked for water or moisture in every ditch. But they were all dry. I had to drag myself on for hours before I came to a village and could satisfy my thirst.

In Bremen I stayed at the hostel that was owned by the union headquarters. It was clean, comfortable, and very well run. You could see the progress of the unions.

I took only three days to get to Osnabrück. At night I slept outside under any convenient bush. It was warm enough in the evening, but in the morning you woke up before sunrise with your teeth chattering. In a village beyond Osnabrück I wanted to buy something to satisfy my gnawing hunger. The woman who ran the shop told me that they also made cigars on the premises. I was allowed to have a look, and there I found my old Dutch friend whom the wind had blown there. We agreed that I would stay there for a while, and that at the beginning of August we would go to Holland together. But then he was able to leave earlier. I finally lost track of him, and no matter how hard I tried I couldn't find a trace of him.

I especially remember the few days before the great mobilization. In the evenings we sat in the pub with our regulars. The intoxication of victory among the young peasant fellows there knew no bounds. They were going to beat everyone in sight in three weeks. When I dared to say that it wouldn't be that easy because the enemy would be armed too, the uproar knew no bounds. They fell upon me like a pack of bloodthirsty hounds and worked me over with their boot heels. The innkeeper managed to slip me out the back door. Otherwise I certainly would have been beaten to death.

And so the War started. Because of my leg injury I didn't have to be a soldier. But later I was called into the auxiliaries and had to put up with a lot. Still, we survived the War. We went hungry and worked ourselves to death, but the fatherland never thanked us.

I've been married for thireen years now.

My wife also comes out of the tobacco industry. Her parents were workers. She had nine brothers and sisters. We live together peaceably with our three children.

I've been writing these lines by the light of a gloomy petroleum lamp while my wife and children sleep in the corner. I want to tell the younger ones that in spite of all the difficulties, *you can, you must proudly continue the fight* for the *new economic and political order* on this earth.

Suggestions for Further Reading
in English

Bonnell, Victoria E., ed. *The Russian Worker: Life and Labor under the Tsarist Regime.* Berkeley and Los Angeles, 1983.

Bry, Gerhard. *Wages in Germany, 1871–1945.* Princeton, 1960.

Burnett, John, ed. *Annals of Labour: Autobiographies of British Working Class People 1820–1920.* Bloomington, Ind. and London, 1974.

Crew, David F. *Town in the Ruhr: A Social History of Bochum, 1860–1914.* New York, 1979.

Davies, Margaret Llewelyn, ed. *Life As We Have Known It.* New York and London, 1975.

Evans, Richard J. "Prostitution, State and Society in Imperial Germany." *Past and Present,* no. 70 (February 1976): 106–29.

Evans, Richard J., and Lee, W. R., eds. *The German Family: Essays on the Social History of the Family in Nineteenth- and Twentieth-Century Germany.* London, 1981.

Evans, Richard J., and Lee, W. R., eds. *The German Peasantry: Conflict and Community in Rural Society from the Eighteenth to the Twentieth Centuries.* London and Sydney, 1986.

Evans, Richard J., and Lee, W. R., eds. *The German Working Class 1888–1933: The Politics of Everyday Life.* London, 1982.

Franzoi, Barbara. *At the Very Least She Pays the Rent: Women and German Industrialization, 1871–1914*. Westport, Conn. and London, 1985.

Göhre, Paul. *Three Months in a Workshop: A Practical Study*. Translated by A. B. Carr. London and New York, 1895.

Henderson, W. O. *The Rise of German Industrial Power, 1834–1914*. Berkeley and Los Angeles, 1975.

Hickey, S. H. F. *Workers in Imperial Germany: The Miners of the Ruhr*. Oxford, 1985.

Iggers, Georg, ed. *The Social History of Politics: Critical Perspectives in West German Historical Writing Since 1945*. New York, 1985.

Joeres, Ruth-Ellen B., and Maynes, Mary Jo, eds. *German Women in the Eighteenth and Nineteenth Centuries: A Social and Literary History*. Bloomington, Ind., 1986.

Kaelble, Hartmut. *Industrialisation and Social Inequality in 19th-Century Europe*. Translated by Bruce Little. New York, 1986.

Lidtke, Vernon L. *The Alternative Culture: Socialist Labor in Imperial Germany*. New York, 1985.

Moeller, Robert G., ed. *Peasants and Lords in Modern Germany: Recent Studies in Agricultural History*. Boston, 1986.

Moore, Barrington, Jr. *Injustice: The Social Bases of Obedience and Revolt*. White Plains, N.Y., 1978.

Neumann, R. P. "Industrialization and Sexual Behavior: Some Aspects of Working-Class Life in Imperial Germany." In *Modern European Social History*, edited by Robert J. Bezucha. Lexington, Mass., Toronto, and London, 1972.

Oberschall, Anthony. *Empirical Social Research in Germany 1848–1914*. New York, 1965.

Pascal, Roy. *Design and Truth in Autobiography*. Cambridge, Mass., 1960.

Quataert, Jean H. *Reluctant Feminists in German Social Democracy, 1885–1917*. Princeton, 1979.

Quataert, Jean H. "A Source Analysis in German Women's History: Factory Inspectors' Reports and the Shaping of Working-Class Lives, 1878–1914." *Central European History* 16, no. 2 (June 1984): 99–121.

Ritter, Gerhard A. "Workers' Culture in Imperial Germany: Problems and Points of Departure for Research." *Journal of Contemporary History* 13 (1978): 165–89.

Roberts, James S. *Drink, Temperance, and the Working Class in Nineteenth Century Germany.* Boston, 1984.

Roth, Guenther. *The Social Democrats in Imperial Germany: A Study in Working-Class Isolation and National Integration.* Totowa, N.J., 1963.

Schorske, Carl E. *German Social Democracy 1905–1917: The Development of the Great Schism.* Cambridge, Mass., 1955.

Stearns, Peter N. "Adaptation to Industrialization: German Workers as a Test Case." *Central European History* 3, no. 4 (December 1970): 303–31.

Stearns, Peter N. *Lives of Labor: Work in a Maturing Industrial Society.* New York, 1975.

Stearns, Peter N. "The Unskilled and Industrialization: A Transformation of Consciousness." *Archiv für Sozialgeschichte* 16 (1976): 248–82.

Vincent, David. *Bread, Knowledge and Freedom: A Study of Nineteenth Century Working Class Autobiography.* London and New York, 1981.

Index

Compositor: Graphic Composition, Inc., Athens, Georgia
Text: 12/13 Garamond
Display: Garamond
Printer: Murray Printing Co.
Binder: Murray Printing Co.